Weekends in New York

WRITTEN BY KAREN CURE

D0829976

BASED ON A CONCEPT BY
ANDREW ANSPACH

PREVIOUSLY PUBLISHED AS
FODOR'S SUNDAY IN NEW YORK

Fodor's Travel Publications, Inc.
New York • Toronto • London • Sydney • Auckland
www.fodors.com

Fodor's Weekends in New York

EDITOR: Steven K. Amsterdam

Editorial Contributors: Paula Bernstein, Andrea Coller, Margaret Mittelbach, Timothy Reynolds, Helayne Schiff, Martha Schulman, Kate Sekules

Editorial Production: Linda K. Schmidt

Maps: David Lindroth, *cartographer*; Steven K. Amsterdam, *map editor*

Design: Fabrizio La Rocca, *creative director*; Steven K. Amsterdam, *cover design*

Production/Manufacturing: Mike Costa

Cover Photograph: Patrick Batchelder

Copyright

Fifth Edition

ISBN 0–679–03546–X

About the Author

Karen Cure has been a New Yorker since 1973. She is the author of *Mini Vacations USA*, *The Travel Catalogue*, *An Old-fashioned Christmas*, and numerous articles for magazines including *Travel & Leisure* and *Diversion*. Now editorial director of Fodor's Travel Guides, she has contributed to many guidebook series and has traveled all over the world, but still believes there's no place like home.

Let Us Hear from You

Fodor's wants to hear about your weekend experiences, both pleasant and unpleasant. When an attraction fails to live up to its billing, let us know and we'll revise our entries where the facts warrant it. Also let us know your suggestions for what to see and do.

Send your letters to the editors of Fodor's Travel Publications, 201 East 50th Street, New York, New York 10022.

Special Sales

Fodor's Travel Publications are available at special discounts for bulk purchases for sales promotions or premiums. Special editions, including personalized covers, excerpts of existing guides, and corporate imprints, can be created in large quantities for special needs. For more information, contact your local bookseller or write to Special Markets, Fodor's Travel Publications, 201 East 50th Street, New York, New York 10022. Inquiries from Canada should be directed to your local Canadian bookseller or sent to Random House of Canada, Ltd., Marketing Department, 1265 Aerowood Drive, Mississauga, Ontario L4W 1B9. Inquiries from the United Kingdom should be sent to Fodor's Travel Publications, 20 Vauxhall Bridge Road, London, England SW1V 2SA.

PRINTED IN THE UNITED STATES OF AMERICA

10 9 8 7 6 5 4 3 2 1

Contents

Poetry Slams, Fancy Linens, and Other Weekend Pleasures   *v*

Manhattan Address Locator   *vi*

Maps

Manhattan *vii*
The Metropolitan Area *viii–ix*
The Five Boroughs *x–xi*
Lower Manhattan *xii–xiii*
Downtown Manhattan (Chambers Street to 14th Street) *xiv–xv*
SoHo and TriBeCa *xvi–xvii*
Chinatown, Little Italy, and the Lower East Side *xviii–xix*
Midtown Manhattan (14th Street to 59th Street) *xx–xxi*
Theater District (and Lincoln Center) *xxii–xxiii*
Upper West Side, Manhattan *xxiv*
Upper East Side, Manhattan *xxv*
Central Park (North) *xxvi*
Central Park (South) *xxvii*
Far Upper West Side *xxviii*
Harlem *xxix*
Far North *xxx*
Bronx Park and Fordham *xxxi*
Long Island City and Astoria, Queens *xxxii*
Jackson Heights, Queens *xxxiii*
Flushing, Queens *xxxiii*
Staten Island *xxxiv*
Hamilton Park (New Brighton), Staten Island *xxxv*
Todt Hill, Staten Island *xxxv*
Prospect Park and Park Slope *xxxvi–xxxvii*
Brooklyn Heights and Cobble Hill, Brooklyn *xxxviii*

1 Essential Information   *1*

Visitor Information *2*
Useful Phone Numbers *2*
Getting to New York City *2*
Getting Around *3*
Manhattan Orientation *5*
Parking *5*
Weekend Hotel Packages *6*
Activities for Children *6*
Places of Worship *7*
Seasonal Pleasures *10*
Where to Find It *12*
Personal and Business Services *14*
Emergencies, Complaints, and Problems *16*

2 Where to Eat   *17*

Restaurants *19*
Sweets and Treats *53*

3 What to Explore 56

Views *57*
Great Walks *58*
Architecture *61*
Explorable Neighborhoods *63*
Small Spaces, Secret Places *71*
Tours *73*
Best Bets for Children *76*

4 What to See 77

Art Museums *78*
Galleries *86*
Historical Treasures *87*
Science and Technology Museums *93*
Best Bets for Children *94*

5 Where to Shop 96

Shopping Hours *97*
Great Neighborhoods for Weekend Shopping *97*
Department Stores *99*
Fashion *101*
Food *105*
Specialty Shops *109*
Auction Exhibitions *125*
Flea Markets *125*
Best Bets for Children *125*

6 Where to Play 128

The Urban Outdoors *129*
Sports and Recreation *143*
Spectator Sports *156*
Best Bets for Children *158*

7 What to Sit Back and Enjoy 159

Theater *161*
Music *165*
Dance *171*
Performance Art *173*
Readings and Lectures *174*
Comedy and Magic *174*
Movies and Video *175*
Summer Arts *177*
Best Bets for Children *178*

Index 180

Poetry Slams, Fancy Linens, and Other Weekend Pleasures

The week may be hectic, but when the weekend comes, there's no better city for unwinding than New York. The pace of the work week dies down, and the best of the city, whatever the season, comes into focus.

Naturally, there is no better way to spend a sunny weekend in the city than in the wilds of our Emerald Empire. Even when the parks seem to fill up, you can still find quiet green paths away from the streets. There are adventures to be had in all five boroughs. And aside from the obvious activities, there are golf, lawn bowling, and tennis; there are trails for hiking and even forests for getting a little bit lost. There is usually enough of a breeze for a kite, and, for those roaming with kids, there are plenty of playgrounds along the way.

Of course the rest of the city comes into the same glorious relief on the weekend, with just as much to offer. The magnificent views— the Hudson River from the George Washington Bridge; Chinatown from Mott Street; the people from anywhere you might be standing; the never-ending array of restaurants, performance spaces, and museums—on Saturday and Sunday, they are what the city is all about.

Now New Yorkers have a marvelously detailed guide to all these weekend offerings. For the wide-eyed novice or even the most seasoned city dweller, this survey of New York's weekend options shows that there is always more to discover. Not just places to savor a drink or check out modern painting, but where to go for church music, for poetry slams, for fancy linens.

With *Weekends in New York*, city explorers have a book that covers everything from megamuseums to Brooklyn bakeries. With comprehensive listings, candid descriptions, and helpful details, this guide should be a bible for weekend wanderers.

Henry J. Stern
Commissioner of Parks and Recreation, City of New York

Manhattan Address Locator

To locate avenue addresses, take the address, cancel the last figure, divide by 2, add or subtract the key number below. The answer is the nearest numbered cross street, approximately. To find addresses on numbered cross streets, remember that numbers increase east or west from 5th Ave., which runs north–south.

Ave. A... *add 3*

Ave. B...*add 3*

Ave. C...*add 3*

Ave. D...*add 3*

1st Ave....*add 3*

2nd Ave....*add 3*

3rd Ave.... *add 10*

4th Ave.... *add 8*

5th Ave.

Up to 200...*add 13*

Up to 400...*add 16*

Up to 600...*add 18*

Up to 775...*add 20*

From 775 to 1286... *cancel last figure and subt. 18*

Ave. of the Americas...*subt. 12*

7th Ave....*add 12*

Above 110th St... *add 20*

8th Ave....*add 9*

9th Ave....*add 13*

10th Ave....*add 14*

Amsterdam Ave. ...*add 59*

Audubon Ave. ...*add 165*

Broadway (23–192 Sts.)...*subt. 30*

Columbus Ave. ...*add 60*

Convent Ave....*add 127*

Central Park West... *divide house number by 10 and add 60*

Edgecombe Ave. ...*add 134*

Ft. Washington Ave. ...*add 158*

Lenox Ave....*add 110*

Lexington Ave....*add 22*

Madison Ave....*add 27*

Manhattan Ave. ...*add 100*

Park Ave....*add 34*

Park Ave. South ...*add 8*

Pleasant Ave....*add 101*

Riverside Drive... *divide house number by 10 and add 72 up to 165 Street*

St. Nicholas Ave. ...*add 110*

Wadsworth Ave. ...*add 173*

West End Ave. ...*add 59*

York Ave....*add 4*

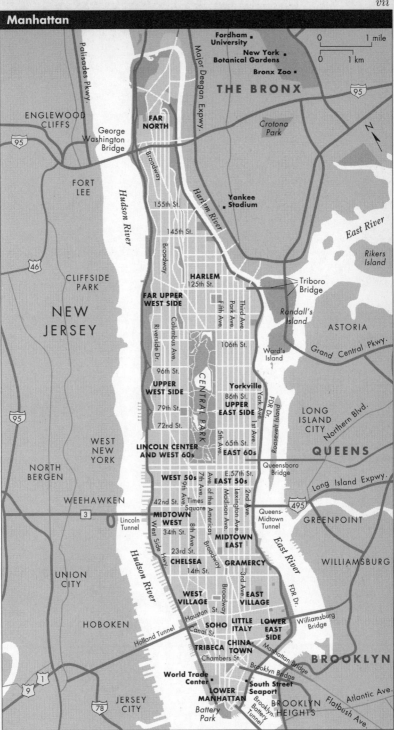

The Metropolitan Area

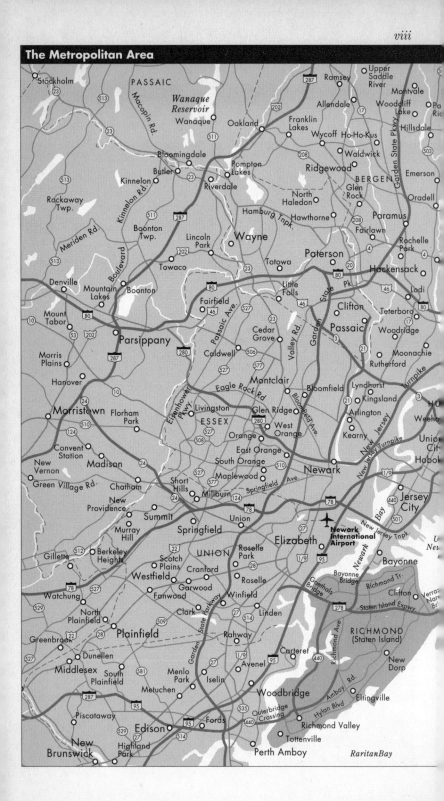

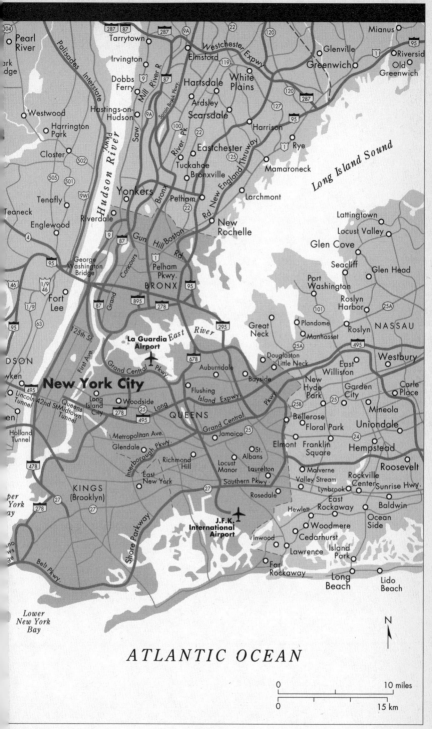

The Five Boroughs

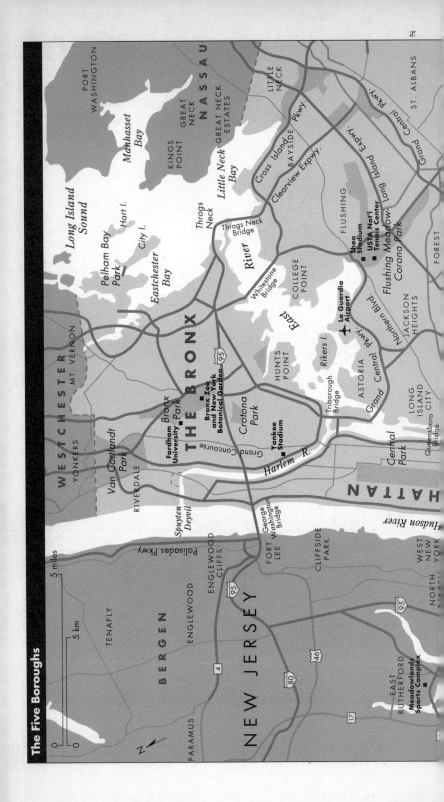

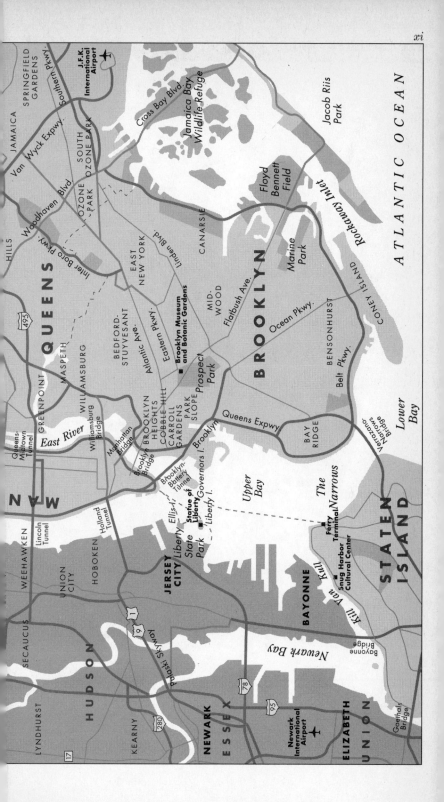

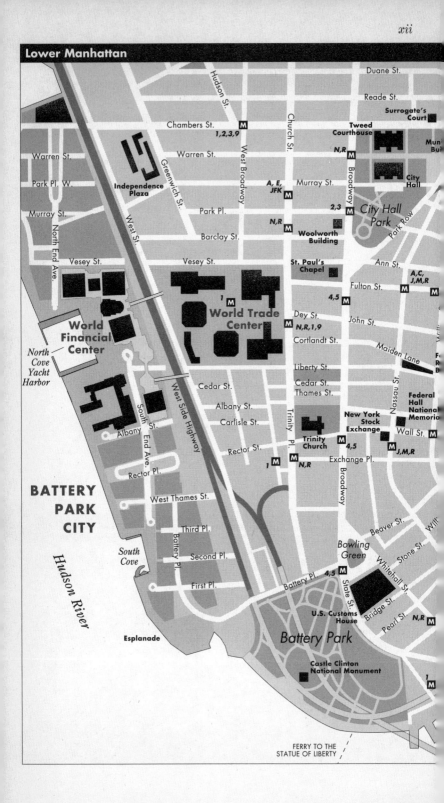

Lower Manhattan

Duane St.

Reade St.

Surrogate's Court

Hudson St.

Chambers St.

1,2,3,9

Warren St.

Church St.

Tweed Courthouse

N,R

Mun Bu

Warren St.

Park Pl. W.

Greenwich St.

Independence Plaza

West Broadway

A, E, JFK

Murray St.

City Hall

Murray St.

West St.

Park Pl.

2,3

City Hall Park

North End Ave.

Barclay St.

N,R

Woolworth Building

Park Row

Vesey St.

Vesey St.

St. Paul's Chapel

Ann St.

A,C, J,M,R

World Financial Center

World Trade Center

Fulton St.

4,5

North Cove Yacht Harbor

Dey St.

N,R,1,9

John St.

West Side Highway

Cortlandt St.

Maiden Lane

Fe R B

Liberty St.

Cedar St.

Thames St.

Federal Hall National Memoria

South End Ave.

Cedar St.

Albany St.

Trinity Pl.

New York Stock Exchange

Nassau St.

Albany

Carlisle St.

Trinity Church

Wall St.

BATTERY PARK CITY

Battery Pl.

Rector Pl.

Rector St.

4,5

J,M,R

N,R

Exchange Pl.

West Thames St.

1

Broadway

Hudson River

Third Pl.

Beaver St.

Stone St.

Wil

Bowling Green

South Cove

Second Pl.

Whitehall St.

Battery Pl.

First Pl.

Battery Pl.

4,5

State St.

Bridge St.

Pearl St.

N,R

U.S. Customs House

Esplanade

Battery Park

Castle Clinton National Monument

J

FERRY TO THE STATUE OF LIBERTY

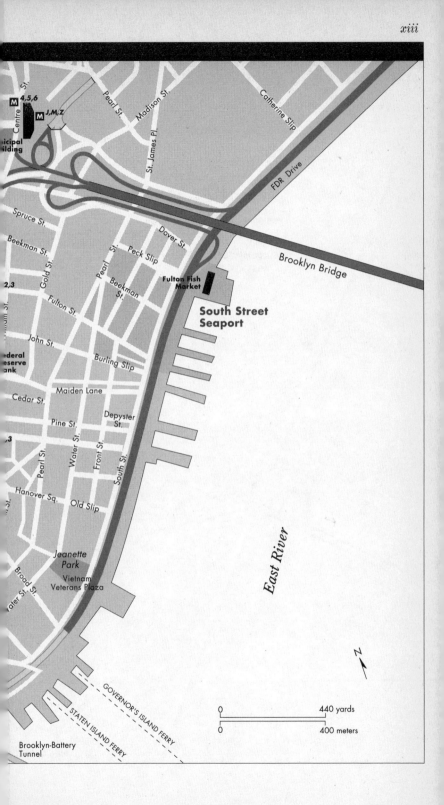

St.

M 4,5,6

Centre

M J,M,Z

icipal
ilding

Pearl St.

Madison St.

St. James Pl.

Catherine Slip

FDR Drive

Spruce St.

Beekman St.

Gold St.

Dover St.

Peck Slip

Pearl St.

Beekman St.

Brooklyn Bridge

2,3

Fulton St.

**Fulton Fish
Market**

John St.

Burling Slip

South Street
Seaport

ederal
eserve
ank

Cedar St.

Maiden Lane

Pine St.

Depyster
St.

3

Pearl St.

Water St.

Front St.

South St.

Hanover Sq.

Old Slip

East River

Broad St.

*Jeanette
Park*

Vietnam
Veterans Plaza

ater St.

N

GOVERNOR'S ISLAND FERRY

STATEN ISLAND FERRY

0   440 yards

0   400 meters

**Brooklyn-Battery
Tunnel**

Downtown Manhattan (Chambers Street to 14th Street)

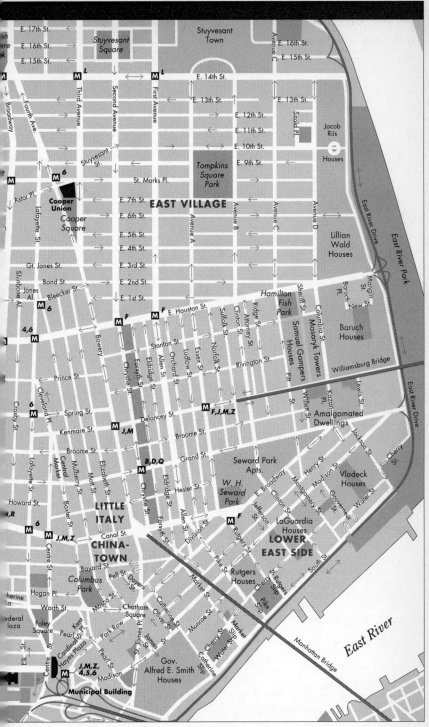

SoHo and TriBeCa

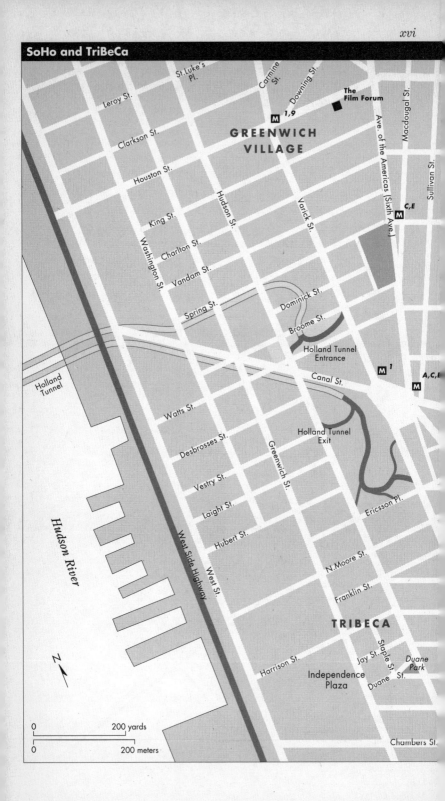

Leroy St.

St. Luke's Pl.

Carmine St.

Downing St.

The Film Forum

Clarkson St.

GREENWICH VILLAGE

M 1, 9

Macdougal St.

Houston St.

Hudson St.

King St.

Varick St.

Ave. of the Americas (Sixth Ave.)

C, E

M

Sullivan St.

Washington St.

Charlton St.

Vandam St.

Spring St.

Dominick St.

Broome St.

Holland Tunnel Entrance

Canal St.

M 1

A, C, E

M

Holland Tunnel

Watts St.

Holland Tunnel Exit

Desbrosses St.

Vestry St.

Greenwich St.

Laight St.

Hudson River

Hubert St.

Ericsson Pl.

N. Moore St.

West Side Highway

West St.

Franklin St.

TRIBECA

Jay St.

Staple St.

Duane Park

Harrison St.

Independence Plaza

Duane St.

N

0   200 yards

0   200 meters

Chambers St.

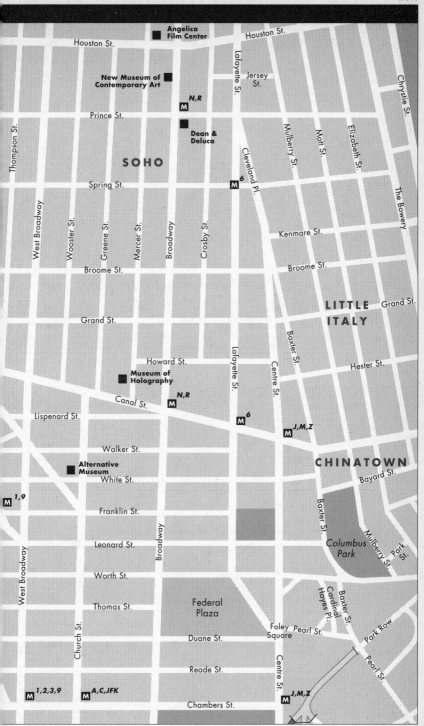

Angelica
Film Center

Houston St.

Houston St.

Lafayette St.

Jersey
St.

Chrystie St.

New Museum of
Contemporary Art

N,R
M

Prince St.

Mulberry St.

Mott St.

Elizabeth St.

Dean &
Deluca

Cleveland Pl.

SOHO

Thompson St.

Spring St.

M 6

The Bowery

West Broadway

Wooster St.

Greene St.

Mercer St.

Broadway

Crosby St.

Kenmare St.

Broome St.

Broome St.

LITTLE
ITALY

Grand St.

Grand St.

Baxter St.

Howard St.

Lafayette St.

Centre St.

Hester St.

Museum of
Holography

Canal St.

N,R
M

M 6

Lispenard St.

J,M,Z
M

CHINATOWN

Walker St.

Bayard St.

Alternative
Museum

White St.

M *1,9*

Franklin St.

Baxter St.

Broadway

Columbus
Park

Mulberry St.

Park St.

Leonard St.

Worth St.

Church St.

West Broadway

Thomas St.

Federal
Plaza

Cardinal
Hayes Pl.

Baxter St.

Park Row

Duane St.

Foley
Square

Pearl St.

Reade St.

Centre St.

Pearl St.

M *1,2,3,9*

M *A,C,JFK*

J,M,Z
M

Chambers St.

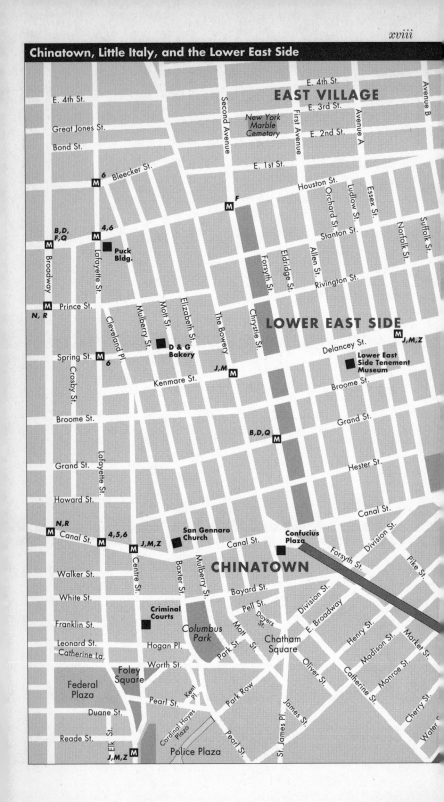

Chinatown, Little Italy, and the Lower East Side

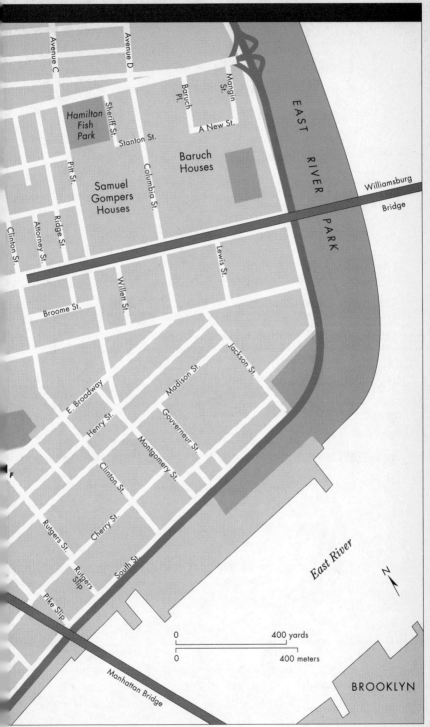

Avenue C

Avenue D

Baruch Pl.

Mangin St.

Hamilton Fish Park

Sheriff St.

Stanton St.

A New St.

EAST

Baruch Houses

Williamsburg

Pitt St.

Columbia St.

Samuel Gompers Houses

RIVER

Bridge

Clinton St.

Attorney St.

Ridge St.

PARK

Lewis St.

Willett St.

Broome St.

Jackson St.

Madison St.

E. Broadway

Gouverneur St.

Henry St.

Montgomery St.

F

Clinton St.

Cherry St.

East River

N

Rutgers St.

Rutgers Slip

South St.

Pike Slip

0   400 yards

0   400 meters

Manhattan Bridge

BROOKLYN

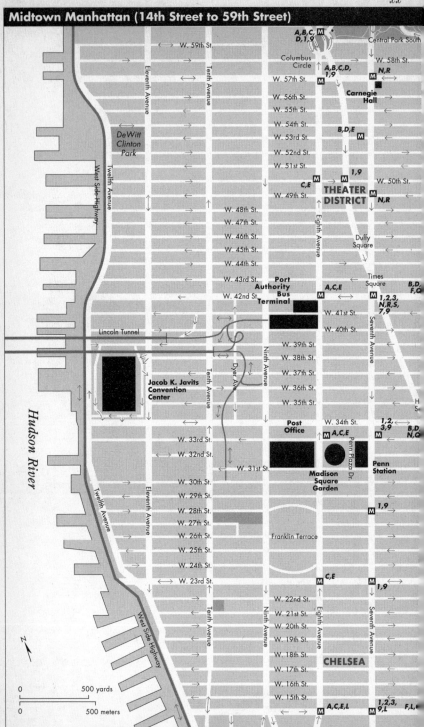

Midtown Manhattan (14th Street to 59th Street)

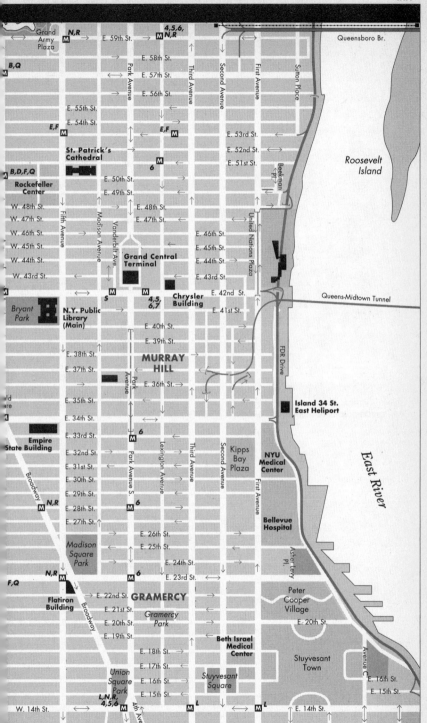

Grand Army Plaza

N,R M

E. 59th St.

4,5,6, N,R M

Queensboro Br.

B,Q M

E. 58th St.

E. 57th St.

E. 56th St.

Park Avenue

Third Avenue

Second Avenue

First Avenue

Sutton Place

E. 55th St.

E. 54th St.

E,F M

E,F M

E. 53rd St.

Roosevelt Island

St. Patrick's Cathedral

6 M

E. 52nd St.

E. 51st St.

B,D,F,Q M

E. 50th St.

Rockefeller Center

E. 49th St.

Beekman Pl.

W. 48th St.

E. 48th St.

W. 47th St.

E. 47th St.

United Nations Plaza

W. 46th St.

Fifth Avenue

Madison Avenue

Vanderbilt Ave.

E. 46th St.

W. 45th St.

E. 45th St.

W. 44th St.

E. 44th St.

Grand Central Terminal

E. 43rd St.

Queens-Midtown Tunnel

W. 43rd St.

M

S

S M

4,5, 6,7 M

E. 42nd St.

Bryant Park

E. 41st St.

N.Y. Public Library (Main)

Chrysler Building

E. 40th St.

E. 39th St.

FDR Drive

E. 38th St.

Park Avenue

MURRAY HILL

E. 37th St.

E. 36th St.

Island 34 St. East Heliport

...ld ...re M

E. 35th St.

E. 34th St.

M

E. 33rd St.

Lexington Avenue

Third Avenue

Second Avenue

First Avenue

Empire State Building

E. 32nd St.

6 M

Kipps Bay Plaza

E. 31st St.

E. 30th St.

NYU Medical Center

E. 29th St.

Broadway

N,R M

E. 28th St.

E. 27th St.

6 M

Bellevue Hospital

E. 26th St.

E. 25th St.

Madison Square Park

E. 24th St.

Asser Levy Pl.

F,Q M

N,R M

6 M

E. 23rd St.

Flatiron Building

Broadway

E. 22nd St.

GRAMERCY

Peter Cooper Village

E. 21st St.

E. 20th St.

Gramercy Park

E. 20th St.

E. 19th St.

Beth Israel Medical Center

Stuyvesant Town

E. 18th St.

Avenue C

E. 17th St.

Union Square Park

E. 16th St.

Stuyvesant Square

E. 16th St.

L,N,R, 4,5,6 M

E. 15th St.

E. 15th St.

W. 14th St.

4th Ave.

M *L*

M *L*

E. 14th St.

East River

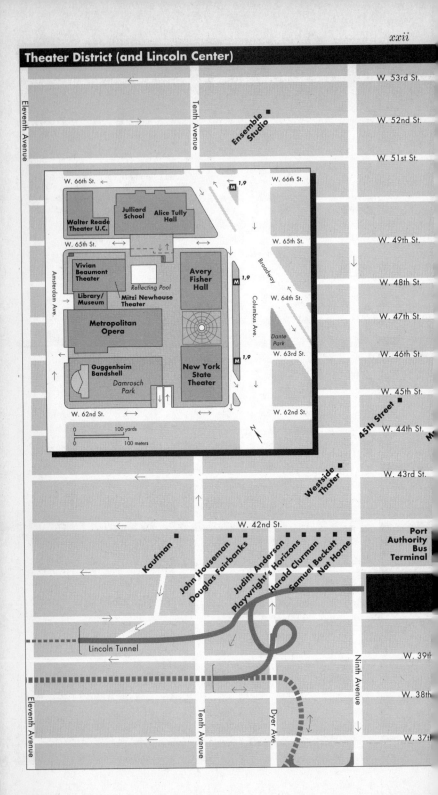

Theater District (and Lincoln Center)

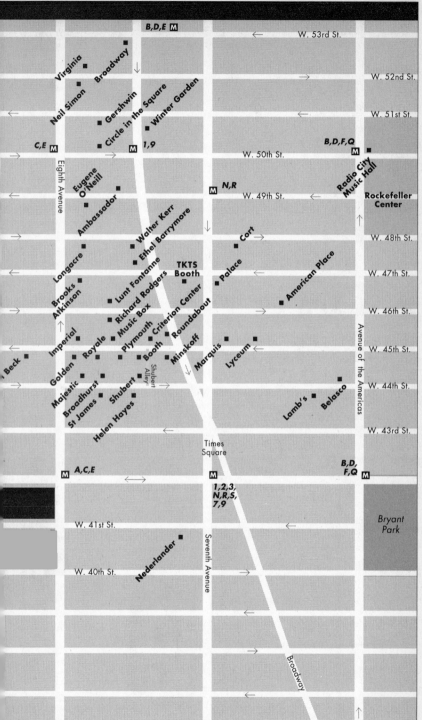

Upper West Side, Manhattan

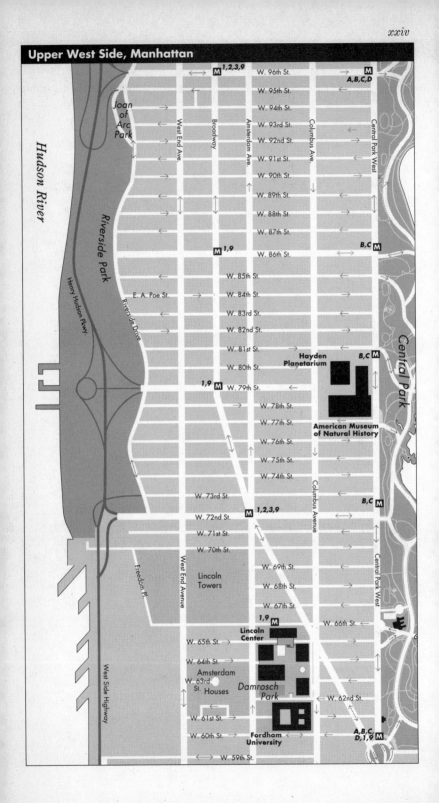

Upper East Side, Manhattan

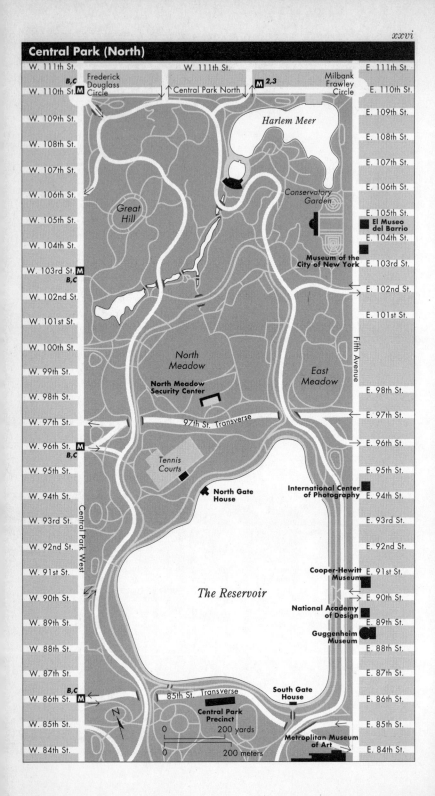

Central Park (North)

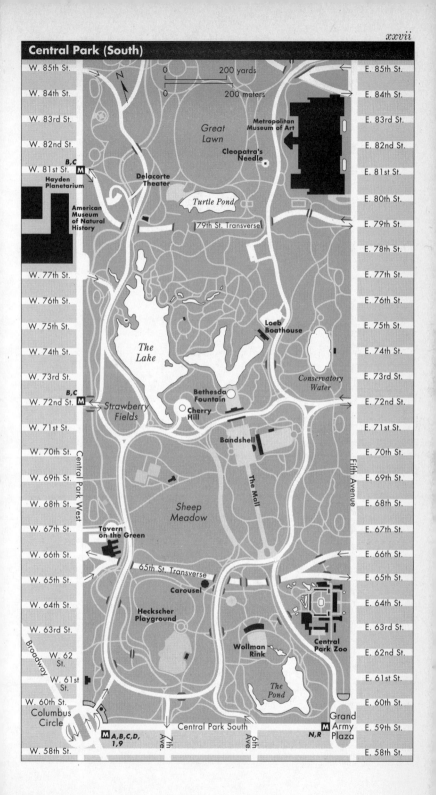

Central Park (South)

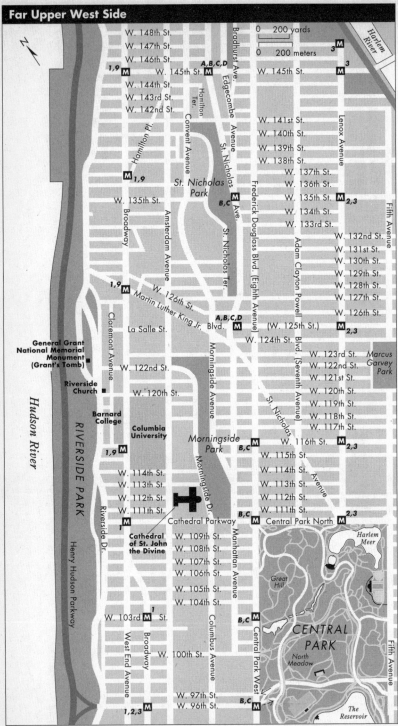

Far Upper West Side

Harlem

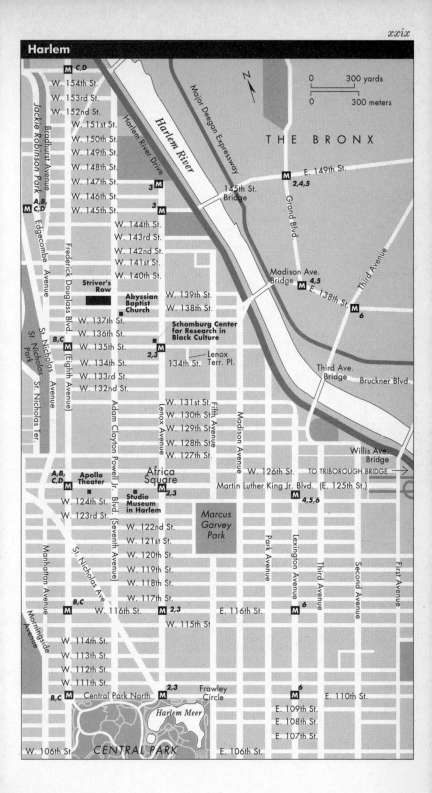

Far North

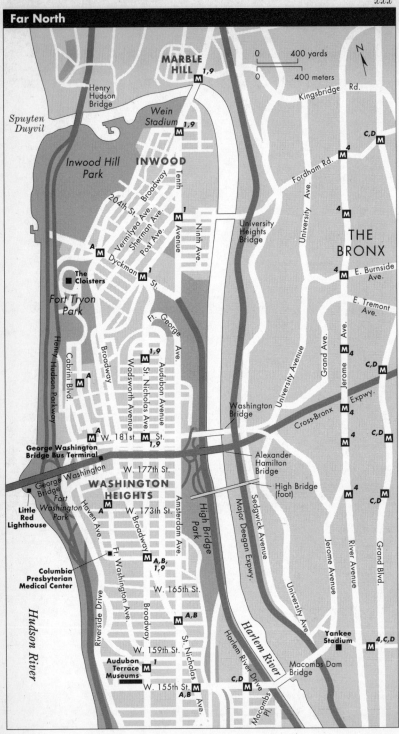

MARBLE HILL

1,9 Ⓜ

Henry Hudson Bridge

Spuyten Duyvil

Wein Stadium **1,9** Ⓜ

Kingsbridge Rd.

Inwood Hill Park

INWOOD

204th St.

Broadway
Vermilyea Ave.
Sherman Ave.
Post Ave.

Tenth Ave.

Ninth Ave.

First Avenue

Ⓜ **1**

University Heights Bridge

Fordham Rd.

C,D Ⓜ

Ⓜ **4**

University Ave.

4 Ⓜ

THE BRONX

Ⓜ **A**
Dyckman

The Cloisters

Ⓜ **1** St.

Fort Tryon Park

Ft. George Ave.

4 Ⓜ E. Burnside Ave.

E. Tremont Ave.

Cabrini Blvd.

Broadway

Wadsworth Avenue
St. Nicholas Ave.

Audubon Avenue

1,9 Ⓜ

Ⓜ **A**

University Avenue

Grand Ave.

Jerome Ave.

Ⓜ **4**

C,D Ⓜ

Henry Hudson Parkway

Ⓜ **A**
W. 181st St.
1,9

Washington Bridge

Cross-Bronx Expwy.

4 Ⓜ

C,D Ⓜ

George Washington Bridge Bus Terminal

W. 177th St.

Alexander Hamilton Bridge

4 Ⓜ

C,D Ⓜ

George Washington Bridge

Fort Washington Park

WASHINGTON HEIGHTS

Ⓜ **A**
W. 173th St.

High Bridge (foot)

Sedgwick Avenue

Major Deegan Expwy.

Little Red Lighthouse

Haven Ave.

Broadway

Amsterdam Ave.

High Bridge Park

Columbia Presbyterian Medical Center

Ⓜ **A,B 1,9**

Ft. Washington Ave.

W. 165th St.

Jerome Avenue

University Ave.

Ⓜ **A,B**

Riverside Drive

Hudson River

Broadway

W. 159th St.

St. Nicholas Ave.

River Avenue

Grand Blvd.

Yankee Stadium

Ⓜ **4,C,D**

Audubon Terrace Museums

Ⓜ **1**

Harlem River Drive

Harlem River

Macombs Dam Bridge

W. 155th St.

Ⓜ **A,B**

C,D Ⓜ

Macombs Pl.

0 ——— 400 yards
0 ——— 400 meters

N

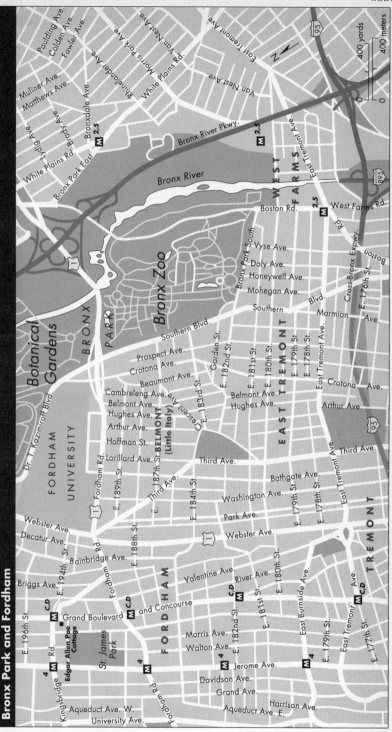

Bronx Park and Fordham

Long Island City and Astoria, Queens

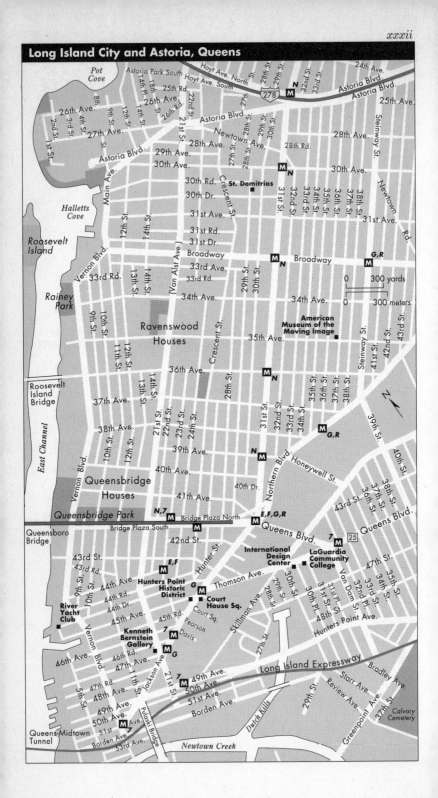

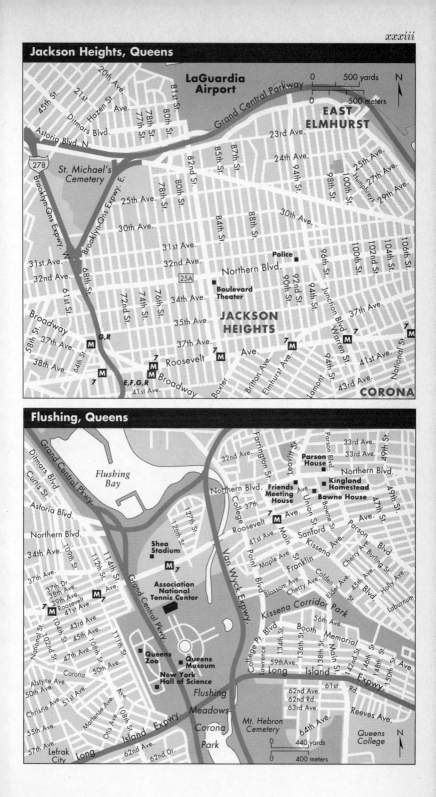

Jackson Heights, Queens

LaGuardia Airport

EAST ELMHURST

0   500 yards
0   500 meters

N

Grand Central Parkway

20th Ave.
21st
Hazen St.
Ditmars Blvd.
45th St.
Astoria Blvd. N
278
St. Michael's Cemetery
Brooklyn-Qns Expwy. W.
Brooklyn-Qns Expwy. E.
81st St.
78th St.
80th St.
77th St.
82nd St.
85th St.
87th St.
78th St.
80th St.
84th St.
88th St.
23rd Ave.
24th Ave.
25th Ave.
27th Ave.
29th Ave.
94th St.
98th St.
100th St.
Humphreys
25th Ave.
30th Ave.
30th Ave.
31st Ave.
32nd Ave.
68th St.
61st St.
25A
31st Ave.
32nd Ave.
34th Ave.
35th Ave.
72nd St.
74th St.
76th St.
Police
Northern Blvd.
Boulevard Theater
92nd St.
90th St.
94th St.
96th St.
100th St.
102nd St.
104th St.
106th St.
JACKSON HEIGHTS
37th Ave.
Broadway
58th St.
49th St.
37th Ave.
38th Ave.
M G,R
M
7
37th Ave.
Roosevelt   Ave.
7
M
7
E,F,G,R
41st St.
Broadway
Baxter
Britton Ave.
Elmhurst Ave.
Lamont
Junction Blvd.
Warren St.
94th St.
37th Ave.
41st Ave.
43rd Ave.
7
National St.
M
7
CORONA

Flushing, Queens

Grand Central Pkwy.
Flushing Bay
Ditmars Blvd.
Curtis Blvd.
Astoria Blvd.
Northern Blvd.
34th Ave.
37th Ave.
37th Dr.
38th Ave.
39th Ave.
Roosevelt
41st Ave.
National St.
102nd St.
104th St.
Corona
Alstyne Ave.
50th Ave.
Christie Ave.
55th Ave.
57th Ave.
Lefrak City
109th St.
114th St.
112th St.
43rd Ave.
45th Ave.
47th Ave.
50th Ave.
108th St.
111th St.
51st St.
Mortense Ave.
Otis Ave.
108th St.
62nd Ave.
62nd Dr.
Long   Island   Expwy.
32nd Ave.
Farrington St.
Leavitt St.
Parson Blvd.
33rd Ave.
33rd Ave.
46th St.
Parson House
Northern Blvd.
Kingland Homestead
49th St.
Northern Blvd.
College
127th St.
126th St.
37th
Friends Meeting House
Roosevelt
Point
41st Ave.
Union St.
Bowne St.
Sanford
Kissena
Bowne House
Ave.
Parson
Cherry Ave.
Burling St.
47th St.
7
M
Shea Stadium
M 7
Association National Tennis Center
Van Wyck Expwy.
Maple Ave.
Blossom Ave.
Cherry Ave.
Franklin
Colden
Elder Ave.
45th Blvd.
Holly Ave.
Laburnum
Kissena Corridor Park
56th Ave.
Booth Memorial
Queens Zoo
Queens Museum
New York Hall of Science
Grand Central Pkwy.
College Pt. Blvd.
Lawrence
134th St.
136th St.
138th St.
59th Ave.
59th Ave.
Long   Island   Expwy.
Main St.
142nd St.
144th St.
146th St.
148th St.
150th St.
Flushing Meadows-Corona Park
Mt. Hebron Cemetery
62nd Ave.
62nd Rd.
63rd Ave.
61st
Rd.
64th Ave.
Reeves Ave.
Queens College
N
440 yards
0   400 meters

Staten Island

The Narrows

NEW JERSEY

Newark Bay

Staten Island–Battery Ferry Terminal

Museum of Staten Island

Snug Harbor Cultural Center Staten Island Children's Museum

ST. GEORGE

Alice Austen House

NEW BRIGHTON

STAPLETON

Garibaldi-Meuci Museum

ROSEBANK

Verrazano Narrows Bridge

Castleton Ave.

Kill Van Kull

Bayonne Bridge

Terr.

Staten Island Zoo

PORT RICHMOND

278

278 Expwy.

GRASMERE

SOUTH BEACH

Richmond

Forest Ave.

Victory Blvd.

Staten Island

GRANT CITY

PORT IVORY

WESTERLEIGH

DONGAN HILLS

Hylan Blvd.

Goethals Bridge

278

440

BULLS HEAD

BLOOMFIELD

95

440

Jaques Marchais Center of Tibetan Art

RICHMONDTOWN

Richmond Rd.

OAKWOOD

Gateway National Recreation Area

Richmondtown Restoration Staten Island Historical Society Museum

La Tourette Park

Amboy Rd.

GREAT KILLS HARBOR

West Shore Expwy.

Arthur Kill

Arthur Kill Rd.

Richmond Rd.

Giffords La.

ELTINGVILLE

Arden Ave.

Ave.

ROSSVILLE

ANNADALE

Huguenot

Woodrow Ave.

Ave.

WOODROW

440

Richmond Pkwy.

Staten Island Rapid Transit

PRINCE'S BAY

95

Outerbridge Crossing

440

Hylan Blvd.

ATLANTIC OCEAN

440

TOTTENVILLE

Conference House

N

Raritan Bay

0   2 miles

0   3 km

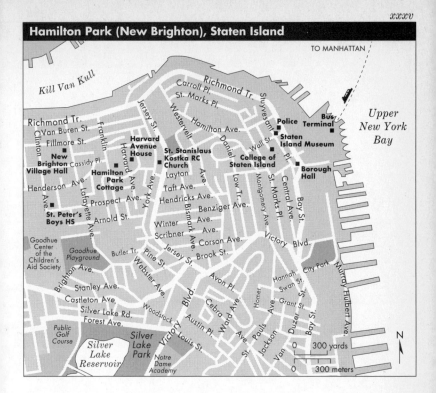

Hamilton Park (New Brighton), Staten Island

TO MANHATTAN

Kill Van Kull

Upper New York Bay

Richmond Tr.

Carroll Pl.
St. Marks Pl.

Richmond Tr.
Van Buren St.
Clinton
Fillmore St.

New Brighton
Village Hall

Cassidy Pl.

Henderson Ave.

St. Peter's
Boys HS

Goodhue
Center
of the
Children's
Aid Society

Goodhue
Playground

Brighton Ave.

Stanley Ave.

Castleton Ave.

Silver Lake Rd.

Forest Ave.

Public
Golf
Course

Silver
Lake
Reservoir

Silver
Lake
Park

Notre
Dame
Academy

Jersey St.

Franklin

Harvard Ave.

York Ave.

Lafayette Ave.

Hamilton
Park Cottage

Prospect Ave.

Arnold St.

Butler Tr.

Pine St.

Webster Ave.

Woodstock Ave.

Victory Blvd.

Louis St.

Westervelt

Harvard Avenue
House

St. Stanislaus
Kostka RC
Church

Layton

Taft Ave.

Hendricks Ave.

Winter Ave.

Scribner Ave.

Jersey St.

Bismark Ave.

Benziger Ave.

Ave.

Corson Ave.

Brook St.

Avon Pl.

Cebra Ave.

Austin Pl.

Hamilton Ave.

Daniel

Low Tr.

Montgomery Ave.

St. Marks Pl.

Ward Ave.

St. Pauls Ave.

Jackson

Carroll Pl.
St. Marks Pl.

Stuyvesant

Wall St.

Central Ave.

Bay St.

Victory Blvd.

Homer

Hannah
Swan St.
Grant St.

Van Duzer

Bay St.

Police

Staten
Island Museum

College of
Staten Island

Borough
Hall

City Park

Murray Hulbert Ave.

Bus
Terminal

N

0   300 yards

0   300 meters

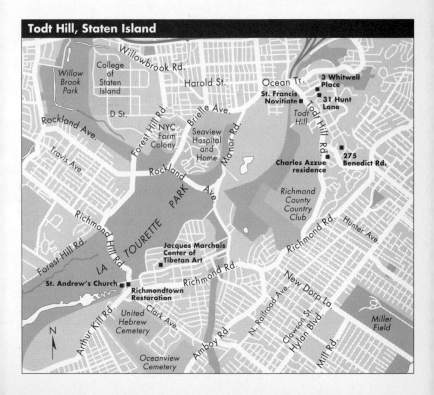

Todt Hill, Staten Island

Willowbrook Rd.

Willow
Brook
Park

College
of
Staten
Island

Harold St.

Ocean Tr.

3 Whitwell
Place

St. Francis
Novitiate

31 Hunt
Lane

Rockland Ave.

Travis Ave.

D St.

Forest Hill Rd.

NYC
Farm
Colony

Brielle Ave.

Seaview
Hospital
and
Home

Manor Rd.

Todt
Hill

Todt Hill Rd.

Charles Azzue
residence

275
Benedict Rd.

Rockland   Ave.

LA TOURETTE   PARK

Richmond Hill Rd.

Forest Hill Rd.

Jacques Marchais
Center of
Tibetan Art

Richmond Rd.

Richmond
County
Country
Club

Richmond Rd.

Hunter Ave.

St. Andrew's Church

Richmondtown
Restoration

United
Hebrew
Cemetery

Clark Ave.

Arthur Kill Rd.

N

Oceanview
Cemetery

Amboy Rd.

New Dorp La.

N. Railroad Ave.

Clawson St.

Hylan Blvd.

Mill Rd.

Miller
Field

Prospect Park and Park Slope

Warren St.
Baltic St.
Butler St.
Douglass St.
DeGraw St.
Sackett St.

Third Ave.

Gowanus Canal

Nevins St.

Prospect Pl.
Park Pl.
St. Johns Pl.
Lincoln Pl.
Berkeley Pl.

Fourth Ave.

Whitwell Pl.
Denton Pl.

N.R. Union St.
President St.
Carroll St.

Prospect Pl.
Park Pl.
Stirling Pl.

Fifth Ave.

Sixth Ave.

Flatbush Ave.

D,Q

Park Pl.

Seventh Ave.

2,3,4

Montauk Club

Vanderbilt Ave.

Eighth Ave.

Carroll St.
Garfield Pl.
1st St.
2nd St.
3rd St.
4th St.
5th St.
6th St.
7th St.
8th St.
9th St.
10th St.
11th St.
12th St.
13th St.
14th St.
15th St.
16th St.

Polhemus Pl. P
Fiske Pl. P
Montgomery

Second Ave.

Third Ave.

N.R.
M
F

Fourth Ave.

Fifth Ave.

Sixth Ave.

Seventh Ave.

Eighth Ave.

M F

N.R.

Prospect Expwy.

Prospect Ave.

Windsor Pl.

B
Pritch

278

18th St.
19th St.
20th St.
21st St.
22nd St.

Third Ave.
Third Ave.

Fourth Ave.

Fifth Ave.

Sixth Ave.

17th St.
18th St.
19th St.
20th St.

Prospec

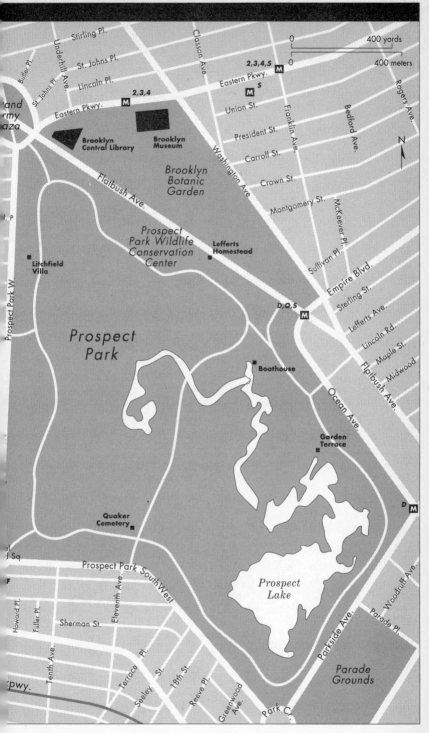

Stirling Pl.
Butler Pl.
Underhill Ave.
St. Johns Pl.
St. Johns Ave.
Lincoln Pl.
Classon Ave.

2,3,4,5
Eastern Pkwy.
M
S

2,3,4
M
Eastern Pkwy.

Union St.

President St.

Carroll St.

Crown St.

Franklin Ave.

Bedford Ave.

Rogers Ave.

N

Brooklyn
Central Library

Brooklyn
Museum

Flatbush Ave.

Brooklyn
Botanic
Garden

Washington Ave.

Montgomery St.

McKeever Pl.

Prospect
Park Wildlife
Conservation
Center

Lefferts
Homestead

Litchfield
Villa

Sullivan Pl.

Empire Blvd.

Sterling St.

Lefferts Ave.

Lincoln Rd.

Maple St.

Midwood

Prospect Park W.

I. P

Prospect
Park

D,Q,5
M

Boathouse

Ocean Ave.

Flatbush Ave.

Garden
Terrace

D
M

Quaker
Cemetery

Prospect Park Southwest

Prospect
Lake

Woodruff Ave.

d Sq.

F

Howard Pl.
Fuller Pl.
Sherman St.
Tenth Ave.
Eleventh Ave.
Terrace Pl.
Seeley St.
18th St.
Reeve Pl.
Greenwood Ave.
Park Cr.

pwy.

Parkside Ave.

Parade Pl.

Parade
Grounds

0   400 yards
0   400 meters

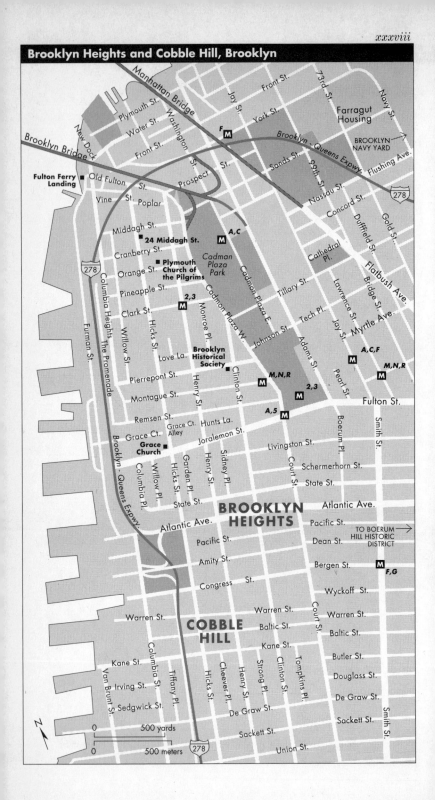

Brooklyn Heights and Cobble Hill, Brooklyn

1 Essential Information

Visitor Information

The **New York Convention and Visitors Bureau** at 59th Street between Broadway and 8th Avenue provides free information, including brochures, subway and bus maps, listings of hotels and weekend packages, and discount coupons for some Broadway shows. *2 Columbus Circle, New York, NY 10019, tel. 212/397–8222 or 800/NYC–VISIT. Open weekdays 9–6, weekends 10–6.*

The **New York Division of Tourism** offers a free series of *I Love New York* booklets, which include a number of New York City attractions and tour packages. *1 Commerce Plaza, Albany, NY 12245, tel. 518/474–4116 or 800/225–5697.*

Fund for the Borough of Brooklyn has several excellent publications about the borough. Their quarterly calendar of events lists entertainment and places of interest. *30 Flatbush Ave., Suite 427, Brooklyn, NY 11217, tel. 718/855–7882.*

Office of the Queens Borough President publishes *Discover Queens*, which covers cultural events, museums, sports and recreation. *What to See and Do in Queens and How To Get There* tells exactly that, and *Queen's World Fare* lists restaurants. *120–55 Queens Blvd., Kew Gardens, NY 11424, tel. 718/286–3000.*

Useful Phone Numbers

Transportation **Amtrak** (tel. 800/872–7245).
Long Island Railroad (tel. 718/217–5477).
Metro-North trains (tel. 212/532–4900).

Local **Metropolitan Transit Authority** (tel. 718/330–1234).
New Jersey Transit (tel. 201/762–5100).
PATH trains (tel. 800/234–7284).
Port Authority Bus Terminal (tel. 212/564–8484).

Tri-State **Port Authority Bridges and Tunnels** (tel. 212/360–3065).

Entertainment **Bryant Park Music and Dance Half-Price Tickets Booth** (tel. 212/382–2323).
Lincoln Center (tel. 212/877–2011).
Madison Square Garden (tel. 212/465–6741).
NYC On Stage (tel. 212/768–1818) lists TKTS Half-Price Theater Tickets, obtainable at Times Square (Broadway and 47th St.) and at Lower Manhattan Theater Center, 2 World Trade Center, Mezzanine.
New York Movie Phone for what's playing—when and where (tel. 212/777–FILM).
Park Events Hot Line (tel. 212/360–3456).
Telecharge (tel. 212/239–6200).
Ticketmaster (tel. 212/307–7171).

Getting to New York City

By Bus Major bus lines serving the city include **Greyhound** (tel. 800/231–2222), serving locations nationwide; **Peter Pan Trailways** (tel. 800/343–9999), serving major cities in the Northeast; **Short Line Bus System** (tel. 212/736–4700), serving upstate New York and New Jersey; **Adirondack/Pine Hill Trailways** (tel. 212/967–2900), serving the Hudson Valley, upstate New York, and Canadian destinations; and **Capitol Trailways** (tel. 800/858–8555), serving points in eastern Pennsylvania.

All long-haul and commuter bus lines feed into the well-policed but still not-very-lovely **Port Authority Terminal,** a mammoth multilevel structure between 40th and 42nd streets and 8th and 9th avenues.

The **George Washington Bridge Bus Station** is located at Fort Washington Avenue and Broadway between 178th and 179th streets in the Washington Heights section of Manhattan. Six bus lines, serving northern New Jersey and New York's Rockland County, operate Sunday from 5 AM to 1 AM. The terminal connects with the 175th Street subway station and the A subway line.

By Car From New Jersey, the **Lincoln Tunnel** (I–495), **Holland Tunnel,** and **George Washington Bridge** (I–95) connect Manhattan to the New Jersey Turnpike system and points west. The Lincoln Tunnel leads to midtown Manhattan, the Holland Tunnel to lower Manhattan, and the George Washington Bridge to upper Manhattan. For each of the three crossings a toll ($4 for cars) is assessed eastbound into New York, but not westbound.

From Long Island, the **Queens–Midtown Tunnel** (I–495) and **Triborough Bridge** (I–278) are the most direct links to Manhattan. Both connect with the east side, but the tunnel comes out in midtown, while the Triborough Bridge enters uptown. Both require tolls ($3.50 for cars) in both directions.

From upstate New York and central Westchester County, the city is accessible via the **New York (Dewey) Thruway** (I–87), a toll road that becomes the **Major Deegan Expressway** through the Bronx. Enter Manhattan via the Triborough Bridge ($3.50 toll). From western Westchester County, the **Sawmill River Parkway** (25¢ toll) leads to the **Henry Hudson Parkway,** which enters Manhattan at the **Henry Hudson Bridge** ($1.50 toll).

From New England, the **Connecticut Turnpike** (I–95) connects to the **New England Thruway** (I–95, toll road) and then the **Bruckner Expressway** (I–278; outbound, follow I–95 signs because the Bruckner isn't marked as I–278 until after its intersection with the Cross Bronx Expressway). Take the Bruckner to the **Triborough Bridge** ($3 toll) or to the **Cross Bronx Expressway,** which crosses upper Manhattan to the west side.

By Train **Amtrak** trains from all points arrive and depart from Pennsylvania Station (31st to 33rd Sts., between 7th and 8th Aves). The **Long Island Railroad,** which serves all of Long Island, also uses Penn Station, as does **New Jersey Transit,** which offers frequent service from the north and central regions of the state. **Metro-North** trains from the northern suburbs and from Connecticut as far east as New Haven stop at Grand Central Terminal (42nd St. and Vanderbilt Ave., between Lexington and Madison Aves.).

PATH trains serve Hoboken, Jersey City, Newark, and Harrison, New Jersey, from the World Trade Center and from stops along 6th Avenue at Christopher, 9th, 14th, 23rd, and 33rd streets. Trains run every 20–30 minutes on weekends; the fare is $1. In New Jersey, PATH trains connect with seven major New Jersey Transit commuter lines at Hoboken, Broad Street (Newark), and Penn (Newark) stations.

Getting Around

By Bus Even with a great many New Yorkers out and about, it's easy to get a bus seat on weekends. Bus fare—which is $1.50, the same as subway fare—may be paid with a token, coins, or Metrocard, but no bills or pennies. This includes one transfer that will permit you to ride at no charge on an intersecting bus route; ask the driver for the transfer slip as you board. Senior citizens pay $1.50, but receive a free return-trip ticket. As in the subways, children under six ride free.

Most routes follow the Manhattan grid: up or down the north–south avenues, east and west on the major crosstown streets. Bus maps are occasionally available in subway token booths but never on buses. The best places to pick one up are the Convention and Visitors Bureau at Columbus Circle or the information kiosks in Grand Central Terminal and Penn Station.

Guide-A-Rides, which show a specific route's map and schedules, are posted at many bus stops in Manhattan and at major stops in the other boroughs.

By Car Driving around Manhattan can be a weekend pleasure. The blocks slip by, almost too quickly, as one neighborhood slowly gives way to the next. You get a sense of how it all fits together, and you can really get around. Friday and Saturday nights can get hectic, though, as revellers from the outer boroughs as well as the suburbs descend, looking for excitement.

Two major north–south arteries run the length of the island. The **West Side Highway** skirts the Hudson River from Battery Park (where it's known as West Street), through midtown to the Upper West Side (where it becomes the Henry Hudson Parkway north of (72nd Street), and past the George Washington Bridge.

The **Franklin D. Roosevelt Drive** (or FDR Drive) runs along the East River from Battery Park into upper Manhattan. (It's called South Street from Battery Park to the Williamsburg Bridge.) It connects with the Triborough Bridge, the Midtown Tunnel, and the Queensboro Bridge.

Most major cross streets in Manhattan (including 14th, 23rd, 34th, 42nd, 57th, 72nd, and 96th) connect with either the West Side Highway or FDR Drive.

By Subway The 704-mile subway system is the fastest and cheapest way to get around the city.

At any hour of the weekend it may still feel like rush hour down under—many people head for beaches or parks or some explorable neighborhood in the late morning, and many more, laden with packages from shopping excursions, pile on the trains homeward bound in the afternoon and go out again at night until the trains are back on their morning schedules.

Trains run 24 hours a day. It's wise to stay alert though; stops are sometimes skipped due to construction or scheduling eccentricities). A single fare is $1.50, regardless of the distance you travel. Children under six travel free; those six and older pay full fare. Reduced rates are available for people who have disabilities and for senior citizens. If you plan a day of traveling around the city by public transportation, buy enough tokens to last. One token permits unlimited transfers within the system until you exit, and tokens can also be used on buses.

The Transit Authority also offers the **Metrocard** in lieu of tokens. The Metrocard acts as a sort of credit card for subway and bus fares, recording cash credit up to $80 on a magnetic strip on the back of the card. The strip is read at the turnstile and a full fare is automatically deducted. Metrocards can be purchased and/or renewed at most token booths and are a handy alternative for those who like to centralize everything in their wallets, or tend to lose change. All stations and buses are expected to be equipped to handle the Metrocard by early 1998.

Maps are posted at both ends of most subway cars and outside token booths, but rarely on the platforms. There's a token clerk in every station to answer questions; some clerks have a few maps to hand out on request (no charge). The New York Convention and Visitors Bureau also has subway maps. For route information, call 718/330–1234. For safety's sake, don't linger on deserted platforms or enter empty cars, and if the train isn't crowded, ride in the same car as the conductor (in the front and middle of the train). For like reason, plan your subway itinerary to avoid changing trains, which may necessitate long walks through sparsely trafficked corridors.

By Taxi Taxis are usually easy to hail on weekend days. Only the ones with the rooftop number lit are available. Taxis cost $1.50 for the first ⅕ mile, 25¢ for each ⅕ mile thereafter, and 20¢ for each minute not in motion, plus a 50¢ evening surcharge (in effect after 8 PM), and the 15% tip that all cabbies expect. Still, New York taxis are mile-for-mile less expensive than those in many cities. A short trip for two or more people may cost less than public transportation for the group, since you pay by the ride, not per person.

Manhattan Orientation

Above 14th Street, Manhattan streets form a regular grid pattern. Consecutively numbered streets run east and west (crosstown), while broad avenues, most of them also numbered, run north or south. Fifth Avenue is the east–west dividing line for street addresses; in both directions, they increase in regular increments from there. For example, on 55th Street, the addresses 1–99 East 55th Street are between 5th, Madison, and Park avenues, 100–199 East 55th would be between Park and 3rd avenues, and so on; the addresses 1–99 West 55th Street are between 5th and 6th avenues, 100–199 West 55th would be between 6th and 7th avenues, and so forth. Above 59th Street, where Central Park interrupts the grid, West Side addresses start numbering at Central Park West, an extension of 8th Avenue. Avenue addresses are much less regular; consult the Manhattan Address Locator that precedes this chapter. South of 14th Street, you'd do best to use a map.

Parking

Parking in New York is no longer a free ride on weekends. Check your metered spot for an "including Saturday and Sunday" regulation. But with many New Yorkers and their cars away for the weekend, you'll have much less competition than during the week.

In addition, many garages throughout the city cut their rates on weekends. Sunday garage rates range from $6 to $21 per day, sometimes even lower.

Check the Manhattan Yellow Pages for an extensive listing of garages. The following are open on weekends and are located near shopping and tourist attractions.

Upper West Side Carousel Garage (201 W. 75th St., tel. 212/874–0581).
Monterey Garage (137 W. 89th St., tel. 212/724–4600).
Omni Parking Corp (155 W. 68th St., tel. 212/874–9664).
79th Street (200 W. 79th St., tel. 212/874–9149).

Upper East Side Continental Towers Garage (301 E. 79th St., tel. 212/650–1936).
Fairmont Garage (300 E. 75th St., tel. 212/650–1416).
Kinney Parking (184 E. 73rd St., tel. 212/650–9625).
Kinney Parking (2 E. 60th St., tel. 212/832–9750).
Park Regis (50 E. 89th St., tel. 212/888–7400).
Square Plus (338 E. 82nd St., tel. 212/327–3430).

Midtown–West Side Belvex (306 W. 44th St., tel. 212/247–5807).
Meyers Parking System (31 W. 52nd St., 212/246–9256).
Sixth Avenue Hippodrome Garage (between W. 43rd and W. 44th Sts. and 5th and 6th Aves., tel. 212/997–9096).

SLL (322 W. 44th St., tel. 212/664–8193).
Tower Parking (140 W. 51st St., tel. 212/560–8232).

Midtown– **Carlton Parking Garage** (443 E. 49th St., tel. 212/688–7666).
East Side **Marlborough Garage** (245 E. 40th St., tel. 212/599–9485).
Murray's Park Garage (230 Lexington Ave. at 34th St., tel. 212/684–9312).
Square Parking (206 E. 59th St., tel. 212/223–9288; 605 Park Ave. at 65th St., tel. 212/650–9220).

West Side **Greenwich Street Parking** (377 Greenwich St., tel. 212/431–4714).
below 23rd **Minetta Garage** (122 W. 3rd St. at 6th Ave., tel. 212/777–3530).
Street **Mutual Garage** (166 Perry St. at West St., tel. 212/741–9773).

East Side **Kinney Systems** (224 Mulberry St., tel. 212/334–3427).
below 23rd **Precise Parking** (150 E. 18th St., tel. 212/254–3955).
Street **Square Parking** (70 E. 10th St. at 4th Ave., entered from 9th St., tel. 212/254–3870).
STAK Service Corp (303 E. 6th St., tel. 212/598–9821).

Weekend Hotel Packages

Many midtown hotels offer special packages that turn a weekend in the city into a wonderful minivacation. These include deluxe suite accommodations, free parking, champagne, luxury chocolates, use of health-club facilities, museum tickets, and/or shopping vouchers. Package offers can sometimes make even the most expensive hotels into a bargain. Call for information and to reserve in advance. The following hotels frequently offer such packages.

Algonquin. The literary round table may be long gone, but recent renovations have preserved this landmark's luxury, in a flowery, Victorian kind of way. *59 W. 44th St., 10036, tel. 212/840–6800.*
Beverly. An imposing lobby with leather couches, mirrored pillars, and piped in classical music hints at the plush grandeur upstairs at this Euro-tourist haven. *125 E. 50th St., 10022, tel. 212/753–2700.*
Doral Court, Doral Park, and **Doral Tuscany.** Three dignified European-style sisters. You can stay at one and sign for meals at the others. All three are cozy with Old World charm. *Court: 130 E. 39th St., 10016, tel. 212/685–1100. Park: 70 Park Ave., 10016, tel. 212/687–7050. Tuscany: 120 E. 39th St., 10016, tel. 212/686–1600.*
Drake. This Swiss-owned high rise is immaculate and modern, if a bit impersonal. *440 Park Ave. at 56th St., 10022, tel. 212/421–0900.*
Le Parker Meridien. Dramatic elegance combines with a warm and friendly staff at this French midtown location. Features include a fitness center and a rooftop pool. *19 W. 56th St., 10019, tel. 212/245–5000.*
Lowell Hotel. Luxurious; suites feature fireplaces, minibars, entertainment centers, and private garden terraces. There's also a fitness center with personal trainers on call. *8 E. 63rd St., 10021, tel. 212/838–1400.*
Marriott Marquis. Big, bright, and gaudy, this 1,800 room giant fits right into its location at the heart of Times Square. A favorite feature—even for locals— is the 46th floor revolving bar and restaurant. *1535 Broadway, 10036, tel. 212/398–1900.*
Mayfair Hotel. Although pricey, every room has a marble bath and a four-line phone with free local service. The traditional tea lounge and friendly service make it a local landmark. *610 Park Ave., 10021, tel. 212/288–0800.*
Morgans. Discreet and chic without being trendy, the rooms lack views but offer fresh flowers and down comforters. *237 Madison Ave. at 37th St., 10016, tel. 212/686–0300.*

New York Hilton. Basic Hilton decor with the added attractions of a fitness center and massage. *1335 Ave. of the Americas at 53rd St., 10019, tel. 212/586–7000.*

Omni Berkshire Place. Everything here is extra large: the lobby, the rooms, even the bathtubs. Electronic controls allow you to dim lights, adjust the air conditioner, and turn on the TV, all from your bed. *21 E. 52nd St., 10022, tel. 212/753–5800 or 800/790–1900.*

Paramount. The Paramount is hyper-trendy with funky Philipe Stark furniture and an "imaginative" lighting scheme in the lobby. Rooms are (small and) even more bizarrely furnished, while the staff are gorgeous to gaze at, if not always efficient. *235 W. 46th St., 10036, tel. 212/764–5500.*

Plaza. This is an excellent location if you plan to shop 5th or Madison or spend a lot of time in the park, but remember the golden rule of location in New York—you always pay for it. *768 5th Ave. at Central Park S., 10019, tel. 212/759–3000.*

Radisson Empire. Nearly on top of Lincoln Center and all that the neighborhood has to offer, with reasonably sized rooms, the Radisson Empire has possibly the most helpful and friendly staff in the city. *44 W. 63rd St., 10023, tel. 212/265–7400.*

UN Plaza–Park Hyatt Hotel. The lobby is small but striking, with charming Japanese floral arrangements. The best feature here is the dramatic East Side views from nearly every room. *44th St. at 1st Ave., 10017, tel. 212/355–3400.*

Vista International. The lobby impresses with a green-granite and marble entrance and curved grand staircase. The health club includes a pool and indoor track. *3 World Trade Center, 10048, tel. 212/938–9100.*

Waldorf-Astoria Hotel. Extensively refurbished several years ago by the Hilton chain, this landmark retains a lot of old New York charm. *301 Park Ave., 10022, tel. 212/355–3000.*

Places of Worship

Even in secular New York City, religion offers weekend solace to followers of every ilk. Beyond moral uplift, weekend services offer an opportunity to study gracious architecture, listen to sacred music, and rub shoulders genteelly with other New Yorkers. Call ahead for information on child care and special hours for summer and holidays. Unless otherwise noted, hours listed are for Sunday services.

Baptist **Abyssinian Baptist Church** (132 W. 138th St., tel. 212/862–7474), a Harlem institution, is known for gospel music and fiery sermons. The 5,000-member congregation now meets to hear the inspiring, liberal pastor Calvin Butts, a powerhouse of Harlem politics and worthy successor to the Adam Clayton Powells, father and son. Services: 11 AM.

Christian Science **Second Church of Christ Scientist** (Central Park West at 68th St., tel. 212/877–6100), this green-domed structure built in 1900, is one of the graceful fixtures of the neighborhood. Service: 11 AM.

Church of Christ **Manhattan Church of Christ** (48 E. 80th St., tel. 212/737–4900), built in 1965 of cast concrete with a stained-glass facade, is conveniently near the Metropolitan Museum. Service: 11 AM.

Eastern Orthodox **Archdiocesan Cathedral of the Holy Trinity** (319 E. 74th St., tel. 212/288–3215), with its golden mosaics and gilded paintings, makes a Sunday service like a vision of Greece. Service: 10:30 AM.

Episcopal **Calvary Episcopal** (Park Ave. at 21st St., tel. 212/475–1216) is a lovely Gramercy Park church designed by James Renwick, who also did St. Patrick's Cathedral. Service: 11 AM.

Cathedral of St. John the Divine (112th St. at Amsterdam Ave., tel. 212/316–7400) is the world's largest Gothic cathedral, though still under construction. The annual blessing of the animals, part of the celebration of St. Francis Day (October 4), is a New York spectacle. There are tours at 12:45 PM on Sunday. Services: 8, 9, 9:30 (Spanish), 11 AM, 7 PM.

Church of the Incarnation (Madison Ave. at 35th St., tel. 212/689–6350) occupies an early Gothic Revival building constructed in 1882 by Marc Eidlitz. There are sculptures by Augustus Saint-Gaudens, carvings from the Daniel Chester French atelier, and fine stained glass. Services: 8:30, 11 AM.

Grace Church (802 Broadway at 10th St., tel. 212/254–2000), topped by an elegant steeple, is another Renwick-designed church. Winston Churchill's mother, Jennie Jerome, was married here. Services: 9, 11 AM, 6 PM.

St. Ann and the Holy Trinity Episcopal Church (Clinton and Montague Sts., Brooklyn, tel. 718/875–6960) has restored Bolton stained-glass windows, some of the oldest that survive. Service: 11 AM.

St. Bartholomew's (Park Ave. at 51st St., tel. 212/751–1616) is a grandiose Byzantine-Romanesque structure with rose windows and mosaics, the Western Hemisphere's fifth-largest pipe organ, and a well-heeled congregation. Services: 9, 11 AM; 8 AM in the chapel without music.

St. Mark's in the Bowery (2nd Ave. at 10th St., tel. 212/674–6377), one of the city's most historic churches, occupies a part of Peter Stuyvesant's estate and is intimately involved in the political and artistic life of this bohemian corner of the East Village. Service: 10:30 AM.

St. Michael's Church (225 W. 99th, tel. 212/222–2700) houses one of the nation's largest collections of works by Louis Comfort Tiffany and boasts a youthful congregation and a lively roster of choral eucharists and festival services. Services: 8, 11 AM.

Trinity Church (Broadway at Wall St., tel. 212/602–0800), chartered in 1697, now occupies a mid-19th-century Gothic building by Richard Upjohn. The church's silhouette has become one of the icons of New York; its time-blackened sandstone is now restored to its original reddish color. Services: 9, 11:15 AM.

Inter-denominational **Judson Memorial Church** (55 Washington Sq. S at Thompson St., tel. 212/477–0351) is an NYU-area landmark, designed by Stanford White with stained-glass windows by John LaFarge and statuary by Augustus Saint Gaudens. It is listed in the National Register of Historic Places. Service: 11 AM.

Riverside Church (Riverside Dr. at 122nd St., tel. 212/222–5900), built in 1930 by John D. Rockefeller, Jr., and inspired by the cathedral at Chartres, features an awesome 215-foot-long nave. Service: 10:45 AM.

Jewish **Park Avenue Synagogue** (50 E. 87th St., tel. 212/369–2600) is a noted Conservative synagogue. Saturday services: 9 AM, 5:45 PM.

Park East Synagogue (164 E. 68th St., tel. 212/737–6900), a Byzantine–Moorish landmark, is presided over by Orthodox rabbi Arthur Schneier, a Holocaust survivor. Saturday service: 9 AM.

Temple Emanu-El (1 E. 65th St., tel. 212/744–1400), founded by a group of German immigrants that included the Guggenheims and Strausses, has the world's largest Reform congregation. Saturday service: 5:30 PM.

Lutheran **Holy Trinity Lutheran Church** (Central Park West at 65th St., tel. 212/877–6815), a neo-French Gothic structure completed in 1903, evokes Paris's Sainte Chapelle. Services: 11 AM, 5 PM.

St. Peter's Lutheran Church (Lexington Ave. at 54th St., tel. 212/ 935–2200) is a lively, contemporary church connected to the Citicorp Center. Some Louise Nevelson sculptures grace the inner sanctum. Services: 8:45, 11 AM, 5 PM jazz vespers.

Methodist **Christ Church United Methodist** (Park Ave. at 60th St., tel. 212/838– 3036), built in 1932, is part Romanesque, part Byzantine, and very imposing. Services: 9, 11 AM.

John Street United Methodist Church (44 John St., between William and Nassau Sts., tel. 212/269–0014) houses the oldest Methodist Society in America, organized in 1766. The current structure, built in Greek Revival style in 1841, holds pristine white pews trimmed in dark wood. Service: 11 AM.

Mormon **Church of Jesus Christ of Latter-Day Saints** (2 Lincoln Sq., Broadway at 65th, tel. 212/875–8197) is opposite Lincoln Center. Services: 9, 11 AM, 1 PM (Spanish), 3 PM (for young singles).

Presbyterian **Fifth Avenue Presbyterian** (5th Ave. at 55th St., tel. 212/247–0490) features almost-opalescent stained-glass windows, some by Louis Comfort Tiffany, others by Maitland Armstrong. Services: 11 AM, 4 PM.

First Presbyterian Church (5th Ave. at 12th St., tel. 212/675–6150) provides restful sanctuary in a structure surrounded by an ornate old cast-iron fence and a fine green yard and gardens. Service: 11 AM.

Madison Avenue Presbyterian Church (921 Madison Ave., at 73rd St., tel. 212/288–8920), a Gothic structure built in 1899, has an exceptional music program. Services: 9:30, 11:15 AM, 6 PM.

Quaker **Society of Friends** (15 Rutherford Pl., between 2nd and 3rd Aves., tel. 212/777–8866). Sunday meetings attract a casual group. Main services: 9:30, 11 AM.

Reformed **Marble Collegiate Church** (5th Ave. at 29th St., tel. 212/686–2770)
Church in held the New World's first communion service on April 7, 1628, in a
America dusty room above a grist mill on what is now William Street, and has been going strong ever since. As many as 1,500 worshippers assemble on Sundays, along with scores of TV cameras, to hear Dr. Arthur Caliandro, who fills the pulpit made famous by Norman Vincent Peale. Service: 11:15 AM.

West End Collegiate (386 West End Ave. at 77th St., tel. 212/787– 1566) looks like something out of old Amsterdam, with its stepped-gable facade. Inside, it's unprepossessing, with massive timbers and stained-glass windows. Service: 11 AM.

Roman **St. Ignatius Loyola** (Park Ave. at 84th St., tel. 212/288–3588) has an
Catholic austere exterior and an interior exuberantly ornamented with mosaics, columns, and Tiffany glass. Services: 7:30, 9:30, 10:45, 11 AM, 12:30, 7:30 PM.

St. Malachy's (239 W. 49th St., tel. 212/489–1340), known as the Actor's Chapel, schedules masses around theater matinees and evening performances. Services: 9, 11 AM.

St. Patrick's Cathedral (5th Ave. at 50th St., tel. 212/753–2261) is the soaring Gothic cathedral where Cardinal O'Connor celebrates the 10:15 mass almost every Sunday. Services: 7, 8, 9, 10:15, noon, 1, 4, 5:30 PM.

St. Vincent Ferrer (869 Lexington Ave. at 66th St., tel. 212/744– 2080) is an immense church with splendid stained glass and a carved altar wall. Services: 8, 10, noon, 5:30 PM.

Unitarian **Church of All Souls** (1157 Lexington Ave. at 80th St., tel. 212/535– 5530) has a large, diverse congregation. Services: 10, 11:15 AM.

Community Church of New York (40 E. 35th St., tel. 212/683–4988), traditionally liberal, is where the late Michael Harrington presided. Service: 11 AM.
The Universalist Church (Central Park West at 76th St., tel. 212/595–8410) is a neo-Gothic church built in 1898, based on designs by William Potter. Service: 11 AM.

Seasonal Pleasures

New York is a city for all seasons. Each month brings a new crop of special happenings in museums, parks, and other institutions, as well as sports events and much more.

Winter In wintertime the great indoors beckons, and the performing arts calendar is usually full. But don't forget about the city's great outdoors, too. There's ice-skating in the parks and at Rockefeller Center. The Bronx Zoo, delightfully uncrowded, offers the opportunity to see animals in their winter coats.

Early Jan.: The **National Boat Show** will awaken the sailor in you. Jacob K. Javits Convention Center, tel. 212/922–1212.
Late Jan. to early Feb.: The **Winter Antiques Show** is one of the top events of its kind in the country. Seventh Regiment Armory, Park Ave. at 67th St., tel. 212/665–5250.
Feb.: Chinese New Year is celebrated with special banquets at nearly every Chinese restaurant in the city, and Chinatown's narrow streets are ankle deep with red firecracker paper.
Mid-Feb.: Westminster Kennel Club Dog Show offers a fascinating showcase for top-of-the-line pooches. Madison Square Garden, tel. 212/465–6741.
Early Mar.: International Cat Show is a feline-lover's delight. Madison Square Garden, tel. 212/465–6741.
Mid-Mar.: Ringling Brothers Barnum & Bailey Circus begins its glittering run here. Madison Square Garden, tel. 212/465–6741.
Late Mar.: Greek Independence Day Parade struts a fabulous show of native costumes. 5th Ave. from 62nd to 79th Sts.

Spring Nature wakes up with a floral show that fairly takes the breath away. Daffodils and forsythia gild Central Park as well as the botanical gardens; the New York Botanical Garden in the Bronx is especially wonderful, particularly the Murray Liasson Narcissus Collection and Daffodil Hill. April brings the neon blaze of azaleas, and May means a pink blizzard of flowering cherry trees, singularly beautiful along the Hudson River in Riverside Park, around the Central Park Reservoir, and in the Brooklyn Botanic Garden.
Mar. or Apr.: Easter festivities occur all over town. Masses of flowers turn Macy's ground floor into an exquisitely fragrant wonderland; the Waldorf-Astoria displays an elaborate chocolate sculpture worth going out of your way to see. On Easter Sunday, exhibitionists don extravagant or improbable hats and saunter down 5th Avenue in the annual Easter Parade.
May: You Gotta Have Park is a special weekend when thousands of volunteers—citizens and celebrities—pitch in to clean up Central Park.
Mid- to late May: Ninth Avenue International Food Festival features food and merchandise from 32 countries. 9th Ave. south of 57th St., tel. 212/581–7217.
Late May to early June: Washington Square Art Show fills Washington Square Park and adjacent side streets in Greenwich Village. Tel. 212/982–6255.

Summer As the hot weather settles in, so does the season of street fairs and block parties. In June, roses bloom by the thousands at the Brooklyn Botanic Garden and at the Bronx's New York Botanical Garden. Later on, perennials come into their own in these two gardens, as well as in Central Park's Conservatory Garden and in community gardens all over the city. Water babies sun at the beaches, fans pray for homers at Yankee and Shea stadiums, theatergoers enjoy Shakespeare in the Park, and music lovers savor the Museum of Modern Art's Summergarden concerts. (For more on the foregoing, *see* Chapters 6 and 7.)

June: Riverside Park Festival features dances, chess tournaments, a bubble-blowing contest, a gospel concert, and other entertainment.
June: Queens Festival brings professional entertainment, games, rides, and exhibits to Flushing Meadows—and a crowd of millions to enjoy it all. Flushing Meadows–Corona Park, Queens, tel. 718/886–5454.
Early to mid-June: Feast of St. Anthony is celebrated with 10 days of canneloni and veal and sausage and things parmigiana. Sullivan St. near Houston St., tel. 212/777–2755.
Mid-June: Puerto Rican Day Parade marches to Latin rhythms and the most exuberant of crowds. 5th Ave., between 42nd and 86th Sts., tel. 212/665–1600.
Late June: Gay and Lesbian Pride Parade vacillates between earnest political protest and free-for-all celebration of attire, music and some politics as it cruises down 5th Avenue and through the heart of Greenwich Village. 5th Ave. from 57th St., to 10th. St., then west on Christopher to the piers.
Late June: The Mermaid Parade celebrates all things funky and fishy on Brooklyn's legendary Coney Island boardwalk, as the Mermaid King and Queen "open up" the Atlantic Ocean for the summer.
Early to mid-July: American Crafts Festival is where spinners spin; weavers weave; and puppeteers, jugglers, and other entertainers keep things lively as hand-crafted goods are "ooh"-ed and "ahh"-ed over, and sometimes bought. Lincoln Center, tel. 212/877–2011.
July to Aug.: Shakespeare in the Park presents free Shakespeare performances on stages in city parks. Tel. 212/861–7277.
Aug.: Tap-O-Mania at Macy's is, according to the *Guinness Book of World Records*, "the world's largest assembly of people tap dancing the same routine at one time." Because the chorus line fills up Herald Square, it can be held only on a Sunday. 34th St. and 6th Ave., tel. 212/695–4400.
Late Aug. to early Sept.: U.S. Open Tennis Championships are aces with the local tennis lovers. National Tennis Center, Flushing Meadows-Corona Park, Queens, tel. 718/271–5100.
Aug.: Harlem Week highlights workshops, street carnivalia, dance, rap, jazz, fairs, gospel singing, and other cultural events. Throughout Harlem, tel. 212/427–7200.

Autumn The street festival season continues as baseball fans wait with bated breath for the outcome of the year's pennant races. With crowds at the beaches thinning out, it's a great time to enjoy the surf in solitude. Later on, the fall foliage is glorious, particularly in the parks. October marks the beginning of Rockefeller Center ice-skating—the first frost of the next season.

Mid-Sept.: New York Is Book Country brings New Yorkers out in droves to enjoy scores of bookstalls and exhibits from major publishers and antiquarian collectors. 5th Ave., between 48th and 57th Sts., tel. 212/522–3074.
Mid-Sept.: Feast of San Gennaro, 10 days honoring the patron saint of Naples, is the biggest of the city's Italian street fairs. Mulberry St., Little Italy, tel. 212/226–9546.
Late Sept. to early Oct.: New York Film Festival is the high point of the local film buff's year. Alice Tully Hall, Lincoln Center, tel. 212/875–5000.
Early Oct.: Pulaski Day Parade commemorates Polish hero Casimir Pulaski. 5th Ave., between 26th and 52nd Sts.

Late Oct. or early Nov.: New York City Marathon begins at the Verrazano-Narrows Bridge and loops through all the boroughs. Tel. 212/860–4455.

Nov.: Virginia Slims Tennis Championships in mid-month brings the stars of women's tennis to town. Madison Square Garden, tel. 212/465–6741.

Nov. 11: Veteran's Day Parade honors our nation's war heroes. 5th Ave., between 24th and 39th Sts., tel. 212/267–1998.

Winter Holidays During the Christmas holidays, many stores that are closed on Sundays through most of the year do a booming Sunday business. In fact, on the two Sundays before Christmas, midtown blocks of 5th Avenue are closed to vehicular traffic, while crowds of shoppers pause en route to admire the giant Christmas tree at Rockefeller Center. Meanwhile, the Cartier building is wrapped in a big red bow, the center mall up Park Avenue is studded with fir trees twinkling with little white lights, and all New York glitters with special events.

The **American Museum of Natural History** decks a wonderful Christmas tree with origami figures. At the **Metropolitan Museum of Art,** exquisite Neapolitan crèche figures ornament the museum's Christmas tree, set against a medieval choir screen. The *Nutcracker*, performed by the **New York City Ballet** at Lincoln Center's New York State Theater, never fails to dazzle (tel. 212/870–5570).

Animated displays depicting Yuletide fantasies fill windows of the great Manhattan stores on 5th Avenue: **Lord & Taylor** at 38th Street, and **Saks** at 50th Street. For the hip, occasionally outrageous version, peer into the Christmas windows at ultra-fashionable **Barneys** on 7th Avenue at 17th Street or uptown at 61st and Madison.

The Christmas Spectacular, a musical extravaganza featuring the high-kicking Rockettes, fills the stage at **Radio City Music Hall** in Rockefeller Center (tel. 212/247–4777).

Brooklyn's visual offering is **Dyker Heights,** a largely Italian neighborhood in Bay Ridge, near the Verrazano-Narrows Bridge, where the tradition of setting up a crèche has spawned extravagant displays of lights. Streets in the 70s between 12th and 14th avenues yield the best viewing. By subway: Take the B train, get off at 71st or 79th St., and head west.

Where to Find It

With so much to do in New York and so much of it changing all the time, the best way to find out what's happening over the weekend is to check updated local listings. The following publications are the easist to find all over the city.

The Weekend section of the Friday **New York Times** (www.nytimes. com) offers solid cultural criticism along with thorough movie listings; theater advertisements and a directory; a regular column for children's events; and museum, gallery, and auction guides. All that for 60¢ and you can buy it absolutely anywhere.

Despite its stuffy reputation, the *New Yorker* magazine has become more *downtown* in the last few years, and its "Goings On About Town" section now lists everything from piano recitals to performance art. Headings include theater; dance; nightlife (rock, jazz, and standard cabaret shows); art (museums, libraries, galleries, and a separate section just for photography); and classical music (with a very thorough list of opera, orchestras, and individual recitals). The Above and Beyond section includes lectures, readings, and special tours. The movie listings are augmented by concise synopses and critical analysis, with special attention paid to revivals and art films. $2.95, weekly, at most newsstands.

New York is slightly lower-brow but nearly as thorough an alternative to the above. What it lacks in high intellect it more than makes up for with loads of photos and extra added sections, including shopping, an extensive restaurant guide, and a whole slew of things to do just for kids. The Cue section brings together listings for movies, galleries, museums, auctions, theater, concerts, nightclubs, comedy and cabaret, even television and radio highlights. $2.95, weekly, at newsstands everywhere.

Geared toward a young trendy market, *Time Out New York* (www.timeoutny.com) purports to be the ultimate listings guide for the entire city (despite the fact that they seem predisposed to putting Hollywood film stars on the cover). The emphasis here is on nightlife for singles, with a whole section for dance clubs and thorough coverage of bars, rock concerts, and restaurants. Art, theater, and movies are also listed along with sports, television, video releases, and lesbian and gay happenings. Feature stories tend to make things out to be a little more glamorous than they actually are. Still, if you are coming to town to sight celebrities or break bread with the beautiful people, this is probably the magazine for you. $1.95, weekly, any newsstand.

A downtown institution, the *Village Voice* (www.villagevoice.com) is the last word on what goes on amongst the city's engaged and enraged. Some of New York's most respected critics write for the Voice's Arts section; Voice Choices, a special pull out section, lists it all. Film includes mainstream movies as well as revivals and avantgarde cinema. Music is limited to rock, alternative, and dance club listings. The art section surveys galleries, photography exhibits, and museums. Thorough theater and dance selections, along with monologues, readings, and lectures, round out all the arts. There's even a big restaurant guide. Everything comes with a nicely encapsulated review so you know what to expect. Blue dispensers for the free weekly dot corners all over the city; or check the vestibules of most book stores.

A younger, brattier, and richer cousin to the **Voice,** the *New York Press* (www.adon.com.nypress) covers a lot of the same territory with a little more collegiate irreverence. The emphasis here is on hip, verging on snotty, twentysomethings and all the things they like to do. Listings include film, live music (divided into "rock," "jazz," and "other"), dance clubs, readings, lectures, an extensive outdoors section with walking tours and street festivals, theater, dance, and art exhibits. The free weekly is distributed in green dispensers all over the city; or check downtown cafes, restaurants, and bars.

Several free weeklies offer listings exclusively for the gay and lesbian community. Check for *H/X, LGNY,* and *Next* in any gay friendly bookstore, bar, restaurant, or boutique.

The **Parents' League of New York** (115 E. 82nd St., 10028, tel. 212/737–7385) offers a listing of events and services for children. *New York Family,* a monthly magazine published 12 times a year (New York Family Publications, 420 E. 79th St., Suite 9E, 10021, tel. 212/744–0309) and the *Big Apple Parents' Paper* (Buffalo-Bunyip, Inc., 928 Broadway, Suite 707, 10010, tel. 212/533–2277) are good sources of information for activities geared to youngsters. Several local publications, including the *Village Voice, New York* magazine, and the Friday edition of the *New York Times,* also offer news of happenings for kids.

Personal and Business Services

The following establishments are open weekends most of the year. Always call ahead, however, since some may close for vacations or holidays or in summer.

Automotive Manhattan gas stations that are open weekends, from downtown
Services northward, include the following.

Gas **Mobil** (Allen and Division Sts., tel. 212/966–0571).
Mobil (Spring St. at 6th Ave., tel. 212/925–6126).
Amoco (Broadway at Houston St., tel. 212/473–5924).
Gulf (FDR Dr. at 23rd St., tel. 212/686–4546).
Mobil (11th Ave. at 51st St., tel. 212/974–0243).
96th Street Autocare (303 W. 96th St., tel. 212/749–2123).

Car Rentals Most car-rental outlets at the major airports and throughout the city are open Saturdays and Sundays. Reserve well in advance for summer weekends. The major companies are **Avis** (tel. 800/331–1212), **Budget** (tel. 212/807–8700), **Hertz** (tel. 800/654–3131), and **National** (tel. 800/328–4567). For more competitive rates, try **All City** on the upper west side (tel. 212/721–0080) or downtown (tel. 212/243–9200).

Towing and The Automobile Club of New York (AAA) provides help to mem-
Repairs bers. To protect other drivers, the City Council sets towing rates for all five boroughs—currently $25 for a hookup plus $1.75 per mile and tolls. Check the Yellow Pages for towing and repair services.

Baby-Sitters The **Babysitters Guild** (60 E. 42nd St., Suite 912, tel. 212/682–0227), in business since 1940, screens sitters rigorously.

Business **Dial-A-Secretary** (126 E. 83rd St., tel. 212/348–8982) offers clerical
Services help.

Computer These organizations have Macintosh and IBM-compatible work sta-
Stations tions for rent by the hour, along with a range of printers.

Key Word Process (37 W. 17th St., tel. 212/206–8060) is open week-ends noon–5 (appointment suggested).
Userfriendly (139 W. 72nd St., tel. 212/580–4433) is open Saturday 11–7 and Sunday noon–8.

Photocopying Most copy shops have fax machines, and many also offer laser type-
and Fax setting, word processing, and other office services. The following are among those open all weekend.

Copy Cats (968 Lexington Ave. at 70th St., tel. 212/734–6236; 1646 2nd Ave. at 84th St., tel. 212/734–6104), is open Saturday 9–8 and PSunday noon–8.
Kinko's the Copy Center (24 E. 12th St., tel. P212/924–0802; 2872 B'way at 111th St., tel.212/316–3390; 191 Madison at 34th St., tel. 212/685–3449; 16 E. 52nd St., tel. 212/308–2679; 245 7th Ave. at 24th St., tel. 212/929–2679; 1122 Lexington Ave. at 78th St., 212/628–5500; 21 Astor Pl., tel. 212/228–9511; all open 24 hours).
Metrocopy (222 E. 45th St., tel. 212/687–6699), open weekends 8 AM–midnight.
Village Copier (20 E. 13th St., between 5th Ave. and University Pl., tel. 212/924–3456), open 24 hours.

Currency **Chequepoint USA** (609 Madison Ave., tel. 212/750–2255) is open
Exchange weekends 9–7.

Delivery **Trin** (158 Rutland Rd., Brooklyn 11225, tel. 718/693–8740) will hand deliver any size package anywhere in New York any time on Satur-day or Sunday. Call for an estimate.

Limousine Services	**Attitude New York** (Box 912, Old Chelsea Station, tel. 212/633–0004). **Surrey Limousine Service** (41–38 Crescent St., Long Island City, Queens, tel. 718/937–5700). **Tel Aviv** (343 E. 21st St., tel. 212/505–0555).
Locksmiths	For keys around the clock, call **All-Time Locksmith** (2206 Broadway, between 78th and 79th Sts., tel. 212/724–2210) or **Night and Day Locksmith** (1335 Lexington Ave., tel. 212/722–1017).
Medical *Dentists*	**Dental Emergency Service** (tel. 212/679–3966, 212/679–4172 after 8 PM) can make referrals in Manhattan.
Minor Medical Emergencies	A number of immediate-care facilities and walk-in clinics specialize in annoying-but-not-life-threatening problems. Those associated with hospitals are usually entered through the emergency room; all have doctors, nurses, and facilities for X-rays and lab tests, including: **The Manhattan Eye, Ear, and Throat Hospital's Emergency Room** (210 E. 64th St., tel. 212/838–9200) is worth remembering for related crises around the clock. **New York Hospital's Urgent Care Center** (520 E. 70th St., tel. 212/746–0795; 212/746–5050 for the emergency room), 24-hour emergency room.
Pharmacies	Aside from the abundance of Rite-Aids and Duane Reades around town, the following pharmacies can fill prescriptions over the weekend. **Apthorp Pharmacy** (2201 Broadway at 78th St., tel. 212/877–3480) is open Saturday 9–8 and Sunday 10–7. **Bigelow Pharmacy** (414 6th Ave., between 8th and 9th Sts., tel. 212/533–2700) is open Saturday 8:30–7 and Sunday 8:30–5:30. **Kaufman's Pharmacy** (Lexington Ave. at 50th St., tel. 212/755–2266), open 24 hours. **Leroy Pharmacy** (342 E. 23rd St., tel. 212/505–1555), open 24 hours. **Plaza Pharmacy** (251 E. 86th St., tel. 212/427–6940) is open Saturday 9–9 and Sunday 10–6. **Village Apothecary** (346 Bleecker St. at 10th St., tel. 212/807–7566) is open Saturday 9–9 and Sunday 10:30–7. **Windsor Pharmacy** (1419 6th Ave. at 58th St., tel. 212/247–1538) is open weekends 9–midnight. **Zitomer Pharmacy** (969 Madison Ave., between 75th and 76th Sts., tel. 212/737–5560) is open Saturday 9–7 and Sunday 10–6.
Physicians	**Doctors on Call** (tel. 212/737–2333), a 24-hour housecall service, can send doctors to Manhattan or the boroughs.
Photographic Services *Darkroom Rental*	Amateurs and professionals alike use the facilities at **Latent Image Workshop** (135 W. 26th St., tel. 212/242–0215, open weekends 10–8) and at **Photographics Unlimited/Dial-A-Darkroom** (17 W. 17th St., tel. 212/255–9678, open Sat. 10–7 and Sun. noon–7). Call ahead to reserve.
Photo Processing, Passport Photos	Passport photos as well as one-hour film processing are available from chain outlets such as **Fromex Photo Systems** (1247 3rd Ave. at 72nd St., tel. 212/288–8897; 182 E. 86th St., tel. 212/369–4821; 2041 Broadway at 71st St., tel. 212/580–8181; 2151 Broadway at 76th St., tel. 212/496–2211), open Saturdays 10–6 and Sundays, generally between noon and 5 PM. For custom photo services, try **Photographics Unlimited** (*see above*) and **Baboo** (37 W. 20th St., tel. 212/807–1574, open weekends 9–8).

Post Office The main post office (421 8th Ave., between 31st and 33rd Sts., tel. 212/967–8585) provides a full range of postal services 24 hours every day. Specific information on many subjects is available to those with touch-tone phones at the automated postal information line (tel. 212/330–4000).

Veterinarians **Animal Medical Center** (510 E. 62nd St., tel. 212/838–8100) is a non-profit clinic open 24 hours; no appointment is necessary.

Emergencies, Complaints, and Problems

Dial **911** for police, fire, or ambulance in an emergency (tel. 800/342–4357 for deaf callers). To reach the nearest **police precinct,** call 212/374–5000).

Complaints **Better Business Bureau** (tel. 212/533–6200).
Crime victims hot line (tel. 212/577–7777).
Gay and Lesbian Anti-Violence Project (tel. 212/807–0187).
Potholes (tel. 212/768–4653).
Sex crimes reports (tel. 212/267–7273).
Taxi complaints (tel. 212/221–8294). Be sure to take the driver's name and medallion number.

Lost and **Amtrak** (tel. 212/630–7389 for Penn Station).
Found **City buses** (tel. 718/625–6200).
Long Island Railroad (tel. 718/558–8384).
Metro-North (tel. 212/340–2555).
New Jersey Transit (tel. 201/714–2739 in Hoboken).
PATH trains (tel. 201/216–2677).
Subways (tel. 718/625–6200).
Taxi and Limousine Commission (tel. 212/221–8294).

2 Where to Eat

What do New Yorkers do on the weekend? Eat out, of course. At least once, and probably three or four times in two days, everyone gets out there to gossip, to schmooze, to have trysts, to make eyes across candlelit linen and argue over the bagels next morning—to do, in short, whatever they'd be doing anyway, only do it in public, while stuffing their faces. The restaurant is this city's living room, social center, fishbowl, and playground, and there are about 300 for every taste. Despite the sheer volume of restaurants, you shouldn't plan to dine out Saturday night without a reservation, not even in the neighborhood joint you found half empty on Monday. Sunday brunch can be almost as oversubscribed at places known for their French toast and mimosas, but instead of calling ahead, standing on line clutching 10 pounds of Sunday *Times* is the popular mode at this time. The exception to the Saturday night "reserve or be damned" ordinance is the month of August, when a table is easier to come by, because many of the city's diners are sitting in traffic on the Montauk Highway en route to the Hamptons.

If you're more of a pioneer than a pack animal, Sunday night is the night to favor for restaurant forays. Our listings are heavily biased toward places that remain open on the seventh day, when a certain mood of replete exhaustion settles over a hushed city, and one can dine in peace. As for what to eat: Hell, this is New York. Chew your way around the world from Afghanistan to Zaire, drop by the deli, hit the gastro-porn high spots (not forgetting to treble the reserve-ahead margin), go for musical accompaniment, sidewalk tables, big skyline views, celeb-spotting, all-you-can-eat Lebanese—anything.

Restaurants are listed by neighborhood corresponding to the maps in the back of this book. The neighborhoods are:

Lower Manhattan
TriBeCa
SoHo
Little Italy and Chinatown
Lower East Side
East Village and NoHo
West Village
Gramercy Park, Flatiron, and Union Square
Chelsea
Midtown East (24th to 49th streets east of 5th Avenue)
Midtown West (24th to 49th streets west of 5th Avenue)
East 50s
West 50s
East 60s
Upper East Side
Yorkville (all of the East 80s and 90s except 5th and Madison avenues)
Lincoln Center
Upper West Side
Far Upper West Side (above 96th Street)
Harlem
The Bronx
Brooklyn
Queens

Smoking New York's Smoke-Free Air Act prohibits smoking in restaurants with more than 35 seats, except in separate rooms, outside, or in the bar area. Certain restaurants, however, especially those with a heavily European or markedly youthful clientele, ignore the law. If either side of the ban bothers you, call ahead to ascertain the smoke-friendliness of your prospective boîte.

Dining Hours Breakfast, when available, usually begins at 7 or 7:30 AM. Brunch customarily runs from 11 AM or 12 PM to 3 or 4 PM and dinner from 5 or 6 to 10 or 11 PM, although many places stay open much later, especially on Saturday night; kitchens often close in the interval between the two services. You usually can't get a drink before 12 PM on Sundays, because New York State law restricts the serving of alcoholic beverages.

Reservations This is the weekend and this is New York. You can face crowds at any time. If you want to be sure you'll have a seat, call *at least* a day or two in advance.

Seasonal Closings Many restaurants close for vacation in summer or close on Sundays when business is slow—often in January and in midsummer. Always call ahead to avoid disappointment.

Prices The price categories outlined below are based on dinner prices:

Category	Dinner entrée	Dinner cost*
$$$$	over $24	over $60
$$$	$16–$25	$40–$60
$$	$10–$16	$20–$40
$	$5–$12	under $20

per person, including drink and tip

Saving Money Lunch and brunch prices are often ⅓ to ½ those at dinner, and prix fixe menus offer an even better value, making a potentially astronomical restaurant more terrestrial. Brunch prix fixe menus usually include at least one drink and coffee. And never let waiters get away with reciting daily specials without announcing their prices!

Credit Cards The following credit card abbreviations are used: AE, American Express; D, Discover; DC, Diners Club; MC, MasterCard; V, Visa.

Restaurants

Lower Manhattan

Tourists flock to South Street Seaport and environs, and locals tend to stay away, but everyone appreciates the boardwalk, river breezes, and tall ships. You can eat decently here, too—it's a bit like leaving town.

American/ Casual **Edward Moran Bar & Grill.** A singles' club for financialites during the week, where omelets and oysters come with mahogany wainscoting, and—the star of the place—sunset on the Hudson. *4 World Financial Center, tel. 212/945–2255. AE, DC, MC, V. Sun. 11:30 AM–9:30 PM. $*

McDonald's. Yes, you read that right. But *this* branch has a doorman, table service, a pianist (until 5 PM Sundays) and a slightly augmented menu. *160 Broadway, between Maiden La. and Liberty St., tel. 212/385–2063. AE, DC, MC, V. Weekends 7:30 AM–9 PM. $*

American/ International **Windows on the World.** From 1993 to 1996, when this restaurant was closed, New York had to gaze on itself from far lower down, but the top–of–the–World Trade Center is back. Use Cellar in the Sky to indulge in a prix fixe with wines that wins raves but breaks banks, or slum it at the Greatest Bar on Earth. Reserve, reserve, reserve. *1 World Trade Center, 107th floor, tel. 212/524–7000. AE, DC, MC, V. Main dining room: Sat. 5 PM–10 PM, Sun. 5 PM–9 PM; Cellars in the Sky: Sat. 7 PM–10 PM. $$–$$$$*

Hudson River Club. Bereft of its starriest chef (Waldy Malouf put it on the map), this is still a promising downtown destination on the second floor of the World Financial Center, where views of Liberty over the bay bring a tear to the eye—especially at sunset. The name tells you all you need to know about decor (clubby) and cuisine (Hudson River Valley produce: game, smoked fish, berries, seasonal). Sunny Sunday lunch nirvana. *4 World Financial Center, tel. 212/ 786–1500. AE. Sat. 5 PM–10 PM, Sun. 11:30 AM–2:30 PM. $$$*

Bridge Café. The Seaport's only wood-frame building (ca. 1801) charms with its pressed-tin ceiling, yellow wood-slat walls, and linoleum floor. Basic brunch fare is spiced with out-of-the-ordinary salads and entrées. The eponymous Brooklyn Bridge is practically overhead. *279 Water St. at Dover St., tel. 212/227–3344. AE, DC, MC, V. Sat. 5 PM–12 PM, Sun. 11:45 AM–10 PM. $$*

Harbour Lights. There may be better options for grills than this South Street Seaport restaurant, but they're not kidding about the lights. Go by night; order shrimp. *Pier 17, South Street Seaport, Fulton and South Sts., tel. 212/227–2800. AE, DC, MC, V. Weekends 10:30 AM–1 AM. $$*

Italian **Gianni's.** This is the Seaport's spot for pasta, garlic bread with Gorgonzola, and people-watching. *15 Fulton St., at South Street Seaport, tel. 212/608–7300. AE, DC, MC, V. Weekends 3 PM–10 PM. $$$*

Ecco. The old mahogany cabinetry, black-and-white tile floor, and bar, bristling with moldings that once attracted well-heeled crowds, are unchanged, as are the abundant antipasto buffet, exquisite Napoleons, and terrific veal chops. *124 Chambers St., between W. Broadway and Church St., tel. 212/227–7074. AE. Sat. 5:30 PM–11 PM. $$–$$$*

TriBeCa

Thanks largely to Drew Nieporent, who gave the world—or the triangle below Canal Street that is *his* world—the TriBeCa Grill, and Montrachet, and Nobu, and Layla, and Zeppole/TriBakery, and goodness knows what else by now, this former warehouse wasteland gobbles up most NYC foodies and scenies most weekends, Hamptons season excepted.

American/ Casual **Bubby's.** TriBeCa's essential (read: *endless* lines) sweet-tooth brunch, where the good build-your-own omelets and average sandwiches are uniformly passed over for fat fruit pies and pancake specials. A decidedly hippy ambience, more dinner-oriented these days. *120 Hudson St. at N. Moore St., tel. 212/219–0666. AE, MC, V. Weekends 8:30 AM–11 PM. $*

Walker's. This relaxed neighborhood corner bistro-saloon beams friendly vibes from a rather desolate corner, and practically never closes. Sundays, jazz musicians liven up the back dining room at 8 and 10 PM. Brunch is a deal. *16 N. Moore St. at Varick St., tel. 212/ 941–0142. AE, MC, V. Weekends 11:45 AM–4 AM. $*

American/ International **Odeon.** Who doesn't love this always-happening bistro/café/bar scene? Defining the evolutions of downtown chic since the arty early '80s, it's one accurate restaurant barometer, serving the seared fish and bitter leaves, the bruschetta and comfort-food pasta *de nos jours* to crowds that know. *145 W. Broadway, between Thomas and Duane Sts., tel. 212/233–0507. AE, DC, MC, V. Weekends 11:30 AM– 3 AM. $$$*

TriBeCa Grill. Part-Nieporent, part- De Niro, part-Maxwell's Plum (the bar part), past its prime, but settled in as a name-dropping neighborhood staple, serving slightly haute American food. Try brunch. *375 Greenwich St. at Franklin St., tel. 212/941–3900. AE, DC, MC, V. Sat. 5:30 PM–11:15 PM, Sun. 11:30 AM–2:45 AM, 5: 30 PM–9:45 PM. $$$*

American Regional **El Teddy's.** Liberty's crown rising out of this flashy Mexican joint's roof is a TriBeCa landmark, known for its frenetic bar crowd (not to mention its margaritas and burritos). The decor looks like Spain's eccentric architect, Antonio Gaudí, had a hand in it. *219 W. Broadway at Franklin St., tel. 212/941–7070. AE, DC, MC, V. Sat. 6 PM–1 AM, Sun. 6 PM–11 PM. $$*

French/ **Alison on Dominick Street.** Warm and tiny with its blue-velvet decor
Continental and deft, friendly service, this restaurant is loved for its sophisticate Francophile menus and understated romance. *38 Dominick St., between Hudson and Varick Sts., tel. 212/727–1188. AE, DC, MC, V. Sat. 5:30 PM–10: 45 PM, Sun. 5:30 PM–9:30 PM. $$$$*

Capsouto Frères. Here's the best brunch, bar none, says the consensus, and a romantic, brick-walled setting for it. Soften focus with any of a dozen single-malt Scotches. *451 Washington St., at Watts St., tel. 212/966–4900. AE, DC, MC, V. Sat. 12 PM–3 AM, 6 PM–11 PM, Sun. 12 PM–3:30 PM, 6 PM–10 PM. $$$*

Indian **Salaam Bombay.** A sight for sore Sunday eyes; these festive mauve walls, tapestry-covered banquettes, and golden ceiling, look especially plush over the bargain brunch buffet of tandooris and curries. *317–319 Greenwich St., between Duane and Reade Sts., tel. 212/ 226–9400. AE, DC, MC, V. Sat. 5:30 PM–11 PM, Sun. 12 PM–3 PM, 5:30 PM–11 PM. $–$$*

Italian **Gigino.** Gigino has an appealing Italian country look and interesting regional dishes, like a black risotto with raspberry vinegar, and *melanzane alla cioccolata* (eggplant in chocolate sauce). *323 Greenwich St., between Duane and Reade Sts., tel. 212/431–1112. AE, DC, MC, V. Sat. 4 PM–12 AM, Sun. 4 PM–11 PM. $$–$$$*

Japanese **Nobu.** The tables are booked solid, especially on Saturday. Seats at the sushi bar overlook the construction of Chef Matsuhisa's patented dishes of beauty. *Omikase* is the only way to go: You set the limits according to your taste buds and your pocket, and the chef takes care of the rest. *105 Hudson St., tel. 212/219–0500. AE, DC, MC, V. Weekends 5:45 PM–10:15 PM. $$$$*

Malaysian- **Franklin Station.** The high-ceiling room and open kitchen of this
French unique gallery-cum-restaurant is the setting for an Asian-French hybrid where satay meets croissants. BYO or get a papaya milk shake from the fresh juice bar. *222 W. Broadway, at Franklin St., tel. 212/274–8525. AE, MC, V. Weekends 10 AM–10 PM. $*

SoHo

On weekends, SoHo is immersed in crowds at all hours—out-of-towners in a shopping frenzy, mostly, with a cache of Euro-singles still animating the West-Broadway/Broome axis. The SoHo Grand hotel is dragging the cursor ever nearer Canal Street.

American/ **Cub Room Cafe.** Eat lovely, friendly American staples, like
Casual macaroni-and-cheese, black bean soup, sandwiches, French toast, in wood-and-brick non-decor. *183 Prince St., at Sullivan St., tel. 212/777–0030. AE. Sat. 12 PM–1 AM, Sun. 12 PM–11 PM. $$*

Jerry's. Probably the first diner-with-a-twist, with its zebra banquettes, mosaic floor, roasted chicken and veggies, and American breakfast, the Jerry's formula still works, now veering away from exhaustingly hip toward cozy. *101 Prince St., between Greene and Mercer Sts., tel. 212/966–9464; also 302 Columbus Ave., tel. 212/ 501–7500. AE, MC, V. Sat. 11 AM–11:30 PM, Sun., 11 PM–5 PM. $$*

Lucky Strike. Tables are veneered wine crates, the bar is copper, the ceiling is stamped tin, and the menu is scrawled on ancient mirrors, but the frantic faux-Paris scene's the thing. Brunchers find pizzetas and pastas, eggs and burgers, and a more laid-back vibe. *59 Grand St., near W. Broadway, tel. 212/941–0479. AE, MC, V. Weekends 12 PM–4 AM. $$*

Aggie's. This funky counterculture coffee shop hops all day, thanks to reasonable prices for sprightly soups and sprouty sandwiches.

146 W. Houston St., at MacDougal St., tel. 212/673–8994. No credit cards. Sat. 10 AM–4 PM, 6 PM–11 PM, Sun. 10 AM–4 PM. $

Café Borgia. This cozy, brick, tin-ceiling, family-run neighborhood institution provides rest for the footsore, all kinds of espresso, cappuccino, hot chocolate, tea, or frappé, and a good selection of sandwiches and pastries. *161 Prince St., between W. Broadway and Thompson St., tel. 212/677–1850. No credit cards. Weekends 10 AM–12 AM. $*

Dean & Deluca. Join the hordes in this large and airy, skylit, white space and try to resist exquisite cakes, muffins, scones, and cookies—or pastas, herb-scattered chicken, and baguette sandwiches from the lunch counter. *121 Prince St., tel. 212/254–8776. No credit cards. Weekends 9 AM–8 PM. $*

Ear Inn. At this artsy hangout by the Hudson, there's one of the city's finest jukeboxes, hit-or-miss comfort food, coziness, and regular literary/musical soirees. *326 Spring St., between Washington and Greenwich Sts., tel. 212/226–9060. AE, DC. Weekends 12 PM–4 AM. $*

Fanelli. Crowds congregate at this smoky Old New York relic for beer and burgers amid yellowing boxing photos. *94 Prince St., at Mercer St., tel. 212/226–9412. AE, DC, MC, V. Sat. 12 PM–2 AM, Sun. 12 PM–12:30 AM. $*

Moondance Diner. Pin-spot lighting, an eclectic soundtrack, and sparkly vinyl banquettes and counter stools, with an a/c-ed summer extension in a *tent*, is the funky setting for veggies, risottos, burgers, chicken, salads and classic brunches. *80 6th Ave., between Canal and Grand Sts., tel. 212/226–1191. No credit cards. Open Sat. 24 hrs, Sun. 8:30 AM– 12 AM. $*

Olive's. A glorified takeout counter serving spectacular sandwiches and "today's" cake or cookie. You can refuel fast and sit down, too, if you grab that red bench first. *120 Prince St., between Greene and Wooster Sts., tel. 212/941–0111. AE, MC, V. Sat. 9 AM–7 PM, Sun. 9 AM–6 PM. $*

Spring Street Natural Restaurant. Hanging plants, huge windows, and ceiling fans, as well as a not-too in-your-face organic ethic make this '70s survivor a sunny, undemanding place to brunch. The never-changing menu has smoked turkey–goat's cheese salads, stir-fries, broiled bluefish, great French toast. Avoid the pasta. *62 Spring St., at Lafayette St., tel. 212/966–0290. AE, DC, MC, V. Sat. 11:30 AM–1 AM, Sun. 11:30 AM–12 AM. $*

American/ International

Cupping Room Café. Exposed brick, a pot-bellied stove, and an antique bar are the ideal breakfast backdrop, and the baked goods here hit the spot. Go early. *359 W. Broadway, between Broome and Grand Sts., tel. 212/925–2898. AE, DC, MC, V. Sat. 7:30 AM–2 AM, Sun. 7:30 AM–12 AM. $$–$$$*

Blue Ribbon. Famed as the chefs-and-the-people-who-love-them late night hang. Don't imagine you can roll up at 2 AM and get a table for the fab *coquillages* (shellfish); you'll have an hour's wait. Sunday's better. *97 Sullivan St., tel. 212/274–0404. AE, DC, MC, V. Sat. 12 PM–4 AM, Sun. 12 PM–2 AM. $$*

Match. A keeper on the northern edge of Soho, with Oriental-ish appetizer-type food served in deconstructed interior to mostly young arty people. The bar is the thing. *160 Mercer St., tel. 212/343–0020. AE, DC, MC, V. Sat. 11:30–4 AM, Sun. 11:30–2 AM. $$*

Savoy. Young owners scour the land for suppliers of the freshest produce for constructing inventive U.S.-regional menus to serve at their tiny, warmly-lit salon. *70 Prince St., tel. 212/219–8570. AE, MC, V. Sat. 12 PM–3 PM, 6 PM–11 PM, Sun. 6 PM–10 PM. $$*

SoHo Kitchen. You can choose from some 90 different wines by the glass—and 14 champagnes—at this lofty brick-walled charmer. Stick to burgers or pasta and try a "flight"—groups of related wines (or beer) in taster sizes. *103 Greene St., between Prince and Spring*

Sts., *tel. 212/925–1866. AE, DC, MC, V. Sat. 11:30 AM–1:30 AM, Sun. 12 PM–10:30 PM. $*

Eastern European **Triplet's Roumanian.** A rollicking place for chopped liver, potato pancakes, and mammoth chops, with ladles of *schmaltz*, in every sense, including singing waiters. *11–17 Grand St., at 6th Ave., tel. 212/925–9303. AE, DC, MC, V. Sat. 6:45 PM–12:30 AM, Sun. 4 PM–9:30 PM. $$$*

French **Provence.** Well known for its stunning garden, consistently fantastic Southern French down-home cuisine in generous portions, and a laid-back, romantic atmosphere. *38 MacDougal St., tel. 212/475–7500. AE, MC, V. Sat. 12 PM–3 PM, 6 PM–12 AM, Sun. 12 PM–3; 6 PM–11:30 PM. $$$*

Raoul's. An everlasting scene, with an elbow-to-elbow bar, and very excellent, authentic Parisian bistro food. The check may be higher than you expect, but you're paying for the ambience. *180 Prince St., near Thompson St., tel. 212/966–3518. AE, MC, V. Sat. 5:30 PM–2 AM, Sun. 5:30 PM–12 PM. $$$*

La Jumelle. Dark, loud, young, and—be warned—smoky, this dive of a bar-resto on Euro-corner is not known for its adequate fodder (chicken breast smothered in Dijon mustard, bland couscous, moules), but on a good night, it's fun city. *55 Grand St., tel. 212/941–9651. AE, MC, V. Sat. 5 PM–2 AM, Sun. 5 PM–12 AM. $$*

Soho Steak. The ideal neighborhood bistro delights a neighborhood that's struggling not to become a theme park. Eat braised pheasant, salade niçoise, perfect *pommes allumettes* (matchstick fries), and, of course, steak many ways, all of them French. *90 Thompson St., tel. 212/226–0602. No credit cards. Sat. 6:30 PM–12 AM, Sun. 6:30 PM–11 PM. $$*

Italian **Mezzogiorno.** An everlasting corner trattoria, where the sidewalk tables provide great people-watching, and the thin-crust pizzas, pasta, and polenta dishes match the Italian rock music for a generic European mood. *195 Spring St., at Sullivan St., tel. 212/334–2112. No credit cards. Sat. 12 PM–2 AM, Sun. 12 PM–1 AM. $$–$$$*

Amici Miei. The only sidewalk garden actually *on* Houston Street is better than it's rich Milanese pasta and meat dishes, but try a trattoria brunch of focaccia and frittata. *475 W. Broadway, at Houston St., tel. 212/533–1933. AE, MC, V. Weekends 12 PM–1 AM. $$*

Arturo's. Get great pizza from the brick-lined, coal-fired oven at this institution with rickety chairs. Nighttime jazz is a plus. *106 W. Houston St., at Thompson St., tel. 212/475–9828. AE, MC, V. Weekends 3 PM–12 AM. $*

Japanese **Honmura An.** There's no contest: When it comes to soba noodles, this is the best place in town, but be prepared to pay. *170 Mercer St., tel. 212/334–5253. AE, DC, MC, V. Sat. 6 PM–10:30 PM, Sun. 6 PM–9:30 PM. $$$*

Blue Ribbon Sushi. A few doors down from its eponymous sibling, this estimable train-shaped booth-lined sushi place has a vast and superior menu, long lines, no sign, and NYC's only sushi smoking room. *119 Sullivan St., tel. 212/343–0404. AE, DC, MC, V. Weekends 6 PM–2 AM. $$–$$$*

Omen. Unusual Japanese fare at this diminutive rustic includes ginger-tangy *omen*, a noodle soup. *113 Thompson St., between Prince and Spring Sts., tel. 212/925–8923. AE, DC. Weekends 5:30 PM–10:30 PM. $$*

Middle Eastern **Casa La Femme.** Either the souk of your dreams, with sexy, annually changing decor (cushions, muslin-draped de-e-ep booths, a communal hookah), and backgammon tables, or a Euro-nightmare of people too gorgeous to live. Still, everyone likes the fantastic tajines: try the roasted red snapper with caramelized onions, potatoes, and tomatoes). Check out Sunday's movie night. *150 Wooster St., tel. 212/505–0005. AE, MC, V. Weekends 5:30 PM–3 AM. $$*

Café Noir. This is Marakesh-in-Soho with crumbling stucco walls, smoke, Moroccan picking food, and hordes of trendies late at night. *32 Grand St., tel. 212/431–7910. AE, MC, V. Weekends 11 AM–4 AM. $–$$*

Portuguese **Pão!** A tiny find that has authentic Lisbon mama's cooking, on the way-west strip by the Ear Inn. It's notably friendly. *322 Spring St., tel. 212/334–5464. AE, MC, V. Sat. 6 PM–12:30 AM, Sun. 6 PM–10:30 PM. $$*

Pseudo- **Pravda.** By now, last year's model-watcher's hangout has settled
Russian into being the nice bar it resembles. All witty battered leather armchairs, Russian constructivist art, own-label flavored vodkas, and an underground buzz, this isn't an eating place, unless fish eggs and *blinis* (savory pancakes) satisfy. *281 Lafayette St., tel. 212/226–4696. AE, MC, V. Sat. 5 PM–3:30 AM, Sun. 5 PM–2:30 AM. $$*

Vegetarian **Souen.** Brunchers at this natural-food old-timer get their waffles made with pounded sweet rice. *210 6th Ave., at Prince St., tel. 212/807–7421. AE, DC, MC, V. Weekends 10 AM–10 PM. $*

Little Italy and Chinatown

The north-eastern end of Little Italy has become a neighborhood unto itself, full of happening little stores selling great design wares, tiny storefront galleries, and equally small-scale restaurants. As for old Mulberry Street, it still rolls on, with its cannoli, the red sauce, the zeppole, and the sidewalk tables crowded with tourists. Chinatown has been threatening to swallow it for years, but the main drag drags on. Chinatown gets going early on Sunday for *dim sum*. If you want a full meal, come around 7 PM, when the pace slows. Note that many restaurants here do not accept credit cards, offer reservations only to groups, and serve no liquor; check ahead.

American/ **M&R Bar.** You'd think this neighborhood fave had been there
Casual forever, but it only opened in 1995, since then the classic bar, the scarlet dining room lined with framed nudes, and the yard—all tiny—have been jumping. The American food's OK; cioppino, broiled fish, Caesar salad. Avoid the risotto, try the appetizer plate. *264 Elizabeth St., tel. 212/226–0559. AE, MC, V. Sat. 5 PM–1 AM, Sun. 11 AM–3:30 PM, 5 PM–1 AM. $$*

Chinese **Beijing Duck House.** Crisp-skinned Beijing duck, which must be ordered ahead elsewhere, is served daily in these basic digs. *22 Mott St., near Bayard St., tel. 212/227–1810. AE. Weekends 11:30 AM–10:30 PM. $$*
Canton. With its powder-blue tablecloths and blond wood walls, this Cantonese seafood specialist turns out consistently good food, reflecting owner-chef Larry Leong's interest in French and Italian cuisine. Go before 6 or after 8. *45 Division St., between Market St. and Bowery, tel. 212/226–4441. No credit cards. BYOB. Weekends 12 PM–9:30 PM. $$*
20 Mott Street Restaurant. Crowds jam this bright, multitiered restaurant for the golden fried crab claws or rice-flour dumplings with pork. The Cantonese menu offered later on is encyclopedic. *20 Mott St., between Bowery and Pell St., tel. 212/964–0380. AE, MC, V. Weekends 9 AM–11 PM. $$*
Bo Ky. Half Thai, half *teo-chew* (indigenous to China's Quangdong province), this absolutely plain storefront restaurant offers fiery main-course soups unique to Chinatown. *80 Bayard St., between Mott and Baxter Sts., tel. 212/406–2292. No credit cards. Weekends 8 AM–9:30 PM. $*
Joe's Shanghai. Famous for its soup dumplings, which must—simply must—be tried to be believed. *9 Pell St., tel. 212/233–8888. No credit cards. Weekends 11 AM–11:30 PM. $*

New York Noodle Town. It's virtually impossible to order wrong at this open secret of a bargain, hideous to behold though it is (bring sunglasses). Roasted meats are sublime. *28½ Bowery, tel. 212/349–0923. No credit cards. Open 24 hrs.* $

Nice Restaurant. In the best Hong Kong style, Nice does well with dim sum and with unusual dishes such as soy-flavored squab and salt-baked chicken. *35 E. Broadway, between Catherine and Market Sts., tel. 212/406–9776. AE. Weekends 8 AM–10:30 PM.* $

Oriental Town Seafood. Sea-fresh fare that stands out even in Chinatown makes it easy to overlook plain-Jane surroundings and hurry-up service. *14 Elizabeth St., between Canal and Bayard Sts., tel. 212/619–0085. No credit cards. Weekends 8:30 AM–10 PM.* $

69 Mott. Any dish composed of pork is the way to go here, whether in soups, over rice, or shredded and blended with a spicy sauce. Very popular, crowded, and not at all distinguished by its finesse in service. *69 Mott St., tel. 212/233–5877. No credit cards. Weekends 9 AM–10 PM.* $

31 Dim Sum House. Possibly the noisiest and tastiest dim sum–eria in all Chinatown. Cheerful servers seat you at shared round tables, coax you to taste every dumpling yet invented, and count plates to tally up your bill. *31 Division St., tel. 212/431–9063. No credit cards. Weekends 7:30 AM–10 PM.* $

Wo Hop. Come here to try *congee*, a soupy rice purée, chunky with beef, chicken, duck, pork, or seafood. *15 Mott St., between Bowery and Park Row, tel. 212/766–9160, Sun. 11–5; 17 Mott St., tel. 212/962–8617; No credit cards at either. Open 24 hrs.* $

French **Le Jardin Bistro.** On the Soho borderline, this has the perfect arbor out back, for the coq au vin, *moules marinieres* (mussels in broth), cassoulet, and steak-frites of your Francophile heart's desire. *25 Cleveland Pl., tel. 212/343–9599. AE, MC, V. Weekends 11:30 AM–3:30 PM, 6 PM–11 PM.* $$

Café Gitane. Light up, they mean it. Maybe it's the nicotine, but there's always a laid-back scene behind the Gitane-pack blue storefront, where great foccacia sandwiches and oily-eggplant salads go down well with coffee and gossip. *242 Mott St., tel. 212/334–9552. No credit cards. Sat. 9 AM–12 AM, Sun. 9 AM–11:30 PM.* $

Italian **Grotta Azzurra.** Blue grotto indeed, with all the tourist trappings of the neighborhood, from lobster fra diavolo to walls of signed celeb photos. *387 Broome St., at Mulberry St., tel. 212/925–8775. No credit cards. Weekends 12 PM–11:30 PM.* $$

Puglia. This vintage red-sauce specialist is rowdy and crowded with seekers of red wine and hefty portions of lasagna, spaghetti, and veal. *189 Hester St., at Mulberry St., tel. 212/966–6006. No credit cards. Weekends 12 PM–12 AM.* $–$$

Vincent's Clam Bar. Seafood and pasta are doused with the hot sauce amid old wood beams and big arched windows at this local legend (now *which* mobster was shot here?). *119 Mott St., at Hester St., tel. 212/226–8133. AE. Weekends 11:30 AM–3:30 AM.* $–$$

Ferrara. It's the best-known of all Little Italy's bakeries, and has now cloned itself all over town, but you can still catch a buzz at the bustling dessert mecca, where the *sfogliatelle* (a "thousand-layer" pastry) and pignoli should be fresh, thanks to rapid turnover. *195 Grand St., tel. 212/226–6150. AE, MC, V. Weekends 8:30 AM–12 AM.* $

Lombardi's. The country's first pizzeria is back with two sizes (large and LARGE) and a choice of eight toppings on the city's best coal-oven pies. *32 Spring St., tel. 212/941–7994. No credit cards. Weekends 11:30 AM–10 PM.* $

Thai **Thailand Restaurant.** A frequently jolly ambience and some of the city's best—and least pricey—Thai food make up for the faded wood paneling and floor tiles, and the Bangkok temple–style booths are irresistible. *106 Bayard St., at Baxter St., tel. 212/349–3132. AE. Weekends 12 PM–12 AM. $*

Vietnamese **Nha Trang.** The usual ugly glass-topped tables, florescent lighting, and plastic chopsticks don't look great, but that's not why you're here. The menu is huge, repetitive, and reliable. Ask for help ordering. *87 Baxter St., tel. 212/233–5948. No credit cards. Weekends 10 AM–10 PM. $*

Pho Bang. This branch of the small, but global, chain, does the best summer rolls in town, so the hideous decor is endurable. *117 Mott St., tel. 212/966–3797. No credit cards. Weekends 10 AM–10 PM. $*

Saigon House Restaurant. The food is good, fresh, and suitably lemongrassed, at this comfortable little cellar hideaway facing Columbus Park, behind the Criminal Courts building. *89 Bayard St., tel. 212/732–8988. AE, DC, MC, V. Weekends 11:30 AM–10:30 PM. $*

Lower East Side

Don't come here Saturday for Eastern European and deli fare–the streets are all but boarded up–but save calories and cash for the Sunday foray into Orchard Street.

Chinese/ Kosher **Bernstein-on-Essex.** A—or is it *the*—kosher-Chinese serves a lean, peppery-smoky pastrami. *135 Essex St., between Delancey and Houston Sts., tel. 212/473–3900. AE, MC, V. Weekends 11 AM–12:30 AM. $$*

Deli **Katz's Deli.** Thanks to that movie, everyone knows the place, but do they realize the meats are still cured on the premises? Sit at the table with the sign: "This is where Meg Ryan sat. . . . Have what she had." *205 Houston St., at Ludlow St., tel. 212/254–2246. AE. Sat. 8 AM–12 AM, Sun. 8 AM–10 PM. $*

Eastern European **Sammy's Roumanian.** To call this Jewish steak house a "hole in the wall" suggests a charm that does not exist. It's simply a clamorous storefront whose chief distinction is the high decibel level of the entertainment and the gargantuan servings of steaks, chops, and traditional flanken, kreplach, and stuffed cabbage. Despite the relatively uncomplicated menu, the bill can add up fast. *157 Chrystie St., near Delancey St., tel. 212/673–5526. AE, DC, MC, V. Weekends 3 PM–11 PM. $$$*

Original Yonah Schimmel Kinshery. The knishery to end all knisheries, this is authentic, from its cracked Formica to its "order anything as long as it's a knish." Or borscht. We're so glad it's still here, but unsure why, since the hunger-blitzing things are like bricks. *137 E. Houston St., near 2nd Ave., tel. 212/477–2858. No credit cards. Weekends 8 AM–6 PM. $*

Jewish Dairy **Ratner's Restaurant.** Potato pancakes or pierogi, gefilte fish and kreplach, baked egg barley with creamed mushrooms, borscht, *matzo brei* (matzo pancake)—all the Jewish dairy favorites are here, and so deeply satisfying that handsome brunch spots elsewhere seem prissy by comparison. *138 Delancey St., between Norfolk and Suffolk Sts., tel. 212/677–5588. AE, MC, V. Sat. 6 PM–2 AM, Sun. 6 AM–12 AM. $*

East Village and NoHo

It's been Ukrainian and Polish, it's been the new Soho, its park has been the site of Wigstock—and riots—it's been grunge and punk and junkie, and what is the East Village now? All those things, plus a restaurant playground. NoHo's artery is Lafayette, with a few veins off of it.

American **First.** Dark, loud, lined with booths and youths, this dining room is best late, for a vast portion of, say, beer-braised short ribs with macaroni and cheese and jicama slaw, and a smoke at the bar. *87 1st Ave., tel. 212/674–3823. AE, MC, V. Sat. 6 PM–3 AM, Sun. 11 PM–1 AM. $$*

Opaline. The biggest thing underground in the E.V., this dim and deconstructed two-tiered cavern beneath Takahachi calls to mind Parisian fin-de-siècle absinthe-drinking decadence, and has a likable menu of bistro-type dishes (duck confit salad, salmon and lentils in red wine). *85 Ave. A, tel. 212/475–5050. AE, DC, MC, V. Sat. 6 PM– 2 AM, Sun. 6 PM–11 PM. $$*

Pisces. One of the East Village's gastronomic highlights from day one—when it was virtually it's *only* gastronomic highlight—this plainly wood-floored, open-in-summer, white-tableclothed eatery, where locals mix with slumming Upper East Siders, serves, yes, fish. They smoke their own too. *95 Ave. A, tel. 212/260–6660. AE, MC, V. Sat. 5:30 PM–1 AM, Sun. 11:30 AM–11:30 PM. $$*

Marion's. In this older sister of M&R Bar, a revival of a JFK (Sr.) haunt, get good martinis and OK '50s retro food, and attend fashion-show brunches the first Sunday of every month. *354 Bowery, between Great Jones and 4th Sts., tel. 212/475–7621. MC, V. Sat. 6 PM– 12:30 AM, Sun. 6 PM–11:30 PM. $–$$*

American/ Casual

Time Café. The best thing here is the Fez bar in back, but actually the vaguely organic food's fine—roast chicken with succotash, smoked salmon quesadilla rolled up like maki. Brunch is way popular, especially when it's warm enough to eat outside. *380 Lafayette St., at Great Jones St., tel. 212/533–7000. AE, DC, MC, V. Sat. 10:30 PM–1 AM, Sun. 12 PM–12 AM. $$*

DoJo. This woodsy, pseudo-Japanese-vegetarian, and surprisingly tasty grunger haunt is cheap and cheerful. *24 St. Mark's Pl., between 2nd and 3rd Aves., tel. 212/674–9821. No credit cards. Weekends. 11 AM–1 AM. $*

NoHo Star. It's been around so long, you forget to admire the decor, with its ceramic tile art, generous light and space, but this stayer is useful all hours—especially brunch. The schizoid American/ Oriental menu is reliable; go for a sandwich or salad—skip the stir-fry. *330 Lafayette St., at Bleecker St., tel. 212/925–0070. AE, DC, MC, V. Weekends 10:30 AM–2 AM. $*

Old Devil Moon. A lovable bargain stuffed with yard-sale treasures, serving vast plates of mom-never-made-it-like-this Southern faves: baked ham and cakes for brunch; collards and meat loaf and spiced gravy and so on. *511 E. 12th St., tel. 212/475–4357. MC, V. Weekends 10 AM–12 AM. $*

Three of Cups. Another dark dive for the Villagers, specializing in thin-crust pizzas, though a lot of other unpretentious food exits the wood-burning oven. Check out the bordello-like downstairs dive bar while you wait. *83 1st Ave., tel. 212/388–0059. MC, V. Sat. 12 PM–2 AM, Sun. 12 PM–1 AM. $*

Two Boots. Italian/Cajun is the conceit, but you wouldn't know it as you order another thin-crust pizza pie amid hipsters and families and wildly colored decor. *37 Ave. A, tel. 212/505–2276. MC, V. Sat. 12 PM–1 AM, Sun. 12 PM–12 AM. $*

Yaffa Café. The funkiest garden in town was maybe done by the Lady Bunny; inside, tiny tables and pitch darkness create grunge at all hours. The food's a 70s time warp, and none the worse for that— Mid-East dips, stir fries, chicken and pasta entrees; a hits-the-spot brunch menu. *97 St. Mark's Pl., tel. 212/674–9302. MC, V. Open 24 hrs. $*

American Regional

Miracle Grill. Fairly sophisticated Southwestern grills, guac and chips, and frozen fruit margaritas are served in an austere dining room, but you'd be crazy to miss the big, tree-shaded, fairy-lighted garden. *112 1st Ave., near 7th St., tel. 212/254–2353. AE, MC, V. Sat. 11:30 AM–12 AM, Sun. 11:30 AM–11 PM. $$*

Great Jones Street Café. Cramped but pleasingly funky, this is a must if you're in the mood for Cajun martinis (spiked with jalapeños), blackened bluefish, a collegial crowd, and a resonant juke-box. *54 Great Jones St., west of Bowery, tel. 212/674–9304. No credit cards. Sat. 11:30 PM–1 AM, Sun. 11:30 PM–12 AM. $*

Deli/Eastern European

Kiev. The essential dive for challah French toast, pierogi, chicken soup and blintzes at 4 AM. It's basic; sometimes friendly, usually full—as you will be after. *117 2nd Ave., tel. 212/674–4040. No credit cards. Open 24 hrs. $*

Second Avenue Kosher Delicatessen. The senseless murder of owner, Abe Liebewohl, vocal opponent of the egregious street fairs that bug and gridlock all New York, did not kill his wonderful deli: Still one of the top three. Lines are probable. *156 2nd Ave., at 10th St., tel. 212/677–0606. AE. Sat. 7 AM–12 AM, Sun. 7 AM–12 AM. $*

Veselka. This institution of a Ukrainian diner is open all hours for stodgy bricks of pierogi, kasha, sweet cheese blintzes, and heart-warming soups. The complete renovation of '96 miraculously failed to kill its brooding ambiance, despite the fishbowl-like walls of window in back. *144 2nd Ave., at 9th St., tel. 212/228–9682. AE, MC, V. Open 24 hrs. $*

English

Telephone Bar & Grill. Bangers, shepherd's pie, a good beer selection, and a facade of three authentic red London phone booths lend an English accent to this popular pub. *149 2nd Ave., between 9th and 10th Sts., tel. 212/529–5000. AE, MC, V. Sat. 11:30 PM–2:30 AM, Sun. 10:30 AM–1:30 AM. $*

Greek

Agrotikon. Do make the trek to the ugliest block in the neighborhood for cuisine bearing nil relation to coffee shop moussaka: snapper with anise and caraway; baked baby goat; chicken with pine nuts, feta, and capers; garlic and cod mashed potato. . . . Repeat visits are necessary to do justice to it all. *322 E. 14th St., tel. 212/473–2602. AE, MC, V. Weekends 5 PM–12 AM. $$*

Indian

Haveli. By popular vote, this beats Indian Row (just around the corner), as its crackle-glass window, and cool decor hint. The cost is only slightly above the rest, and uncommon extras like tomato-and-mustard-seed soup make up for the difference. *100 2nd Ave., between 5th and 6th Sts., tel. 212/982–0533. AE, DC, MC, V. Weekends 12 PM–12 AM. $*

Mitali East. The brunch buffet is a steal at this snug Indian standby. *334 E. 6th St., between 1st and 2nd Aves., tel. 212/533–2508. AE, MC, V. Sat. 12 PM–12:30 AM, Sun. 12 PM–12 AM. $*

Rose of India. This is one of the best, and cheapest, spots on the curry block. *308 E. 6th St., tel. 212/533–5011. No credit cards. Weekends 12 PM–12 AM. $*

Italian

Col Legno. The wood-burning oven that lends a homey feeling to this spare eatery imparts a smoky flavor to some very good grills, the standouts here. *231 E. 9th St., between 2nd and 3rd Aves., tel. 212/777–4650. AE. Weekends 6 PM–11:30 PM. $$*

Cucina di Pesce. Free antipasto and robust pastas and seafoods draw crowds to this rococo downstairs room full of antique mirrors and decorative trinkets. *87 E. 4th St., between 2nd and 3rd Aves., tel. 212/260–6800. No credit cards. Sat. 3 PM–1 AM, Sun. 2:30 PM–12 AM. $*

In Padella. Drop in and join local students and artists for well-executed pasta dishes, fresh seafood specials, and delicious focaccia. *145 2nd Ave., at 9th St., tel. 212/598–9800. No credit cards. Sat. 11 AM–1 AM, Sun. 11 AM–12 AM. $*

John's of 12th Street. Candles stuck in raffia-wrapped Chianti bottles barely illuminate this hole-in-the-wall established in 1908. It draws companionable crowds of old and young at peak hours, so go early if you haven't reserved. *302 E. 12th St., just east of 2nd Ave., tel. 212/475–9531. No credit cards. Sat. 4:30 PM–11:30 PM, Sun. 3:30 PM–10:30 PM. $*

Lanza Restaurant. Ceiling fans, paintings of Italian scenes, a tile floor, flowers, and an inviting garden create the feel of an authentic trattoria. The hungry crowds know this is one of Manhattan's greatest restaurant bargains. *168 1st Ave., between 10th and 11th Sts., tel. 212/674–7014. AE, DC, MC, V. Sat. 12 PM–11 PM, Sun. 12 PM–10 PM. $*

Veniero's. The correct after-dinner dessert-and-espresso call, or useful for a decadently sugary breakfast, this ancient bakery has lines down the block in warmer seasons. *342 E. 11th St., tel.212/674–7264. AE, MC, V. Sat. 8 AM–1 AM, Sun. 8 AM–12 AM. $*

Japanese **Takahachi.** Simply, super sushi in the usual bright-lights, pine tables setting. The crab shumai are unmissable, as are the more traditional country appetizers. *85 Ave. A, tel. 212/505–6524. AE, MC, V. Weekends 5:30 PM–12:30 AM. $$*

Korean **Dok Suni's Korean Home Cooking.** A notch more hep than many other Korean BBQ places. Come here for the do-your-own BBQing on the table meats, Korean tacos (thinly sliced beef to top with hot sauce and wrap in lettuce leaves), cold beer, and crowds. *119 1st Ave., between 7th and 8th Sts., tel. 212/477–9506. No credit cards. Sat. 4:30 PM–1 AM, Sun. 4:30 PM–11 PM. $*

Thai **Siam Square.** This cramped, unassuming, family-run place serves up surprisingly fresh and flavorful curries. A note on the menu invites you to alter the heat and meat levels to your taste. *92 2nd Ave., between 5th and 6th Sts., tel. 212/505–1240. AE, DC, MC, V. Sat. 11:30 AM–12 AM, Sun. 11:30 AM–11 PM. $*

Vegetarian **Souen.** This branch of the Soho eatery (*see above*) pleases serious vegetarians. *28 E. 13th St., tel. 212/627–7150. AE, DC, MC, V. Sat. 10 AM–11 PM, Sun. 10 AM–10 PM. $–$$*

Angelika Kitchen. This serene, pine-table café makes macrobiotic taste exciting. Theater types and dancers flock for minutely described specials, organic greens and sea vegetable combos, as well as spectacular cornbread. *300 E. 12th St., between 1st and 2nd Aves., tel. 212/228–2909. No credit cards. Weekends 11:30 AM–10:30 PM. $*

Vietnamese/ **Indochine.** It's ba-a-ack. The Asian-colonial place-to-be-seen in the **Cambodian** Eighties got a second wind. Is it still humming? If you can make reservations on the weekend, it's not. *430 Lafayette St., between Astor Pl. and 4th St., tel. 212/505–5111. AE, DC, MC, V. Weekends 5:30 PM–12:30 AM. $$$*

West Village

The West Village is thick with restaurants—and with crowds on Saturday nights. Most keep late hours, and do a roaring brunch trade, both days.

American **Gotham Bar & Grill.** Home of Alfred Portale and his piled-high entrées. Reserve way ahead, because it's still among the best in town. Beware the bar scene on Saturday. *12 E. 12th St., between 5th Ave. and University Pl., tel. 212/620–4020. AE, DC, MC, V. Sat. 5:30 PM–11 PM, Sun. 5:30 PM–10 PM. $$$$*

One If By Land, Two If By Sea. Aaron Burr's former carriage house stands out for its fireside bar, a romantic idyll with its velvet settees, piano music, and exquisite flowers. *11 Barrow St., between 7th Ave. and W. 4th St., tel. 212/228–0822. AE, DC, MC, V. Sat. 5:30 PM–12 AM, Sun. 5:30 PM–11 PM. $$$*

Grove. An unpretentious neighborhood staple that's best for its big garden, though the food—things like grilled fish, lamb shank, peach cobbler—is perfectly OK. *314 Bleecker St., tel. 212/675–9463. AE, DC, MC, V. Sat. 11 AM–12 AM, Sun. 11 AM–11 PM. $$*

Home. Its name conjures images of hearth-side cocooning, homemade stews and roasts, onion rings, big plates of cookies and—this being Manhattan—tiny spaces, and that's exactly what you get. Plus a minute garden and lovely service. *20 Cornelia St., tel. 212/243–9579. AE. Sat. 11 AM–11 PM, Sun. 11 AM–10 PM. $$*

Knickerbocker Bar & Grill. Hung with vintage posters and Hirschfeld drawings, this large room serves a bargain brunch, then dinner until 12 AM. *33 University Pl., at 9th St., tel. 212/228–8490. AE, DC, MC, V. Weekends 12 PM–2 AM. $$*

La Bohème. Design freethinker Sam Lopata's charming little faux-Provençal bistro has colander-shaded light bulbs, thin-crust pizzas, good steak-frites, and first-rate apple tart and roast chicken. *24 Minetta La., near 6th Ave., tel. 212/473–6442. AE, V. Sat. 12 PM–12 AM, Sun. 12 PM–11 PM. $$*

Le Zoo. A happening, hopping, friendly wooden-floored, candlelit, white-table-clothed Villager, with ambitious French-American bistro food for fortyish Calvin Klein wearers and gay mafia. *314 W. 11th St., tel. 212/620–0393. AE, DC, MC, V. Sat. 6 PM–12 AM, Sun. 11 AM–11 PM. $$*

Thomas Scott's. This jewel box of a restaurant is outfitted with Schott & Zwiesel crystal, Villeroy & Boch china, mahogany corkedwood floors, and then candlelit. Try duck and lentil soup, salmon steak, and "Seven Degrees of Orgasm" chocolate cake. *72–74 Bedford St., at Commerce St., tel. 212/627–4011. AE, DC, MC, V. Sat. 6 PM–11 PM, Sun. 12 PM–10 PM. $$*

American/ Casual

Nadine's. Large windows make this corner place especially pleasant at brunch time, when salads and sandwiches team with breakfast fare for diverting results, and it's all served with buttermilk biscuits and fruit butters. *99 Bank St., at Greenwich St., tel. 212/924–3165. AE, DC, MC, V. Sat. 11 PM–1 AM, Sun. 11 AM–12 AM. $$*

Sweet Basil. Brunch at this brick-and-wood spot with a pressed-tin ceiling features not only burgers but some of the city's best jazz (there's a music charge from 10 PM to 2 AM). *88 7th Ave. S, between Grove and Bleecker Sts., tel. 212/242–1785. AE, MC, V. Weekends 11 AM–2 AM. $$*

Village Grill. Thankfully large, with tons of sidewalk tables, this serves standard Yankee-Frenchie food, but is best for watching the world go by. *518 La Guardia Pl., tel. 212/228–1001. AE, MC, V. Weekends 12 PM–2 AM. $$*

Anglers & Writers Salon de Thé. At this charmer, few can resist the French toast made from raisin-walnut bread, the pecan waffles, or the blueberry or cherry pancakes; others go for open-faced turkey sandwiches with stuffing, pastas, and antipasto platters. *420 Hudson St., at St. Luke's Pl., tel. 212/675–0810. No credit cards. Sat. 9 AM–12 AM, Sun. 10 AM–10 PM. $*

Chumley's. This former speakeasy, still without a sign outside, is seductively cozy for burgers served hearthside. *86 Bedford St., at Barrow St., tel. 212/675–4449. No credit cards. Sat. 12 PM–2 AM, Sun. 2 PM–12 AM. $*

Corner Bistro. Burger mecca, to say nothing of the fries. *331 W. 4th St., tel. 212/242–9502. No credit cards. Sat. 11 AM–4 AM, Sun. 11 AM–2 AM. $*

White Horse Tavern. A rickety favorite of Dylan Thomas, this genial saloon draws a non–New York crowd. *567 Hudson St., at 11th St., tel. 212/243–9260. No credit cards. Sat. 11 AM–4 AM, Sun. 11 AM–2 AM. $*

American Regional

Fannie's Oyster Bar. With its pleasant garden, this is a bit of New Orleans, complete with bead curtains, gumbo, jambalaya, oysters, Cajun martinis, and live jazz and blues. *765 Washington St., between 12th and W. Bethune Sts., tel. 212/255–5101. No credit cards. Sat. 6 PM–12 AM. Closed Sun. $$*

Ye Waverly Inn. Yankee pot roast, Southern fried chicken, and chicken pot pie recall Sunday dinners of 30 years ago. Of the four low-ceiling rooms in this 180-year-old town house, two of have fireplaces.

A guitarist entertains during brunch. *16 Bank St., at Waverly Pl., tel. 212/929–4377. AE, DC, MC, V. Weekends 11 AM-3:30 PM and 5 PM-11:30 PM. $$*

Sazerac House Bar & Grill. The everlasting Cajun place for Sazerac cocktails (a Pernod-zapped bourbon drink) and Creole crab cakes. *533 Hudson St., at Charles St., tel. 212/989–0313. AE, DC, MC, V. Sat. 11 AM– 12 AM, Sun. 11 AM–11 PM. $–$$*

Brother's Bar-B-Q. Heaping plates of bad-for-you comfort food, free hush puppies, and brightly colored cocktails come at you fast in this relocated and now less-divey (a bad thing), frat-like dive. Ignore dry ribs and tasteless chicken and go for pulled pork. *225 Varick St., tel. 212/727–2775. AE, MC, V. Sat. 11 AM–12:30 AM, Sun. 11 AM–11 PM. $*

Cowgirl Hall of Fame. They're not kidding—menu notes pluck female cowpokes from obscurity and a festive atmosphere is assisted by cheerful staff and kitsch decor complete with a shop selling silly Western baubles. Pitchers of beer and OK Tex-Mex are really not the point. *519 Hudson St., at 10th St., tel. 212/633–1133. AE. Sat. 11 AM–12 AM, Sun. 11 AM–11 PM. $*

Pink Tea Cup. In this pink soul-food café, photos of Martin Luther King and the Supremes gaze down on platters full of pork chops, hash, pigs' feet, grits, and biscuits. *42 Grove St., near Bleecker St., tel. 212/807–6755. No credit cards. Weekends 8 AM–12 AM. $*

Asian **Cuisine de Saigon.** This quiet brownstone restaurant offers shrimp on a sugarcane stalk and other culinary adventures. *154 W. 13th St., between 6th and 7th Aves., tel. 212/255–6003. AE, DC, MC, V. Sat. 5 PM–11 PM, Sun. 5 PM–10:30 PM. $$*

E&O. Nell Campbell's boîte on Houston looks gorgeous, from its kingfisher-blue and scarlet ceiling to its glamorous population. Authentic Vietnamese dishes mix with generic Westernized-Asian (satay) at treble the Chinatown tab. Drink Susie Wongs (watermelon martini); go downstairs for the nightclubby bar. *100 W. Houston., tel. 212/254–7000. AE, DC, MC, V. Sat. 12 PM–1 AM, Sun. 12 PM–12 AM. $$*

Belgian **Café de Bruxelles.** Hearty French and Belgian dishes—*boudin blanc* (white meat sausage) and *waterzooi* fish stew—are the specialties at this lace-curtained brasserie with a zinc bar. Beer and fries are, of course, the highlights. *118 Greenwich Ave., at 13th St., tel. 212/206–1830. AE, DC, MC, V. Sat. 12 PM–12 AM, Sun. 12 PM– 10:30 PM. $$–$$$*

English **Tea and Sympathy.** Owner Nicky (English, of course) does the traditional Sunday lunch of roast beef, Yorkshire pudding, and all the trimmings, then blackberry and apple crumble or sherry trifle, the English fry-up for breakfast, and proper tea after 12 PM at her tiny, ultrapopular expat trendies' home-away-from-home. *108 Greenwich Ave., tel. 212/807–8329. No credit cards. Weekends 10 AM–10 PM. $*

French **Black Sheep.** This nook, with exposed brick walls and rustic wood tables, shines at brunch, when you can devise your own omelet, order smoked trout, or sample Amaretto French toast made with nutty whole wheat bread and served with sautéed grapes. *344 W. 11th St., at Washington St., tel. 212/242–1010. AE, MC, V (cash only at brunch). Sat. 5:30 PM–12 AM, Sun. 12 PM–3:30 PM, 5:30 PM–12 AM. $$–$$$*

Chez Ma Tante. Small and usually bustling, this classic French bistro with crisp white tablecloths serves food of a high order at fair prices. Regulars call it the best in the neighborhood. *189 W. 10th St., between W. 4th and Bleecker Sts., tel. 212/620–0223. AE, DC, MC, V. Sat. 5 PM–12 AM, Sun. 12 PM–11 PM. $$–$$$*

Café Loup. This longtime favorite keeps regulars happy with French bistro fare such as cassoulet and roast duck with green peppercorns. At brunch, grills and roasts supplement the usual eggs.

105 W. 13th St., between 6th and 7th Aves., tel. 212/255–4746. AE, DC, MC, V. Sat. 4 PM–11:30 PM, Sun. 11 AM–10:30 PM. $$

Florent. Drag queens, disco gods, Russian tourists, slackers, schlemiels, and starlets squeeze in together at the original meat-district diner: onion soup and eggs with kippers for breakfast; charcuteries, grills, and choucroute for dinner. It's always busy. *69 Gansevoort St., between Greenwich and Washington Sts., tel. 212/989–5779. No credit cards. Open 24 hrs Sat., Sun. 9 AM–5 AM. $$*

Italian **Cent'Anni.** This bright, streamlined trattoria with close-together tables has a delicious menu of Florentine dishes such as capellini with lobster and clams. *50 Carmine St., between Bleecker and Bedford Sts., tel. 212/989–9494. AE, MC, V. Sat. 5:30 PM–11 PM, Sun. 5 PM–10:30 PM. $$$*

Il Cantinori. It's hard to go wrong in this wonderful dining room with dark beams and white stucco walls, and on occasion—if grilled wild mushrooms are available, for instance—the Tuscan fare here is sublime. *32 E. 10th St., between University Pl. and Broadway, tel. 212/673–6044. AE, DC, MC, V. Sat. 5:30 PM–12 AM, Sun. 5:30 PM–11 PM. $$$*

Zinno. Peach-painted brick walls, fresh flowers, flattering lighting, and expertly executed pastas and grills make this spot a pleasure. Terrific jazz is frosting on the cake. *126 W. 13th St., between 6th and 7th Aves., tel. 212/924–5182. AE, DC, MC, V. Sat. 5 PM–11:30 PM, Sun. 5 PM–11 PM. $$–$$$*

Bar Pitti. Next door to much pricier and fancier Da Silvano, this is at its best in summer for the sidewalk scene. All Tuscan dishes are fine here, especially those—lentil salad, grilled shrimp, garlic spinach—chalked on the specials board. Sweet waiters make the deal even sweeter. *268 6th Ave., tel. 212/982–3300. No credit cards. Weekends 12 PM–12 AM. $$*

La Focaccia. Its chairs are hard, its tables jammed together, but there's compensatory diversion: the chic crowd, unusual pastas, good grills, and scrumptious breads. *51 Bank St., at W. 4th St., tel. 212/675–3754. AE, MC, V. Weekends 5:30 PM–11:30 PM. $$*

Piadina. A rollicking good time of a smoker-friendly (read, tiny) dive. Share many appetizers, pastas, and *piadina*—the eponymous bread. *57 W. 10th St., tel. 212/460–8017. No credit cards. Weekends 6:30 AM–11:30 PM. $$*

Pó. The little railroad-car-shaped, white-walled, somehow sophisticated place cares passionately about regional dishes, fresh produce, unexpected specials, and pleasing you. 31 Cornelia St., tel. 212/645–2189. AE. Sat. 5:30 PM–11 PM, Sun. 5 PM–9:30 PM. $$

Cucina Stagionale. Is terrific food in intimate surroundings at miniscule prices worth waiting in line for? Fans of this "seasonal kitchen" say yes. Go early to avoid the rush. *275 Bleecker St., between 6th and 7th Aves., tel. 212/924–2707. No credit cards. Weekends 12 PM–12 AM. $*

John's Pizzeria. It's hard to find better pizza than at this rough-around-the-edges, half-century-old Villager with its coal-fired brick ovens. *278 Bleecker St., between 6th and 7th Aves., tel. 212/243–1680. No credit cards. Sat. 11 AM–12:30 AM, Sun. 11 AM–11:30 PM. $*

Mappamondo. These twin sisters offer a fresh, modern style of Italian cooking, heavy on the vegetables and with much marinading behind the scenes. Decor consists, of course, of antique maps, with deep green stained-wood walls at **Due** (on Hudson) and hordes of young arty types. *11 Abington Sq., at 8th Ave., tel. 212/675–3100; Due, 581 Hudson St., at Bank St., tel. 212/675–7474. No credit cards. Weekends 12 PM–12 AM. $*

Osso Buco. This striking three-level restaurant dishes up Italian food family-style. All entrées are sized to serve two to eight hungry people. The 40-ounce Porterhouse steak may be the biggest in town. *88 University Pl., between 11th and 12th Sts., tel. 212/645–4525. AE, DC, MC, V. Sat. 4:30 PM–11:30 PM, Sun. 4:30 PM–10 PM. $*

Tanti Baci Cafe. For the time being, bring your own booze, and enjoy it with the bargain-priced pasta and homey specials. One of the best buys in the pasta parade. *163 W. 10th St., tel. 212/647–9651. MC, V. Sat. 11 AM–12 AM, Sun. 11 AM–11 PM. $*

Japanese **Japonica.** Sundays provide a rare chance to avoid the perennial line at this greenery-swagged, homey sushi bar (not a contradiction in terms here), serving some of NYC's freshest and *biggest* raw fish confections. *100 University Pl., between 11th and 12th Sts., tel. 212/ 243–7752. AE. Sat. 1 PM–11 PM, Sun. 1 PM–1:30 AM. $$*

Mexican **Benny's Burritos.** This funky, '60s corner café is true Cal-Mex: Everything is made without lard, preservatives, microwaves, or MSG. The vast tortillas come in whole wheat and white versions, and brunch stars burritos with chorizo, green eggs, and omelets with smoked ham, cheese, and jalapeños. *113 Greenwich Ave., at Jane St., tel. 212/727–0584. No credit cards. Sat. 11:30 AM–1 AM, Sun. 11:30 AM–12 AM. $*

Tortilla Flats. A young crowd of regulars jams this café on Sundays for *huevos rancheros* (fried eggs with beans and hot sauce), biscuits, grits, and good times. *767 Washington St., at 12th St., tel. 212/243–1053. AE. Sat. 12 PM–1 AM, Sun. 12 PM–11 PM. $*

Spanish **Café Español.** Typical of the Greenwich Village genre of Spanish restaurant, there's also a Mexican side to the menu, but stick to simple grilled dishes: pork chop, chicken, or two-pound lobster (prices are rock bottom). *172 Bleecker St., tel. 212/505–0657. AE, DC, MC, V. Sat. 12 PM–1 AM, Sun. 12 PM–12 AM. $$*

El Rincón de España. Gazpacho, grilled chorizos, and garlicky shellfish stews are good choices in this stucco-walled neighborhood saloon festooned with bullfight art. A guitarist serenades at dinner. *226 Thompson St., between 3rd and Bleecker Sts., tel. 212/260–4950. AE, DC, MC, V. Weekends 12 PM–12 AM. $$*

Rio Mar. This bright, tidy and out-of-the-way restaurant with a loyal following and terrific seafood stews was here in meat-packing land way before it was hip. Try the *caldo gallego* (a brew of potatoes, white beans, kale, and meats). *7 9th Ave., at Little W. 12th St., tel. 212/243–9015. AE. Sat. 12 PM–3 AM, Sun. 12–2 AM. $$*

Gramercy Park, Flatiron, and Union Square

If Park Avenue South, and environs, is restaurant row, then Union Square is restaurant square. Don't overlook Gramercy, especially if you're after a bit of peace and quiet.

American **Aja.** A spacious, light, peculiarly eclectic interior, with a comfy armchair bar, showcases Gary Robins' startling American/Asian food, heavy on the cilantro. *937 Broadway, tel. 212/473–8388. AE, DC, MC, V. Sat. 6 PM–11 PM, Sun. 6 PM–10 PM. $$$*

Union Square Cafe. About the hottest, hippest, most-talked-about kitchen of recent years has such a well-loved, spaciously elegant restaurant attached that you need to book about two weeks ahead to catch dinner here, even on Sunday. *21 E. 16th St., between 5th Ave. and Union Sq., tel. 212/243–4020. AE, DC, MC, V. Sat. 6–11:30, Sun. 5:30 PM–11:30 PM. $$$*

Verbena. This small, cunning restaurant in the historic Inn at Irving Place pays homage to the humble herb and honest American cooking. The garden with its glass screens with pressed flowers is charm itself. Chef/owner Diane Forley worships freshness and clear flavors. *54 Irving Pl., at 17th St., tel. 212/260–5454. AE, DC, MC, V. Sat. 5:30 PM–10:30 PM, Sun. 12 PM–9:30 PM. $$$*

Gramercy Tavern. A classic the moment it opened, because of Danny "Union Square" Meyer and Tom Colicchio, here you choose the restaurant for an expensive, grown-up's meal, the bar in front for a more casual, still culinarily impressive experience, available without advance planning. *42 E. 20th St., tel. 212/477-0777. AE, DC, MC, V. Sat. 12 PM-11 PM, Sun. 5 PM-11 PM. $$-$$$*

Alva. Kind of ironic that this is named for the light-bulb inventor, because it's *dark* in here. On the other hand, it's lovable, and the rich, slightly Mediterranean Yankee comfort food rarely misses. *36 E. 22nd St., tel. 212/228-4399. AE, DC, MC, V. Weekends 5:30 PM-12 AM. $$*

American/ Casual

Pete's Tavern. Don't come for anything more exciting than a burger. Do come, not for the food, but for the low-ceiling antiquity of the spot where O. Henry supposedly penned "The Gift of the Magi." *129 E. 18th St., tel. 212/473-7676. AE, DC, MC, V. Sat. 11 AM-12:30 AM, Sun. 11 AM-12 AM. $$*

Friend of a Farmer. At this countrified, chintzy little restaurant on Irving Place, you get homey, rustic fare—apple butter and cheddar cheese omelets, buckwheat pancakes with walnuts, and muffins and cinnamon rolls from the restaurant's own talented bakers. *77 Irving Pl., tel. 212/477-2188. AE, MC, V. Sat. 10 AM-11 PM, Sun. 10 AM-10 PM. $*

Heartland Brewery. This frat house/white collar microbrewery specializes in fruit-flavored ales and pub food. *35 Union Sq. W, between 16th and 17th Sts., tel. 212/645-3400. AE, DC, MC, V. Sat. 12 PM-12 AM, Sun. 12 PM-10 PM. $*

Old Town Bar. Time-blackened tin ceilings and a long mahogany bar scuffed and ringed by a century of drinkers make this unrenovated old-timer one of a vanishing breed. Cuisine is strictly burger-and-fries. *45 E. 18th St., tel., 212/529-6732. AE, MC, V. Sat. 12:30 PM-11:30 PM, Sun. 1 PM-10 PM. $*

American Regional

America. Take the kids to this stadium-sized café. Adults can order spicy and ethnic fare while small fry go for peanut butter-and-marshmallow-whip sandwiches. Portions are huge. *9 E. 18th St., tel. 212/505-2110. AE, DC, MC, V. Sat. 11:30 AM-12:30 AM, Sun. 11:30 AM-11:30 PM. $$*

City Crab. This vast and bustling slice of Maryland looks like it's going to be really inexpensive; but it isn't. People seem happy though, especially on the loud first floor or at the bar. *235 Park Ave. S, tel. 212/529-3800. AE, DC, MC, V. Sat. 11 AM-12:30 AM, Sun. 11 AM- 11 PM. $$*

Coffee Shop. Not one of those Greek standbys, but a smokin' (literally) faux-Brazilian melting pot of scenesters. It jumps for brunch, with live samba music and very edible crossover Latin-soul-Italian cooking. *29 Union Sq. W, tel. 212/243-7969. AE, MC, V. Weekends 8 AM-5 AM. $$*

Live Bait. Dixieland faves, gravy on everything, catfish po'boys, and shellfish (all good) are not the point when you're still wearing your frat ring or you have legs to your armpits. *14 E. 23rd St., between Broadway and Madison Ave., tel. 212/353-2400. AE, MC, V. Sat. 12 PM-1 AM, Sun. 12:30 PM-11 PM. $-$$*

Asian

Republic. Ultrasuccessful, huge, stark, modern, high-decibel youngsters' haunt where you share benches at long wooden tables for big bowls of satisfying noodles and soups and curries. *37 Union Sq. W, tel. 212/627-7172. AE, DC, MC, V. Sat. 12 PM-12 AM, Sun. 12 PM-11 PM. $*

French

Park Bistro. An inviting, gently lit spot with gray walls and red banquettes, this restaurant draws raves for Provençal dishes, such as sautéed codfish on mashed potatoes with an onion sauce. *414 Park Ave. S, at 28th St., tel. 212/689-1360. AE, DC, MC, V. Weekends 5:30 PM-10:30 PM. $$$*

La Colombe D'or. This restaurant takes the cuisine of Southern France and Americanizes it: dishes such as excellent grilled calf's liver with carrots and parsnips cooked in cream, and ginger custard with almond pralines are typical. *134 E. 26th St., near Lexington*

Ave., tel. 212/689–0666. AE, DC, MC, V. Weekends 5:30 PM–11 PM. $$

Les Halles. Recalling the Gauloise-smoky joints where Parisians congregate for onion soup, this trendy bistro serves such hearty fare as steak-frites, tripe, and cassoulet. *411 Park Ave. S, between 28th and 29th Sts., tel. 212/679–4111. AE, DC, MC, V. Weekends 12 PM–12 AM. $$*

Italian   **Sal Anthony's.** This townhouse dining room opened in 1966, and a loyal cadre has stayed, drawn by the deferential service, thick veal chops, and inviting decor: oil paintings on brick walls, huge bouquets, and crisp white cloths on well-spaced tables. *55 Irving Pl., tel. 212/982–9030. AE, DC, MC, V. Sat. 12 PM–12 AM, Sun. 12 PM–10 PM. $$*

Latin   **Patria.** Doug Rodriguez invented this genre he calls "Nuevo Latino", now copied everywhere, but still the best in this glamorous three-tiered soaring room. Have: many seviches, sugarcane-speared tuna, a chocolate cigar, a ball. *250 Park Ave. S, tel. 212/777–6211. AE, DC, MC, V. Sat. 5:30 PM–11:30 PM, Sun. 5:30 PM–10:30 PM. $$$*

Mediterranean   **Luna Park.** It fulfilled a long-felt want, this outdoor café in Union Square, but not for gourmets. Its moules, salads, grills, and pastas are adequate; slow service is not even that, but here beneath a *luna*, who cares? *Union Sq., tel. 212/475–8464. AE, MC, V. Closed Oct.–Mar. Hrs unavailable at press time.*

Soul Food   **Cafe Beulah.** Chef-owner Alexander Smalls makes merry with soul food: black-eyed pea cakes with creole mayonnaise, sautéed chicken livers with peppered turnip greens, and she-crab soup. *39 E. 19th St., near 5th Ave., tel. 212/777–9700. AE, DC, MC, V. Sat. 5:30 PM–12 AM, Sun. 11 AM–10 PM. $$*

Chelsea

Boytown, as ever, Chelsea is brunchland too, but eclipsing both faces is the retail resurgence along former Ladies' Mile, where the megastores line up to stress your plastic. Don't forget the ever-growing fleamarket along 6th Avenue.

American   **Cal's.** White tablecloths, pretty bouquets, and a mirrored mahogany bar transform a former warehouse, where saffron-scented fish soup, juicy veal T-bone, and eggs Benedict on smoked salmon are representative. Don't miss the mashed potatoes. *55 W. 21st St., tel. 212/929–0740. AE, DC, MC, V. Weekends 5 PM–12 AM. $$*

Man Ray. This bistro next to the Joyce Theater serves goat cheese tarts, crisp calamari, thin-crusted pizzas, and cinnamon ice cream on apple tartlets to a gay crowd. *169 8th Ave., at 18th St., tel. 212/627–4220. AE, DC, MC, V. Sat. 11 AM–12 AM, Sun. 11 AM–11 PM. $$*

The Viceroy. Regulars from the neighborhood enjoy the oversize cocktails and friendly atmosphere at this nouvelle-American gay joint. *160 8th Ave. near 18th St., tel. 212/633–8484. AE, DC, MC, V. Sat. 11:30 AM–1 AM, Sun. 11:30 AM–12 AM. $*

American/ Casual   **Empire Diner.** This stainless steel diner is as au courant as ever, with its eclectic cuisine, terrific beer menu, and live music. *210 10th Ave., at 22nd St., tel. 212/243–2736. AE, MC, V. Open 24 hrs. $$*

Big Cup. The essential brunch scene assists with all-day-and-evening lounging too. The cups are indeed big, the coffee inside them good, and the boys thick on the ground. *228 8th Ave., tel. 212/206–0059. No credit cards. Weekends 7 AM–3 AM. $*

Chelsea Commons. This corner bar stands out in Chelsea for its good pub grub and great atmosphere: Exposed brick makes its dim interior cozy when it's blustery outdoors, and its walled garden a lovely escape when the weather's torrid. *242 10th Ave., at 24th St., tel. 212/929–9424. AE, MC, V. Weekends 12 PM–1 AM. $*

Caribbean   **Lola.** Brunch time gospel singers keep the house rolling and shaking while happy diners down thin, cayenne-peppered onion rings, baby-back ribs with scrambled eggs and healthy tuna burgers. Amen! *30 W. 22nd St., tel. 212/675–6700. AE, DC, MC, V. Sat. 6 PM–11 PM, Sun. 9:30 AM–3 PM, 6 PM–10 PM. $$–$$$*

Claire. Amid lattices, greenery, and ceiling fans, you can sample the food of the tropics, including conch chowder, Chelsea's best grilled fish, and terrific key lime pie in this casual café. *156 7th Ave., between 19th and 20th Sts., tel. 212/255–1955. AE, DC, MC, V. Sat. 11:30 AM–12:30 AM, Sun. 11:30 AM–12 AM. $$*

French   **L'Acajou.** Were it not for the low lighting and the hearty, slightly Germanic Alsatian menu, you'd take this austere little bistro for a coffee shop. *53 W. 19th St., tel. 212/645–1706. AE, MC, V. Sat. 6:30 PM–12:00 AM, Sun. 6:30 PM–11 PM. $$–$$$*

Italian   **Le Madri.** Order the marinated vegetables, grilled squid, or veal chop on arugula-ricotta foccacia with truffle oil at this long-lived, expensive Tuscan restaurant. The awning-shaded patio offers quiet. *168 W. 18th St., tel. 212/727–8022. AE, DC, MC, V. Sat. 12 PM–11 PM, Sun. 12 PM–2:30 PM, 5:30 PM–10 PM. $$$$*

Tiziano. Chic but affable, this Joyce Theater neighbor serves brick-oven pizzas, pastas, veal, and other Mediterranean dishes. *165 8th Ave., between 18th and 19th Sts., tel. 212/989–2330. AE, DC, MC, V. Sat. 11 AM–1 AM, Sun. 11 AM–12 AM. $$*

Twigs. A sleek little Italian café, all marble and brass, this is a neighborhood favorite for individual pizzas with well-blistered crusts and toppings such as fennel-perfumed sausage and eggplant. *196 8th Ave., at 20th St., tel. 212/633–6735. AE, MC, V. Weekends 12 PM–12 AM. $*

Mexican   **Mary Ann's.** Tex-Mex standbys, carefully prepared and gently priced, come from this casual (and often crowded) cantina with barn-board walls and hanging plants. Bring your best weekend appetite. *116 8th Ave., at 16th St., tel. 212/633–0877. No credit cards. Sat. 12 PM–11 PM, Sun. 12 PM–10 PM. $*

Midtown East

Though office workers are absent on weekends, many restaurants in this area are open for business—some all day long and some in the evening. Hotel dining rooms can also be good bets.

American   **Ambassador Grill.** A striking contemporary space in the UN Plaza Hotel, with deep wine-colored banquettes and artful bouquets, this is best for its Lucullan Sunday brunch buffet. *1 UN Plaza, 44th St., at 1st Ave., tel. 212/702–5014. AE, DC, MC, V. Sat. 7 PM–10:30 PM, Sun. 7 PM–10:30 PM. $$$*

Smith & Wollensky. Boisterous and noisy, this wood-paneled, wood-floored steak house blankets plates with huge slabs of meat; lamb chops, prime rib with crisp hash browns, and pecan-bourbon pie are a carnivore's perfect Sunday dinner. *797 3rd Ave., tel. 212/753–1530. AE, DC, MC, V. Weekends 5 PM–11:30 PM. $$$*

Comfort Diner. This cute little homey, eccentric place is exactly what its name announces, except that its decor is more attention-grabbing. *214 E. 45th St., tel. 212/867–4555. AE, DC, MC, V. Weekends 9 AM–9 PM. $*

British   **The British Open.** Even if you don't play golf, this place is still great fun for its fake British pub ambiance and matching menu: steak and kidney pie, fish and chips, and beer on tap. *320 E. 59th St., near 1st Ave., tel. 212/355–8467. AE, MC, V. Weekends 12 PM–11 PM. $*

Chinese   **Chin Chin.** A rust-and-peach front room, hung with turn-of-the-century family photographs of the ancestral Chins, and an airy back room that's all snowy white is the setting for above-average dumplings, hot-and-sour and corn-and-crabmeat soups, and tea-smoked duck. *216 E. 49th St., tel. 212/888–4555. AE, DC, MC, V. Sat. 5 PM–12 AM, Sun. 5 PM–11 PM. $$$*

Drinks **Top of the Tower.** This viewful lounge is one of the city's best-kept secrets, with an open-air terrace that's sheer heaven in summer. *Beekman Tower Hotel, 49th St. at 1st Ave., tel. 212/355–7300. AE, D, DC, MC, V. Weekends 5 PM–2 AM.*

French **Box Tree.** At this intimate, exquisite town house restaurant, setting, service, and food are refined and elegant to the *n*th degree. *250 E. 49th St., tel. 212/758–8320. AE. Weekends 6 PM–9:30 PM. $$$$*

Japanese **Sushi Hatsu.** Don't eat anything unless it's raw. Sit only at the sushi bar, and be ready to blow plenty of bucks on the best sushi, sashimi, and exotica imaginable. *1143 1st Ave., between 62nd and 63rd Sts., tel. 212/371–0238. AE, MC, V. Sat. 5:30 PM–3:30 AM, Sun. 5:30 PM–10:30 PM. $$$*

Seafood **Water Club.** The view of Queens that you get from Manhattan's yacht-clubbiest restaurant may not excite, but the waterside location makes brunches a special delight, whether you go for leg of lamb, smoked salmon, omelets, or Irish oatmeal. *500 E. 30th St., tel. 212/683–3333. AE, DC, MC, V. Sat. 12 PM–2:30 PM, 5:30 PM–11 PM, Sun. 11 AM–3 PM, 5:30 PM–10 PM. $$$$*

Dock's. This giant, high-ceiling fish house–saloon is an oyster eater's delight, though brunch is more eggy than you might expect. *633 3rd Ave., at 40th St., tel. 212/986–8080. AE, DC, MC, V. Sat. 5 PM–12 AM, Sun.11:30 AM–3 PM, 5 PM–11 PM. $$–$$$*

Midtown West

This neighborhood encompasses the southwestern fringes of Rockefeller Center, the theater district's Restaurant Row, the area in and around the Manhattan Towers artists' housing complex, and Hell's Kitchen. Restaurant pickings are correspondingly rich and unpretentious.

American **44.** The menu of this Royalton Hotel sophisticate mates with Philippe Starck's fantastic decor and the look-at-me print media stars to give you one big catwalk. Weekday lunch is still its shining hour though. *44 W. 44th St., tel. 212/944–8844. AE, DC, MC, V. Sat. 8 AM–3 PM, 6 PM–11:30 PM, Sun. 8 AM–3 PM, 6 PM–10:30 PM. $$$$*

Algonquin Hotel. The Round Table still stands; the Rose Room and Edwardian Lounge still have fans, especially for brunch time apple pancakes and corned beef hash. The walnut-paneled lobby-lounge remains one of the city's most charming spots for drinks. *59 W. 44th St., tel. 212/840–6800. AE, DC, MC, V. Weekends 7 AM–10 AM, 5:30 PM–11 PM. $$$*

The View. Times Square vistas dazzle in the city's only revolving rooftop restaurant, in the Marriott Marquis Hotel, so go for an all-you-can-eat brunch buffet or a festive dinner. *1535 Broadway, at 45th St., tel. 212/704–8900. AE, DC, MC, V. Sat. 5:30 PM–11:30 PM, Sun. 10:30 AM–2 PM, 5:30 PM–10:30 PM. $$$*

American/ Casual **Landmark Tavern.** A fireplace and potbellied stove warm this Old New York relic with a burnished bar and smoke-darkened pressed-tin ceiling. The terrific brunch features Irish oatmeal pancakes and traditional soda bread. Anglo-Irish dinner is less of a deal. *626 11th Ave., at 46th St., tel. 212/757–8595. AE, DC, MC, V. Sat. 12 PM–12 AM, Sun.12 PM–11 PM. $$$*

Joe Allen. This Restaurant Row institution is fun for elevated pub fare and late-night noshing. *326 W. 46th St., tel. 212/581–6464. MC, V. Weekends 11:30 AM–11:30 PM. $$*

Mike's American Bar and Grill. Here's a bright light in Hell's Kitchen, where they mix the strongest margaritas, serve up goat cheese salad, corn bread, and grills; and where the decor changes radically every few months. *650 10th Ave., at 46th St., tel. 212/246–4115. AE. Weekends 11 AM–4 PM, 5:30 PM–12 AM. $*

New World Grill. Fine looking and perfect for alfresco dining (although the interior and horseshoe bars are also attractive). Food is a symbiotic mix; the wine list and cocktails are outstanding. *329 W. p49th St., tel. 212/957–4745. AE, MC,V. Sat. 12 PM–12 AM, Sun. 12 PM–10 PM. $*

American Regional

B. Smith. Sunday matinee-goers brunch on pecan pancakes and Pfried whiting and grits with homemade biscuits in a shiny post-modern room punctuated by huge earth-toned urns and gigantic bouquets. At dinner, good grills complement eccentric preparations such as scampi with mango glacé. *771 8th Ave., at 47th St., tel. 212/247–2222. AE, DC, MC, V. Sat. 11:30 AM–11:30 PM, Sun. 12 PM–10:30 PM. $$*

Brazilian

Cabana Carioca. In this dim, unpromising spot where Portuguese is the lingua franca, the exuberant Brazilian cooking, which crosses Portuguese, Indian, and West African flavors, warrants a visit. *123 W. 45th St., tel. 212/581–8088. AE, DC, MC, V. Weekends 12 PM–11 PM. $$*

Chinese

Mee Noodle Shop. This informal chain of noodle shops promotes the joys of steamed and fried dumplings and heart-warming and filling noodle soups. *795 9th Ave., tel. 212/765–2929; also at 922 2nd Ave. and 219 1st Ave. AE. Sat. 11:30 AM–12 AM, Sun. 11:30 AM–11:30 PM. $*

French

Le Madeleine. Behind lace curtains, this Theater Row café features an ivy-walled garden, tables with white umbrellas, and a bistro menu. Try the apple-almond and banana-walnut pancakes at brunch. *403 W. 43rd St., tel. 212/246–2993. AE, MC, V. Sat. 12 PM–3:30 PM, 5 PM–11:30 PM, Sun. 12 PM–3:30 PM, 5 PM–10 PM. $$*

Italian

Orso. This convivial, relaxed-yet-upmarket Italian spot has long been popular with theater-makers as much as theater-goers. A daily-changing bilingual menu—from pizza and pasta to boned, roasted quail—is served on hand-painted Portuguese dishes. *322 W. 46th, tel. 212/489–7212. MC, V. Sat. 11:30 AM–11:30 PM, Sun. 12 AM–10:30 PM. $$–$$$*

Becco. Be hungry for this Restaurant Row newcomer. They bring 'round a ton of assorted antipasti, then pasta and risotto, and you take as much as you want. After that, talented eaters can attempt an entrée at only a couple of bucks more than the fixed price, before the fruit tart arrives. *355 W. 46th St., between 8th and 9th Aves., tel. 212/397–7597. AE, DC, MC, V. Sat. 12 PM–3 PM, 5 PM–12 PM, Sun. 12 PM–3 PM, 5 PM–10 PM. $$*

Peruvian

Peruvian Restaurant. In this hole in the wall full of plastic plants, the adventurous can sample beef-and-rice *sancochado* soup, ceviche, mashed potato pies, and terrific tamales. *688 10th Ave. near 49th St., tel. 212/581–5814. No credit cards. Weekends 8:30 AM–10:30 PM. $*

Thai

Siam Grill. This small, neat restaurant offers fare worth a trip from outside the neighborhood—spicy grills, such as beef satay and curry-spiked chicken *gai yang. 585 9th Ave., between 42nd and 43rd Sts., tel. 212/307–1363. AE, DC, MC, V. Sat. 4:30 PM–11 PM, Sun. 4:30 PM–10:30 PM. $*

East 50s

This is prime territory for hotel dining rooms and their fabulous, no-holds-barred, all-you-can-eat brunches. To the east, along 1st and 2nd avenues, simple neighborhood restaurants abound: snug, comfortable, and sedate.

American/ Casual

Billy's. In this mahogany-paneled bit of Old New York, the menu of honest roasts, chops, and seafood says "home" to a crowd of politicos and personalities. *948 1st Ave., between 52nd and 53rd Sts., tel. 212/ 753–1870. AE, DC, MC, V. Sat. 11:30 AM–11:30 PM, Sun. 11:30 AM– 11 PM. $$–$$$*

Neary's. Affluent East Siders know a good deal when they see it. Drinks are generous, service is friendly, and the first-rate corned beef hash is famous. The portions are huge, but save room for some of the best rice pudding in town. *358 E. 57th St., tel. 212/751–1434. AE, DC, MC, V. Sat. 11 AM–4 PM, Sun. 12 AM–4 PM. $$*

Wylie's Ribs & Co. Big, greasy platters of barbecued ribs and chicken are the reason to come here. *891 1st Ave., at 50th St., tel. 212/751– 0700. AE, DC, MC, V. Weekends 11 AM–11 PM. $*

Chinese

Fu's House. This relocated longtime uptown favorite has low-fat, low-salt specials. *972 2nd Ave., between 51st and 52nd Sts., tel. 212/ 517–9670. AE, DC, MC, V. Weekends 11:30 AM–11:30 PM. $$–$$$*

Deli

Kaplan's. The best bet for simple deli in the neighborhood, this spot serves terrific potato pancakes and smoked fish. *59 E. 59th St., tel. 212/755–5959. AE, DC, MC, V. Weekends 8 AM–10 PM. $*

Indian

Dāwat. Actress-author Madhur Jaffrey offers a number of her intriguing, innovative preparations at this sophisticated, serene restaurant. Eggplant with tamarind sauce or chicken *makhani*, aromatic with ginger and coriander, are a change from the usual curries. *210 E. 58th St., tel. 212/355–7555. AE, DC, MC, V. Sat. 11:30 AM–11:30 PM, Sun. 5 PM–11 PM. $$*

Italian

Bice. Manhattan's version of the Milan original serves fine risottos in a contemporary, subtly lighted room, open to the sidewalk in fair weather. *7 E. 54th St., tel. 212/688–1999. AE, DC, MC, V. Weekends 12 PM–12 AM. $$$*

Mediterranean

Meltemi. A sunny Greek island of a place, where fresh fish, simply charbroiled with a spritz of lemon is the thing to order, after the hummus. *905 1st Ave., tel. 212/355–4040. AE, DC, MC, V. Weekends 12 PM–11 PM. $$*

Pescatore. Non-specific Mediterranean fare is cooked here by a Turkish chef: mostly fish, as you'd expect, of which the simplest are the best; also chopped Mediterranean salad; and homemade pasta with mixed seafood and white beans. *955 2nd Ave., between 50th and 51st Sts., tel. 212/752–7151. AE. Weekends 5 PM–11 PM. $$*

Mexican

Rosa Mexicano. Margaritas with pomegranate juice keep the bar packed, while diners in the rosy-stuccoed back room devour tortillas with pork, piquant grills, and tasty guacamole prepared tableside. *1063 1st Ave., at 58th St., tel. 212/753–7407. AE, DC, MC, V. Weekends 5 PM–12 AM. $$–$$$*

Zarela. Gutsy red snapper hash, tuna with mole sauce, and the trademark chicken *chilaquiles* (chicken layered with fried tortillas) will expand your view of Mexican cuisine. *953 2nd Ave., between 50th and 51st Sts., tel. 212/644–6740. AE, DC. Sat. 5 PM–11:30 PM, Sun. 5 PM–10 PM. $$–$$$*

Spanish

Tapas Lounge. A sexy, candlelit Spanish hideaway by the 59th Street Bridge, where you dine handsomely on little dishes, sprawl on couches, and sip sangria. There's a communal table for lone diners. *1078 1st Ave., tel. 212/223–2322. AE, DC, MC, V. Sat. 5 PM–5 AM, Sun. 3 PM–12 AM. $$*

West 50s

The West 50s, home to Rockefeller Center, Carnegie Hall, and Central Park South, also contains great Italian restaurants, New York's premier caviar purveyor, wonderful ethnic nooks, and grand hotels that are gala settings for drinks or brunch. The million theme eateries of 57th Street start here too, but we don't list many of them—they're not hard to find.

American **Edwardian Room.** This stately Plaza Hotel dining room is unabashedly romantic with its ornate paneling, coffered wood ceilings, burgundy brocade walls, and fat bouquets. Central Park views from the tall windows make it grand for brunch. *5th Ave., at Central Park S, tel. 212/759–3000. AE, D, DC, MC, V. Sat. 7 PM–10 PM, Sun. 7 AM–2 PM. $$$$*

Palm Court. This lofty roomful of potted palms and gold leaf in the Plaza Hotel serves one of the city's most lavish Sunday brunch buffets, with a pianist to set the mood. *5th Ave. at Central Park S, tel. 212/546–5350. AE, D, DC, MC, V. Sat. 6:30 AM–12 AM, Sun. 6:30 AM–2 PM, 4 PM–12 AM. $$$$*

Petrossian. With mink-trimmed banquettes, rosy granite floors, and rté etched glass, this Paris-based caviar shop is heaven for the affordable Sunday brunch and champagne by the glass; or splurge for a French dinner with Russian accent. *182 W. 58th St., tel. 12/245–2214. AE, DC, MC, V. Sat. 11:30 AM–3:30 PM, 5 PM–11:30 PM, Sun. 11:30 AM–10:30 PM. $$$$*

Rainbow. This glamorous restaurant complex atop the GE Building in Rockefeller Center stars the two-story-high *Rainbow Room*, a lavish, romantic spot with aubergine silk walls, cast-glass balusters, and silver lamé tablecloths. Choral groups serenade during the lavish brunch; during dinner you can waltz and cha-cha on the revolving dance floor to the music of oldies and Latin bands. At the *Rainbow Promenade*, a splendidly viewful bar, you can opt for less expensive pleasures: lively little meals accompanied by classical guitar. *30 Rockefeller Plaza, tel. 212/632–5100. AE, DC. Sat. 5 PM–1 AM, Sun. 5 PM–10:30 PM. $$$$*

China Grill. In this jumbo brasserie with black granite walls and bleached-wood floors, the culinary East meets West on a menu offering wonders like lobster spiced with ginger and curry. *60 W. 53rd pSt., tel. 212/333–7788. AE, DC, MC, V. Sat. 5:30 PM–12 AM, Sun. 5 PM–10:30 PM. $$$*

American/ **Gallagher's.** The West Side's best steak house, this has long been a
Casual hangout for sports figures, whose photos hang on the wood-paneled pwalls. You'll also find unquestionably fine aged prime beef, displayed by the side out front. *228 W. 52nd St., tel. 212/245–5336. AE, DC, pMC, V. Weekends 12 PM–12 AM. $$$*

Harley Davidson Cafe. Loud and crowded as you'd expect, but here the service is pleasant, prices are low, and the food is more than a pcasual afterthought. *1370 6th Ave., at 56th St., tel. 212/245–6000. pAE, DC, MC,V. Weekends 11:30 AM–2 AM. $$*

Mickey Mantle's. Eggs-and-bagels brunches and chicken-fried steak and hickory-smoked ribs at dinner take second place to the World Series footage on video monitors and a bartender who talks batting averages. *42 Central Park S, between 5th and 6th Aves., tel. 212/688–7777. AE, D, DC, MC, V. Weekends 12 PM–12 AM. $$*

Planet Hollywood. You know. *140 W. 57th St., between 6th and 7th Aves., tel. 212/333–7827. AE, D, DC, MC, V. Sat. 10:30 AM–1 AM, Sun. 11 AM–1 AM. $–$$*

Hard Rock Café. You know. As with all these things, go between 4 and 6 for the shortest line out front. *221 W. 57th St., tel. 212/459–9320. AE, D, DC, MC, V. Sat. 11:30 AM–2 AM, Sun. 11:30 AM–12 AM. $*

American **American Festival Café.** American regional classics are served here
Regional amid folk art and patchwork quilts. Brunch on orange-vanilla French toast or roast beef hash; dine on Baltimore crab cakes with homemade potato chips and do it alfresco in summer, alongside the famous Rockefeller Plaza ice rink. *20 W. 50th St., tel. 212/332–7620. AE, DC, MC, V. Weekends 9 AM–10 PM. $$*

Deli **Carnegie Deli.** Pastrami is served in mile-high sandwiches at this institution, founded in 1934 and immortalized in Woody Allen's *Broadway Danny Rose*, though there were already lines outside. *854 7th Ave., between 54th and 55th Sts., tel. 212/757–2245. No credit cards. Weekends 6:30 AM–4 AM. $*

Stage Deli. Fans dispute whether the Stage or the Carnegie does a better job, but they're both in the same league. *834 7th Ave., between 53rd and 54th Sts., tel. 212/245–7850. AE, MC. Weekends 6 AM–1 AM. $*

French **La Bonne Soupe.** A sweet Seventies time warp of checkered tablecloths and Chianti bottle candlesticks. Eat onion soup, quiche, grilled salmon, lemon tart. A midtown bargain. *48 W. 55th St., tel. 212/586–7650. AE, MC, V. Sat. 11:30 AM–11:30 PM, Sun. 11:30 AM–10:30 PM. $*

Indian **Darbár.** Persian carpets hung against dusky rose velvet walls and carved wooden screens create a hushed, elegant setting for northern Indian cuisine: chicken tandoori; biryani with lamb, raisins, and spices. *44 W. 56th St., tel. 212/432–7227. AE, D, DC, MC, V. Sat. 12 PM–11 PM, Sun. 12 PM–10 PM. $$*

Italian **San Domenico.** Veteran New York restaurateur Tony May still earns raves for ravioli with hazelnut butter and sage, shrimp and beans with Tuscan olive oil, and venison with juniper berries. It's luxurious and sometimes starry. *240 Central Park S, between 7th Ave. and Broadway, tel. 212/265–5959. AE, DC, MC, V. Sat. 5:30 PM–11 PM, Sun. 5:30 PM–10 PM. $$$$*

Remi. Curved walls, Venetian glass chandeliers, and an 18-foot-high mural celebrating Venice set the scene for fashionable clientele and northern Italian cuisine. Sample one of the 40 grappas. *145 W. 53rd St., tel. 212/581–4242. AE, DC, MC, V. Sat. 5:30 PM–11:30 PM, Sun. 5:30 PM–10 PM. $$$*

Trattoria dell'Arte. Designer Milton Glaser filled this huge space with giant bas-relief lips and breasts and sepia prints of oversized eyes and noses. Equally diverting are the carefully prepared antipasti and pastas Chianti with uncommon sauces. *900 7th Ave., tel. 212/245–9800. AE, D, DC, MC, V. Sat. 12 PM–11:30 PM, Sun. 12 PM–10:30 PM. $$$*

Da Tommaso. One of the most pleasant options for traditional Italian food, this is the place to visit for delicious pasta, warm service, and Old World charm. The wine list has some rare bargains. *903 8th Ave., between 53rd and 54th Sts., tel. 212/265–1890. AE, DC, MC, V. Weekends 4:30 PM–11 PM. $$*

Japanese **Menchanko-tei.** Japanese noodle soup is just the thing before a winter concert at nearby Carnegie Hall. The price is right. *39 W. 55th St., tel. 212/247–1585. AE, DC, MC, V. Sat. 7 AM–12:30 AM, Sun. 7 AM–11:30 PM. $*

Russian **Russian Samovar.** Hearty eggplant dishes and good grills soothe theater folk in this snug, unprepossessing little dining room with long banquettes and comfortably spaced tables. *256 W. 52nd St., tel. 212/757–0168. AE, MC, V. Sat. 12 PM–12 AM, Sun. 5 PM–11:30 PM. $$*

Seafood **Manhattan Ocean Club.** This attractive pastel dining room continues to do a roaring trade in, say, mahi-mahi with scallions and orange vinaigrette. An excellent wine list reflects the expertise of Alan Stillman, who also owns Smith & Wollensky. *57 W. 58th St., tel. 212/371–7777. AE, D, DC, MC, V. Sat. 5 PM–11:30 PM, Sun. 5 PM–10:30 PM. $$$$*

Thai **Bangkok Cuisine.** Eighth Avenue in the 50s is full of Thai restaurants, but this is among the best. Order a Thai beer to accompany steamed fish or crispy *mee krob* noodles. *885 8th Ave., between 52nd and 53rd Sts., tel. 212/581–6370. AE, MC, V. Weekends 4 PM–11:30 PM. $*

East 60s

Though many luxury restaurants in the blocks between 5th and Park avenues close on Sunday, Saturday night is busy. Farther east, brunch is popular, especially along 1st and 3rd avenues.

American   **Café Pierre.** Soothing and civilized, with ornate mirrors and cloud murals overhead, this has long been a sumptuous place for breakfast, and other meals, too. *2 E. 61st St., tel. 212/940–8185. AE, D, DC, MC, V. Weekends 7 AM–11:30 PM. $$$$*

Post House. This long-standing institution, a comfortably masculine spot, serves some of the city's best steaks, chops, and lobsters. *28 E. 63rd St., tel. 212/935–2888. AE, DC, MC, V. Weekends 5:30 PM–10:30 PM. $$$$*

Sign of the Dove. Consider this long-standing ultraromantic place for a brunch of scrambled eggs with warmed smoked salmon, caviar, and fried quail eggs. Skylights keep daytime bright, and there's music all day. *1110 3rd Ave., at 65th St., tel. 212/861–8080. AE, DC, MC, V. Sat. 11:30 AM–11 PM, Sun. 11:30 AM–10 PM. $$$$*

Matthew's. This is Matthew Kenney's original place, where his trademark Mediterranean/Moroccan vegetable-friendly food is served in a gently colonial setting, nice and bright in the daytime. *1030 3rd Ave., tel. 212/838–4343. AE, DC, MC, V. Sat. 12 PM–11 PM, Sun. 12 PM–10 PM. $$$*

American/ Casual   **Boathouse Café.** Of several places to eat in Central Park, this restaurant is the finest. Seating is indoors and out. (Open March to October; otherwise, fast-food concessions will suffice). *74th St. near 5th Ave. entrance, tel. 212/517–2233. AE, D, MC, V. Sat. 12 PM–10:30 PM, Sun. 11 AM–10:30 PM. $$*

Jackson Hole. There are a few of these good-value burger joints around town, perfect for kids needing a "cow on a bun" and brownies. *232 E. 64th St., tel. 212/371–7187. AE. Sat. 10:30 AM–1 AM, Sun. 10:30 AM–12 AM. $*

Serendipity 3. This happy mix of ice cream parlor and general store has been going strong since 1954. Moviegoers and models, families and singles come for casseroles, pastas, and sandwiches—and frozen hot chocolate. *225 E. 60th St., tel. 212/838–3531. AE, D, DC, MC, V. Sat. 11:30 AM–2 AM, Sun. 11:30 AM–12 AM. $*

American Regional   **Arizona 206.** Barbecued foie gras with cactus pears is the rich flavor of Southwestern cuisine here. Spicy chili and a fireplace keep diners warm in winter. Pop into the café for less expensive fare. *206 E. 60th St., tel. 212/838–0440. AE, DC, MC, V. Sat. 12 PM–11:30 PM, Sun. 5:30 PM–10:30 PM. $$–$$$*

French   **Le Régence.** This lavish Plaza Athénée Hotel restaurant features light, refined fare as opulent as the ornate, pale blue Louis XV decor. Sunday brunches are positively artful. *37 E. 64th St., tel. 212/606–4647. AE, DC, MC, V. Weekends 12 PM–9:30 PM. $$$$*

Ferrier. Garlicky snails, roast Cornish hen, and good fish specials team to keep this bistro happily, noisily full. Pink tablecloths and golden lighting create a flattering tableau, reflected in a mirrored wall. *29 E. 65th St., tel. 212/772–9000. AE, DC, MC, V. Sat. 12 PM–2 AM, Sun. 12 PM–12 AM. $$$*

Le Relais. Eating takes a back seat to people-watching inside this bistro and its summertime outdoor café. *712 Madison Ave., between 63rd and 64th Sts., tel. 212/751–5108. AE, DC, MC, V. Weekends 12 PM–11 PM. $$$*

Madame Romaine de Lyon. This old-timer prepares omelets with a delightfully light touch—in 500 varieties. *132 E. 61st St., tel. 212/758–2422. AE, DC. Sat. 10:30 AM–10 PM, Sun. 10 AM–12 AM. $$*

Italian   **Primola.** A good-looking European crowd appreciates the lively cooking served in this spare, pale yellow dining room. Salmon marinated with fennel, quail with polenta, lamb chops come in giant portions, and the minestrone is fabulous. *1226 2nd Ave., between 64th and 65th Sts., tel. 212/758–1775. AE, DC, MC, V. Sat. 5 PM–12 AM, Sun. 5 AM–11 PM. $$$*

Contrapunto. This casual, bright-white upstairs restaurant focuses on pasta, with 20-odd options ranging from angel hair with clams and dried tomatoes to fettuccine with sage and lobster. *200 E. 60th St., tel. 212/751–8616. AE, DC, MC, V. Sat. 11:30 AM–2 AM, Sun. 11:30 AM–12 AM. $$*

Gino's. Fuchsia Scalamandre zebra wallpaper is the trademark of this swank and busy room crowded with regulars, who happily tuck into bluefish oreganato, pasta e fagioli, and osso buco with risotto. *780 Lexington Ave., between 60th and 61st Sts., tel. 212/758–4466. No credit cards. Weekends 12 PM–10:30 PM. $$*

Upper East Side

There is no shortage of places to stop to eat in this neighborhood before or after an expedition to Central Park or along Museum Mile. Besides the museums' own cafés, which are often quite good, you'll find chic, sleek trendsetting restaurants alternating with a few warm ethnic nooks.

Afghan **Pamir.** This tiny, dimly lit eatery, hung with rugs and shawls, is aromatic with the spices of its cuisine, which is a cross between Middle Eastern and Indian: kabobs, meat pastries, and rice dishes. *1437 2nd Ave., at 75th St., tel. 212/734–3791; also 1065 1st Ave., at 58th St., tel. 212/644–9258. AE, DC, MC, V. Weekends 5 PM–11 PM. $$*

American **Carlyle Restaurant.** Comfortable chairs and beautiful appointments would make this salon luxurious for brunch even without its superb buffet. The kitchen takes a classic approach. *35 E. 76th St., tel. 212/744–1600. AE, DC, MC, V. Sat. 7 AM–11 PM, Sun. 8 AM–11 PM. $$$$*

Hi-Life Bar and Grill. Soothing prices for huge portions and some of the best martinis in town. Eat steak au poivre, and blackened swordfish. Or order sushi from the raw bar. *1340 1st Ave., at 72nd St., tel. 212/249–3600. DC, MC, V. Sat. 11 AM–11:30 PM, Sun. 11 AM–4 PM. $$*

The Kiosk. Nell's (Campbell; E&O) uptown place, with more look-you-up-and-down attitude than you might like, and lots of smoothies and cool things (we don't mean drinks). *1007 Lexington Ave., tel. 212/535–6000. AE, DC, MC, V. Weekends 11:30 AM–12 PM. $$*

American/ **E.A.T. Café.** With Eli Zabar of the gourmet food store dynasty in
Casual charge, you're sure to be pleased with the sandwiches, salads, and entrées here, not to mention the superlative hard-crusted breads. Breakfast is the quietest and least expensive time to make the marbled, mirrored scene. *1064 Madison Ave., between 80th and 81st Sts., tel. 212/772–0022. AE, MC. Sat., Sun. 7 AM–10 PM. $$$*

Jim McMullen. This clubby spot draws a well-heeled crowd spanning several generations. Reliable plain fare is served at gentle prices; best for brunch. *1341 3rd Ave., between 76th and 77th Sts., tel. 212/861–4700. AE, MC, V. Sat. 11:30 AM–12 AM, Sun. 11 AM–12 AM. $$*

Barbecue **Brother Jimmy's BBQ.** Exposed pipes, ceiling fans, and lots of neon set the mood for down-home service. Brother Jimmy's dry-style ribs are amazingly tender and grease-free. *1461 1st Ave., at 76th St., tel. 212/288–0999. AE, DC, MC, V. Sat. 12 PM–4 AM, Sun. 12 PM–2 AM. $*

Caribbean **Mo's Caribbean Bar & Grill.** Drop in for the rum drinks, the reggae music, and the funky food: conch fritters with red-pepper mayo, coconut shrimp, jerk-chicken wings. Sunday brunch includes two drinks and music. *1454 2nd Ave., at 76th St., tel. 212/650–0561. AE, DC, MC, V. Sat. 11:30 AM–12 AM, Sun. 11:30 AM–12 AM. $*

French **Mark's.** In this salon in the Mark Hotel, brocade pillows roost on cushy banquettes, prints and mirrors bejewel the walls, and the chef turns out complex creations unusual even in Manhattan. This is not for the rich but for the very rich. Desserts are wonderful, as is tea. *25 E. 77th St., tel. 212/879–1864. AE, DC, MC, V. Weekends 7 AM–10 PM. $$$$*

Bistro du Nord. Good, light bistro dishes keep an Upper East Side set coming back to this stylish Carnegie Hill nook. Black-and-white photographs by Avedon, Beaton, and Horst punctuate the yellow walls. *1312 Madison Ave. near 93rd St., tel. 212/289–0997. AE, DC, MC, V. Sat. 11:30 AM–10:30 PM, Sun. 11:30 AM–10 PM. $$$*

Table d'Hôte. Those who like this sliver of a restaurant rave about its brunches, where eggs reign in frittatas, omelets, and nestled in fried bread pockets with provolone and ham. A barn-red floor, white wainscoting, and antique tables and silverplate create a country-house aura. *44 E. 92nd St., tel. 212/348–8125. AE, DC, MC. Sat. 11:30 AM–10:30 PM, Sun. 10:30 AM–9 PM. $$$*

Voulez-Vous. Brunch at this mirrored, bouquet-scattered dining room could be cheese soufflé or pizza with mozzarella, banana, cocoa, and cinnamon. Later on, cassoulet and smoked fish choucroute are a homey way to end a blustery Sunday. *1462 1st Ave., at 76th St., tel. 212/249–1776. AE, DC, MC, V. Sat. 11:30 AM–12 AM, Sun. 11:30 AM–11 PM. $$*

Italian **Coco Pazzo.** This, one of New York's celebrity-spotting restaurants, explores the cuisine of all Italian regions. Levi's are as acceptable as Chanel, and the staff adds to the pleasure of the zestful, herbaceous food. The ever-changing appetizer plate is a good way to sample the chef's prowess, but it's hard to go too far wrong anywhere on the menu. *23 E. 74th St., tel. 212/794–0205. AE, DC, MC, V. Sat. 12:30 PM–12 AM, Sun. 5:30 AM–11:30 PM. $$$*

Lusardi's. This attractive restaurant with mahogany paneling and original posters on pale yellow walls attracts regulars for Sunday dinner—favorite entrées are Cornish hen and tortellini with four cheeses. *1494 2nd Ave., between 77th and 78th Sts., tel. 212/249–2020. AE, DC, MC, V. Sat. 5 PM–12 AM, Sun. 4 PM–11 PM. $$$*

Petaluma. A pastel dining room where Yuppies once grazed on California fare now offers grills, thin-crusted pizzas from the brick oven, and pastas *puttanesca* (redolent of olives and capers) and *amatriciana* (with tomato, onions, and pancetta). *1356 1st Ave., at 73rd St., tel. 212/772–8800. AE, DC, MC, V. Sat. 12 PM–3:30 PM, 5:30 PM–12 AM, Sun. 12 PM–4 PM, 5:30 PM–12 AM. $$–$$$*

Mezzaluna. Despite the incessant din and wait for tables, many people love this casual, ultrachic trattoria with a clouds-and-sky motif on the ceiling and a menu that offers good carpaccios, pizzas, and out-of-the-ordinary pastas. *1295 3rd Ave., between 74th and 75th Sts., tel. 212/535–9600. Weekends 12 PM–4 PM, 6 PM–12 AM. $$*

Sant Ambroeus. The most chic little ice cream parlor in existence, also dispensing dainty, pricey panini. *1000 Madison Ave., tel. 212/570–2211. AE, DC, MC, V. Sat. 9:30 AM–10:30 PM, Sun. 10:30 AM–6 PM. $$*

Japanese **Shabu-Tatsu.** Way east is this cook-your-own place for healthy eaters, where you opt either to barbecue or swish and simmer your paper-thin beef and mounds of veggies in tabletop pots of boiling water. *1414 York Ave., tel. 212/472–3322. AE, DC, MC, V. Sat. 12 PM–11 PM, Sun. 12 PM–10 PM. $$*

Mediterranean **Island.** On Sundays, a chic young neighborhood clientele settles into comfortable wicker bistro chairs and lingers at the terrazzo tables here over French-American brunches and dinners stamped with the robust flavors of Provence and Italy. *1305 Madison Ave., between 92nd and 93rd Sts., tel. 212/996–1200. AE, DC, MC, V. Sat. 12 PM–12 AM, Sun. 10 AM–11 PM. $$–$$$*

Thai **Bangkok House.** This comfortable, deep purple favorite offers a long menu of dishes, such as cucumber salad, beef satay, spring rolls, and hot-lemony squid salad. *1485 1st Ave., between 77th and 78th Sts., tel. 212/249–5700. AE, DC, MC, V. Weekends 5 PM–11:30 PM. $*

Turkish **Uskudar.** Stews, sautés, and grills at this pastel nook full of native crafts provide authentic tastes and aromas. *1405 2nd Ave., between 73rd and 74th Sts., tel. 212/988–2641. AE, MC, V. Weekends 12 PM–11:30 PM. $–$$*

Yorkville

Once New York's Little Germany, Little Hungary, and Little Bohemia, this area is worth visiting these days for a couple of dozen excellent—and expensive—Italian restaurants. There's a cluster of other attractive little restaurants as well.

American/ **Sarabeth's.** Join the legions of baked-goodie fiends prepared to line
Casual up for an hour at this Hotel Wales branch of the tiny chain for the tweedy brunch they dream of all week. *1295 Madison Ave., tel. 212/410–7335. AE, MC, V. Sat. 9 AM–4 PM, 6 PM–10:30 PM, Sun. 9 AM–4 PM, 6 PM–9:30 PM. $$*

Jackson Hole. Another branch of the small chain of efficient and bright burger spots makes a fine child-friendly refuelling station for Museum Mile crawls. *1270 Madison Ave., at 91st St., tel. 212/427–2820. AE. Sat. 7:30 AM–11 PM, Sun. 8:30 AM–10 PM. $*

Chinese **Our Place.** The two sleek, white-and-gray rooms of this restaurant are decidedly western in appearance. The china is Mikasa, the service nurturing, the food "uptown Chinese." Uptown or downtown, you'll find no better tangerine beef or Yang chow pan-fried noodles with shrimp, chicken, and vegetables. *1444 3rd Ave., at 82nd St., tel. 212/288–4888. AE, DC, MC, V. Weekends 11:30 AM–11 PM. $$*

Pig Heaven. Pig-snout mugs, dancing-pig mural, and the terrific Cantonese fare emphasize pork, from the scallion-pancake dim sum to the heavenly roast suckling pig, though there are nonporcine options as well. *1540 2nd Ave., between 80th and 81st Sts., tel. 212/744–4887. AE, DC, MC, V. Weekends 11:30 AM–12 AM. $$*

Eastern **Mocca Hungarian Restaurant.** Robust Hungarian food and wines
European make this café as convivial as a Hungarian wedding. Savor hearty goulashes and the preserve-filled crêpes called *palacsinta*—you won't be hungry again for hours. *1588 2nd Ave., between 82nd and 83rd Sts., tel. 212/734–6470. No credit cards. Weekends 11:30 AM–10:30 PM. $*

French **Le Boeuf à la Mode.** This bistro with etched-glass partitions and white tablecloths pleases a conservative crowd with classics such as duck à l'orange and chateaubriand. *539 E. 81st St., tel. 212/249–1473. AE, DC, MC, V. Weekends 5:30 PM–11 PM. $$$*

Le Refuge. Romantic decor and consistently good renditions of homey lamb and veal chops and roasts make this a favorite of a dressed-up East Side group. *166 E. 82nd St., tel. 212/861–4505. AE. Sat. 12 PM–3 PM, 5 PM–11 PM, Sun. 12 PM–4 PM, 5 PM–9:30 PM. $$$*

Italian **Primavera.** Pampering service and a polished setting keep the rich
Northern and famous coming back here. Specialties include roast marinated kid, succulent and sweeter than lamb, and fresh fruit carved into fanciful shapes for dessert. *1578 1st Ave., at 82nd St., tel. 212/861–8608. AE, DC, MC, V. Sat. 5:30 PM–12 AM, Sun. 5 PM–12 AM. $$$$*

Sistina. East Siders line up at this genial café full of blond wood and white linen. Romeo-waiters describe the esoteric fare from the untranslated Italian menu: "Fantastico!" they exclaim. The spaghetti *alla carbonara* is authentic, but be sure to come here in the fall, white truffle season. *1555 2nd Ave., between 80th and 81st Sts., tel. 212/861–7660. AE, DC, MC, V. Weekends 12 PM–2:30 PM, 5 PM–12 AM. $$$$*

Elaine's. Go early Sunday evening and you'll be seated speedily, albeit in some ignominious position; linger until 9 and you may spot a celebrity basking in the proprietress's warmth. Don't bother with Saturday, unless you are a celeb; leave your taste buds at home. *1703*

2nd Ave., between 88th and 89th Sts., tel. 212/534–8103. AE, DC, MC, V. Weekends 6 PM–2 AM. $$$

Girasole. This spare trattoria in a town house, with gray walls and a star-spangled silvery blue ceiling, turns out succulent grills for a crowd of young professionals. Gorgonzola-topped polenta, quail on risotto, and ricotta cheesecake are good bets. *151 E. 82nd St., tel. 212/772–6690. AE. Sat. 12 PM–3 PM, 5:30 PM–12 AM, Sun. 12 PM–3 PM, 5:30 PM–11 PM. $$$*

Paola's. In this romantic, dollhouse-sized charmer, little mirrors on the walls show off a flotsam of bric-a-brac and allow a genteel crowd to preen surreptitiously over pastas, soups, and grills. *343 E. 85th St., tel. 212/794–1890. AE, MC, V. Weekends 5 PM–11 PM. $$$*

Divino. Good pastas and herb-aromatic grills cost a shade less here than elsewhere in the neighborhood. *1556 2nd Ave., between 80th and 81st Sts., tel. 212/861–1096. AE, DC, MC, V. Sat. 12 PM–12 AM, Sun. 12 PM–11 PM. $$*

Due. It's mobbed and modern, with an airy, geometric design by architect Charles Gwathmey and a menu that stars focaccia breads with many toppings. *1396 3rd Ave., between 79th and 80th Sts., tel. 212/772–3331. No credit cards. Sat. 12 PM–1 AM, Sun. 12 PM–12 AM. $$*

Ecco-La. This family-owned eatery offering inexpensive homemade pastas and other lively northern Italian fare is small and noisy—but reasonable prices compensate. *1660 3rd Ave., at 93rd St., tel. 212/860–5609. AE. Sat. 11:30 AM–12 AM, Sun. 11:30 AM–11:30 PM. $*

Southern **Azzurro.** This friendly storefront café, with a star-scattered blue ceiling, offers beautiful renditions of unusual Sicilian dishes: bucatini tossed with sardines and fennel or penne with roasted eggplant and tomato. It can be noisy, but diners love the happy hubbub. *245 E. 84th St., tel. 212/517–8365. AE, DC, MC, V. Sat. 5:30 PM–11:30 PM, Sun. 4 PM–10 PM. $$$*

Lincoln Center

Cafés have been sprouting like crazy along Columbus Avenue and on adjacent side streets in the past few years—in fine weather there must be more sidewalk seating per block here than on any other avenue in the city.

American/ International **Café des Artistes.** Howard Chandler Christy's lush murals of nudes would draw crowds to George Lang, saint of Hungarian cuisine's, romantic West Side institution even if the food were not as good as it is. The fine Sunday brunch is a legend, and late Saturday supper is heaven. Chocoholics like the ridiculous "Chocolatissimo" extravaganza. *1 W. 67th St., tel. 212/877–3500. AE, DC, MC, V. Sat. 11 AM–2:30 PM, 5:30 PM–11:30 PM, Sun. 10 AM–2:30 PM, 5:30 PM–10:30 PM. $$$$*

Café Luxembourg. In this hip sister of even hipper Odeon, a sophisticated, good-natured staff offers well-honed brasserie standbys salted with nouvelle American ideas. The setting is pure Paris bistro, the buzzing crowd pure New York—mainly prosperous-looking concertgoers on Sundays. *200 W. 70th St., tel. 212/873–7411. AE, DC, MC, V. Sat. 12 PM–12 AM, Sun. 11 AM–12 AM. $$$*

Tavern on the Green. This clichéd, but irresistible Central Park fantasy offers contemporary cuisine such as omelets with crabmeat and chives, eggs Benedict with pancetta, and stuffed breast of veal with sage sauce and rösti at brunch time. The Chestnut Room is cozy, the chandelier-hung Crystal Room sparkles, and the terrace delights in pleasant weather. *Central Park W at 67th St., tel. 212/873–3200. AE, DC, MC, V. Weekends 10 AM–11 PM. $$$*

Josephina. A new chef gussied up the blah organic menus, and there's nothing not to like at this big-portion eating station with several large rooms. The front is coziest. *1900 Broadway, tel. 212/799–*

1000. *AE, DC, MC, V. Sat. 11:30 AM–12 AM, Sun. 11:30 AM–11 PM. $$*

O'Neals'. A pub in front and a big dining room in back serve average bistro-type food—black bean soup, burgers, grilled Cornish hen—but the atmosphere is warm, and Lincoln Center is nearby. *49 W. 64th St., tel. 212/787–4663. AE, DC, MC, V. Sat. 10 AM–12 PM, Sun. 10 AM–10 PM. $$*

The Saloon. This cavernous saloon, with some waiters on skates, is conveniently opposite Lincoln Center. The menu is inventive but immense; stick to simpler dishes and you'll call it a find. *1920 Broadway, at 64th St., tel. 212/874–1500. AE, DC, MC, V. Weekends 10 AM–11 PM. $$*

Vince & Eddie's. Brick walls, oilcloth-covered tables, a sprinkling of antiques, and a working fireplace make this West Sider feel pleasantly cozy, for bean soup, onion tart, roast chicken with savoy cabbage, mashed turnips, and plum tart with hazelnut ice cream. A tiny garden charms in fine weather. *70 W. 68th St., tel. 212/721–0068. AE, DC, MC, V. Sat. 12 PM–3 PM, 5 PM–12 AM, Sun. 11 AM–3 PM, 5 PM–11 PM. $$*

Chinese **Shun Lee Café.** This sleek black-and-white spot is the area's dim sum darling, related to the far pricier midtown Palace, and just as Hong Kong glamorous. *43 W. 65th St., tel. 212/769–3888. AE, DC, MC, V. Sat. 11:30 AM–2:30 PM, 5 PM–12 AM, Sun. 12 PM–10 PM. $$*

French **La Boîte en Bois.** At this tiny country French restaurant monkfish in green peppercorn sauce and zesty fish soup reveal cooks of a high order at work—not often true in this area. *75 W. 68th St., tel. 212/874–2705. No credit cards. Sat. 5:30 PM–10:30 PM, Sun. 4 PM–9 PM. $$$*

Italian **Sfuzzi.** Fanciful faux-Pompeii decor sets the scene for the fun food: savory, clear-flavored pasta dishes, grilled fish and chops, and an antipasto bar. Try the frozen Sfuzzis, which mix sparkling wine, peach schnapps, and peach purée. *58 W. 65th St., tel. 212/873–3700. AE, DC, MC, V. Sat. 11:30 AM–3 PM, 5 PM–12 AM, Sun. 11:30 AM–3 PM, 5 PM–11 PM. $$$*

Fiorello's Roman Café. This bustling restaurant across from Lincoln Center offers outdoor seating and cozy, comfortable tables inside. Specialties include thin-crusted individual pizzas and he-man veal chops. *1900 Broadway, between 63rd and 64th Sts., tel. 212/595–5330. AE, DC, MC, V. Sat. 11 AM–12:30 AM, Sun. 11:30 AM–10:30 PM. $$*

Japanese **Lenge.** This local landmark offers diverting Japanese fare, including the hearty *nabe* (noodle soups). *200 Columbus Ave., at 69th St., tel. 212/799–9188. AE, DC, MC, V. Sat. 12 PM–11:30 PM, Sun. 11 AM–11 PM. $*

Mediterranean **Picholine.** This deeply carpeted, striped, banquetted Lincoln Center neighbor is the very definition of sophisticated, as is Terry Brennan's understated cuisine. The whole fish for two eases the pain of choosing. *35 W. 64th St., tel. 212/724–8585. AE, DC, MC, V. Sat. 12 PM–2:30 PM, 5:30 PM–11:30 PM, Sun. 5 PM–10:30 PM. $$$*

Mexican/ Southwestern **Santa Fe.** The desert-sunset color scheme is sophisticated, fish dishes have real zest, and the margaritas kill. What's for brunch? Try Southwestern omelets and enchiladas suizas. *72 W. 69th St., tel. 212/724–0822. AE, MC, V. Weekends 11:30 AM–12 AM. $$–$$$*

Upper West Side

There are so many restaurants here that you wonder whether the local folk ever eat in. Many are the kind of ordinary spots that you pop into only because they're there, but a few stand out for prices, ambience, or honest-to-goodness good food.

American

Ansonia. Around here, one of the hottest openings of recent years was this glitzy place, with an ambitious kitchen under the aegis of Bill Telepan. Huge, galleried, and with a whole separate bar scene to drop into. *329 Columbus Ave., tel. 212/579–0505. AE, DC, MC,V. Sat. 5:30 PM–2 AM, Sun. 5:30 PM–11:30 PM. $$$*

Fishin Eddie. The back room here is like a conservatory in Maine; the big menu will give seafood fans anxiety; so may the big check. Get dessert next door at Cafe La Fortuna. *73 W. 71st St., tel. 212/874–3474. AE, DC, MC, V. Sat. 5 PM–12 AM, Sun. 5 PM–11 PM. $$*

Savann. A roaring success (now cloned on the east side) this brick-walled casual space has tiny tables loaded with modestly priced fascinating food—melon soup with prosciutto, lime and cilantro; potato-crusted skate with spring vegetable ratatouille; grilled squid with parsnip horseradish puree should give you the idea. *414 Amsterdam Ave., tel. 212/580–0202. MC, V. Sat. 6 PM–12 AM, Sun. 6 PM–11 PM. $$*

Dallas BBQ. Onion rings and barbecue headline here. But for the buck, you won't do better. Especially recommended for families or groups, the brisket sandwich is almost classy. No desserts, so don't plan to hang out. *27 W. 72nd St., tel. 212/873–2004; also 1265 3rd Ave., at 72nd St., tel. 212/772–9393; 21 University Pl., tel. 212/674–4450; 132 2nd Ave., at St. Mark's Pl., tel. 212/777–5574. AE, MC, V. Weekends 11 AM–2 AM. $*

American/ Casual

Stingray. Where Amsterdam's once stood, here's a welcoming seafood place, where shrimp and scallops come in oversized martini glasses, fish is nut-crusted or chargrilled, and pizza has toppings like brie and pear. Nice bar too. *428 Amsterdam Ave., between 80th and 81st Sts., tel. 212/501–7515. AE, DC, MC, V. Sat. 6 PM–12 PM, Sun. 5 PM–11 PM. $$*

Sarabeth's Kitchen. This beige-and-peach tea room beguiles the brunch set with pumpkin waffles, apple-cinnamon French toast, and green-and-white eggs—scrambled with scallions and cream cheese. *423 Amsterdam Ave., between 80th and 81st Sts., tel. 212/496–6280. AE, DC, MC, V. Weekends 9 AM–4 PM, 6 PM–11 PM. $–$$*

Shark Bar. Soul-stirring food with all the trimmings and a terrific Sunday jazz brunch. Very popular. *307 Amsterdam Ave., tel. 212/874–8500. AE, DC, MC, V. Sat. 11:30 AM–3:30 PM, 5:30 PM–1:30 AM, Sun. 11:30 AM–3:30 PM, 5:30 PM–11:30 PM. $–$$*

All State Café. This low-ceiling, brick-walled old-timer with a good jukebox, rickety chairs, and '60s charm serves good fish, poultry, and pastas at pleasant prices. *250 W. 72nd St., tel. 212/874–1883. No credit cards. Weekends 11:30 AM–12:30 AM. $*

Good Enough to Eat. Baskets, quilts, and farm tools make this nook feel like Vermont, and set the scene for farmhouse brunch—apple pancakes, pecan waffles, meat loaf, and chicken pot pie. Go early to avoid lines. *483 Amsterdam Ave., between 83rd and 84th Sts., tel. 212/496–0163. MC, V. Sat. 9 AM–4 PM, 6 PM–10:30 PM, Sun. 9 AM–4 PM, 5:30 PM–10 PM. $*

Museum Café. This sunny café has spent the past 20 years serving its own versions of whatever's most fashionable on the New York food scene. At present, it's something-for-everyone American regional-Chinese–Mexican–Italian. *366 Columbus Ave., at 77th St., tel. 212/799–0150. AE, DC, MC, V. Sat. 11 AM–1 AM, Sun. 11 AM–12 AM. $*

Popover Café. This once-tiny eatery, built around an airy puff of eggs and flour and decked with troops of teddy bears, delights New Yorkers and Europeans who come to enjoy the eponymous popovers' accompaniments: soups, sandwiches, salads, and omelets. Try the cappuccino eggs, cooked to fluffiness in the shell by steam from the espresso maker. *551 Amsterdam Ave., at 87th St., tel. 212/595–8555. AE, MC, V. Sat. 9 AM–11 PM, Sun. 9 AM–10 PM. $*

Royal Canadian Restaurant and Pancake House. Waffles, French toast, omelets, and 54 kinds of pancakes (the large ones drape over the edge of the oversize plates) are all doused with real Canadian maple syrup. Come early. This funky weekend hot spot draws huge crowds. *2286 Broadway, between 82nd and 83rd Sts., tel. 212/873–6052; also 180 3rd Ave., tel. 212/777–9288, and 1004 2nd Ave., tel. 212/980–4131. No credit cards. Weekends 7 AM–12 AM. $*

Asian **Rain.** Is it Malaysian? Thai? Vietnamese? Yes, all of them, with duck fajitas. Add to that a gorgeously dim and decadent bar up front. Shelter from the monsoons with some pad thai and a cocktail. *100 W. 82nd St., tel. 212/501–0776. AE, DC, MC, V. Sat. 12 PM–4 PM, 5 PM–12 AM, Sun. 12 PM–4 PM, 5 PM–10 PM. $$*

Shabu-Tatsu. Just like the one on the Upper East Side. *483 Columbus Ave., tel. 212/874–5633. AE, DC, MC, V. Sat. 12 PM–11 PM, Sun. 12 PM–10:30 PM. $$*

Deli **Barney Greengrass.** "The Sturgeon King" he calls himself, and he does not tell a lie. Mountains of sturgeon, sable, lox, whitefish and all the trimmings, plus matzo ball soup and whatever is here in horrible surroundings. *541 Amsterdam Ave., tel. 212/724–4707. No credit cards. Weekends 9 AM–5 PM. $*

Chinese **Ollie's.** Decor is basic, but regulars swear by the fried dumplings and noodles at this crowded uptown eatery. Grilled shrimp rates praise, too. *2315 Broadway, at 84th St., tel. 212/362–3712. AE, MC, V. Sat. 11:30 AM–1 AM, Sun. 11:30 AM–12 AM. $*

Ethiopian **Blue Nile.** The stools may be a little uncomfortable but this is a delightfully quiet reward for adventurous taste buds. *103 W. 77th St., tel. 212/580–3232. AE, DC, MC, V. Sat. 12 PM–11 PM, Sun. 12 PM–10 PM. $*

Italian **Baci.** In this storefront hangout, a raked-glass ceiling and terrazzo-topped tables add up to a supremely stylish setting for gutsy Sicilian fare such as penne with eggplant and bucatini with sardines and pine nuts. *412 Amsterdam Ave., between 79th and 80th Sts., tel. 212/496–1550. AE, DC, MC, V. Sat. 12 PM–12 AM, Sun. 12 PM–10:30 PM. $$*

Carmine's. Sure, it's an institution, a tourist trap, a zoo, a brawl, a calorie nightmare, but even William Hurt has been seen queuing up for the gargantuan garlic and red sauce pastas, the kind that are hard to find away from the Bronx's Arthur Avenue. *2450 Broadway, near 91st St., tel. 212/362–2200. AE, MC, V. Sat. 5 PM–12 AM, Sun. 2 PM–10 PM. $$*

Japanese **Fujiyama Mama.** White-slipcovered chairs, a loud DJ, stupid menu puns, and lots of chrome and aluminum make this stand out a mile from regular sushi joints. When the deep-fried ice cream flambé is served for a birthday, it comes with a sparkler, and several versions of "Happy Birthday" in quick succession on the speakers. Believe it or not, the sushi isn't bad at all. *467 Columbus Ave., between 82nd and 83rd Sts., tel. 212/769–1144. AE, MC, V. Sat. 6 PM–12:30 AM, Sun. 5 PM–10:30 PM. $$*

Bon 75. Daily, monthly, and seasonal specials supplement the menu at this unassuming black-and-gray restaurant. The extensive appetizer list lets you create a meal Japanese-style, with several tasty small-portion dishes. Broiled fish is good, too. *2140 Broadway, at 75th St., tel. 212/724–1414. AE, MC, V. Sat. 1 PM–12 AM, Sun. 1 PM–11 PM. $*

Latin-Chinese **La Caridad.** Formica dominates the decor in this favorite of savvy cabbies, where the prices are low and the atmosphere is warm. Specialties include the Cuban pot roast known as *ropa vieja*, garlicky squid fried rice, and banana egg foo young. The orange juice is fresh-squeezed and the espresso inky and thick. *2199 Broadway, at 78th St., tel. 212/874–2780. No credit cards. Sat. 11:30 AM–12 AM, Sun. 11:30 AM–10:30 PM. $*

Seafood **Dock's Oyster Bar and Seafood Grill.** The long bar and black-and-white tiled floors are relics of the old West Side, but this fish house is au courant with its changing menu of grills, stews, and sautéed dishes. Poached eggs with smoked salmon and hollandaise on a bagel is appealing at brunch; if you want fresh fish, have the seafood salad. *2427 Broadway, between 89th and 90th Sts., tel. 212/724–5588. AE, DC, MC, V. Sat. 11:30 AM–11:30 PM, Sun. 10:30 AM–10:30 PM. $$–$$$*

Far Upper West Side

The neighborhood from 96th Street north to Columbia University, rapidly gentrifying, is thick with Chinese restaurants, and inexpensive eating abounds.

American Regional

107 West. Local residents congregate for jambalaya, fried catfish, and other good Southern food zapped by Cajun spices. *2787 Broadway, at 107th St., tel. 212/864–1555. AE, MC, V. Sat. 11 AM–12 AM, Sun. 11 AM–10:30 PM. $$*

Chinese

Columbia Cottage. As you might assume, this is full of students, especially since wine arrives free with dinner and dinner itself is good (and inexpensive, too). *1034 Amsterdam Ave., at 111th St., tel. 212/662–1800. AE, MC, V. Sat. 11:30 AM–12 AM, Sun. 11:30 AM–11:30 PM. $*

Hunan Balcony. Decor is standard—chrome, glass, blond wood, hanging plants—and the extensive menu virtually the same as that of most non-Chinatown Szechuan and Hunan spots. The difference here is reliably careful preparation: crisply steamed vegetables, non-greasy sauces, and no stinting on the meat or fish. *2596 Broadway, at 98th St., tel. 212/865–0400. AE, DC, MC, V. Sat. 11 AM–1:30 AM, Sun. 11 AM–1 AM. $*

Ollie's. The plain-Jane decor and noodles-and-dumplings menu at this Columbia student favorite duplicates Ollie's sister café downtown (*see* Upper West Side). *2957 Broadway, at 116th St., tel. 212/932–3300. AE, MC, V. Weekends 12 PM–2 AM. $*

V & T Restaurant. The substantial pizza comes with an array of toppings as old-fashioned as the oilcloth on the tables. A Columbia students' hangout since 1945, it's opposite St. John the Divine. *1024 Amsterdam Ave., between 110th and 111th Sts., tel. 212/663–1708. AE, DC, MC, V. Sat. 11:30 AM–1 AM, Sun. 11:30 AM–10:30 PM. $*

Harlem

American Southern

The Cotton Club. Although the famous original was torn down in the '30s, the name still draws tourists, many foreign, to the prix fixe Sunday brunch, which features Southern staples such as fried chicken, barbecued ribs, collards, and pecan pie. But the real attraction is the joyful noise of gospel singers who will keep you clapping your hands and smiling till next Sunday. *656 W. 125th St., at West Side Hwy., tel. 212/663–7980. MC, V. Sat. 12 PM–12 AM, Sun. 12 PM–9 PM. $*

Emily's. There's a great bar with potent, islandy drinks, a short but really inexpensive wine list, and oh, those chopped barbecue sandwiches, incredible deep-fried chicken livers (dunk them into the zesty house sauce), Emily's mouth-watering corn-bread stuffing (worth the trip in itself), and an out-of-this world batter-fried whiting. *1325 5th Ave., at 111th St., tel. 212/996–1212. AE, DC, MC, V. Sat. 7:30 AM–11:30 PM, Sun. 7:30 AM–9 PM. $*

Sylvia's Soul Food Restaurant. People come from all over the city to feast in this Harlem legend. For years it has been serving zesty collard greens, black-eyed peas, candied sweet potatoes, and gritty homemade corn bread with terrific pork chops, smothered chicken, tender braised short ribs, and pecan pie. *329 Lenox Ave. near 126th St., tel. 212/996–0660. AE, MC, V. Sat. 7:30 AM–10:30 PM, Sun. 12:30 PM–7 PM. $*

The Bronx

Arthur Avenue in the Belmont section is like an old-fashioned Italian Restaurant Row; it will change your ideas about the Bronx forver.

Italian **Amerigo's.** This half-century-old restaurant feeds hungry diners in two rooms, one casual and one formally filled with Italian sculpture. You'll find anchovy-sauced fried mozzarella, gnocchi with a verdant pesto, prime steaks, first-class osso buco, and sublime pork chops with vinegar peppers. All this comes in huge portions—at fair prices. *3587 E. Tremont Ave., between Sullivan Pl. and Lafayette St., Throgs Neck, tel. 718/792–3600. AE, DC, MC, V. Sat. 12 PM–11 PM, Sun. 12 PM–10 PM. $$$*

Dominick's. It's always crowded at this pasta house where platters of spaghetti come saturated with freshly made sauce to down with crusty bread and rough red wine. Everyone sits at long communal tables to feast on shrimp, calamari in red sauce, and fettuccine with bacon-mushroom cream sauce. There is no menu, and waiters keep the running tabs in their heads. The draw is simply honest fare at honest prices. *2335 Arthur Ave., tel. 718/733–2807. No credit cards. Sat. 2 PM–10 PM, Sun. 1 PM–9 PM. $*

Brooklyn

Brooklyn restaurants reflect the tastes both of its deeply rooted ethnic populations and of the newcomers to its gentrifying neighborhoods. Montague Street in Brooklyn Heights; 5th Avenue in Park Slope; and Court Street in Cobble Hill, south of Atlantic Avenue, are full of tiny little restaurants that serve casual American fare with international accents in quaint surroundings. Flatbush Avenue is an outpost of Jamaica, while Brighton Beach, down by Coney Island and the Aquarium, is full of boisterous Russian restaurants.

American/ Casual **Café on Clinton.** This casual nook is sophisticated enough to serve a dozen wines by the glass and friendly enough to provide high chairs. With its custom-made cherry bar and floral tablecloths, it's pretty besides. Seafood features prominently at dinner, and brunch includes a good 10-green salad. Burgers are always available. *268 Clinton St., between Warren and Congress Sts., Cobble Hill, tel. 718/625–5908. MC, V. Sat. 11:30 AM–3:30 PM, 5 PM–10:30 PM, Sun. 11:30 AM–10:30 PM. $–$$*

American/ International **River Café.** From this elegantly unassuming barge-restaurant in the shadow of the Brooklyn Bridge, Manhattan seems close enough to touch. Go for a festive brunch or for dinner or drinks with music and the glittering after-dark view—any time at all. *1 Water St., tel. 718/ 522–5200. AE, DC, MC, V. Sat. 11 AM–3 PM, 5:30 PM–11 PM, Sun. 11 AM–10 PM. $$$$*

Henry's End. After a sunset stroll across the Brooklyn Bridge, this favorite welcomes you with wild game, great desserts, and other tasty edibles. *44 Henry St., at Cranberry St., Brooklyn Heights, tel. 718/834–1776. AE, DC, MC, V. Sat. 5:30 PM–11:30 PM, Sun. 5 PM–10 PM. $$*

12th Street Bar and Grill. The menu changes bimonthly in this cozy restaurant with a pressed-tin ceiling, black-and-white tile floor, and vintage bar. But you can count on interesting fare—perhaps a black-eyed-pea cassoulet or stuffed calamari with polenta. *1123 8th Ave., at 12th St., Park Slope, tel. 718/965–9526. AE, MC, V. Sat. 12 PM– 2:30 PM, 6 PM–11 PM, Sun. 11:30 AM–2:30 PM, 6 PM–11 PM. $$*

Clover Hill. Fans who got into the Clover Hill habit while the restaurant was in Brooklyn Heights are only too happy to travel a few blocks farther to its minuscule new home to the south. The menu, which changes according to what's in the market, shows the influence of East and West, but there are touches of home in dishes like the apple Cheddar crisp and pumpkin bread pudding. *272 Court St., between Kane and Degraw Sts., Cobble Hill, tel. 718/875–0895. No credit cards. Weekends 10 AM–3 PM, 6 PM–11 PM.* $

Italian **Monte's Venetian Room.** At this amiable old-timer with antique murals, scarlet banquettes, and snowy tablecloths, waiters bring fried zucchini and garlic bread before they bring the enormous menu of reliable Neapolitan fare. Go for straightforward pasta dishes, filet mignon, or shrimp with tomato, olives, and garlic. *451 Carroll St., between 3rd Ave. and Nevins St., Red Hook, tel. 718/624–8984. AE, MC, V. Sat. 4:30 PM–10:30 PM, Sun. 2 PM–10 PM.* $$$$

Gargiulio's. At this venerable restaurant, one of a handful of tidy eateries in this less than ravishing corner of New York, there's an octopus on the ceiling, a colorful clientele, and waiters who remain relics of a brighter day on Coney Island. The southern Italian fare is prejudiced to red-sauce, mozzarella, and garlic; the Aquarium is nearby, families are welcomed, and attended parking is available. *2911 W. 15th St., between 5th and Mermaid Aves., Coney Island, tel. 718/266–4891. AE, DC, MC, V. Sat. 11:30 AM–11 PM, Sun. 11:30 AM–11 PM.* $$

Tommaso. The traditional fare here includes stuffed squid on linguini and rabbit with cornmeal; wine lovers come for the vast selection of wines at prices that haven't been seen in stores for a decade. Regulars pile in for their big meal of the day, and Italian singing fills the room. *1464 86th St., between 14th and 15th Aves., Bay Ridge, tel. 718/236–9883. AE, DC, MC, V. Weekends 4:30 PM–11 PM.* $$

Middle **Moroccan Star.** This simple, neat nook stands out for its lamb steaks,
Eastern chicken pie with spices and garlic, and robust lamb stew with almonds, prunes, and carrots. *205 Atlantic Ave., Brooklyn Heights, tel. 718/643–0800. MC, V. Weekends 11 AM–11 PM.* $

Russian **Odessa.** This Russian nightclub-restaurant is like a Las Vegas revue, an Italian wedding, a glitzy bar mitzvah, and a trip to Moscow all rolled into one. Waiters deliver platters filled with stuffed cabbage and apple-and-celery Russian salad. *1113 Brighton Beach Ave., Brighton Beach, tel. 718/332–3223. AE, MC, V. Sat. 8 PM–4 AM, Sun. 6 PM–12 AM.* $$

Steak **Peter Luger.** Giant, aged tenderloins and extra-thick lamb chops are the attractions at this bit of culinary Old New York, an austere dining room full of oak wainscoting and beer-hall tables. *178 Broadway, Williamsburg, tel. 718/387–7400. No credit cards. Sat. 11:30 AM–9:30 PM, Sun. 1 PM–8:30 PM.* $$$

Queens

This sprawling borough is full of ethnic neighborhoods, each with a complement of restaurants where robust flavors can be enjoyed for a song. Roosevelt Avenue, in the shadow of the elevated train, shows off food from Argentina, Colombia, Cuba, and the Philippines. Elmhurst is full of Thai spots, Flushing is home to New York's second-largest Chinese community, and in Astoria, Greek restaurants line the streets.

Chinese **Goody's.** Worth the schlep for dumplings, noodles, and regional dishes that surpass many offered in Chinatown. Don't expect the Ritz. *94–03B 63rd Dr., Rego Park, tel. 718/896–7159. No credit cards. Weekends 11:30 AM–10:30 PM.* $

German **Chalet Alpina.** An accordionist strolls, and waitresses in embroidered blouses serve draft Spaten and Dinckelmann beers, robust schnitzels, and bacon-infused potato salad. *98–35 Metropolitan Ave., at 70th Ave., Forest Hills, tel. 718/793–3774. AE, MC, V. Sat. 4:30 PM–11 PM, Sun. 1 PM–9 PM.* $$

Greek **Karyatis.** After a visit to the American Museum of the Moving Image (*see* Art Museums in Chapter 4), it's fun to stop at this little Athens for solid Greek fare at reasonable prices. *35–03 Broadway, between 35th and 36th Sts., Astoria, tel. 718/204–0666. AE, DC, MC, V. Sat. 12 PM–12 AM, Sun. 12 PM–10:30 PM. $$*

Elia's Corner. This honest family-run operation, with fresh and carefully prepared seafood, is a major contender for title of best Greek restaurant in New York (it also prepares some of the tastiest seafood available at any price). There's no written menu. Start with fried smelts (they melt in your mouth) or amazingly tender grilled octopus. Then, whole red snapper, St. Pierre fish, salmon, bass, or shrimp—all timed to the second and accompanied by incredible potatoes: mashed with garlic or fried with cheese. *24–01 31st St., Astoria, tel. 718/932–1510. No credit cards. Sat. 4 PM–12 AM, Sun. 3 PM–12 AM. $*

Italian **Quartière.** This find gives Forest Hills explorers a good-looking option for out-of-the-ordinary pizzas and grills at prices as relaxing as the neighborhood. *107–02 Queens Blvd. at 70th Ave., tel. 718/520–8037. AE, DC, V. Sat. 12 PM–1 AM, Sun. 12 PM–12 AM. $$*

Latin **18 de Julio Carnicería y Parrillada.** This is the place to go for sensuous tango, decent pasta, and typical Argentine grilled steak dishes, despite the fact that this is a Uruguayan restaurant, one of the few in this ethnic-rich area. *77–05 37th Ave., tel. 718/429–5495. DC, MC, V. Weekends 11 AM–11 PM. $$*

La Fusta. *Parrillada*—huge Argentine mixed grills barbecued tableside—are the specialty at this neighborhood favorite with riding crops ("la fusta" in Spanish) on the walls. Start with the garlicky meat dumplings and end with caramelized milk flan. *80–32 Baxter Ave., Elmhurst, tel. 718/429–8222. No credit cards. Sat. 11:30 AM–11:30 PM, Sun. 2 PM–11:30 PM. $$*

Thai **Jai Ya Thai.** This diner's Thai food is about as authentic as you can get this side of Bangkok. *81–11 Broadway, between 74th St. and Queens Blvd., Elmhurst, tel. 718/651–1330. AE, DC, MC, V. Sat. 11 AM–11:30 PM. $*

Sweets and Treats

Downtown **Minter's Fun Food and Drink** offers six kinds of chocolate chip cookies and exotic chocolate martinis. *4 World Financial Center, tel. 212/945–4455. AE, MC, V. Weekends 8 AM–6 PM.*

SoHo **Dean & DeLuca,** the famous gourmet foods emporium, brews superb espresso and cappuccino to go with the sublime pastries. *560 Broadway, at Prince St., tel. 212/431–1691. AE, MC, V. Sat. 10 AM–8 PM, Sun. 10 AM–7 PM.*

Eileen's is a cheesecake-addict's dream, with about 15 flavors (coconut custard, butter pecan, cherry . . .); pies and desserts, too. There's practically no room inside, so eat in the vest-pocket park out front. *17 Cleveland Pl., at Centre St., tel. 212/966–5585. AE, MC, V. Weekends 10 AM–6 PM.*

Chinatown **Caffè Roma,** an authentic old Italian coffeehouse straight out of *The* **and Little** *Godfather* has marble-topped tables and a long pastry case. *385* **Italy** *Broome St., at Mulberry St., tel. 212/226–8413. No credit cards. Weekends 8 AM–12 AM.*

Ceci-Cela is a taste of France with the most authentic patisseries, almond croissant, and house-made sorbets in town. *55 Spring St., tel. 212/274–9179. Sat. 8 AM–7 PM, Sun. 9 AM–7 PM.*

Chinatown Ice Cream Factory satisfies the urge for green tea, coconut, or red bean ice cream. *65 Bayard St., near Mott St., tel. 212/608–4170. No credit cards. Weekends 11:30 AM–11:30 PM.*

Ferrara, a New York institution, is still fun for espresso, dessert, and people-watching. *195 Grand St., at Mulberry St., tel. 212/226–6150. AE, DC, MC, V. Sat. 8 AM–1 AM, Sun. 8 AM–12 AM.*

East Village **Bruno Bakery.** The biscotti at this (remodeled and too glossy) pasticceria are in contention for the city's best. *506 La Guardia Pl., between Houston and Bleecker Sts., tel. 212/982–5854. MC, V. Sat. 7 AM–2 AM, Sun. 7 AM–12 AM.*

De Robertis Pastry Shop, a mosaic-tiled coffeehouse, has been around forever—and looks it. Try the biscotti or the very good pignoli, but give the sorbetti a miss. *176 1st Ave., at 10th St., tel. 212/674–7137. MC, V. Weekends 9 AM–11 PM.*

Gem Spa, basically a newsstand, is one of the first places in New York to serve egg creams and still pours some of the best. *131 2nd Ave., at St. Mark's Pl., tel. 212/529–1146. No credit cards. Open 24 hrs.*

Veniero, now a century old, is the bustling home of every kind of Italian sweet—plus irresistible gelati, cheesecakes, and chocolate mousse cake. *342 E. 11th St., between 1st and 2nd Aves., tel. 212/674–7264. AE, MC, V. Sat. 8 AM–12 AM.*

West Village **Anglers & Writers Salon de Thé** (*see* West Village Restaurants, *above*) pours brews from Fortnum & Mason as well as specialty coffees.

Caffè Dante a convivial spot, serves superlative espresso and wonderful hazelnut gelato. *79–81 MacDougal St., between Houston and Bleecker Sts., tel. 212/982–5275. No credit cards. Sat. 10 AM–3 AM, Sun. 10 AM–2 AM.*

Caffè Reggio, a smoke-darkened, vintage-1927 room, stands out for its huge, fanciful espresso machine and old Italian art. *119 MacDougal St., between W. 3rd and Bleecker Sts., tel. 212/475–9557. No credit cards. Sat. 10 AM–3 AM, Sun. 10 AM–2 AM..*

Caffè Vivaldi is a pleasant place to soak up Greenwich Village atmosphere anytime. In summer, its quiet side street makes for peaceful sidewalk-sitting. *32 Jones St., at Bleecker St., tel. 212/691–7538. No credit cards. Weekends 11 AM–2 AM.*

Pravinie Gourmet Ice Cream dishes out 32 exotic ice creams. *193 Bleecker St., between 6th Ave. and MacDougal St., tel. 212/475–1968. Sun. 12 PM–12 AM. No credit cards.*

Tea and Sympathy (*see* West Village restaurants, *above*) is the place to go for the authentic English after noon.

Midtown West **Cupcake Café** fans swear that whole-wheat doughnuts warrant the trip to Hell's Kitchen, but the rainbow-colored butter-icing bouquets on the buttery gateaux are more incredible still. *522 9th Ave., at 39th St., tel. 212/465–1530. No credit cards. Sat. 8 AM–6 PM, Sun. 9 AM–5 PM.*

West 50s The **Palm Court,** in the Plaza Hotel, **Petrossian,** and the **Rainbow Promenade** (*see* East 50s and West 50s restaurants, *above*) are all fine refueling spots: The Palm Court serves the quintessential tea, though some call it touristy, and Petrossian has a bar where you can snack in style—on caviar and champagne.

Gotham Lounge, Hotel Peninsula. New York at its elegant best. Tea for two (or more) and the service is dear, in every sense of the word. *700 5th Ave., tel. 212/247–2200. AE, DC, MC, V. Weekends 11 AM–12 AM.*

East 60s **Les Friandises.** Tops for Francophiles. *972 Lexington Ave., tel. 212/988–1616. AE. Sat. 8 AM–7 PM, Sun. 10 AM–6 PM.*

The Rotunda, with murals and a ceiling painted with sky and clouds, has a clientele that fits the setting. Move in for tea. *Pierre Hotel, 5th Ave., at 61st St., tel. 212/940–8185. AE, DC, MC, V. Weekends 3 PM–5 PM.*

Lincoln Center **Café La Fortuna** offers refuge, espresso, opera music, and pastries to weary Columbus Avenue strollers. *69 W. 71st St., tel. 212/724–5846. Sat. 12 PM–1:30 AM, Sun. 12 PM–12:30 AM.*

Houlihan's, a casual chain pub, will serve you an adolescent-pleasing dessert even if you don't have a meal. Go for the fudge-and-caramel-doused caramel-nut-crunch pie, its crust made of crushed Oreos and Snickers with peanut butter. *Broadway and 63rd St., tel. 212/339–8862. AE, DC, MC, V. Sat. 11:30 AM–12 AM, Sun. 11:30 AM–10 PM.*

Upper West Side

Café Lalo. So many gateaux, so little time. Peak times see lines; otherwise, the cakes, pies, tortes, croissants, desserts, and cookies are best at one of the little round tables here, maybe late at night. It's utterly Continental. *201 W. 83rd St., tel. 212/496–6031. No credit cards. Sat. 9 AM–4 AM, Sun. 9 AM–2 AM. $*

Good Enough to Eat and **Sarabeth's Kitchen** are also good for sweets. (*see* Upper West Side restaurants, *above*).

Zabar's, with seating on high stools, is awkward and uncomfortable, but it's also *the* spot for coffee and pastries in the neighborhood. *2245 Broadway, at 81st St., tel. 212/787–2000. No credit cards. Sat. 8 AM–8 PM, Sun. 9 AM–6 PM.*

Upper East Side

Café Word of Mouth, a good bet for the area, though not cheap or easy to find. Great brownies! *1012 Lexington Ave., between 72nd and 73rd Sts., tel. 212/249–5351. AE, MC, V. Sat. 9 AM–6 PM, Sun. 10 AM–5 PM.*

Mark's, in the Mark Hotel, offers tea-takers desserts as opulent as the setting (*see* Upper East Side restaurants, *above*).

Sant' Ambroeus, a brass-and-marbled outpost of the Milan gelateria/pasticceria, tempts with incredibly opulent sweets. *1000 Madison Ave., near 77th St., tel. 212/570–2211. AE, MC, V. Sat. 9:30 AM–10:30 PM, Sun. 10:30 AM–6 PM.*

Far North

Carrot Top Pastries is the place to get the carrot cake you are likely to find at tony downtown bake shops fresh from the oven. It's rich, moist, stuffed with raisins and walnuts, topped with thick cream-cheese frosting, and the absolute best in town. *3931 Broadway, between 164th and 165th Sts., tel. 212/927–4800; 5025 Broadway, between 214th and 215th Sts., tel. 212/569–1532. No credit cards. Weekends 6 AM–11 PM.*

3 What to Explore

With the working crowds gone, weekends become the time to see the city from a fresh perspective. Circle around it, get an overview from up high or from down below, or explore a new neighborhood. There are as many ways to see the city as there are means of locomotion.

The attractions in this chapter are open Saturday and Sunday unless otherwise indicated. Call for hours, which are often seasonal.

Views

New York is grander and more expansive from on high than it seems from street level. There are small buildings and tall ones, bits of green, cars like flashing beetles, and water all around. On a clear afternoon, when the sun glints on the sea or flashes on a million panes of glass, or at sunset as the building facades turn first to gold and then to rose, there's no finer spectacle. Though weekends are busy, lines for the elevators to observation decks are not usually a problem. Go later in the day: When most of the crowds are trudging off to dinner, you can catch an early sunset.

Rooftop Panoramas

No longer the world's tallest building, as it was when it debuted in 1931, the **Empire State Building** is still synonymous with New York City. Measuring 1,454 feet high, this limestone, granite, and stainless steel tower designed by Shreve, Lamb & Harmon, offers a view from the heart of Manhattan, and retains a symbolic stature no other Big Apple building, however tall, has since achieved. Its observation decks on the 86th and 102nd floors still give a sense of New York's huge scope: Central Park, the George Washington Bridge, and the Bronx to the north; Queens and the ocean to the east; New Jersey to the west; and, to the south—oh yes, the World Trade Center's twin towers. A strong-walled open-air terrace around the deck on the 102nd floor offers views of up to 80 miles on a clear day. *350 5th Ave. at 34th St., tel. 212/736–3100. Admission: $4.50 adults, $2.25 children 5–11 and senior citizens.*

From its perch on the southern tip of the island, the **World Trade Center** offers a watery view that emphasizes New York's importance as a port. Directly below is New York Bay; the mighty Hudson lies just to the west. To the north, midtown's skyscrapers rise like Emerald City from the jumble of low rises in the Village and SoHo. Inch up to the floor-to-ceiling windows; the view straight down the side of the building is dizzying. Take the escalator to the Rooftop Promenade, the world's highest outdoor observation platform. When it's open, it's just you, the breezes, the birds, and the occasional helicopter or private airplane, many of which are flying below your feet. The tower's restaurant, Windows on the World (*see* Chapter 2), has reopened, so you can also savor the breathtaking view from a table indoors. *2 World Trade Center, tel. 212/435–7397. Admission: $10 adults, $5 children 6–12, $8 senior citizens.*

Other Views

If you're coming in to Manhattan from Brooklyn, Staten Island, New Jersey or points south, one of the best views of the lower Manhattan skyline can be had from the **Brooklyn–Queens Expressway.** If you're already in Manhattan, scoot through the Battery Tunnel (toll $3.50) just for the sake of coming back via the BQE over the Brooklyn Bridge (where, as an added bonus, you'll get a lengthy look at the South Street Seaport's Pier 17). This vista is especially stellar at night.

After a day trekking around Greenwich Village, head over to the 3-mile-long **Hudson River Park Esplanade** (tel. 212/353–0366), a bike and pedestrian walkway that offers fabulous views of the Hudson and even the Statue of Liberty on a clear day. The walkway already stretches from 29th Street to Battery Park City, and it is still growing; Manhattanites are trying to convince the city to extend it all the way up the west side, and eventually around the entire island.

For a supremely comfortable take on a classic midtown panorama sweeping down 5th Avenue, try the rooftop bar at the **Peninsula** (700 5th Ave. at 55th St., tel. 212/247–2200).

Head to the **Iris and B. Gerald Cantor Roof Garden** atop the Metropolitan Museum of Art's Wallace Wing (5th Ave. at 82nd St., tel. 212/535–7710; open May–Oct., weather permitting) for a romantic vista of Central Park to the west and south amid a setting of contemporary artwork. Take in the trees and tall buildings, but don't forget the sculptures.

The **Memorial Arch** in Brooklyn's Grand Army Plaza, has fine views of Prospect Park, south Brooklyn, and lower Manhattan. The arch is open when funding allows, or by appointment, so call ahead (tel. 718/965–8952).

At the highest spot in **Green-Wood Cemetery,** the Manhattan skyline is framed in trees (*see* Cemeteries in Chapter 6).

The **Fulton Ferry Landing** nestled just south of the Brooklyn base of the Brooklyn Bridge on Old Fulton Street, offers a water-level look at the East River bridges, the Statue of Liberty, and all those skyscrapers. Go for brunch, dinner, or just a drink at the bar on the terrace at the **River Café** (1 Water St., tel. 718/522–5200; *see* Chapter 2) next door, or head north into the neighborhood locally known as DUMBO (for Down Under the Manhattan and Brooklyn Bridge Overpasses), and picnic by the water in Empire State Park (so close to the Seaport, you can almost see the ties on the yuppies).

The tower at **Riverside Church** is a mere 21 stories high—not much in the pantheon of New York panoramas. But from here, the Hudson is practically at your feet, along with views of the George Washington Bridge a couple of miles uptown and the crenellated Palisades of New Jersey to the west. An elevator leads to the 20th floor. Walk the last flight up on a twisty staircase that winds among the 74 bells of the world's largest carillon. *122nd St. and Riverside Dr., tel. 212/870–6700. Admission: $2.*

Great Walks

While the country-weekend contingent flees the city for state park and forest trails on weekends, their urban counterparts—dedicated walkers—know that there's no time like the weekend for hoofing it up and down the city streets. Do as they do. Step into your best walking shoes, choose any avenue or street, and follow it from one end to the other or from river to river, observing how the neighborhoods blend into one another. Or hike across one of the city's 2,098 bridges for a fresh look at scenery that usually speeds by in a blur.

George Washington Bridge

The noted architect Le Corbusier called the George Washington Bridge "the most beautiful bridge in the world. Made of cables and steel beams, it gleams in the sky like a reversed arch . . . the only seat of grace in the disordered city . . ." It's an apt description, as anyone who ever walks across it will discover. Not many people do; joggers are the most frequent travelers. And it's a little scary because the bridge is more than 200 feet above the water level and the only thing that separates walkers from water is a steel railing on either walkway. From one end of the 3,500-foot span to the other, this bridge offers the best of all possible views up and down the Hudson.

Brooklyn Bridge

This 1,595½-foot East River crossing, designed by John Augustus Roebling, is both airy and monumental. Its great towers and cables form an elegant frame for city and river, with the Williamsburg and Manhattan bridges to the north.

Although the bridge was acclaimed as the "Eighth Wonder of the World" when it was completed in 1883, Brooklynites and other New Yorkers were skeptical that a span so long and airy could really be sound. The year after it opened, P. T. Barnum took 21 elephants across to prove its strength.

Since the fanfare of the bridge's centennial celebration in 1983, it has been lovingly tended. The filigree of cables, long a cold battleship gray, has been repainted in the original warm pale brown. The bicycle/pedestrian path that runs down the middle—raised for better viewing—is now surfaced with smooth wood planks, and the stairways that once punctuated this route have been removed. The vehicular roadway has been paved, thereby eliminating the high whine that car tires used to make as they rolled across the metal grates. At the south end, stop for a bite at the legendary **Patsy Grimaldi's Pizzeria** (19 Fulton St., tel. 718/858–4300), and then amble into Brooklyn Heights, itself a charmer full of brownstones as stately as any on Washington Square (*see* Explorable Neighborhoods, *below*). On the Manhattan end, stroll a bit farther downtown to South Street Seaport for some window-shopping and snacking. *Take the 4, 5, 6, J, M, N, R or Z train to the Chambers St./City Hall station. The pedestrian entrance to the bridge is directly across Centre Street from City Hall.*

Brooklyn Heights Promenade

When the Brooklyn–Queens Expressway was built, it was placed below grade between Middagh Street and Atlantic Avenue and covered by a cantilevered roof. In this one stroke, the already handsome and architecturally distinguished Brooklyn Heights acquired a wide ⅓-mile-long river-edge promenade that remains one of the few spots for New Yorkers to enjoy the waterfront with picture postcard views of the city. Honey locust trees, shrubs, ornamental lampposts, and a delicate iron railing frame a view of spiky masts, short red-brick buildings, and a great mass of glittering skyscrapers in the backdrop. Take a picnic and linger to enjoy this panorama of the Seaport and Lower Manhattan to the accompaniment of bird songs and tugboats' braying. Manhattan, as close as it is, seems very far away.

42nd Street

While most New Yorkers would admit that the West 42nd Street of old was sleazy (and sometimes even downright nasty), you will find a scant few who don't mourn its passing—at least a little bit. Most of the porn shops and peep shows are gone or going; the XXX theaters have already been cleared out and cleaned up. Still, after you pass some of the thoroughfare's new "legitimate" tenants (whose storefronts are in some cases far more garish than any porn marquee ever was), a stroll from river to river on this cross-street will reveal a surprising smattering of the diverse wonders the city has to offer.

Between 9th and 10th avenues is **Manhattan Plaza,** subsidized housing for actors and artists, with **Theater Row** and its Off-Broadway playhouses across the street. Between 8th and 9th avenues are **Holy Cross Roman Catholic Church,** and, across the street, the **Port Authority Bus Terminal** (the world's largest, but no place to visit unless you are taking a trip). At press time most of the old movie theaters between 7th and 8th avenues were empty, their marquees glowing but blank. The locked gates were painted in primary colors, symbolic of the continuing "family entertainment" overhaul taking place, but the fundamental architecture of the buildings remains worth seeing. The old **Selwyn Theater** (229 W. 42nd St.) has become a visitor center that offers information about sights, tours, and transit. The **New Amsterdam** (214 W. 42nd St.), once considered the country's most opulent theater, is landmarked inside and out and is a must-see. The refurbished **New Victory** theater (207 W. 42nd St.) has opened and now purveys children's plays. **Times Square,** where 7th Avenue crosses Broadway, was once the focal point of the carriage dealers' district, the Longacre. It was renamed when the *New York Times* moved to the building on the triangle between 42nd Street, Broadway, and 7th Avenue (its New Year's Eve opening in 1904, celebrated with fireworks, inaugurated a city tradition). The building's early Beaux Arts style has been obscured by concrete and a so-called Zipper, which flashes headlines across some 15,000 blinking bulbs. The police station that once stood across the street has been replaced by a gargantuan yuppie brewery/restaurant: another sign of changing times.

The **Graduate Center** of the City University of New York, between 5th and 6th avenues, redone in 1970, was built in 1912; its third-floor Aeolian Hall hosted the premiere of George Gershwin's *Rhapsody in Blue*. The **New York Public Library's** central research facility, on 5th Avenue, is equaled in its Beaux Arts splendor only by **Grand Central Terminal** at Vanderbilt Avenue, a short block and a half farther east (*see* Architecture, *below*). The ultracontemporary **Philip Morris Building,** across the street from the terminal, houses a branch of the Whitney Museum of American Art, and the sculpture court is open on Sundays. The Art Deco **Chanin Building** at Lexington Avenue is embellished with bas reliefs, and it's just catty-corner from the **Chrysler Building,** one of the most splendid of the city's skyscrapers from its radiator-cap decorations and stainless steel spire to the African marble lobby and its muraled ceiling. Continuing east are the Art Deco **Daily News Building,** former headquarters of New York's "hometown paper" (the lobby still contains the world's largest interior globe), and the greenhouselike **Ford Foundation Building** at 43rd Street, generally acknowledged to be one of the most elegant modern office buildings in the city. Just beyond that is the **Tudor City** apartment complex, designed in the mid-1920s as a self-contained city. The **United Nations,** along the East River, has gardens and fine views.

5th Avenue

Grand prewar apartment buildings, fabulous mansions, swank hotels, museums, and exclusive shops line 5th Avenue between the Metropolitan Museum of Art at 81st Street and the Empire State Building. The impression is of one great long parade of New York City's wealth, past and present. Residential buildings opposite Central Park feature marble columns and voluted capitals, delicate wrought-iron railings and doorways, French windows and leaded panes, elaborate cornices, porticoes, balconies, entablatures, and roof balustrades; they cost fortunes to build. Particularly splendid are the François I mansion at 79th Street, now the Ukrainian Institute of America; the Duke mansion at 78th Street, now part of New York University (N.Y.U.); the Frick Collection at 70th Street, Pittsburgh industrialist and art collector Henry Clay Frick's former home; and the Metropolitan Club at 60th Street, which McKim, Mead & White designed for J. P. Morgan and his cronies. On the side streets there are others—most notably the former Charles Scribner residence at 9 East 66th Street and coal magnate Edward Berwind's house at 2 East 64th Street (now co-op apartments). Grand mansions like these used to inhabit 5th Avenue farther south as well—the current Cartier Building at 52nd Street is among these stately structures.

Below **St. Patrick's Cathedral** and **Rockefeller Center,** the avenue changes. There's a procession of designer boutiques and luggage, lace, and a few electronics stores where going-out-of-business sales are a way of life; you'll also find a clutch of smaller, not so pricey shops that don't look like much. But in their gracious Beaux Arts and Gothic Revival styles, what's overhead speaks eloquent volumes to those who bother to look up. Passing the **New York Public Library** and **Lord & Taylor** the avenue leads to the **Empire State Building,** where visitors can collect their thoughts about it all from a loftier perspective.

Architecture

There's only one way to appreciate a great building: Look it up and down, admire its proportions, and notice its detailing—the hood-ornament decorations on the Chrysler Building, for instance, or the constellation-studded ceiling in Grand Central.

Great Buildings

550 Madison (1984). The Philip Johnson/John Burgee–designed former AT&T Building, nicknamed "the Chippendale skyscraper" for its broken keyhole pediment, is one of a kind. A stroll around the base of the building, which is now occupied by Sony, makes it seem even larger, even grander. The lobby's statue, "The Spirit of Communication," by Evelyn Longworth, is a stroke of gold. *550 Madison Ave., between 55th and 56th Sts.*

Chrysler Building (1930). William Van Alen's streamlined tour de force, with its crown-shape illumination at the top, is a New York icon. The stainless-steel frills, a decorative band emblazoned with cars, and the varied stonework are only part of the architect's accomplishment. The 480 fluorescent tubes that show off the tower were added in recent years. *405 Lexington Ave. at 42nd St.*

City Hall (1811). One of the city's architectural treasures, City Hall was designed by Joseph François Mangin and John McComb Jr. in the French Renaissance and Federal styles. The rear elevation was originally brownstoned to cut costs—the architects believed that nobody important would ever live north of City Hall. *City Hall Park, between Broadway and Park Row.*

Federal Hall (1834–42). George Washington took the oath of office on the site of this Manhattan Parthenon, designed by Town & Davis and built of Westchester marble around the foundations of a previous city hall. The building itself is closed on weekends, but don't miss the view from the top of the steps near the John Quincy Adams Ward statue of Washington. *28 Wall St. at Nassau St.*

Grand Central (1903–13). In truth, Grand Central is not a *station*—that is, a stop on the way to somewhere else—but a *terminal*, the end of the line. Its grand proportions, the airiness created by its immense windows, and a ceiling resplendent with the constellations of the zodiac make this one of the city's truly great spaces. This Warren & Wetmore masterpiece offers two special experiences. Behind the window at the terminal's west end, which is really a sandwich of two windows, you can walk along cast-glass sidewalk-bridges accessible via the stairway near Vanderbilt Avenue. And outside the entrance to the Oyster Bar (on the lower level) a whisper into one corner of the Guastavino tile vaulting will be heard perfectly in the opposite corner. *42nd St. at Vanderbilt Ave., between Park and Madison Aves.*

Metropolitan Life Building (1963). New Yorkers will continue to refer to this landmark as the Pan Am Building, even though the sign atop the 59-story tower now reads "Met Life" (the insurance company purchased the building in 1981 and replaced the sign in 1993). Designed by Walter Gropius, Emery Roth & Sons, and Pietro Belluschi, the precast curtain-wall constructed building created a stir when it first appeared and obscured the Park Avenue view of Grand Central station. *200 Park Ave. at 45th St.*

Radio City Music Hall (1932). The home of the Rockettes and one of the showpieces of Rockefeller Center was threatened with demolition a few years ago, and it took the work of dedicated preservationists to stay the wrecker's ball. This is a grandiose space, with some 6,000 seats, three cantilevered mezzanines, a soaring four-story lobby, and a shimmering gold curtain—all three tons of it. *6th Ave. at 50th St., tel. 212/632-4041. Admission for guided tours: $13.75 adults, $9 children under 12.*

Rockefeller Center (1932–40). On 22 acres of prime Manhattan real estate, this is a city in its own right, with the Channel Gardens, the Lower Plaza, the sleek 850-foot former RCA Building (now NBC's headquarters and, officially, "the General Electric Building"), and, all around, mid-rise buildings such as the former Time & Life Building at 1 Rockefeller Plaza and the Associated Press Building. The gray limestone structures are at once modern and historic, and the sculptures and plaques communicate a romantic view of capitalism, the city, and the workplace. Terrific sculpture, including Paul Manship's colossal *Prometheus* and Isamu Noguchi's 10-ton stainless steel panel *News*, are the grace notes. *47th–50th Sts., between 5th and 6th Aves.*

Seagram Building (1958). This great Mies van der Rohe structure looks as modern as the day it was built. The proportions and detailing exude calm and stability; the now common additon of an expansive plaza was a fresh idea when the building went up. *375 Park Ave., between 52nd and 53rd Sts.*

Woolworth Building (1913). Architect Cass Gilbert's imposing tower for dime-store king F. W. Woolworth was known as the "Cathedral of Commerce" when it was built (and paid for with $13.5 million cash). This gothic-style skyscraper—the world's tallest building when it opened—is embellished with bas-reliefs representing the continents on the second story and a Noah's ark of gargoyles outside the 26th, 49th, and 51st floors. *233 Broadway, between Barclay St. and Park Pl.*

Lobbies

Some of the city's most palatial architecture can be seen in the lobbies of its office buildings. Mirrors and gilt, ceilings painted with clouds, glossy marble, Beaux Arts and rococo: It's all there, and no two are quite alike. Although most lobbies are officially closed on weekends, the guards on duty will often accommodate sightseers.

Chrysler Building (1930). The lobby is practically paved in African marble with touches of chrome, and the Art Deco motifs are as abundant inside as out (*see* Great Buildings, *above*).

Film Center Building (1929). Mosaics in gold and other colors fill the lobby with light and texture—part Art Deco, part Islamic. *630 9th Ave., between 44th and 45th Sts.*

551 Fifth (1927). Formerly the Fred F. French building, it was once the headquarters of the Tudor City apartment complex's designer and builder. It has been beautifully restored by new owners, Met

Life. Brass, gilt, and marble all gleam under a coffered ceiling. *551 5th Ave., at 45th St.*

570 Lex (1931). Formerly the General Electric Building, GE has since donated this Art Deco palace to Columbia University and moved to 30 Rockefeller Plaza. It's recently been restored, with tan marble and stainless steel. *570 Lexington Ave., at 51st St.*

Helmsley Building (1929). The interior of Warren & Wetmore's former New York Central Building is another study in gleaming splendor. The elevators have clouds painted on the ceilings. *230 Park Ave., between 45th and 46th Sts.*

New York County Courthouse (1926). Footsteps echo and voices reverberate in the central lobby of this hexagonal structure, fronted by a Corinthian portico, although jurors who come on weekdays see a plainer side of the building—the utilitarian courtrooms and the labyrinthine corridors and stairways. *60 Centre St., between Pearl and Worth Sts. in Foley Sq.*

127 John St., at Water St. (1969), offers the 20th-century counterpart to these elaborate details: neon. A tunnel full of it makes designer Rudolph de Harak's lobby as playful as the others are grand.

Surrogate's Court/Hall of Records (1899–1911). Impressing the small citizen with the power of government was what public architecture was all about at the turn of the century, and it shows in the extremely grand entry space of this building. *31 Chambers St., between Centre and Elk Sts.*

Woolworth Building (1913). This structure is even more lavish inside than outside, with jewel-like mosaics, lacy wrought-iron cornices covered with pure gold leaf, three-story high arches, and fanciful sculptures: Mr. Woolworth counting his dimes, the renting agent closing a deal, the architect cradling a model of the building. The helpful guards usually proffer the building brochure; if they don't, ask for one (*see* Great Buildings, *above*).

Explorable Neighborhoods

People come from all over the tristate area to sample the cultural, culinary, and commercial pleasures of Sundays on the Upper West Side, SoHo, and Greenwich Village, and we've included some of the highlights of these areas here. But other city treasures are a subway ride away, neighborhoods that for most people are just names in real estate ads. There may be a small museum, a restaurant, or shop worth exploring. Or you may find an endless block of perfect brownstones shaded by fine old trees, or an exotic cultural enclave that makes you feel a world away from your home ground.

Manhattan

Ladies' Mile The gaslight era's premier shopping and entertainment district (Broadway from 8th to 23rd Sts. and 6th Ave. from 14th to 23rd Sts.) was where Benjamin Altman, Paul J. Bonwit and Edmund D. Teller, Samuel Lord and George Washington Taylor, and others built drygoods stores into retail institutions that changed the face of American merchandising. The much-photographed **Flatiron Building**, Daniel Burnham's 1902 wedge-shaped office tower at 23rd Street and 5th Avenue, is this area's magnificent mascot. Photographers, architecture firms, publishing houses, and advertising agencies have moved into the neighborhood's lofts and once-decrepit office buildings and have turned it into a commercial center for the media arts. Unfortunately, with the renaissance have come giant chain stores, like Staples and the Burlington Coat Factory. The former **Siegel-Cooper Dry Goods Store** (620 6th Ave.) now houses the interminable Bed, Bath & Beyond, as well as a Filene's Basement and a T. J. Maxx. And the former headquarters building of the **B. Altman**

Dry Goods Store (621 6th Ave.) is now occupied by a Today's Man. Try to concentrate on the architecture.

Marble Hill The Harlem River at the northern tip of the island hasn't always flowed as it does now. In 1859, to cut the distance between the East River and the Hudson, the loop that the river used to make was filled in. A new, more direct waterway was dredged out, thereby severing Marble Hill, south of the old arc, from Manhattan. Though it officially remained part of the borough, Marble Hill has had an air of separateness ever since.

The old Victorian villas were never spit-and-polished into gentrification, and the mood is quiet and small-town. **St. Stephen's Methodist Episcopal Church** (211–213 W. 134th St.), an arresting Shingle-style structure, is the major landmark along the twisting lanes. It's pleasant just to ramble and admire the towers and turrets and verandas of the old homes.

Harlem Well-to-do Germans, Irish, Jews, and Italians came in successive waves to the ornate, late-19th-century apartment houses and brownstones of Harlem, once a quiet country village. The black population of the Tenderloin District in the West 30s, dislocated by the construction of Macy's, Penn Station, and other buildings in the neighborhood, also began to settle here during the 1920s. Harlem's important influence on many aspects of American culture and its architectural treasures make it well worth a visit.

Turn-of-the-century churches endure. Among them: the **First Corinthian Baptist Church,** formerly the Regent Theatre (7th Ave. at 116th St.); wildly eclectic **St. Thomas the Apostle Church** (262 W. 118th St.); **St. Martin's Episcopal Church,** a massive Romanesque structure with the city's largest hand-played carillon (122nd St. and Lenox Ave.); and the **Metropolitan Baptist Church** (151 W. 128th St.). **St. Philip's Church** (204 W. 134th St.) was designed by Vertner W. Tandy, the first registered black architect in New York State. And gothic **Abyssinian Baptist Church** (132 W. 138th St.) is where the charismatic Adam Clayton Powell Jr. once preached. Fine residential buildings include numerous row houses dating to the late 19th century along 130th Street between Lenox and 7th avenues, at 136th and 137th streets between 7th and 8th avenues, at 26–46 Edgecombe Avenue between 136th and 137th streets, and 321 W. 136th Street between Edgecome and 8th avenues. The late-19th-century King Model Houses of the St. Nicholas Historic District are now better known as **Strivers' Row** (roughly 138th to 139th Sts., between 7th and 8th Aves.). Most celebrated is the establishment that opened in 1914 as Hurtig and Seamens New Burlesque Theater and Opera House, but in 1934 became the **Apollo Theatre** (253 W. 125th St.), sponsoring its famously raucous and talent-filled amateur nights, and hosting performers like Bessie Smith, Billie Holiday, Duke Ellington, Count Basie, Aretha Franklin—and, more recently, New Edition, Mary J. Blige, and the Fugees.

The Upper West Side The ornate pre-war buildings that line the boulevards of Broadway, West End Avenue, Riverside Drive, and Central Park West provide a stately backdrop for glitzy boutiques and the scads of wannabe soap actors hustling off to their auditions at **ABC-TV** (Columbus Ave. and 66th St.) and hopeful performers and aficionados making the pilgrimage to **Lincoln Center** (Amsterdam Ave. and 64th St.). A stroll up tony Columbus Avenue should stretch at least as far as the **Museum of Natural History** (Central Park West and 81st St.), whose lavish grounds and pink granite corner towers occupy a four-block tract. **Zabar's** (Broadway at 80th St.) is a bustling landmark for gourmets and gourmands who crave anything from smoked fish to obscure Belgian chocolates. Head down Broadway and peer into the towering wrought iron gates and serene courtyard of the

Apthorp (2211 Broadway), a private residence housing many prominent New Yorkers, such as writer Nora Ephron. If you cut over to Central Park West at 72nd Street, you can join the throngs admiring the **Dakota,** in front of which John Lennon was shot in 1980, and in which *Rosemary's Baby* was set. Farther uptown are the ivied buildings of **Columbia University** (116th St. and Broadway), where you can absorb the flavor of student fervor in the cafés around the campus, before you ramble over to the **Cathedral of St. John the Divine** (Amsterdam Ave. and 112th St., tel. 212/316–7540 for tour and events information), a magnificent Episcopal church that will be the world's largest gothic cathedral once it's finished (it's currently two-thirds done) around 2250.

Lower Manhattan   Some of the best small corners of the city are down here, set against some of its biggest buildings. The streets, by turns narrow and wide, are reminiscent of those the early settlers remembered from the medieval quarters of their European homelands. Each turn reveals a different perspective on the buildings along its route. There is some wonderful public art here, along with fine new buildings and enough terrific old-timers to make the area a sort of museum without walls.

Start at the **World Financial Center** on the west or at **South Street Seaport** on the east and work your way from river to river, lingering on the west side long enough to take in the new **Hudson River Park Esplanade,** a bike and pedestrian path that offers soothing vistas of (yes!) New Jersey and the Statue of Liberty (*see* Views, *above*). Some sights to see: **Castle Clinton** in **Battery Park;** the Beaux Arts **Alexander Hamilton Custom House** (1 Bowling Green), with its statues symbolizing Asia, the Americas, Europe, and Africa, and which now houses the National Museum of the American Indian; the out-of-the-ordinary lobby of the **Broad Financial Center** (33 Whitehall St.); the **South Cove** esplanade in Battery Park City with its boardwalk and 3-acre waterside park; the imposing **Federal Hall National Memorial,** closed on weekends but still interesting outside (Nassau St. at Wall St.); and **Trinity Church** (Broadway at Wall St.; *see* Chapter 6). Stop by the **Fraunces Tavern** museum (54 Pearl St. at Broad St.; *see* Chapter 4) for a tour, but don't plan to dine in the restaurant—it's closed on weekends. Stroll down **Water Street,** built on landfill that widened Manhattan into the East River after Trinity Parish was chartered in 1697. Don't miss the **Vietnam Veterans Memorial** (near 55 Water St.), a wallful of glass blocks etched with excerpts from soldiers' letters. Inland, the great **Woolworth Building** (*see* Architecture, *above*) stands at the foot of **City Hall Park.** The Horace Greeley and Benjamin Franklin statues across Park Row (formerly Newspaper Row) recall the area's days as the city's publishing center—home of the *New York World, Sun, Tribune, Recorder, Evening Post, American,* and other papers. The *Sun* later moved to **280 Broadway,** at Chambers Street, earlier occupied by A.T. Stewart's eponymous dry-goods store–the first department store in New York. The building still sports the old *Sun* clock, although today it houses a Modell's. At the top of the park is the Georgian-Renaissance **City Hall.** The **Municipal Building** (Chambers St. at Centre St.) is only slightly less grand, and the statue of Civic Fame atop it has been recently burnished. **Foley Square** impresses with its flotilla of courthouses, including the hexagonal **New York County Courthouse** and **U.S. Courthouse** with their column porticoes. Northwest of Foley Square, on Duane Street, is the site of the 18th-century **Negro Burial Ground;** a community protest in 1990 prevented the recently rediscovered graves from being unearthed to make room for a government building.

TriBeCa   The Triangle Below Canal Street (hence the acronym) is a former warehouse district turned trendy artists' neighborhood, some of which has (so far) managed to maintain its semi-desolate, urban frontier feel. It has beckoned the likes of Harry Belafonte, Laurie Anderson, Isabella Rosellini and, more recently, newlyweds J.F.K. Jr. and Carolyn Bessette. Interesting streets to explore include **Staple Street** and **Harrison Street** between Greenwich and Hudson, where Federal row houses provide an anachronistic contrast to the newer architecture by the water. Get an eyeful of the magnificent Beaux Arts exterior and avant-garde art inside the **Clock Tower Gallery** (108 Leonard St. at Broadway), then climb the stairs to the terrace 14 floors above City Hall Park. Also worth a visit are the **Franklin Furnace Archives** (112 Franklin St., tel. 212/925–4671), an alternative gallery, **El Teddy's** (219 W. Broadway, tel. 212/941–7070), a former mob haunt that is now enjoying a new, more respectable life as an outrageously decorated Mexican restaurant and bar (fronted by an enormous Statue of Liberty crown), and **Let There Be Neon** (38 White St., tel. 212/226–4883), a shop that vibrates with neon art and signs of all shapes and sizes. Note the building at **2 White Street,** a still-standing Federal-era store built in 1809 that serves as the obligatory local dive, the Liquor Store Bar. The **TriBeCa Film Center** (375 Greenwich St.), housed in an old coffee warehouse, is the production and development complex for Robert De Niro, whose restaurant, the **TriBeCa Grill** (*see* Chapter 2) occupies the bottom floor. Just south on this cobblestoned street, stop by the 110-year-old **Bazzini** (339 Greenwich St.) nut, chocolate, and coffee emporium, for the smell of fresh-roasted nuts and a look at a classic TriBeCa warehouse, complete with loading docks and corrugated awnings.

The Lower East Side Although the neighborhood seems to shrink by the year, the landmarks that remain describe this area's rich history as the hub of Jewish immigration to America from the 1880s through World War I. Although much of the area that used to be considered the Jewish Lower East Side is now more truly part of Chinatown, or given over to Hispanic residents, the core of the old Jewish Lower East Side remains a bustling center of commerce and tradition on Sundays. (Don't even think about checking out the area on a Saturday–nearly everything is closed for the Sabbath).

Just off Canal Street is the **Eldridge Street Synagogue** (12 Eldridge St., tel. 212/219–0888), a Moorish structure with a Gothic-style rose window built in 1886. It was the first synagogue built by Eastern European Jews in America (who had previously worshipped in converted churches). Ira Gershwin prayed here, as did Jonas Salk and Linus Pauling. (Also in the area is the **Bialystocker Synagogue,** an Orthodox shul on Willett Street, which was originally a Methodist Church.) The former headquarters of the preeminent Yiddish newspaper, the **Daily Forward** (175 E. Broadway), still has its name inscribed in the stone, although the paper has moved and the space is now occupied by a Chinese church and Bible factory. The century-old **Weinfeld's Skull Cap Mfg.** (19 Essex St., tel. 212/254–9260) is one of numerous purveyors of religious goods in the area, selling yarmulkes and tallit, or prayer shawls, to Jews from all over the city. For an establishment that caters to an even broader clientele, stop at **Guss's Pickles** (35 Essex St.), for garlicky sour or half-sour pickles, pickled tomatoes, or just about anything fished out of the pungent brine in the street-side barrels.

Orchard Street is closed to traffic between Delancey and Houston streets on weekends, allowing merchants to extend their shops via racks on the sidewalks—and pushing throngs of would-be patrons into the streets. There is nothing genteel about the bustle here. and haggling that takes place on Orchard Street. Shopping is not for the timid (and on Sundays, with the unbearable crowds, it is nearly impossible, even for the brazen) but the scene is worth seeing, and the cut-rate prices keep pulling customers in.

To get a better idea of what life used to be like in the area, take a tour of the nearby **Lower East Side Tenement Museum,** which depicts the lives of the various tenants who once inhabited the tenement apartment building at 97 Orchard Street (built in 1864). *90 Orchard St., tel. 212/431–0233. Gallery admission: $3. Tour: $8 adults, $6 students and senior citizens, children under 6 free.*

And, of course, stop for lunch at **Ratner's Dairy Restaurant** (138 Delancey St., tel. 212/677–5588), where the onion rolls and vegetarian veal cutlet have made this restaurant a Jewish culinary landmark for nearly a century.

Chinatown and Little Italy If you head east along Canal Street, you will run into the ever-expanding and frenetic Chinatown, which has over the years engulfed much of the Lower East Side's Jewish neighborhood. (Chinatown occupies the area south of Canal on the east side; Little Italy starts to the north.) One of the biggest attractions here is simply the carnival-like atmosphere on the small streets, which are packed with people and purveyors of untold varieties of pungent fish and exotic vegetables. The **Museum of Chinese in the Americas** (70 Mulberry St. tel. 212/619–4785) preserves an interesting collection of documents and personal letters of the local inhabitants. **Quong Yeun Shing & Co** (32 Mott St., tel. 212/962–6280), one of the oldest stores in Chinatown, still maintains its original pagoda roof and facade. The red, gold, and green exterior of the **Sun Wei Association** (24 Pell St., tel. 212/233–4080) is a slice of Chinese symbolism. The landmark **First Shearith Israel Graveyard** (55 St. James Pl., near Chatham Sq.) is the oldest Jewish cemetery in the United States and a reminder of the multiethnic history of the neighborhood.

In Little Italy the feel is distinctly different, and today not as Italian as it used to be. Still, **Mulberry Street** and famous—and in some cases, infamous—eateries like **Ferrara's** (195 Grand St., 212/226–6150), *the* place to go for cannoli, and **Umberto's Clam House** (129 Mulberry St., 212/431–7545), where mobster Joey Gallo was whacked in 1973, are rife with atmosphere. Perhaps the best time to explore this area is in mid-September, during the Feast of San Gennaro, when the streets are closed off for revelers.

East Village and NoHo In what many find the island's most colorful neighborhood, holdouts from the 1960s coexist with a deeply entrenched Eastern European community. Artists, punks, and account executives move freely between the Polish and Ukrainian coffee shops and trendy tapas bars. Galleries, designer's boutiques, and real egg creams—to say nothing of St. Mark's Place itself—provide ample diversion.

In **Astor Place,** the northern tip of the triangle that's more recently been known as NoHo, four of the colonnaded town houses that were home to the fashionable Astors, Vanderbilts, and Delanos can still be found across the boulevard from the Joseph Papp Public Theater. Many a speaker made history in the basement of **Cooper Union,** the country's oldest building framed with steel beams. (Here, in 1860, Abraham Lincoln made the "Right Makes Right" speech that catapulted him into the White House.) **St. Mark's-in-the-Bowery Church** and the red brick **Merchant's House Museum** (*see* Historical Treasures *in* Chapter 4) are both in the area (the Merchant's House is open for tours on Saturday). The city's only building by the Chicago architect Louis Sullivan, Frank Lloyd Wright's teacher, is the **Bayard Building** at 65 Bleecker Street between Crosby Street and Broadway. **Stuyvesant Street, East 10th Street,** and **East 11th Street** are worth exploring for their pretty Federal houses. Three more blocks and you hit **Union Square,** home of socialism and the *Daily Worker* in the '20s, of Warhol's Factory in the '60s, of the Farmer's Market and raised park in the '90s. Tack east along 8th Street, **St. Mark's Place,** the spine of the East Village. Packed with funky shops and funkier people, St. Mark's Place extends from Lafayette Street to Avenue A (the border of what used to be called Alphabet City before the N.Y.U. students moved in) and **Tompkins Square Park,** the site of riots over the rights of the homeless in 1990. Generally crowded with children, in-line skaters, and eccentrically shorn musicians, the park is a more peaceful spot these days.

The Bronx

The Bronx as depicted in the film *Fort Apache: The Bronx* and Tom Wolfe's novel *The Bonfire of the Vanities* is not the only Bronx. Many of the lovely multiethnic neighborhoods merit independent exploration. The colorful food markets in **Belmont,** as the thoroughly Italian neighborhood around **Arthur Avenue** is known, are more or less shuttered tight on Sundays. But the restaurants do a booming business on Saturdays, and after dinner it's pleasant to explore the almost surrealistically tidy streets full of shops and small apartment buildings. **City Island,** a 230-acre landfall just south of the Westchester County line that feels like a New England fishing village, is a lively, offbeat place for dining out and a favorite destination for waterlovers; it also has a growing artist community. Stroll down **City Island Avenue,** the main drag, and enjoy the festive spirit, the salt tang in the air, yacht clubs, and the handful of old homes and appropriately nautical new condos, all shipshape. Gulls wheel and cry, and off in the distance, Manhattan's skyscrapers appear like a mirage. Hilly **Riverdale** reveals a treasure house of architectural feats and fantasies, both antique and modern: neo-Georgian and Stick style, contemporary and English Tudor. The Hudson River and the dramatic Palisades form a backdrop to these former summer homes of millionaires, erected in the early 20th century. For quintessential Riverdale scenery, meander along **Palisade Avenue, Sycamore Avenue** north of 252nd Street, and **Independence Avenue** from 248th to 254th streets. Of the estates, **Wave Hill** (W. 249th St. and Independence Ave.) is open to the public. The mansion is handsome and the gardens are superlative, the lawns graced with giant elms and maples (*see* Chapter 6). Drive past other estates, including **Alderbrook** (circa 1880; 4715 Independence Ave., near 248th St.), where the artist Elie Nadelman once lived. John F. Kennedy attended **Riverdale Country School** on Fieldston Road, the main thoroughfare of **Fieldston,** where charming English cottages date from the '20s.

Brooklyn

A neighborly spirit, nearly absent in Manhattan, makes Brooklyn seem almost like a small town grown up. It also feels greener than most of Manhattan and more varied.

Brooklyn Heights Over the Brooklyn Bridge and just south of the up-and-coming Fulton Ferry landing area, Brooklyn Heights has long been one of the city's most genteel neighborhoods. It's not surprising that the Landmarks Preservation Commission designated it a historic district before any other neighborhood in the city.

Montague Street, the east-west commercial thoroughfare, sets the tone. It is vibrant, lively, and, above all, neighborly—a place where the stoops are tall and photocopied handbills flutter on lampposts. Shops in row houses purvey Yuppie necessities (coffee beans, imported cheeses, books, and stylish clothing), and restaurants bustle at brunch time.

On other streets, stately brownstones prevail, with stoops of stone or curled wrought-iron railings and high windows. Many streets bear the names of fruits and trees, the legacy of a certain influential Miss Middagh, who despised the practice of honoring city fathers by emblazoning their surnames on street signs. **Willow Street,** between Clark and Pierrepont streets, is pretty and architecturally varied, with bay windows, turrets, towers, and terra-cotta; **Columbia Heights,** is particularly graceful. And note the landmarks: At **2–3 Pierrepont Street,** mid-19th-century brownstone palaces were used in John Huston's film *Prizzi's Honor;* the **Plymouth Church** is where preacher Henry Ward Beecher once auctioned off a nine-year-old girl to dramatize the evils of slavery; the Romanesque Revival **Our Lady of Lebanon Roman Catholic Church** (113 Remsen St.) shows off doors salvaged from the wrecked ocean liner *Normandie;* and the Gothic Revival **Grace Church** (254 Hicks St.), shaded by an 80-foot elm, presides over **Grace Court** and **Grace Alley,** a mews full of restored carriage houses. Scores of creative people have called the Heights home, including W. H. Auden, Benjamin Britten, Hart Crane, Truman Capote, Gypsy Rose Lee, Arthur Miller, Walt Whitman, Thomas Wolfe, and Richard Wright.

Cobble Hill and Carroll Gardens This charming brownstone district, more varied and less formal than the Heights, was farming country in the 17th century and became a strategic point in the Revolutionary War. Bounded by **Atlantic Avenue** on the north (worth a stroll for its Middle Eastern spice shops and antiques stores), De Graw Street on the south, Hicks Street on the west, and Court Street on the east, **Cobble Hill** filled with comfortable row houses in the 19th century. Germans and Italians swelled the population before World War I, and Syrians and Lebanese came just afterwards. The neighborhood has been so stable and so carefully maintained for so many years that the New York City Landmarks Commission has declared 22 blocks of the area the Cobble Hill Historic District. **Clinton Street,** which runs right down the center of it all, makes for pleasant strolling, with its varied Victorian houses and stoops with stone or wrought-iron balustrades. Landmarks include **197 Amity Street,** where Jennie Jerome, Winston Churchill's mother, was born; **40 Verandah Place,** where the novelist Thomas Wolfe once lived; and the **Workingmen's Cottages** and adjoining **Tower and Home Apartments** (near Warren, Baltic, and Hicks Sts.), a group of cottages and apartments put up by the philanthropist Alfred Tredway White in 1879. The nearby **Christ Church and the Holy Family** Episcopal church (Kane St. at Strong Pl.) was one of several churches designed by the architect Richard Upjohn, who also did Manhattan's Trinity Church. In fact, all of **Kane Street** is worth a look, with its Italianate row houses and fine wrought-iron work.

Carroll Gardens, which adjoins Cobble Hill to the south, is a deeply Italian neighborhood, where octogenarians play bocce in the park and congregate on corners. Many of the row houses have little front yards, and the scene has scarcely changed since the turn of the century on streets like **1st Place, Carroll Street,** and **President Street.** The **Cammereri Brothers Bakery** (502 Henry St.) is where Nicholas Cage labored over a hot oven in the 1987 film *Moonstruck.*

Park Slope This area, bounded by Flatbush Avenue and Prospect Park on the east and 5th or 6th Avenue on the west, St. Mark's Place on the north, and 15th Street on the south, eventually became Brooklyn's Gold Coast; it was designated a historic district in 1973. Yet it was largely farmland until the Brooklyn Bridge connected Brooklyn to Manhattan, and thus its architecture is late Victorian, characterized by excess and elaboration. Along Prospect Park West, each house is more heavily embellished than its neighbor, with bay windows, stained glass, and other accoutrements of Italianate, Gothic Revival, Romanesque Revival, Queen Anne, and other styles.

The gateway to Park Slope is **Grand Army Plaza,** an oval of roadways radiating from the 80-foot-high **Soldiers' and Sailors' Memorial Arch;** the commercial center of the area is lively **7th Avenue.** But the real character of the Slope is best seen on its side streets, particularly those south of Grand Army Plaza between 8th Avenue and Prospect Park West. **Carroll Street** is the site of work by some of the city's best architects. **Montgomery Place,** with most of its houses designed by C. P. H. Gilbert, is known as the "block beautiful"; there's hardly a street in the city with forms so strong and textures so rich. The **Henry Carlton Hulbert Mansion** and the **William Childs Mansion** near Montgomery Place bristle with Flemish brickwork and gargoyles. Another exceptional building is the old **Montauk Club,** a Venetian Gothic palazzo at the intersection of Lincoln Place and 8th Avenue. The Park Slope skyline is spiked by splendid churches. **St. Augustine's Roman Catholic Church,** on 6th Avenue near Sterling Place, is like a cantata in mottled sandstone, brick, copper, and marble, with a jubilant chorus of gargoyles and statues. Mosaics, paintings, and stained-glass windows complete the effect.

Queens

While mostly residential, this second most populous of the five boroughs still offers a few less-trodden attractions and quiet neighborhoods for those willing to get on the subway or the 59th Street bus (the Q32).

In the vital ethnic neighborhood of **Astoria,** Greek is more commonly spoken than English. Pastry shops (*xaxaroplasteion*) and coffeehouses (*kaffenion*) send their heady fragrances into the streets, and there are Greek restaurants and nightclubs galore. The heart of it all is the Greek Orthodox Church of **St. Demitrios** (30–11 30th Dr.), a sprawling yellow brick building with a red-tile roof and the largest congregation of the sect outside Greece. The monumentally columned **Kaufman Astoria Studios** (34–12 36th St.) have come to life again to make movies, although they are not open to the public. Next door, the **American Museum of the Moving Image** (35th Ave., between 36th and 37th Sts; *see* Chapter 4) welcomes film fans. **Flushing,** now a thriving Asian community, still has many historic landmarks, including the 1661 **Bowne House Historical Society,** (37–01 Bowne St., between 37th and 38th Aves.). The shingle-sided, hiproofed **Friends' Quaker Meetinghouse** (137–16 Northern Blvd., between Main and Union Sts.) was built in 1694, which makes it the city's oldest house of worship in continuous use. Not far away is the pleasantly aged **Waldheim** residential neighborhood, a few small-town Victorian blocks north of the **Queens Botanical Garden** and southwest of Parsons Boulevard and Franklin Avenue.

Long Island City, across the 59th Street Bridge (or the Queensboro Bridge, depending on your perspective) is the latest district to attract artists with its low rents and big spaces. The community has an energy all its own; its beauty is of the practical, stark sort, with the midtown skyline a glorious backdrop. In the **Hunters Point Historic District,** well-kept row houses, constructed of tough Westchester stone, retain their original stoops and cornices; an oversize metal sculpture—Daniel Sinclair's "Bigger Bird"—in the center of the small park at 21st Street proclaims the artistic spirit of the local residents. By comparison, **Vernon Boulevard,** particularly around its intersection with **Jackson Avenue,** is an incongruous mix of shingled homes, butcher shops, diners, and art galleries cowering beneath the four-barreled stacks of the behemoth Pennsylvania Railroad generating plant. **Silvercup Studios,** west of Vernon at the intersection of 21st Street and 43rd Avenue, has 14 soundstages; *Broadway Danny Rose, When Harry Met Sally,* and other films were shot here (sorry, no tours). **Court House Square,** at 21st Street and 45th Avenue, is overshadowed by I. M. Pei's greenish 48-story **Citicorp Building.** It's the largest building in Queens and it may permanently change the character of this low-key, rarely visited neighborhood.

Staten Island

Staten Islanders are perpetually lobbying to secede from the rest of the city (they were recently thwarted again by the state's highest court), and it is true that the feel of this borough is as different as if it were in another state. Most off-islanders who ride the ferry return on the same boat, without ever setting foot on the 13.9-by-7.5-mile island. Still, it's well worth exploring the land where Aaron Burr died and Joan Baez was born. Take in a concert or visit one of the local museums; then, with a good street map in hand, stroll around a little. And have fun getting lost—an almost inevitable prospect because Staten Island's streets are hard to follow. Good routes to explore are along the North Shore, home of the **Snug Harbor Cultural Center** (1000 Richmond Terr., tel. 718/448–2500), which includes a theater, botanic gardens, and other attractions, and the **Staten Island Institute of Arts and Sciences** (75 Stuyvesant Pl., tel. 718/727–1135), where one of the galleries open to the public specializes in images of night birds. Another good outing is along the East Shore, where you'll find the **Alice Austen House** (*see* Chapter 4). Beaches edge the shore, and the interior is lush with parks, thanks to the Greenbelt system which protects 1,000 acres of forest and wetlands all over the island (*see* Chapter 6).

The **Hamilton Park** corner of Staten Island is impressive for its cluster of stuccoed Italianate villas trimmed in gingerbread and its huge Shingle-style "cottages" put up just before and just after the Civil War. Streets to explore—all a little more than a mile from the ferry terminal—are **Harvard Avenue, Pendleton Place, Prospect Avenue, Lafayette Street,** and **Ellicott Place.** The Tudoresque **110 and 120 Longfellow Avenue** was Casa Corleone in Francis Ford Coppola's 1971 movie *The Godfather;* the wedding scene was shot in the garden at 120.

Todt Hill is, at 409 feet, the loftiest point along the Atlantic seaboard south of Maine. It's also the island's most prestigious residential neighborhood, particularly the area between **Flagg Place** and **Todt Hill Road,** just south of the **Richmond County Country Club** (135 Flagg Pl.). Here there are handsome homes, modern and antique, including works by the highly respected architects Ernest Flagg (1857–1947) and Robert A. M. Stern. One of the prettiest spots is the 80-acre **Moravian Cemetery,** adjoining the **High Rock Park** (100 Nevada Ave.; *see* Chapter 6).

Small Spaces, Secret Places

These cul-de-sacs, mews, exceptional blocks, and special streets are like neighborhoods in miniature; intimate and charming, they show off city living at its most intimate.

Manhattan

Mott Street in Chinatown is narrow, curving, and jammed with stores selling roots and herbs, rice bowls, cheap wind-up toys, and paper parasols.
Grove Court, a half dozen three-story Federal red-brick town houses built in the 1850s around a Greenwich Village courtyard, inspired O. Henry's short story *The Last Leaf.* Peek through its entrance gate, between 10 and 12 Grove Street.
MacDougal Alley, a Greenwich Village alcove blocked off by an iron fence, is lined with houses built in the 1830s as stables for the mansions of Washington Square North. Artists took over the horses' quarters in the 1920s, and past residents have included painter Jackson Pollock, actor John Carradine, buffalo-nickel designer James

Earle Fraser, and arts patroness Gertrude Vanderbilt Whitney. From West 8th Street, go south on MacDougal Street and look to your left.

Milligan Place is another Village charmer—a triangular courtyard with a trio of brick houses. Enter on the west side of 6th Avenue, around the corner from Patchin Place (*see below*).

Patchin Place, lined by 10 tan brick three-story town houses dating from the 19th century, was once the home of the poet e. e. cummings. You'll find it off West 10th Street in Greenwich Village, just north of the Jefferson Market Courthouse (now the Jefferson Market Library).

Washington Mews is a private, 19th-century, cobblestoned street, but gawkers are generally tolerated. The buildings on the north side are the former stables for the residents of the fancier brownstones and townhouses along 8th Street and Washington Square. Gertrude Vanderbilt Whitney (as in the Whitney Museum), the writers John Dos Passos and Sherwood Anderson, and the artist Edward Hopper all lived in the mews. Now, the buildings mostly house N.Y.U. faculty. The street runs from 5th Avenue to University Place, just south of 8th Street.

St. Luke's Place, shaded by a canopy of lacy-leafed gingko trees, is one of the prettiest Village streets. The city's colorful mayor, James J. Walker, lived at 6 St. Luke's Place. It's actually Leroy Street, which changes its name between Hudson Street and 7th Avenue.

Sniffen Court, a well-kept midtown mews with 10 diminutive Romanesque Revival town houses, is on the south side of 36th Street between 3rd and Lexington avenues.

Beekman Place is one of the abodes of Manhattan's quiet money. Its houses, in English Tudor, French Renaissance, and Georgian styles, have been home to songwriter Irving Berlin and socialite Mary Astor, among others. On a bluff above the East River, it's tucked away between 51st Street and Mitchell Place (as 49th Street is known east of 1st Avenue).

Riverview Terrace, a cobblestoned East Side nook, is visible through its iron gates on Sutton Square. To get there, walk north on Sutton Place to Sutton Square and then turn right and left again.

Henderson Place, a group of circa-1881 vine-entwined brick town houses in Queen Anne style, is even more charming for its position alongside an apartment tower, between 86th and 87th streets off East End Avenue.

Pomander Walk, two rows of Tudoresque town houses facing each other across a common walkway, was inspired by the sets for a play by the same name and intended for the use of stage folk. Actress Madeline Carroll lived here, as did Humphrey Bogart, Lillian and Dorothy Gish, and Rosalind Russell. Look for it on the Upper West Side, between 94th and 95th streets, West End Avenue, and Broadway.

Hudson View Gardens, a cluster of vine-covered Gothic-style apartment buildings from the 1920s, is private property, but occasional visitors do enter to admire the exuberantly gardened interior and catch one of the romantic panoramas that gave the complex its name. It's in Washington Heights, at 116 Pinehurst Avenue between 183rd and 185th streets.

Brooklyn

Grace Court Alley, a Brooklyn Heights mews east of Hicks Street, near Grace Church, is where residents of Remsen and Joralemon streets' mansions once kept their carriages. The iron hay cranes are now used for hanging plants. West of Hicks Street is **Grace Court**.

Hunts Lane is almost more like London than London. You'll find this Brooklyn Heights mews full of window boxes just across Henry Street from Grace Court Alley.

Tours

Although it's fun to discover the city on your own, serendipitously, it can also be rewarding to explore more methodically. You may want to take one of the dozens of sightseeing tours that form on street corners and piers all over the city every weekend or pick up one of the handful of printed tours published by various organizations, both public and private.

Guided Tours

From the Water
Sailing

The Pioneer, a 102-foot two-masted schooner built in 1885 to carry cargo along the Delaware River, sails regularly for two-hour tours in season. If the spirit moves you, you can help the crew raise her sails—or even take the helm. *South St. Seaport, tel. 212/748–8590 weekdays. Fare: $16 adults, $13 senior citizens, $12 students, $6 children ages 2–12, under 2 free. Call to reserve at least two weeks before sailing.*

Motor Cruises

Circle Line. More than 40 million passengers have steamed around Manhattan on the eight 165-foot Circle Line yachts since the three-hour cruises were inaugurated in 1945. The 35-mile trip takes in such sights as the Little Red Lighthouse, the Palisades, Spuyten Duyvil, Grant's Tomb, Harlem, the *Intrepid*, the Javits Center, and, of course, the Statue of Liberty—never so fine as when seen from close up. The company's **Harbor Lights** cruises take in the sunset and Manhattan's lighted skyline. *Pier 83, 12th Ave. at 42nd St., tel. 212/563–3200. Fare: $20 adults, $16 senior citizens, $10 children 2–12, children under 2 free.*

Seaport Liberty Cruises. Several Coast Guard cutters pull out of their South Street Seaport piers several times every Saturday and Sunday. *Pier 16, South St. Seaport, tel. 212/425–3737. Fare: $12 adults, $10 students and senior citizens, $6 children under 12. 60-min cruises Mar.–Dec.*

Staten Island Ferry. Even if you've ridden the ferry before, a new crop of sailing ships, a cluster of new buildings on shore, or a blazing sunset can completely transform the experience. Complete the round-trip right away for an hour of fine views and fresh air, or stay on Staten Island for awhile. *Staten Island Ferry Terminal near Battery Park, tel. 212/806–6940. Fare: 50¢ round-trip, pay in Staten Island only). Around the clock, year-round.*

Neighborhood and Theme Tours

The following organizations regularly sponsor special tours. Write in advance for a brochure or call to find out what's on when you want to go and make reservations if necessary. Meeting places vary from tour to tour, so be sure of the rendezvous point. Fees range from $5 up to about $35.

Adventure on a Shoestring takes in oddball as well as better-known corners of the city—perhaps Hell's Kitchen, Yorkville, Chelsea, Murray Hill, Roosevelt Island, or other areas. Its motto is "exploring the world within our reach . . . within our means." Tours are rain or shine, and the price is $5—as it was when they started 34 years ago. *300 W. 53rd St., New York 10019, tel. 212/265–2663.*

Art Deco Society of New York explores the Art Deco details of Central Park South, the East and West 50s, 42nd Street, and other locations. *385 5th Ave., Suite 501, New York 10016, tel. 212/679–3326.*

Art Tours of Manhattan provides tours of museums, studios, and galleries with private guides—mainly Ph.D.s. *28 Scott La., Princeton, NJ 08540, tel. 609/921–2647.*

Big Onion offers 25 tours, including a twilight walk across the Brooklyn Bridge into Brooklyn Heights in summer and a multi-ethnic eating tour that covers the historic and gastronomic delights of the Lower East Side, Chinatown, and Little Italy. Tours are led by graduate students in American urban and ethnic history. *Box 20561, New York 10021, tel. 212/439–1090.*

Brooklyn Center for the Urban Environment offers Brooklyn tours of neighborhoods like Williamsburg and Greenpoint (as well as tours of Manhattan nabes like the Lower East Side) most weekends year-round. *Tennis House, Prospect Park, Brooklyn 11215, tel. 718/788–8549.*

The Brooklyn Historical Society offers walking (and noshing) tours of the borough's multiethnic neighborhoods several times a month during the warmer seasons. *128 Pierrepont St., Brooklyn 11201, tel. 718/624–0890.*

Doorway to Design specializes in behind-the-scenes tours emphasizing entree to private homes, clubs, and other not-available-to-the-general-public sneak peeks. See the inside of an artist's studio in Manhattan or Brooklyn, or shop a private sale. Itineraries are custom designed for groups or individuals. *1441 Broadway, Suite 338, New York 10018, tel. 212/221–1111 or 718/339–1542.*

Harlem Renaissance Tours offers customized tours for groups, focusing on history, culture, gospel music, Harlem nightlife—you name it. *34 Hamilton Terrace, New York 10031, tel. 212/722–9534.*

Harlem Spirituals concentrates on gospel music, as sung by parishioners at Sunday morning services. *1697 Broadway, Room 203, New York 10019, tel. 212/757–0425.*

Harlem Your Way! has regular weekend walking tours, gospel music tours, and tours that focus on antiques, galleries, or soul food. *129 W. 130th St., New York 10027, tel. 212/690–1687.*

Joyce Gold History Tours of New York, offered intermittently throughout the year (or book a private tour any time), take in one of 20 neighborhoods, like Ladies' Mile or old Dutch New York. Gold, a local historian, has also written a couple of good miniguides to these areas. *141 W. 17th St., New York 10011, tel. 212/242–5762.*

Kramer's Reality Tour is for serious *Seinfeld* fans only. Kenny Kramer, the real-life model for Cosmo, offers this 3-hour tour of people and places made famous by the show. *Box 391, Times Square Station, New York 10036, tel. 212/268–5525.*

Lower East Side Tenement Museum's Streets Where We Lived tours, offered most weekends (April through December), are led by historians who tell participants about life in the multiethnic immigrant neighborhood as they stroll through the historic streets. *90 Orchard St., between Delancey and Broome Sts., New York 10002, tel. 212/431–0233.*

Manhattan Passport offers custom group tours and provides knowledgeable guides for sightseeing, shopping, and gallery hopping. *112 E. 71st St., New York 10021, tel. 212/861–2746*

Municipal Art Society, one of New York's principal preservation groups, offers tours focusing on architecture, history, and urban planning intermittently during the year. *457 Madison Ave., New York 10022, tel. 212/935–3960.*

Museum of the City of New York Walking Tours take architecture as a vehicle for understanding the social and political history of New York neighborhoods, ranging from Park Slope to Tompkins Square. *1220 5th Ave., New York 10029, tel. 212/534–1672. Tours offered every other Sat., Apr.– Oct.*

New York City Department of Parks & Recreation's Urban Rangers lead dozens of guided weekend strolls all over the city. *1234 5th Ave., Room 111, New York 10029, tel. 718/383–6363 or 800/201–PARK.*

92nd Street Y sponsors one of the city's richest and most varied arrays of walking tours. You might stop at sites that inspired Antoine de Saint-Exupéry to write *The Little Prince* or revisit Tammany haunts or famous New York disaster sites. Tours are sometimes led by well-known local figures. *1395 Lexington Ave., New York 10128, tel. 212/996–1100. Offered every Sun. year-round.*

Radical Walking Tours will teach you the radical history of Tompkins

Square Park, or tell you what the IRA and Sacco and Vanzetti have to do with the City Hall area. A leftist antidote to the routine stops on the typical sightseeing tour. *Tel. 718/492–0069.*

River to River Downtown Walking Tours, led by a chatty retired schoolteacher named Ruth Alscher-Green, cover lower Manhattan concentrating with a sense of fun on historical gossip, quirky detail, and landmarks both old and new. *375 South End Ave., Suite 19U, New York 10280, tel. 212/321–2823.*

SoHo Art Experience, includes a visit to a loft, the best art shows of the moment, and the finest of SoHo's cast-iron architecture, with side dishes of shops and other sights; led by Joy Jacobs. *101 Wooster St., Loft 5R, New York 10012, tel. 212/219–0810.*

South Street Seaport Walks show off the adjacent unrestored district, which looks the way the entire area did before the current boom. *207 Front St., New York 10038, tel. 212/748–8757. Abbreviated tour offered in winter.*

A Walk of the Town customizes walks with themes for small groups—like a tour of Opera Lovers' New York, for instance, or Cops, Crooks, and the Courts. Gather a group of friends, and proprietor Marvin Gelfand will work out an itinerary. *280 Riverside Dr., New York 10025, tel. 212/222–5343.*

Citywide Bus Tours Tours, ranging in length from 2 to 8½ hours, are available from **Gray Line** (1740 Broadway, New York 10019, tel. 212/397–2600).

Helicopter Tours A tour by the city's main helicopter sightseeing outfit, **Island Helicopter Sightseeing,** is definitely an eye-opening experience. Four different tours are available, each longer (and more expensive) than the one before. The longest is 34 miles and circumnavigates Manhattan. *Departures from heliport at 34th St. and East River, tel. 212/683–4575 for recorded information. Fare: $44–$134. Year-round, weather permitting.*

Tours on Tape

Pathfinder Productions has 90-minute cassettes covering midtown, lower Manhattan, the Village, Chinatown to SoHo, and 5th Avenue's Millionaire's Mile. *Box 3426, Noroton, CT 06820, tel. 203/854–0880. $10.95 per tour plus $3 postage.*

Talk-A-Walk has four cassette-recorded walking tours through lower Manhattan: "Gotham's Markets," "Gotham's Expanding Waistline," "The Power Structure," and "Across the Brooklyn Bridge." Each tape covers history, culture, architecture, legends, and lore. *Sound Publishers, 30 Waterside Plaza, Suite 10D, New York 10010, tel. 212/686–0356. $9.95 per cassette.*

Sightseeing from City Buses

The slow pace of city buses, so aggravating on busy weekdays, is just right for taking in the scenery on a leisurely weekend day. Riding from one end of the route to the other not only provides a glimpse of a succession of neighborhoods, but gives an overview of how they fit together. Two routes are recommended:

The **M-10** rolls down Central Park West to Columbus Circle, sails down 7th Avenue to Varick Street and West Broadway, curls around up Church and Hudson streets, then heads straight up 8th Avenue all the way to 159th Street. Along the route are the American Museum of Natural History at 81st Street; a string of ornate old apartment buildings, including the Beresford at 81st Street and the gabled Dakota at 72nd Street; Times Square; low-key Chelsea; and the World Trade Center.

The **M5** meanders up and down curving, slightly hilly Riverside Drive, with the Hudson River a constant presence to the west and miles of fine prewar apartment houses on the other side. **Grant's**

Tomb is at 122nd Street, the **Soldiers' and Sailors' Monument** at 89th Street. The bus crosses 72nd Street, turns south on Broadway, heads east on 57th Street, and then goes straight south on 5th Avenue, passing **Tiffany's, St. Patrick's Cathedral, Rockefeller Center, Lord & Taylor** department store, and the **Flatiron Building.** Turning across 8th Street and then down Broadway, the bus rolls finally to Houston and SoHo. If you stay on the bus, you ride up 6th Avenue, where there's a whole different scene: the **Flower District, Macy's** department store, **Bryant Park,** and skyscrapers.

Horse-Drawn Carriage Rides

Whether the air is frosty and crisp or soft and warm, it's extremely pleasant to lean back, watch the scenery slip by, and listen to the clip-clop-clip-clop of horses' hoofs on pavement.

Catch one of these cabs on 59th Street near the Plaza Hotel, at the southeast corner of the park. The cost is city-regulated at $34 for the first half-hour, $10 for each quarter-hour after that; the fare is calculated by time, not per passenger.

Best Bets for Children

Transportation and tall buildings are two of the most exciting things about sightseeing in New York for children. Just riding in a taxicab or bus can be a thrill; so is the subway (especially the first car of the train, with its view of the tunnels and track).

The city's helicopters, horse-drawn carriages, sailboats, and ferryboats are also child-pleasers. Try the tram ride to Roosevelt Island, too, or the Circle Line boat trip around Manhattan, which takes in the Little Red Lighthouse, known to youngsters all over America from Hildegarde Hoyt Swift's book, *The Little Red Lighthouse and the Great Gray Bridge*.

A trip to the top of one of New York's viewing platforms is another must. Should you do the Empire State Building or the World Trade Center? In deciding, consider the view you want and proximity to other sites. On its lower level, the **Empire State Building** boasts an exhibit devoted to esoteric facts and figures from "Guinness World of Records Exhibit Hall" columns, and you're a 20-minute walk from the aircraft carrier *Intrepid.* Or you're a quick cab ride away from **Grand Central Terminal**—kids love its constellation-studded ceiling, glass-paved footbridges, and whispering gallery. The **World Trade Center's** view of the harbor and its scattering of big ships gets raves, as does the rest of Lower Manhattan, which also offers the **South Street Seaport, Fraunces Tavern,** and the **Brooklyn Bridge.** The **Woolworth Building,** also in the area, is like every child's fantasy of a fairy-tale palace, with its gold-mosaic lobby and ornate stonework.

4 What to See

First thing in the morning you might stand face to face with the emperor Tutankhamen. After lunch, languish in the drawing room of a French bordello with Toulouse Lautrec. Weegee could take you on a flashbulb-lit tour of New York's seedy underbelly, or Romaire Beardon could introduce you to the city's jazzy rhythms. By the end of the day you may need to take a break from all the stimuli and stare into the cold, mathematical heart of a modernist Mondrian composition. Two days with the endless resources of New York's vast array of museums and galleries can be both a dramatic, eye-opening experience and one of the most contemplative, restful activities the city has to offer.

Weekends are the bustling prime time for exhibits, lectures, concerts, films, and tours but always call ahead. If you're making a special trip to see a specific item, make certain that it will be on display when you get there. Also check opening times, for many museums close on holidays or on Sundays in summer. Admission fees, given below, are usually waived for members, babies, and toddlers, and students and senior citizens can show IDs to qualify for reduced rates. Special rates for children ordinarily prevail only when they are accompanied by a parent or guardian.

Art Museums

How long has it been since you looked at Claude Monet's *Water Lilies* or Jean-Honore Fragonard's *Progress of Love* or Paul Klee's *Red Balloon*? Or had Jenny Holzer inform you that 'YOU ARE A VICTIM OF THE RULES YOU LIVE BY'? To see these works or their peers you need not travel far.

Megamuseums

New York City's megamuseums are really more like several museums under one roof, with a huge variety of collections ranging from Egyptiana to European painting, sculpture, and decorative arts. They are usually humming on Sundays, with crowds spilling over into the gift shops and nearby restaurants.

Metropolitan Museum of Art There isn't another museum in the city that covers so much so thoroughly: 2,000 European paintings, 3,000 European drawings, an equal number of American paintings and statues, 4,000 medieval objects and a comparable group of musical instruments, a million prints, as well as decorative arts and quite a lot more. Temporary exhibitions are mounted with great regularity, and items go in and out of storage constantly, for even with its 32 acres of floor space, only a quarter of what the Met actually owns is on view at any given time.

There's too much here to see it all in one visit and the big traveling shows can be overwhelmingly crowded on weekends. However, with all its nooks and crannies, dramatic arrangements and small surprises, there's always something previously undiscovered that makes a trip to the Met worthwhile.

Highlights **American wing** (first, second, and third floors) centered on the Astor Court, is green, cool, and restful regardless of the day of the week, regardless of the weather outside. The 20 room settings never seem too crowded, and there are wonderful paintings as well.
Arms and armor (first floor) has handsomely wrought artifacts that children often find entertaining.
Egyptian wing (first floor) is full of bas reliefs, sculptures, and artifacts covering nearly four millennia. The imposing Temple of Dendur and surrounding pool are focal points of this area.
Medieval art (first floor) is especially noteworthy for its cavernous sculpture hall. Built to resemble a church and divided by a wrought-

iron choir screen, it feels cool and quiet no matter how busy the day.
Primitive art (first floor, in the Michael C. Rockefeller Wing), with
7,000 sculptures, ritual objects, and everyday artifacts, spans 3,000
years of the history of Africa, the Americas, and the Pacific Islands.
Greek and Roman art (first and second floors) has dazzling displays
of gold and silver tableware and ceremonial vessels counterpointing
a collection of Grecian urns.
Lehman Pavilion (first floor), a group of seven period rooms, shows
off 18th-century French furniture, as well as Flemish, Italian, and
French paintings, drawings, and tapestries.
Dutch painters are displayed in galleries 11–15 (second floor), including creations by Jan Vermeer, Frans Hals, Gerard Ter Borch,
and others to restore the soul; there are 19 Rembrandts.
Musical instruments (second floor) is a spot for music lovers. Pick up
an Acoustiguide on your way into the museum, and you can hear how
exquisite craftsmanship has translated into centuries of sound.
19th-century paintings and sculpture (second floor) is one of the glo-
ries of New York. Painting after world-famous painting by Corot,
Millet, Turner, Rodin, Renoir, Pissaro, Van Gogh, Cézanne, and
others can be seen.
European sculpture and decorative arts (in a new five-story south
wing) includes sculpture, glass, ceramics, furniture, textiles, and
jewelry that date from the 16th to the 20th centuries. The outdoor
sculpture garden on the second floor has Rodins and a view out to the
backdrop of Central Park.

Weekend   Lectures, films, and panel discussions take place almost hourly in
Programs   the Grace Rainey Rogers and Uris Center auditoriums on topics as
diverse as the collections. There are also special programs for families. Strollers are fine on Saturday, but not on Sunday.

Facilities   The **Museum Dining Room** serves brunch on Sunday (tel. 212/879–
5500 for reservations).

The **Great Hall Balcony Bar** serves drinks on Friday and Saturday
from 4:00 to 8:30 with live music from 5–8.

A parking **garage** on the premises makes the Met a good bet for out-
of-towners.

*5th Ave. and 82nd St., tel. 212/535–7710, 212/570–3932 for special
programs, or 212/570–3711 for recorded tours. Suggested contribution: $8 adults, $4 students and senior citizens, children under 12
free. Open Sat. 9:30–8:45, Sun. 9:30–5:15.*

Brooklyn   A little off the beaten path but well worth the trip, the Brooklyn Mu-
Museum   seum offers an encyclopedic collection, in many areas comparable to
of Art   the Met, spread through a gorgeous, turn-of-the-century Beaux
Arts monument that lacks the Met's crowds and noise. Many of those
who do make the trip come for blockbuster exhibitions: "Monet &
the Mediterranean" (through January 1998) and "The Qajar Epoch:
2000 Years of Painting from the Royal Persian Courts" (through January 1999). But its own collections—2 million items running the
gamut from plastic-and-metal Elsa Schiaparelli jewelry to Brooklyn
Dodgers uniforms to Winslow Homer watercolors—are of international caliber. Recent reinstallation of the permanent galleries of
Chinese art has given new emphasis to a fine and wide-ranging collection of Asian artifacts. Other long-term installations include
20th-century decorative arts and an excellent Egyptian collection.
An extensive project by architects Arata Isozaki and James Stewart
Polshek restored the museum's interior and doubled the museum's
450,000 square feet, adding a new auditorium that has given the museum its first formal gathering place in half a century.

Highlights   **Grand Lobby installations** (first floor) feature work created specifically for this grandiose space by contemporary artists.

Asian art (second floor) includes pieces from Afghanistan to Qajar via China, the Islamic world, and India. The installation features highlights from the museum's vast collection of Chinese artifacts, focussing on the Chinese cultural pattern of renewal from the past. On view are objects prepared for the tomb and burial, ritual and religious icons, and a large number of fine ceramics. Also well represented are Japanese statuary, Islamic tapestry and manuscripts, as well as Indian and Afghan art.

Egyptian galleries (third floor), guarded by massive Assyrian wall sculptures, contain incredible treasures from ancient Egypt's tombs and royal cities from the Predynastic period (4000–3000 BC) to the Muslim conquest (7th century AD). Besides mummies in glorious sarcophagi, there are jewelry; pots; tools; solemn statues of queens, kings, cats, and dogs; and small precious objects in bright blue faïence, alabaster, black basalt, limestone, or ivory.

Period rooms (fourth floor) include 21 parlors, sitting rooms, and dining rooms from plantation mansions and New England cottages from 1675 to 1830. Viewing the Jan Martense Schenck House, the oldest, is like stepping into a painting by a Dutch master. The somber, exotic Moorish Room from John D. Rockefeller's town house is a tycoon's Alhambra. Costume galleries and decorative arts complement the period rooms.

Old Masters and French impressionists (fifth floor) show works by Hals, Reynolds, Monet, Degas, Pissaro, Cassatt, Toulouse-Lautrec, and others.

American collection (fifth floor) chronicles American art from its origins to the present. With paintings by Copley, Sargent, Lafarge, Sloan and Eakins, the collection rivals the Met's.

Iris and Gerald Cantor Gallery (fifth floor) showcases 58 sculptures by Auguste Rodin, including works relating to *The Gates of Hell*, *The Burghers of Calais*, and *Balzac*.

Frieda Schiff Warburg Memorial Sculpture Garden (behind the building) is studded with architectural artifacts rescued from elaborately ornamented buildings built in the 19th century and demolished in the 20th: theatrical masks, cherubs, lions, scrolls, capitals, Medusas, and columns in bronze, copper, limestone, brownstone, and terra-cotta. Look for the lamppost from Coney Island's now-defunct Steeplechase Park (circa 1897), the white goddess that once cradled the Penn Station clock, and the butterfly with a face like Puck's.

Weekend Programs Making art captivating for children is the business of the Sunday gallery explorations: "Arty Facts" at 11 AM for kids 4–7 years old and "What's Up" for kids 8–12 at 2 PM. Raiders of the Fine Arts is the title of their multiweek courses—Boisterous Books, Sculpture Speaks, Paper Possibilities. For adults, there are movie matinees and gallery talks on many subjects.

200 Eastern Pkwy., Brooklyn, tel. 718/638–5000. Admission: $4 adults, $2 students, $1.50 senior citizens, children under 12 free. Open weekends 10–5. Parking on premises, or take the No. 2 or 3 subway downtown from Manhattan to the Eastern Pkwy./Brooklyn Museum stop.

Other Major Museums

At the **Frick Collection,** a small but exquisite set of Rembrandts, Holbeins, Vermeers, Fragonards, and Bouchers is beautifully set off by industrialist Henry Clay Frick's splendid Beaux Arts mansion facing Central Park. The luxuriant, cultured atmosphere of the Frick could make an art lover of any Philistine and creates an impressive context for viewing some of the great masters of the western canon. The neoclassic garden court with its burbling fountain, Ionic columns, stone benches, and ivy is the oasis within this oasis, possibly one of the most soothing public rooms in New York City. A 20-minute audiovisual introduction to the collection, including the history of H.C. Frick and the mansion, is shown on the half hour. *1 E. 70th St., tel. 212/288–0700. Admission: $5 adults, $3 students and senior citizens. Children under 10 not admitted, under 16 must be accompanied by adult. Open Sat. 10–6, Sun. 1–6.*

At the **Guggenheim Museum,** the architecture is as important as the art. The building, a Frank Lloyd Wright creation that opened in 1959, the year its architect died, still looks modern. The interior is made up of a quarter-mile long ramp which winds, Dr. Seuss-like, up and up for four levels around a lobby fountain and shafts of sunlight streaming in from the six-lobed skylight. A major restoration and expansion completed in 1992 added a 10-story tower annex, designed by Gwathmey Siegel, that is part of Wright's original conception and provides more space to display copper magnate Solomon Guggenheim's collection. The collection is particularly strong in the works of Klee and Kandinsky and, to a lesser extent, of Chagall, Delaunay, and Léger. Picasso and others are represented in the Thannhauser Wing. While the architecture and art are often breathtaking, senior citizens and visitors with children may want to note that it can also be rather tiring. One solution is to start your visit with a trip up in the elevator and work your way **down.** *1071 5th Ave. at 89th St., tel. 212/423–3500 for recorded exhibition information. Admission: $8 adults, $5 students and senior citizens, children under 12 free. Open Sat. 10–8, Sun. 10–6.*

J. Pierpont Morgan Library, housed in tycoon J. P. Morgan's lavish Renaissance-style palazzo, displays his collection of books, manuscripts, incunabula, and works of art on paper, one of the country's finest. You might see a Gutenberg Bible, or manuscripts and letters from the likes of Balzac, Byron, Dickens, Keats, Dürer in the changing exhibitions. And the West Room's carved 16th-century ceiling, the library's fine hardwood cabinets, and the marble, tapestries, and Italian furniture throughout the library are eloquent testament to what it must have been like to be wealthy at the turn of the century. *29 E. 36th St., tel. 212/685–0008 or 212/685–0610 for recorded information. Suggested contribution: $5 adults, $3 students and senior citizens. Open Sat. 10:30–6, Sun. 12–6.*

The **Museum of Modern Art,** founded a few days after the Crash of '29, addresses itself to the history and the present status of modern and postmodern art. Paintings represent nearly every movement since the late 19th century: Bauhaus, Pop, Minimalism, De Stijl, abstract expressionism, Impressionism, Dadaism, surrealism, Cubism, and others; and the collection includes celebrated works such as Monet's *Water Lilies*, Van Gogh's *The Starry Night*, Rousseau's *Sleeping Gypsy*, Picasso's *Les Demoiselles d'Avignon* and *Three Musicians*, and Wyeth's *Christina's World*. Photographs by Henri Cartier-Bresson and other greats continue to inspire awe, as do the architectural models and objects of design exhibited around the museum. The Sculpture Garden offers peaceful moments, and the film department, with its huge library of prints, most screened nowhere else, is a city treasure. (*See* Movies *in* Chapter 7.) Even the two restaurants (upscale and downscale) and the expansive gift shops are pleasant (if crowded). *11 W. 53rd St., tel. 212/708–9480 for recorded information; 212/708–9490 for film schedules. Admission: $8.50 adults, $5.50 students and senior citizens, children under 16 free. Open weekends 11–6.*

Gertrude Vanderbilt Whitney founded the **Whitney Museum of American Art** in 1930 with the idea of celebrating the work of artists while they were still alive. The result is one of Manhattan's most dynamic institutions, a veritable textbook of the nation's current artistic output. Mrs. Whitney's own collection is the nucleus of the permanent collection of some 8,000 20th-century paintings, sculpture, and works on paper by such artists as Thomas Hart Benton, Stuart Davis, Alex Katz, Ellsworth Kelly, Roy Lichtenstein, Georgia

O'Keeffe, Maurice B. Prendergast, Jackson Pollock, Mark Rothko, and Frank Stella. There are always lively special exhibitions: the Shakers' elegantly simple furniture, Edward Hopper's existential Americana, Red Grooms's huge sculpto-pictoramas, to name a few entries. The biennial invitational exhibition, surveying the previous two years on the art scene, adds controversy and excitement in the spring of odd-numbered years. The second floor film and video gallery shows experimental pieces rarely available anywhere else and in the past has presented retrospectives of Andy Warhol and No Wave Cinema. Weekend gallery talks are at 2 and 3:30. You can get refreshments in the museum restaurant and, in summer, in the outdoor sculpture court. *945 Madison Ave. at 75th St., tel. 212/570–3676, 212/570–0537 for film schedules, or 212/570–3652 for gallery talks. Admission: $8 adults, $5 students and senior citizens, children under 12 free. Open weekends 11–6.*

Small Surprises

Bronx Museum of the Arts, housed since 1982 in a former synagogue, was founded in 1972. Intriguing exhibitions show off new American art, particularly works by Bronx artists. The building stands on the Grand Concourse, a great boulevard lined with mid-rise Art Deco buildings. *1040 Grand Concourse, at 166th St., the Bronx, tel. 718/681–6000. Admission: $3 adults, $2 students, $1 senior citizens. Open weekends 10–6.*

DIA Center for the Arts, since moving from its original SoHo digs to Chelsea, has expanded it's mission as well as its square footage. The new center includes three floors of galleries and a roof garden with outdoor installation space, all dedicated to exposing the public to contemporary art and literature. Beyond exhibitions, a wide variety of lectures, readings, and performances take place all weekend long. *548 W. 22 St., tel. 212/989–5566 or 212/989–5912. Admission: $4 adults, $2 students and senior citizens, children under 10 free. Open weekends 12 PM–6.*

Guggenheim Museum SoHo, the uptown institution's downtown sister, showcases gems from the permanent collection and hosts special exhibitions in a bright, lofty space designed by architect Arata Isozaki. *575 Broadway, at Prince St., tel. 212/360–3500 or 212/423–3500 for recorded exhibit information. Admission: $6 adults, $4 students and senior citizens, children under 12 free. Open Sat. 11–8, Sun. 11–6.*

National Academy of Design, modeled on Europe's great art academies, has asked every new associate member to contribute a self-portrait since it was founded in 1825 by Samuel F. B. Morse, Thomas Cole, and Rembrandt Peale; it now has the country's largest collection of American portraits. Sculpture, prints, and other paintings are also featured. *1083 5th Ave. between 89th and 90th Sts., tel. 212/369–4880. Admission: $5 adults, $3.50 students and senior citizens. Open weekends 12 PM–5.*

Snug Harbor Cultural Center, a onetime sailors' retirement home on Staten Island, is the site of the city's largest collection of Greek Revival buildings. Together with other equally charming late-19th- and early 20th-century structures, these are home to the Newhouse Gallery, the Staten Island Children's Museum, an art school, the Staten Island Botanical Garden, and Veteran's Memorial Hall. Special trolleys and city bus service make it easy to get there. *914 Richmond Terr., Livingston, Staten Island, tel. 718/448–2500. Admission free. Open weekends 9–5; tours at 2.*

Studio Museum in Harlem exhibits art, photography, sculpture, and artifacts from Africa, the Caribbean, and the Americas in this lively and sophisticated small institution founded in the late 1960s. Watch for the long-planned T. F. Bing Sculpture Garden. *144 W. 125th St., tel. 212/864–4500. Admission: $5 adults, $3 senior citizens, $1 children under 12. Open weekends 1–6.*

Specialty Museums

American Craft Museum. The displays of 20th-century art made of clay, fiber, glass, metal, and wood in this museum pay homage to the hand, material, and process of creating crafts. The decade-long exhibition series, *The History of 20th Century American Craft: A Centenary Project*, documents the contributions of craft artists to our nation's cultural history. *40 W. 53rd St., tel. 212/956–3535. Admission: $5 adults, $2.50 students and senior citizens, children under 12 free. Open weekends 10–6.*

American Museum of the Moving Image. Situated on the Astoria Studios site, in the building where Paramount Pictures once produced silents and talkies starring the likes of Rudolph Valentino, Gloria Swanson, and Claudette Colbert, this is the first public museum in the country devoted solely to the history of the movies and film production, promotion, and exhibition. It curates TV history as an art museum would, interprets its material like a history museum, and emphasizes technology like a science center. Static and interactive displays explore what goes on behind the scenes—the work of directors, actors, set directors, makeup artists, and other industry specialists—and show off selections from the 83,000-item collection of cameras, projectors, costumes, scenery, production logs, studio business documents, lobby cards, licensed artifacts, and much more. On weekends there are two or three screenings in the 195-seat main theater; meanwhile, old serials from *Captain America* to *Tigerman* play in the smaller screening/conference rooms, the shag-rug-and-vinyl-sofa TV Lounge, and in the Tut's Fever Theater, a work of art in its own right, in which artists Red Grooms and Lysiane Luong pay witty homage to neo-Egyptian picture palaces of the 1920s. *35th Ave. at 36th St., Astoria, Queens, tel. 718/784–4520 or 718/784–0077 for recorded information. Admission: $7 adults, $4 students, senior citizens, and children under 12 (includes screenings; small extra fees for celebrity appearances). Open weekends 11–6.*

Cloisters. The Metropolitan Museum's upper Manhattan branch for medieval art occupies a cool, silent building that could be transported from Europe's medieval past. Once called the crowning achievement in American museology, the museum, which incorporates elements of five medieval cloisters, is spectacularly situated overlooking the Hudson River, at the high point of Fort Tryon Park. (John D. Rockefeller Jr., who donated the 4-acre site, also purchased 700 acres of New Jersey's Palisades to protect the view.) The collection of medieval European art, the country's best, includes icons and chalices, the superb Unicorn Tapestries, altarpieces, paintings and wood sculptures from the Middle Ages, illuminated manuscripts and works in stained glass, metal, enamel, and ivory. The formal gardens (*see* Gardens *in* Chapter 6) are exquisite. From fall through spring, there are special concerts of medieval and Renaissance music. Weekends, which draw a more diverse crowd than weekdays, are busiest in spring, when the gardens come into bloom, and less crowded in cold months, except during December when there are concerts. If you want to see a quieter side of the Cloisters, come in the morning. *Fort Tryon Park, tel. 212/923–3700. Suggested contribution: $8 adults, $4 students and senior citizens. Open Nov.–Feb., weekends 9:30–4:45; Mar.–Oct., weekends 9:30–5:15.*

Cooper-Hewitt National Design Museum. The only museum in the country devoted exclusively to historical and contemporary design, the permanent collection at this delightful institution includes some 250,000 objects that represent 3,000 years of design: ceramics, woodwork, furniture, glass, porcelain, and textiles ranging from fine lace to tapestries, not to mention some 30,000 drawings and prints, and enchanting miscellany—bird cages, valentines, pressed flowers, and even Christmas tree ornaments. The museum's home, the landmark neo-Georgian 1901 Andrew Carnegie mansion, full of wonderful old oak paneling, coffered ceilings, and parquet floors, is being remodelled to adjoin the new Design Resource Center and Agnes Bourne Bridge Gallery, both slated to open in late 1997, just in time for the museum's centennial. Recent exhibits have been forward thinking as well, often focussing on contemporary media and advertising as well as the impact of the computer age on graphic design and typography. Tours of the mansion are offered every other Sunday at 1 and 2:30. *2 E. 91st St., tel. 212/860–6868. Admission: $3 adults, $1.50 students and senior citizens, children under 12 free. Open Sat. 10–5, Sun. 12 PM–5.*

International Center of Photography. This focal point of the American photographic community displays works from around the world, emerging talents and masters from the earliest days to the present, both at its main branch on Museum Mile and a smaller, midtown location (1133 6th Ave. at 43rd St., tel. 212/768–4680) for special exhibits. It was founded in 1974 by Cornell Capa, brother of the famous photographer Robert Capa. The permanent collection includes 10,000 prints from greats such as Eugene Smith, Diane Arbus, Eugene Atget, Edward Weston, Cindy Sherman, and Alfred Steiglitz, and major holdings include the works of Henri Cartier-Bresson, Robert Capra, Roman Vishniac, and Weegee. *1130 5th Ave. at 94th St., tel. 212/860–1777. Admission at each location: $4 adults, $2.50 students and senior citizens, $1 children under 12. Open (both locations) weekends 11–6.*

Museum of American Folk Art. Founded in 1961, this institution in a space near Lincoln Center with a quartet of well-lighted galleries, displays such eclectic objects as a 9-foot Indian chief weather vane, carousel animals, a stars-and-stripes quilt, trade signs, decoys, rag dolls, cigar store figurines, and more. *2 Lincoln Sq. (Columbus Ave. between 65th and 66th Sts.), tel. 212/977–7170 . Admission free. Open weekends 11:30–7:30.*

New Museum of Contemporary Art. The temporary exhibitions at this maze of rooms and galleries can be catergorized as eclectic, but always exuberant and original. They have included "Bad Girls," a series of two exhibitions of feminist art, and the first museum retrospective of photographer André Serrano's work. At Weekend Dialogues, museum docents conduct informal discussions with interested visitors, which could provide an excellent springboard when diving into the sometimes murky waters of the contemporary art galleries in surrounding SoHo. *583 Broadway, between Houston and Prince Sts., tel. 212/219–1222 or 212/219–1355 for recorded information. Admission: $4 adults, $3 artists, students, and senior citizens; children under 12 free. Open Sat. 12 PM–8, Sun. 12 PM–6.*

Nicholas Roerich Museum. The eponymous Russian artist enjoyed a varied career that included archaeological excavations, Asian journeys over antique caravan routes, and set design for Diaghilev's *Prince Igor* and Stravinsky's *Rite of Spring*. His paintings of the Himalayas—serene presences in rich colors, grand and majestic, vast and isolated, and unquestionably awe inspiring—are the focal point of the work displayed in the museum's mansion home (circa 1898), designed by Clarence True. The frequent Sunday concerts are usually, but not always, at 5 and sometimes, but not always, classical. The museum is small; some think it weird. You won't have to fight crowds to enjoy the special tranquility here. *319 W. 107th St., tel. 212/864–7752. Admission free. Open weekends 2–5.*

Showcasing World Cultures

Asia Society. John D. Rockefeller III's considerable Asian art collection, one of the great ones in the field, is the backdrop for changing exhibitions in a stunning modern building. *725 Park Ave. at 70th St., tel. 212/288–6400. Admission: $3 adults, $1 students and senior citizens. Children under 12 free. Open Sat. 11–6, Sun. 12 PM–5.*

Chinatown History Museum. A former elementary school, in use from 1893 to 1976, now houses a gallery where you can browse through changing exhibitions—for example, a German's antique photographs of San Francisco's Chinatown. The focus is on the heritage of New York's Chinese community of over 230,000 people. Occasional walking tours illuminating the area are available on weekends by appointment; reserve in advance. *70 Mulberry St. at Bayard St., 2nd floor, tel. 212/619–4785. Admission: $2 adults, $1 students and senior citizens. Children under 17 free. Open weekends 10:30–5.*

El Museo del Barrio. The country's only museum dedicated to Puerto Rico's culture—and one of the most important institutions of Latin American arts—exhibits dozens of hand-carved Santos de Palo (saints). Special exhibitions may showcase works by folk artists living in New York or replicate studios of craftsmen from Caribbean states. In November the museum provides space for a community altar commemorating the Latin American Day of the Dead. Concerts are occasionally held on weekends, and usually during the summer. *1230 5th Ave., between 104th and 105th Sts., tel. 212/831–7272. Admission: $4 adults, $2 students and senior citizens, children under 12 free. Open weekends 11–5.*

Hispanic Society of America. Visiting the Spanish Renaissance-style terra-cotta court here is like taking a quick trip to the Alhambra. Subtly hued, hand-painted tiles, carved wood screens and statues, elaborately worked gold and silver, original opera scores, ivories, textiles, and wrought-iron pieces are the backdrop for magnificent paintings by such artists as Diego Velásquez, El Greco, and José Ribera. Francisco de Goya's *Duchess of Alba* and the room full of murals by 20th-century realist Joaquín de Sorolla y Bastida are among the best known. Thousands of manuscripts and books make this also a superb center for research on Spanish and Portuguese history, art, and literature. But it is an appealing place for casual visitors as well—and practically unknown (visited by only 10,000 people a year). No more than 35 visitors are permitted inside the building at any one time, so it's always quiet, even on weekends. *613 W. 155th St., tel. 212/926–2234. Admission free. Open Sat. 10–4:30, Sun. 1–4.*

Jacques Marchais Museum of Tibetan Art. There is a heady Oriental air to this institution in the Staten Island hills. The square stone buildings have the feeling of temples; the gardens are studies in tranquility with a lotus pond, terraces, and view of lower New York Bay; and the collection is this hemisphere's largest private grouping of Tibetan art. You can admire exquisite metalwork, the many manifestations of Buddha and Hindu deities, a temple altar surrounded by prayer wheels and lamps where priests once burned yak butter. There are also weekend lectures, demonstrations, and recitals in the serene main gallery. *338 Lighthouse Ave., near Richmond Rd., Richmondtown, Staten Island, tel. 718/987–3500. Admission: $3 adults, $2.50 senior citizens, $1 children under 12. Open Apr.–Nov., weekends 1–5.*

Japan Society Gallery. Housed in a Japanese-style building designed by architect Junzo Yoshimura and enhanced by a placid pool, this museum is one of the few in this country devoted to the exhibition of the arts in Japan. Three times a year special exhibitions are mounted that explore the breadth and diversity of the Japanese aesthetic and encompass painting, sculpture, architecture and textile design, ceramics, woodblock prints, lacquerware, and folk arts. *333 E. 47th St., tel. 212/832–1155. Admission free. Open Sat. 11–5 only during special exhibitions, closed Sun.; call for schedule.*

Jewish Museum. This institution, the largest in the Western Hemisphere dedicated to preserving and interpreting Jewish culture, has an appeal that transcends religion, for it concentrates not just on art and artifacts but on the society—and the individuals—who produced or used them. Special history- and issue-oriented exhibitions may deal with works of African Americans and American Jews, and women photographers of the Weimar Republic; the permanent collection contains more than 27,000 works of art, artifacts, and broadcast media material covering four millennia of Jewish history. *1109 5th Ave. at 92nd St., tel. 212/423–3200 or 212/423–3230 for recorded information. Admission: $7 adults, $5 students and senior citizens, children under 12 free. Open Sun. 11–5:45; closed Sat.*

Museum for African Art. A new museum dedicated to African art, both contemporary and traditional, is at home in a handsome, two-story space designed by Maya Lin, who also designed the Vietnam Veterans Memorial in Washington, DC. Exhibits include contemporary sculpture, ceremonial masks, architectural details, costumes, and textiles. Guided tours are offered at 2 every Sunday, and other weekend activities include storytelling and movement workshops to acquaint visitors with the oral traditions and public rituals that form a large part of many African cultural aesthetics. *593 Broadway, between Houston and Prince Sts., tel. 212/966–1313. Admission: $4 adults; $2 students, senior citizens, and children under 12. Open weekends 12 PM–6.*

National Museum of the American Indian. Gustav Heye is the man responsible for this vast collection, which includes baskets, bead and quill work, costumes, carvings, peyote paraphernalia, ritual objects, tomahawks, and wampum. *1 Bowling Green St., near Battery Park, tel. 212/283–2420. Admission free. Open weekends 10–5.*

Ukrainian Museum. Located in the midst of a still-thriving Ukrainian community, this museum, founded in 1976, collects, preserves, displays, and interprets the culture of this southwestern corner of the Ukraine through paintings, drawings, and watercolors by Ukrainian artists living here and abroad, as well as photographs focussing on Ukrainian immigration, costumes, textiles, coins, kilims, decorative ceramics, brass and silver jewelry, and over 1,000 brilliantly colored Easter eggs. Weekend courses, held in winter and spring, give visitors the chance to try their hand at Ukrainian embroidery, bake traditional Ukrainian Easter breads, and make *gerdany* (bead necklaces) and *pysanky* (Easter eggs). Parking lots along 3rd and 4th avenues are less crowded on weekends, and there's plenty of free parking along side streets. *203 2nd Ave., between 12th and 13th Sts., tel. 212/228–0110. Admission: $1 adults, 50¢ students and senior citizens, children under 6 free. Open weekends 1–5.*

Yeshiva University Museum. Housed in the Yeshiva University library, the collection and the special exhibits on topics ranging from Jewish weddings to Shtetl customs emphasize Jewish life throughout history. Models illustrate synagogue architecture in different cultures. *2520 Amsterdam Ave., between 185th and 186th Sts., tel. 212/960–5390. Admission: $3 adults, $2 children under 12 and senior citizens. Open Sun. 12 PM–6; closed Sat.*

Galleries

A large part of what makes the visual arts in New York so vibrant is the community of contemporary artists studying, working, and showing in the city. While museums provide a cultural history, galleries give visitors a view of culture in the making, showing us the trends, follies, statements, and hype that will decide what appears in the museums tomorrow, and what will end up in the dumpster.

Traditionally New York galleries have been open to the public Tuesday through Saturday, making them a better touring bet during the first half of the weekend. However, there are many exceptions (as well as unexpected openings and closings) so it's always best to call first when you want to visit. Or simply take a stroll through the main neighborhoods and stick your head in for whatever looks intriguing.

Of course art galleries are by no means restricted to any particular neighborhoods; they can and do turn up everywhere. For a comprehensive listing of galleries and what they're showing, check *Art in America/New York: Galleries and Museums* published four times a year by Brant Art Publications (575 Broadway, tel. 212/941–2800). Or go to the periodical section of the nearest bookstore and pick up a copy of *Artforum, Artnews,* or any of the other national magazines that cover the New York art scene.

SoHo

The 19th-century cast iron architecture of SoHo provides the setting for what most people think of as a "New York art gallery." Iron pillared facades, large, display-front windows, and glassily polished hardwood floors have set the scene for the rise and fall of artists, critics, and trends for several decades. It is the site of the Reagan-era art boom, which fostered the careers of 1980s "art stars" like Julian Schnabel, Robert Longo, Jean-Michel Basquiat, and Barbara Kruger. While the artists' scene still thrives today, ensuing gentrification and proliferation of boutiques, cafes, and bistros has made SoHo an excellent setting for a day's aimless browsing from gallery to gallery. The following is a list of neighborhood dealers.

Prince Street: Thorp (No. 103), Leslie-Lohman (No. 127), Luhring Augustine (No. 130).
Wooster Street: The Drawing Center (No. 35), Klein (No. 40), Printed Matter (No. 77), Gallery 292 (No. 120), Greenberg (No. 120), Gagosian (No. 136).
Greene Street: Zwirner (No. 43), Postmasters (No. 80), Gorney (No. 100).
Broadway: Fung (No. 537), Ross (No. 568), Marcus (No. 578).
Grand Street: Kasmin (No. 74), Deitch Projects (No. 76), SoHo Triad Fine Arts (No. 107).

Chelsea

Since 1990, many of the most established dealers have left SoHo, and other parts of town, to recongregate between 10th and 11th avenues, from 20th to 29th streets, in upper Chelsea. The look here is more industrial, with huge garage and factory spaces converted to white-on-white showrooms with concrete floors and minimal architectural detail. This minimalism also extends to the immediately surrounding neighborhood where, although some fine art may be seen, there's not much else to do.

Three highly respected dealers, **Barbara Gladstone, Matthew Marks,** and **Metro Pictures** have set up house side by side in one very large complex (515–523 W. 24th St.), and their enclave has informally adopted the name of another powerhouse: MGM. Other major galleries in the area include **Stefan Stux** (535 W. 20th St.), **Paula Cooper** (534 W. 21st St.), **Morris-Healy** (530 W. 22nd St.), **303** (525 W. 22nd St.), and **Team Gallery** (527 W. 26th St.).

Historical Treasures

Rushing from here to there and back in your weekday life, it's easy to forget that New York is one of the most historic cities in the nation. But if you look, the evidence is all around: the brick warehouse reflected in the glass-walled skyscraper, the bronze plaque on the side of an apartment tower, the great mansion that no amount of money could replicate today. Weekends are a perfect time for visiting the institutions that preserve the city's historic riches.

Museums

American Numismatic Society. Founded in 1858, this institution showcases one of the world's foremost collections of coins and medals. Among the million objects, you might see a bronze medal of Marchese Leonello d'Este designed by Pisanello (1397–1455), a dinar from 7th-century Damascus, or a $2 note issued by the Paterson, New Jersey, Cataract City Bank. *Broadway at 155th St., tel. 212/234–3130. Admission free. Open Sat. 9–4:30, Sun. 1–4.*

Boathouse. Jacopo Sansovino's Library of St. Mark in Venice inspired this terra-cotta building on the meandering Lullwater in Brooklyn's Prospect Park. The graceful steps, below a row of arched windows and illuminated by reproductions of the original 1,500-pound dolphin lamps, make a fine place to sit and contemplate the lake and Olmsted's great park beyond. Inside is a nature center geared towards children, and outside, paddle boats are available to rent. *East Lake Dr. at Lincoln Rd., Prospect Park, Brooklyn, tel. 718/287–3474. Admission free. Open Memorial Day–Labor Day, weekends 11–6.*

Ellis Island. From 1892 to 1954, some 12 million immigrants took their first steps on U.S. soil on this 27½-acre island in New York harbor. Now, after many years of restoration, Ellis Island is a museum devoted to immigration. At its heart is the Registry Room, where inspectors once decided the fate of arrivals. The cavernous Great Hall, where the immigrants were registered, has amazing tiled arches by Rafael Guastavino. White-tiled dormitory rooms overlook this grand space; the Railroad Ticket Office at the back of the main building houses exhibits on the "Peopling of America," recounting 400 years of immigration history, and "Forced Migration," focussing on the slave trade. The many-columned baggage room, now replastered, is an orientation area. The old kitchen and laundry building has been stabilized, rather than restored, so that you can see what the whole place looked like just a few years ago. Even if your ancestors did not arrive here, the visit leaves a powerful impression. *Ferries leave from Castle Clinton in Battery Park, Manhattan. Ellis Island, tel. 212/269–5755 for ferry schedules. Fares: $7 adults, $5 senior citizens, $3 children 3–17. Open Oct.–Apr., weekends 9:30–3:30; May–Sept., Sun. 9–4:30.*

***Intrepid* Sea-Air-Space Museum.** The spiffy modern marquee and ticket booth in front of the USS *Intrepid* send up the red flag of caution: "Tourist trap!" you may say to yourself, and drive on. Think again. The 150,000-square-foot veteran of World War II, Vietnam, and NASA recovery missions is stuffed with artifacts, exhibits, and movies of surprising interest. Beginning with the impressive film that explains just what an aircraft carrier is all about, the exhibits sweep you along from battle to battle, war to war, era to era, and hero to hero. Narrow-bodied, needle-nosed fighter planes from several eras fill the windswept deck; some 70 historic planes, rockets, capsules, satellites, and mock-ups are scattered around the ship, whose deck alone is as big as many a city park. Great for hyper kids. *Intrepid Sq., Pier 86, 12th Ave. and 46th St., tel. 212/245–0072. Admission: $10 adults, $7.50 children 12–17 and senior citizens, $5 children 6–11. Open weekends 10–5 (ticket booth closes at 4).*

Museum of the City of New York. Housed in an impressive neo-Georgian red brick building, this repository of New York City history and culture contains art, photographs, handicrafts, arcana, and historic printed documents. Anything and everything that helps tell the story of the city can be found here, from period furniture to political cartoons to models of the city's port to a dollhouse collection. In 1998 the Museum is set to open its New Museum for a New Century, which will include a digital library of historic documents, city records, and other primary source materials for in-depth research.

1220 5th Ave., at 103rd St., tel. 212/534–1676, or 212/534–1034 for current programs. Suggested contribution: $5 adults, $3 students, children, and senior citizens. Open Sat. 10–5, Sun. 1–5.

Queens Museum. The star here is the Panorama of the City of New York, an amazing creation that Parks Commissioner Robert Moses conceived for the 1964 World's Fair. It takes up 9,000 square feet, and every detail in every borough is there, right down to the planes taking off at La Guardia Airport. New buildings are added as they go up, to keep the vision current. *New York City Building, Flushing Meadows-Corona Park, Flushing, Queens, tel. 718/592–5555. Admission: $2 adults, $1 students and senior citizens, children under 5 free. Open weekends 12 PM–5.*

Richmondtown Restoration. A modest hamlet in the late 17th century, the Staten Island county seat 50 years later, and a major civic center during the Industrial Revolution, the village of Richmond faded from the public eye after the island became a part of New York City in 1898. But this oblivion means the salvation of some wonderful structures—the oldest surviving elementary school in the country (circa 1695), the Queen Anne–style New Dorp Railroad Station (circa 1850), and 25 other historic buildings representing architectural styles ranging from Greek Revival to Victorian. Restoration has been going on since 1939, and today, on 100 acres in Staten Island's Greenbelt, 15 of the historic structures are open to the public during guided tours. Museum exhibits show off Staten Island history. Children enjoy the antique dolls, toys, and small-scale furniture on exhibit in the Bennett House. Special events, an integral part of the presentation, usually take place on Sundays. *441 Clarke Ave., La Tourette Park, Staten Island, tel. 718/351–1611. Admission: $4 adults, $2.50 students and senior citizens, children under 6 free. Open Apr.–Dec., weekends 1–5.*

South Street Seaport

One of the busiest places in the city on weekends, it's all too easy to forget that the Seaport offers more than a terrific opportunity to drop a couple of hundred bucks on gizmos and gadgets. It's also a museum—a cobblestone complex of small galleries and exhibit buildings that tell the story of the days when South Street really was the Street of Ships. While the Fulton Fish Market, founded in 1922, stabilized the area after years of decline, preservationists prevailed in establishing the South Street Seaport Historic District and South Street Seaport Museum. Following hard upon this was a large-scale development project by the Rouse Company that brought the area to the state in which you find it today.

Among the museum's attractions are several ships moored at Pier 16, including *Peking,* a 347-foot four-masted bark built in 1911 and the second-largest sailing ship in existence; *Wavertree,* a 293½-foot full-rigged ship currently being restored to continue her sailing career; and *Ambrose,* a 135-foot steel lightship that guided vessels coming into New York harbor until 1963. At the **Children's Center** (165 John St.), your youngsters can watch a 15-minute film of sailors battling a storm off Cape Horn six decades ago and then visit one of the maritime workshops. **Bowne & Co.** (211 Water St.) is an old print shop, where several vintage presses use antique type to print items to order.

At the **Boat Building Shop** (Burling Slip), craftsmen construct replicas of historic vessels while others whittle away on ship models, figureheads, and other carvings at the **Maritime Crafts Center** (head of Pier 15, under the *Wavertree* bowsprit). In the **A. A. Low Building** (171 John St.), **Visitors' Center** (207 Water St.), and **Museum Gallery** (213 Water St.), there are changing exhibitions of paintings, photographs, models, and tools from the museum's collections. *South Street Seaport Museum ticket sales at visitor center near Titanic*

Memorial Tower at Fulton and Water Sts. and on Pier 16 at the Pilothouse, tel. 212/748–8600 or 212/732–7678 for recorded information. Admission: $6 adults, $5 senior citizens, $4 students, $3 children 4–13. Open Apr.–Sept, weekends 10–6, Oct.–Mar. 10–5.

Statue of Liberty

For tristate residents, the idea of this great monument, modeled after the sculptor's mother, is almost a cliché—the thing you take out-of-towners to see. But France's gift to America, officially entitled *Liberty Enlightening the World*, retains the power to impress even the most jaded New Yorker. From close up, she seems even taller than her 151 feet, with her position atop an 89-foot pedestal, which itself rests on the 65-foot-high star-shaped ramparts of the old Fort Wood. If you arrive early enough, before the crowds, you may be able to get to the top without undue waiting. First take the elevator to the viewing platform atop the pedestal (for terrific views over the harbor) and from there, trek up (12 stories and 171 steps) through the statue's body to the crown for even better views. With the wind whipping at your face, the harbor humming with boats and ships, and the torch shining over it all from 305 feet up, it's easy to bask in the patriotic glow. *Ferries leave from Castle Clinton in Battery Park. Liberty Island, New York Bay, tel. 212/363–3200 for the statue, 212/363–8832 for the museum, or 212/269–5755 for ferry schedules. Statue admission free. Ferry: $7 adults, $5 senior citizens, $3 children under 17. Open weekends 9–5.*

Restored Houses

Manhattan **Abigail Adams Smith House.** Abigail Adams Smith was the second U.S. president's daughter and the sixth president's sister. In the shadow of the Queensboro Bridge, this former carriage house, midtown Manhattan's only historic home, has nine rooms of Federal and Empire furniture and 18th-century-style gardens planted by the current owners, the Colonial Dames of America. There are special programs on the second Sunday of every month. *421 E. 61st St., tel. 212/838–6878. Admission: $3 adults, $2 students and senior citizens, children under 12 free. Open Sept.–May, weekends 11–4.*

Lower East Side Tenement Museum. At this new Lower East Side institution, housed in an authentic tenement building, you can see an exhibit of photographs about tenement life. There are two special programs, both on Sundays. In an hour-long play, "Family Matters: An Immigrant Memoir," characters tell you about their lives and their world—Hester Street, the synagogue and yeshiva, and that greatest of all luxuries, the public baths. Walking tours explore the streets where immigrants haggled over eggs and argued about politics. Many other events take place weekends—slide shows, lectures with discussions, and genealogical workshops among them. *197 Orchard St., between Delancey and Broome Sts., tel. 212/431–0233. Suggested general admission: $3. Tours: $8 adults, $6 students and senior citizens.*

Morris-Jumel Mansion. The knoll known as Mount Morris, the site of this columned Palladian house, is Manhattan's second-highest elevation and once had a view up to Westchester, over to New Jersey, and down to the tip of Manhattan. The view exists no longer, but the history makes up for it. Renovated over the years, this mansion—which was built by an English loyalist, bought by a French merchant, and inherited by his wife (who was in her later years briefly married to Aaron Burr)—is now a splendid structure, a place where a time warp takes over and the 18th century prevails. Manhattan's oldest residential building—a Georgian country villa—sets a gracious tone consistent with the furnishings. The octagonal drawing room has hand-painted wallpaper from China and mahogany Chip-

Pick up the phone.
Pick up the miles.

1-800-FLY-FREE

Now when you sign up with MCI you can receive up to 8,000 bonus frequent flyer miles on one of seven major airlines.

Then earn another 5 miles for every dollar you spend on a variety of MCI services, including MCI Card® calls from virtually anywhere in the world.*

You're going to use these services anyway. Why not rack up the miles while you're doing it?

Is this a great time, or what? :-)

pendale mirrors with gilt phoenix finials. There's also a bed that is said to have belonged to Napoleon. Surrounding the mansion is the **Jumel Terrace Historic District** (between 160th and 162nd Sts. and Edgecombe and St. Nicholas Aves.), where some 50 late-19th-century row houses in limestone, brownstone, clapboard, and brick line up along Jumel Terrace and Sylvan Terrace, and other streets. *65 Jumel Terr. at 160th St. near St. Nicholas Ave., in Roger Morris Park, tel. 212/923–8008. Admission: $3 adults, $1.50 students, children under 12 free. Open weekends 10–4.*

Merchant's House Museum. This extraordinarily solid redbrick 1832 town house is the only historic house in the city with the original furniture. It's a family home, and guided tours show it as that, from the Greek Revival parlors to the Rococo Revival bedrooms and plain-Jane servants' rooms; they open the closets stuffed with antique clothing and wrinkled old gloves and point out the bed in which the last surviving family member, Gertrude, was born, slept every night of her life, and died. *29 E. 4th St., between Lafayette St. and the Bowery, tel. 212/777–1089. Admission: $2 adults, $1 students and senior citizens, children under 13 free. Open Sun. 1–4; closed Sat.*

Theodore Roosevelt Birthplace. The actual birthplace of the 26th president was demolished in 1916, but this reconstruction, dating from 1923, holds much original furniture and re-creates the environment of prosperous polish in which the man who gave his name to the teddy bear spent his first 14 years. The cut-glass prisms of the parlor chandelier glitter as they did when they delighted the young TR; the library is full of the overstuffed chairs and lavish silk hangings that TR associated with "gloomy respectability"; and the dining room chairs have horsehair coverings that "scratched the bare legs," as he later recalled. *28 E. 20th St., tel. 212/260–1616. Admission: $2 adults, children under 12 free. Open weekends 9–5, with tours until 4.*

The Bronx   **Bartow-Pell Mansion Museum.** This tranquil spot in Pelham Bay Park, one of the last of the summer houses that old New Yorkers built on Long Island Sound, is only a mile from a snarl of Bronx highways. Yet with its perimeter border of woods and marshes and its fine formal gardens, carriage house, and stable, the mansion feels very much the country estate it was in 1842, when Robert Bartow built the 10-room gray stone Greek Revival structure on 200 acres. An allée of chestnut trees, a path lined with rhododendrons, a lily pond, an herb garden, and lawns show off the presiding horticultural talents of the International Garden Club, headquartered here. An indoor porch is occasionally the setting for high tea and chamber music concerts. *Shore Rd., Pelham Bay Park, tel. 718/885–1461. Admission: $2.50 adults, $1.25 students and senior citizens, children under 12 free. Open weekends 12 PM–4.*

Poe Cottage. Not only is this the last home of American poet, novelist, and storyteller Edgar Allan Poe and his wife, Virginia, but it is also the last remaining house of what used to be the village of Fordham. With its sparkling white clapboards and forest-green trim, it's in congruously tiny and countrified amid the anonymous high rises of the Grand Concourse. A slide show tells the story of the author's life here from 1846 to 1849. *Poe Park, 2460 Grand Concourse, tel. 718/881–8900. Admission: $2. Open Sat. 10–4, Sun. 1–5.*

Valentine-Varian House. This two-story Georgian-vernacular structure (1758), the second-oldest house in the borough, is a relic of the days when most of the Bronx was farmland and carriages lumbered along the nearby Boston Post Road. It's a good place to get a feel for the history of the Bronx from the time of the Indians and the Dutch through the Revolutionary War. Two galleries house changing exhibitions; the third is a permanent display on Bronx history. *3266 Bainbridge Ave. at E. 208th St., tel. 718/881–8900. Admission: $2. Open Sat. 10–4, Sun. 1–5.*

Van Cortlandt Museum. Occupying a beautiful valley in the city's third-largest park, this three-story fieldstone mansion built by Frederick Van Cortlandt in 1748, is an airy, comfortable home, with high ceilings, wide-planked floors, many fireplaces, a central hallway, and an abundance of Dutch and English furniture dating from the 18th and 19th centuries. Windows look out over the flower gardens to the marshes beyond, and there are herb gardens and fine old trees on the property. *Broadway and 246th St. in Van Cortlandt Park, tel. 718/543-3344. Admission: $2 adults, $1.50 students and senior citizens, children under 14 free. Open weekends 11-4.*

Brooklyn **Lefferts Homestead.** One of Brooklyn's last Dutch colonial farmhouses, this home was built by Peter Lefferts between 1777 and 1783 and presented to the city by his descendants in 1918. With its sloping eaves, high gambrel roof, rag rugs, colonnaded porches, carved woodwork, and split front door, it's a handsome structure. The most entertaining aspect of a visit here is the chance to watch craftspeople shearing sheep, spinning flax, quilting, tape-weaving, casting pewter, caning chairs, coopering, making shoes, dipping candles, and tending an herb and vegetable garden. Changing exhibits explore local Dutch-American farm life, and there are occasional seasonal events, such as cider-making parties and games days. Sunday is the busiest day of the week; come early. *Flatbush Ave. and Empire Blvd., Prospect Park, tel. 718/965-6505. Admission free. Open weekends 12 PM-4 (until 5 in summer).*

Queens **Bowne House.** The borough's oldest house, a 1661 saltbox, has pegged floors, old beams, and fine furniture that date from the days when Quakers held their meetings here and when John Bowne stood up against the persecutions of then-governor Peter Stuyvesant. Inside you'll see a great deal of furniture that was handed down through the nine generations of Bownes who owned the house after their ancestor's death. *37-01 Bowne St., Flushing, tel. 718/359-0528. Admission: $2 adults, $1 senior citizens, students, and children under 12. Open weekends 2:30-4:30.*

King Manor. This stately 10-room clapboard home, with a Greek Revival portico and fluted Doric columns, belonged to one of the most distinguished figures in this nation's early history. Rufus King, the first U.S. senator from New York, who was known for his stance against slavery, lived here in the early part of the 19th century. Careful restoration of the manor house, with its distinctive gambrel roof, recall that time. The 5,000-volume library—King's favorite room—features a trompe l'oeil painting of oak paneling. *150th St. and Jamaica Ave., King Park, Jamaica, tel. 718/206-0545. Suggested contribution: $2 adults, $1 students and senior citizens. Open Apr.-Dec., weekends 12 PM-4.*

Kingsland House. This 2½-story home of a wealthy 18th-century Quaker named Benjamin Doughty stands today only because history-minded supporters arranged for it to be moved to its present site on property that once belonged to the Flushing nurseryman Samuel Parsons. Immense and serene, the now-landmarked Weeping Beech Tree, the oldest in America, which Parson's son brought from Belgium as a cutting in a flowerpot in 1847, is one of the attractions of a visit to the house; the other is a group of modest exhibits of local interest on local automotive history, trousseaux, the 1964 World's Fair, and more. *143-35 37th Ave., Flushing, tel. 718/939-0647. Admission: $2 adults; $1 students, senior citizens, and children under 12. Open weekends 2:30-4:30.*

Quaker Meeting House. A familiar sight on a busy street, this is the city's oldest continuously used meeting house; the spare, quiet interior, though still used regularly for Sunday meetings, is on view only one day a month—a Sunday. There's a tiny cemetery in back. *137-16 Northern Blvd., Flushing., tel. 718/358-9636. Admission free. Open for worship Sun. at 11; open for sightseers 2-4 1st Sun. of month.*

Queens County Farm Museum. From the 17th through the 18th centuries, farming was a way of life in Queens. This museum, in a spreading old house acquired by the city in 1981 and subsequently restored, recalls that era. The property's 53 acres yield apples and herbs, tomatoes and squash. There are cows, chickens, goats, pigs and sheep, and you can buy fresh produce and baked goods at the occasional old-fashioned county fairs. There are even occasional hayrides. *73–50 Little Neck Pkwy., Floral Park, tel. 718/347–FARM. Admission free. Open weekends 10–5; house tours on the hr.*

Staten Island **Alice Austen House Museum and Park.** Photographer Alice Austen's Victorian cottage, with its steeply peaked dormer windows, gingerbread trim, gardens, breathtaking view of the harbor and the Verrazano Narrows, and lush turf sweeping to the shore makes for a restful afternoon visit. Some of the rooms re-create the house as it was when Austen lived there—the parlor is full of Victorian furniture, for instance—and you can also see exhibits of her photographs, which document rural Staten Island life at the turn of the century. A 20-minute video narrated by Helen Hayes on Alice and her house is also shown. *2 Hylan Blvd., tel. 718/816–4506. Suggested contribution: $3. Open weekends 12 PM–5.*

Conference House. The 226-acre Conference House Park is right on the water at the point where the Raritan River meets the Arthur Kill and flows into the Atlantic. The fieldstone manor's considerable historical importance derives from a dramatic meeting that took place here two months after the signing of the Declaration of Independence, at which a contingent of Americans, including Benjamin Franklin, refused a British peace offer, the terms of which demanded that the Colonies return to British control. The rest is history. The house's furnishings, including a sea chest that belonged to the family who built the house in the 17th century, look quite simple today, but were considered luxurious at the time. On the grounds are beautiful rose and herb gardens. *7455 Hylan Blvd., tel. 718/984–2086. Admission: $2 adults, $1 senior citizens and children 6–12. Open Apr.–Nov., weekends 1–4.*

Garibaldi Meucci Museum. Before unifying Italy in the mid-19th century, Giueseppi Garibaldi spent an enforced exile in the home of his friend, Antonio Meucci. Meucci, a hero in his own right, was a Florence native who developed a working model of the telephone long before Alexander Graham Bell. Five small rooms of exhibits honor the house's two prestigious occupants and provide a glimpse into an odd corner of New York's past. A 10-minute video on the museum, Meucci, and his invention of the telephone is shown. The museum is owned and operated by the Sons of Italy in America. *420 Tomkins Ave., tel. 718/442–1608. Suggested contribution: $3. Open weekends 1–5, winter months by appt. only.*

Science and Technology Museums

Manhattan **American Museum of Natural History.** Weekends are busy at this beloved institution, but with over 36 million artifacts and specimens in 40 halls and galleries, there's something to divert everyone, and more than enough room to absorb the scrambling hordes of excited kids and tolerant parents. The museum, still on the cutting edge of research in its fields, is a giant encompassing a whole world of anthropology and natural history; recently renovated dinosaur exhibits; a 1,300-year-old giant sequoia tree; Aztecs and Incas, Eskimos and Plains Indians, with their teepees, totems, and temples; a herd of stuffed wild elephants and a diving whale 94 feet long; the Star of India sapphire and the largest meteorite ever retrieved. Free museum highlights tours provide a good overview for first-timers. From September through June, weekend programs examine world cultures several times daily, and there are additional performances, films, and lectures. Films on the Naturemax Theater's 40-foot-high and 66-foot-wide screen are vivid, whether the footage explores the Grand Canyon or the magic of flight. The adjacent **Hayden Planetarium** is closed for a major renovation until 2000. *Central Park West and 79th St., tel. 212/769–5100 for general information, 212/769–5000 or 212/769–5315 for Leonhardt People Center events. Suggested contribution to the museum: $8 adults, $6 students and senior citizens, $4.50 children under 12. Theater: $6 adults, $5 students and senior citizens, $3 children under 12. Open Sat. 10–8:45, Sun. 10–5:45.*

Sony Wonder Technology Lab. A walk through the hands-on Wonder Lab will wow visitors of any age, and perhaps change one's perception of the technological age. The adventure starts in the entry lobby, where visitors log onto a communications network by recording their name, image, and voice, and then proceed to a series of interactive displays with six "professional studios" ranging from medical diagnostics to television production to environmental research technology to video-game design. Visitors are encouraged to use the hands-on exhibits to learn about communication technologies and create their own compositions. In the nation's first fully interactive High Definition Theater, the audience orchestrates a video adventure from their seats. They actually determine the outcome of the feature they are watching by voting with a futuristic joystick attached to the arm of their chair. *550 Madison Ave., between 55th and 56th Sts., tel. 212/833–8100. Admission free. Open Sat. 10–6, Sun. 12 PM–6.*

Queens **New York Hall of Science.** This museum, stuffed with hands-on exhibits, is all about scientific fundamentals—with an emphasis on the "fun." Here you can pedal an airplane propeller into motion, control a windmill, make yourself disappear on TV, build an arched bridge that will hold your weight, watch atoms collide, and create shadows on a glowing wall. Specially trained college students, "Explainers," lead weekend workshops and answer questions in languages ranging from Ga and Hindi to Spanish and French. There are special festivals and events all the time—"Science Halloween," "Science Book and Toy Fest," and so on. *47–01 111th St., Flushing Meadows-Corona Park, tel. 718/699–0005. Admission: $4.50 adults, $3 children under 17 and senior citizens. Open weekends 10–5.*

Staten Island **Staten Island Institute of Arts and Sciences.** The oldest of Staten Island's cultural institutions encompasses not just art, local history, or natural science but all three. This wonderful community resource introduces children to textiles, American paintings and prints, European silver and decorative arts, the Staten Island Ferry, entomology, birds, seashells, geology, and lots of other exhibits that make the museum fairly burst at the seams. The galleries are rarely crowded here, but weekends are lively with families and small groups who come for the regular programs and special exhibitions. *5-min walk from Staten Island Ferry at 75 Stuyvesant Pl., tel. 718/727–1135. Suggested contribution: $2.50 adults, $1.50 students and senior citizens. Open Sat. 9–5, Sun. 1–5.*

Best Bets for Children

There are children's sections in the major museums—most notably the **Junior Museum** at the **Metropolitan Museum of Art** and the **Discovery Room** at the **American Museum of Natural History.** Other museums offer special programs for kids or families; among them are the **Brooklyn Museum of Art,** the **Jewish Museum,** and the **Museum of the City of New York,** home of wonderful dollhouses and antique toys. At the **Whitney Museum of American Art,** children like the Calder Circus and the film that goes along with it. The *Intrepid* **Sea-Air-**

Space Museum, the **New York Hall of Science,** and the **Staten Island Institute of Arts and Sciences** are hits as well.

In addition, New York has its complement of so-called children's museums:

People from all over the borough bring their small fry to the active **Brooklyn Children's Museum,** where neon-resplendent "people tubes" funnel visitors through the museum's four levels, each of which demonstrates some facet of the world—for example, weights and measures or music. Shrieks of delight prove just how effective it all is. In one area, youngsters use their five senses to understand unfamiliar objects; in another, they play a walking piano or other instruments; and in still another, they learn about sleep, dreams, and nightmares. There's also an Early Learners Area for children under six. *145 Brooklyn Ave., Crown Heights, Brooklyn, tel. 718/735–4400. Suggested contribution: $3. Open weekends 12 PM–5.*

The lively **Children's Museum of Manhattan,** designed for toddlers through age 10, exposes children to different cultures through interactive exhibits. The Community Gallery exhibits children's artwork from around the world. Kids can paint, make collages, learn about animation, become newscasters, and generally stay amused for hours on end. (For adults, the noise can be traumatic.) *212 W. 83rd St., tel. 212/721–1223. Admission: $5, children under 3 free. Open weekends 10–5.*

The **Staten Island Children's Museum,** occupying the former maintenance building at what is now the Snug Harbor Cultural Center (see Art Museums, above), is stuffed with interactive displays, and on Sundays the place is a hive of activity, with kids swarming and buzzing around each exhibit. These have included "Building Buildings" (by an architect) and "What if you couldn't . . . ?" (to illuminate what it's like to be disabled). *1000 Richmond Terr., Snug Harbor Cultural Center, Staten Island, tel. 718/273–2060. Admission: $4, children under 3 free. Open weekends 12 PM–5.*

5 Where to Shop

Sometimes it seems that whatever else New Yorkers and visitors are doing on the weekend, they're also shopping. If shopping in New York was ever limited to certain neighborhoods or days of the week, it is now an all-area, all-hours, all-weather activity. Shoppers can browse and buy at small, unusual stores that reflect the taste of their owners, at department stores, increasingly at national chains and the flagship stores of major catalog houses.

Shopping Hours

The following stores, which usually do a full day of business on Saturday, are generally open on Sunday from noon to 5 or 6. Some shops open an hour or two earlier or later, while others may close as late as 8 or 9. Book and record stores and those catering to hipsters often stay open past 10, especially on Saturdays. On the Lower East Side, where businesses are closed on the Jewish Sabbath (Saturday), stores may open as early as 8:30 and close as late as 9 on Sunday. When a store is closed on either Saturday or Sunday, it's indicated. Some stores normally closed on Sundays will open during the holiday shopping season. When in doubt, it's best to call ahead.

Great Neighborhoods for Weekend Shopping

World Financial Center On the weekends the stores stay open but the work-a-day crowds are gone, making it easier to enjoy both the shopping and the setting, which combines the grandiose (vaulted ceilings, cathedral-like steps) with the grand (the river, that city skyline). Familiar names such as **Ann Taylor, Tahari, Joan and David, GAP Kids, Godiva,** and **Mimi Maternity** nestle next to more unusual spots such as **Quest Toys, Sabine Roy Florist and Ornaments,** and **Georgiou,** which offers upscale day and evening wear. Readers will enjoy the **Civilized Traveller** and the well-stocked branch of **Rizzoli Bookstore.** There's even an outpost of **Barneys New York.**

South Street Seaport The Seaport, once a working port, has adapted well to its new life as a mall, with stores along the cobbled extension to Fulton Street, in the Fulton Market Building (once the fish market) and in Pier 17. You can enjoy the area while shopping a good selection of national chain stores, including **Ann Taylor, Liz Claiborne/Elizabeth,** the **Limited** and **Express** for women's clothing and the **Gap, Old Navy, Banana Republic, J. Crew, Country Road,** and **Abercrombie & Fitch** for men's and women's wear, from rugged to formal. Gadget fiends will enjoy **Brookstone** and the **Sharper Image,** and handbags and fragrances can be found at **Coach** and **Caswell-Massey,** respectively. Distinctive cards and stationary can be found at **Bowne & Co.** and **Greetings Earthlings.**

Lower East Side The first home to millions of Russian and Eastern European Jewish immigrants, this area has long been New Yorkers' bargain beat. The center of it all—narrow, unprepossessing Orchard Street—draws crowds on nice days. Merchandise ranges from kitsch to elegant, and service is businesslike. Start at Houston Street, walk down one side of Orchard Street as far as Canal Street, and then walk back up the other. Essential stops include **Fine & Klein** for handbags and leather goods (between Delancey and Rivington Sts.) and **Forman's** for women's clothing (with three stores between Grand and Broome Sts.). Grand Street (off Orchard St., south of Delancey St.) is jammed with shops for linens, towels, and other household items. Outstanding is the century-old **Harris Levy,** where many a celebrity comes for fine and pricey bedding.

SoHo On West Broadway, SoHo's main drag, and on Wooster, Greene, Mercer, Prince, Spring, Broome, and Grand streets, major art galleries alternate with chic clothing stores, such as **Comme des Garç-**

ons (118 Wooster, between Prince and Spring Sts.), where avant-garde clothing for men and women by Japanese designer Rei Kawakubo is the lure. Other well-known stops include decorative-items specialist **Wolfman-Gold & Good Company** (Mercer St.) and Southwest-themed **Zona** (Greene St., both are between Spring and Prince Sts.) and gourmet food emporium **Dean & DeLuca** (Broadway at Prince St.). There's also **Portico** (W. Broadway, between Spring and Broome) and **Portico Bed & Bath** (Spring St. at Wooster): The former offers contemporary furniture with a classic look, ranging from cushy sofas to oversized armoires; the latter, elegant linens and bath accessories. Lovely furniture from foreign climes can be found at **Boca Grande** (Greene St. between Spring and Broome) and **Sarajo** (Prince at Mercer). **Peter Roberts Antiques** (134 Spring St., between Wooster and Greene) is a major resource for furniture and pottery produced by the American Arts and Crafts movement.

Other Options From Lincoln Center north to 86th Street, this boulevard mixes
Columbus brunch, museums, and proximity to Central Park with a cluster of
Avenue stores catering to the young couples and singles who now live in this gentrified neighborhood. You can buy clothing ranging from the clubby, suave (**Frank Stella Ltd.** at 81st St., for men) and bright funk (**Betsey Johnson** between 71st and 72nd Sts.) to high style (**Charivari** at 72nd St.) and find brightly patterned linens at **April Cornell** (between 84th and 85th Sts.) and **Pondicherri** (between 81st and 82nd Sts.). On Sundays, one of the city's biggest flea markets brings crowds to the schoolyard of I.S. 44 (between 76th and 77th Sts.); you can browse for hours. Children (and adults) will enjoy browsing the toys at nearby **Penny Whistle Toys** and fossils across the avenue at **Maxilla and Mandible** (both between 81st and 82nd Sts.). Restorative caffeine and sweets are available at the charming **Columbus Bakery** (between 81st and 82nd Sts.): try the chocolate almond bark.

5th Avenue Shopping on this famous avenue begins at 59th Street and ranges south, and though some of the department stores are closed on Sundays, the window shopping is always rewarding, not to mention a great money saver. This is the home of many of New York's most fabled emporia, and you can start with the jewel-like salons of **Bergdorf Goodman** and **Bergdorf Goodman Men** (at 59th St.) and then head down to **Henri Bendel** (55th St.). If it's Saturday, don't miss **Takashimaya** (between 55th and 54th Sts.) which offers a delightful and revivifying lunch at its Tea Box Cafe. The **Versace Boutique** (between 50th and 52nd St.) and the glitzy faux-royalty frills on all of its goods make for a lively shopping diversion. Next stop is **Saks Fifth Avenue** (at 50th St.), and you can finish the bulk of your browsing at **Lord & Taylor** (at 38th St.). If children are in your party, you'll want to include **F.A.O. Schwarz** (at 58th St.).

57th Street This thoroughfare offers all kinds of goodies: outrageous games at the **Compleat Strategist** (between 8th and 9th Aves.), records and books at **Rizzoli** (between 5th and 6th Aves.), and high-tech gizmos at **The Sharper Image** (between 5th and 6th Aves.). At the corner of 5th Avenue is the **Warner Bros. Studio Store,** an interactive festival with coffee mugs, golf shirts, jewelry, toys, not to mention limited-edition production cels, all featuring Looney Tunes characters. Eastward on 57th Street, there's lingerie at **Victoria's Secret** (between Park and Madison Aves.). From there, it's hard not to end up dropping into **Bloomingdale's,** just two blocks north (between Lexington and 3rd Aves.).

Madison This upscale avenue is actually a great place to buy books. Starting
Avenue at the **Corner Bookstore** (at 93rd St.) you can proceed to the charming **Crawford Doyle Booksellers** (between 81st and 82nd Sts.) find design, architecture, and gardening books at **Archiva** (both between

74th and 75th Sts.) and farther south, at 35th Street, pick up travel books at the **Complete Traveller.** On the journey, other needs can easily be met: pretty household objets at **Adrien Linford** (between 93rd and 94th Sts. and at 74th St.), delectable bread and cookies at **Ecce Panis** (at 90th St.), children's clothing at **Chocolate Soup** (between 74th and 75th Sts.) and well-priced, well-designed housewares and furnishings at **Crate & Barrel** (at 59th St.). From 68th Street down to 60th you'll be in the land of the designer stores, and you can choose between **Armani, Moschino, Barneys New York,** and **Calvin Klein,** among others.

East Village   This neighborbood, roughly 9th Street south to Houston Street, 3rd Avenue to the East River, is a magnet for the young and hip, which makes it a great place to shop for rare records, objets de kitsch, and vintage clothing. Check out **Little Rickie** (49½ 1st Ave., at 3rd St.) and **Love Saves the Day** (119 2nd Ave at 7th St.) for Godzilla lunch boxes and '70s Jesus paraphernalia, and a lot of baby boomers; don't miss **A-1 Record Shop** (439 E. 6th St., between 1st Ave. and Ave. A) for vinyl rarities. **Kentucky 7** (45 E. 7th St.) has interesting antiques from rural America, and **Dinosaur Hill** (306 E. 9th St.) offers toys and clothes with a hand-crafted appeal.

Atlantic   Wide and busy, this street is a delight for antiquers and people who
Avenue,   love to eat. The block between Hoyt and Bond streets offers over 20
Brooklyn   antique stores, bound to have the armoire or old church pew of your dreams. A few blocks closer to Brooklyn Heights is a one-block "town" of Middle Eastern stores, fragrant with spices and pastries. Try **Sahadi** (at 187–9) for Lebanese specialties, dried fruit, and virtually everything else, **Damascus Breads & Pastry** (195) for fresh spinach pies and pita breads, and **El-Asmar International Delights** (197) for halvah.

Department Stores

ABC Carpet & Home. The ultimate home furnishings store meets Miss Havisham's attic, with merchandise ranging from delicate items for bedroom, bath, and baby to gargantuan pieces of antique furniture. Contemporary furniture too, along with rugs galore and an excellent selection of upholstery fabric. Luxury is the watchword here, and if the sheer profusion of items can be overwhelming, this is still a store where a serious shopper can easily while away an afternoon. *881 and 888 Broadway, at 19th St., tel. 212/473–3000. Open Sat. 10–7, Sun. 11–6:30.*

Barneys New York. Founded some 60 years ago by Barney Pressman as a discount outlet for men's clothing, Barneys is one of the city's retail trendsetters. Its huge selection of menswear ranges from made-to-measure and top European and American designer clothing to traditional tweeds and pinstripes. The women's collection is a showcase of current fashion. The Chelsea Passage area can be counted on for distinctive handmade linens, small leather goods, and accessories for the home. Watch for the fabled Barneys Warehouse Sales around Labor Day and Presidents' Day; devotees say the discounts of 50% to 70% are worth the frenzy. *660 Madison Ave. at 61st St., tel. 212/826–8900. Open Sat. 10–7, Sun. noon–6. World Financial Center, tel. 212/945–1600. Open Sat. 11–5, Sun. 12 PM–5.*

Bed, Bath & Beyond This giant goes beyond the call of duty when stocking its shelves with household supplies at reasonable prices. It keeps expanding its wares, and now carries linens, towels, bath mats, lamps, cookware, magnets, lamp bases, pillows, bathroom fixtures, and cookbooks, making it a great place for one-stop shopping whether you're furnishing a house, apartment, or dorm room. *620 6th Ave., between 18th and 19th Sts., tel. 212/255–3550. Open Sat. 9:30–9, Sun. 10–8.*

Bergdorf Goodman and **Bergdorf Goodman Men** These stores seem like a collection of tiny boutiques, each with its own look and product line. Expect lovely, expensive merchandise, much of it by famous designers. The decorative accessories, fancy foods, china, and other housewares in the main store make perfect hostess gifts and should ensure that you'll be invited back. *754 and 745 5th Ave., at 59th St., tel. 212/753–7300. Open Sat. 10–6.*

Bloomingdale's. The main floor seems a stupefying maze, but once you reach the elevators, the going gets easier. The selection of everything from clothing and housewares to tabletop furnishings and gourmet gadgetry is peerless. The store is notable for the designer rooms on the fifth floor, with state-of-the-art home furnishings, ranging from fine period reproductions to off-beat pieces from the Far East to the sleekest of contemporary offerings. *1000 3rd Ave., at 59th St., tel. 212/355–5900. Open Sat. 10–7, Sun. 11–7.*

Century 21. Think of this as a discount department store. You can get cosmetics and accessories, the well-known and well-marked-down designer wear for men and women, shoes, linens, luggage, and small appliances. *22 Cortlandt St., between Broadway and Church Sts., tel. 212/227–9092. Open weekends 10–7.*

Crate & Barrel. Shoppers pour into this Chicago chain's first New York City branch for reasonably priced housewares downstairs and simple comfy furniture upstairs. The look is unobtrusive and blends with American, French Provincial, and other countrified decorating styles. *650 Madison Ave., at 59th St., tel. 212/308–0004. Open Sat. 10–7, Sun. 12 PM–6.*

Henri Bendel. Owned by the Limited, this longtime trendsetter, now on 5th Avenue, offers savvy, stylish women's clothing by both established and up-and-coming designers, and a first floor notable for its sophisticated displays. *712 5th Ave., between 55th and 56th Sts., tel. 212/247–1100. Open Sat. 10–7, Sun. 12 PM–6.*

Lord & Taylor. This store can be relied upon for classic clothes and accessories for both men and women. It's refined, never overwhelming, has a good-looking and affordable line of private label clothes, and recently it has been having significant 20–30%-off sales. *424 5th Ave., between 38th and 39th Sts., tel. 212/391–3344. Open Sat. 10–7, Sun. 11–6.*

Macy's. This miracle on 34th Street is the largest retail store in America and one of the biggest on earth. Appropriately hectic, the merchandise represents practically every trend, size, and color. Still, there's something majestically institutional about the place, with its beige travertine columns touched with brass and escalators with wide wood grooves. Estate Jewelry, on the mezzanine, is a pleasure. If you need cooking equipment, the Cellar is one of the city's best bets. *Herald Sq., Broadway at 34th St., tel. 212/695–4400. Open Sat. 10–8:30, Sun. 11–7.*

Saks Fifth Avenue. This wonderful store still embodies the moneyed spirit and style with which it opened in 1926. Contemporary designers such as Calvin Klein and Donna Karan have boutiques that are showpieces of store display. Saks believes in good manners, the ceremonies of life, and dressing for the part; the selections for men, women, and children reflect this. *611 5th Ave., between 49th and 50th Sts., tel. 212/753–4000. Open Sat. 10–6, Sun. 12 PM–6.*

Takashimaya New York. This store is an odd hybrid of Japanese sensibilities, French imports, and international elegance. Its six floors feature hyper-worldly accessories, bed, bath, and beauty products, one-of-a kind gardening implements, dried flowers, and delicate chocolates. Understand: There may not be anything you need, strictly speaking, but you'll find lots to admire and to covet. Best of all, even if you only buy two dollars worth of fragrant Indian tea you'll still get the trademark tissue wrap and tri-cornered Takashimaya bag. *693 5th Ave., between 54th and 55th Sts. tel. 212/350–0100. Open Sat. 10–8.*

Fashion

Clothing for Men and Women

Designers

Agnès B (116–118 Prince St., between Wooster and Greene, tel. 212/925–4649; 79 Greene St., between Broome and Spring Sts., tel. 212/431–4339; 13 E. 16th St., tel. 212/741–2585; 1063 Madison Ave., at 80th St., tel. 212/570–9333). Spacious and spare clothes made in France and very circa now. (Greene St. store is menswear only.)

Calvin Klein (654 Madison Ave., at 60th St., tel. 212/292–9000). Austere tastefulness is the watchword here as Klein displays his men's, women's and home designs in a roomy and minimalist white space.

Charivari (18 W. 57th St., tel. 212/333–4040). The three branches of this store, one of the first in the city to cater to those who want seriously avant-garde styles, are still a must for the fashion forward.

Comme des Garçons (116 Wooster St., between Prince and Spring Sts., tel. 212/219–0660). A blank white store retails some of the choice output of designer Rei Kawakubo.

Emporio Armani (110 5th Ave., between 16th and 17th Sts., tel. 212/727–3240). The big-name Italian designer displays suits to shoes in his large store with 17-foot ceilings and arched windows and doors.

Gianni Versace (817 Madison Ave., at 68th St., tel. 212/744–6868, women; 212/744–5572, men); **Boutique** (647 5th Ave., between 51st and 52nd St., tel. 212/317–0224). For men, lace mesh jeans mingle with somewhat more traditional clothes, while at the women's store, beautiful suits in astonishing colors mix with bold evening wear. The five-floor 5th Avenue location proffers the full line, up to and including pillows with gold fringe and really pricey rompers. *Closed Sun.*

Giorgio Armani (760 Madison Ave., between 65th and 66th Sts., tel. 212/988–9191). Four attractive floors display Armani for men and women, including day and evening wear. The hard-core fan can even purchase black peds bearing the designer's name.

Moschino (803 Madison Ave., between 67th and 68th Sts., tel. 212/639–9600). An extremely colorful shop offering the full range of this whimsical designer's collection, from babywear to swimwear all the way to his couture line. *Closed Sun.*

Patricia Field (10 E. 8th St., between 5th Ave. and University Pl., tel. 212/254–1699). This is the home of funky clubwear as seen by a single inventive designer.

Todd Oldham Store (123 Wooster St., off Prince St., tel. 212/219–3531). The bright, almost tie-dyed floor tiles set the stage for Oldham's colorful clothes meant for women whose sense of humor goes hand in hand with their sense of style.

Yohji Yamamoto (103 Grand St., at Mercer St., tel. 212/966–9066). Using unusual fabrics and textures, this designer creates clothes that are extremely offbeat and beautiful.

Discount

Daffy's (111 5th Ave., at 18th St., tel. 212/529–4477; 335 Madison Ave., at 44th St., tel. 212/557–4422; 1311 Broadway, at 34th St., tel. 212/736–4477; 135 E. 57th St., tel. 212/376–4477). The wares here mix the cheap, priced cheaper, and the pricey, marked way down.

Syms (42 Trinity Pl., near Rector St., tel. 212/797–1199; 400 Park Ave., at 54th St., tel. 212/317–8200). The longer an item remains in the store, the lower its price. Shoppers hunt for the bargains among unbeautiful surroundings but the payoff is designer clothing at prices that are either good, great, or fabulous.

Resale and Secondhand

Designer's Resale (324 E. 81st St., between 1st and 2nd Aves., tel. 212/734–3639). Off the avenue, you can find secondhand but recent Armani, Chanel, and Versace for (relatively) reasonable prices.

Encore (1132 Madison Ave., at 84th St., tel. 212/879–2850) New York's cast-off Karans and Alaïas all end up here.

Ina (101 Thompson St., between Prince and Spring Sts., tel. 212/941–4757). At this consignment shop, the owner, Ina, collects designer-label clothes from uptowners and sells them to downtowners.

Vintage **Antique Boutique** (712 Broadway, near Washington Pl., tel. 212/460–8830). Hip teens love the baggy overcoats, minis, and other oldies.

Harriet Love (126 Prince St., between Greene and Wooster Sts., tel. 212/966–2280). The proprietress presents a selection of resucitated styles and garments in excellent condition.

Screaming Mimi's (382 Lafayette St., between E. 4th and Great Jones Sts., tel. 212/677–6464). The black bustiers, vintage clothing, and funky styles on which this shop built its reputation are as audacious as ever.

Young and Hip **Canal Jean** (504 Broadway, between Spring and Broome Sts., tel. 212/226–1130). Dyed cotton knits, a huge selection of vintage clothing, and other casual funk fill this cavernous downtown institution.

Diesel (770 Lexington Ave., at 68th St., tel. 212/308–0055). Leather distressed to look like vinyl, orange patent book bags, and rave/industrial wear for those too young to remember when people wore this stuff for real.

Reminiscence (74 5th Ave., between 13th and 14th Sts., tel. 212/243–2292). The theme is strictly '50s and '60s, in vintage and casual new clothing, with appropriate kitsch accessories.

Trash and Vaudeville (4 St. Mark's Pl., between 2nd and 3rd Aves., tel. 212/982–3590). Black, white, and electric colors create the look upstairs and down. Most of the clothing is for teenagers and up, but even shopping for with-it babies, you may find a chartreuse swimsuit or jet-black rompers.

Menswear **Camouflage** (141 8th Ave., at 17th St., tel. 212/741–9118). The look here is updated classic, as designed by Calvin Klein, Reiss of London, and Hartland; private-label items are also available.

Frank Stella Ltd. (440 Columbus Ave., at 81st St., tel. 212/877–5566). This shop offers classic business clothing and casual wear in subtle variations for conservative types.

Jekyll & Hyde (93 Greene St., between Spring and Prince Sts., tel. 212/966–8503). Dashing clothes for men unafraid of color, texture, and rich fabrics such as velvet and silk.

New Republic (93 Spring St., between Mercer St. and Broadway, tel. 212/219–3005). A small store, but what there is, is choice. A well-edited collection of work clothes for hip bankers, savvy art directors, and the like.

Paul Smith (108 5th Ave., at 16th St., tel. 212/627–9770). The English designer makes clothes and accessories just this side of normal, but God is in the details, like the buttons on the cuffs, the elongated line of the jackets, and the quite handsome shoes.

Paul Stuart (Madison Ave., at 45th St., tel. 212/682–0320). The Paul Stuart line, much of which is made in Italy, features classic clothes for men who work in the spiffier offices of Wall Street and Midtown. If they don't have what you want, check out the even preppier Brooks Brothers and J. Press down the block.

Peter Elliott Ltd. (1070 Madison Ave., at 81st St., tel. 212/570–2300). This shop features classic clothing and accessories, including some outstanding jackets, sweaters, and ties made to the store's specifications.

Saint Laurie, Ltd. (895 Broadway, between 19th and 20th Sts., 3rd floor, tel.212/473-0100). This family-owned business sells suits manufactured on the premises, using natural fabrics and old-fashioned tailoring.

Discount **Eisenberg and Eisenberg** (85 5th Ave., at 16th St., tel. 212/627–1290). This dependable store has been offering bargains on classic clothing since 1898.

Moe Ginsburg (162 5th Ave., at 21st St., tel. 212/242–3482). A stock of suits, shoes, shirts, sweaters, coats, and accessories make this one-stop shopping for men who hate paying retail.

Rothman's (200 Park Ave. S, at 17th St., tel. 212/777–7400). Reaching for a youthful market, this shop offers suits by some of the big names in contemporary men's clothing.

Today's Man (529 5th Ave., at E. 44th St., tel. 212/557–3111; 625 6th Ave., between 18th and 19th Sts., tel. 212/924–0200). This large menswear store offers low prices on suits, coats, sports jackets, slacks, and sweaters.

Womenswear **Anna Sui** (113 Greene St., between Prince and Spring Sts., tel. 212/941–8406). The mode here varies from vivid daytime wear to glitzier outfits for the evening.

Betsey Johnson (130 Thompson St., between Houston and Prince Sts., tel. 212/420–0169; 251 E. 60th St., between 2nd and 3rd Aves., tel. 212/319–7699; 1060 Madison Ave., at 80th St., tel. 212/734–1257; 248 Columbus Ave., at 71st St., tel. 212/362–3364). Having made her name during the '60s, Betsey Johnson is back, showing young New Yorkers how much fun dressing up can be with frills, ruffles, wild patterns, and Day-Glo colors.

Chelsea Atelier (128 W. 23rd St., between 6th and 7th Aves., tel. 212/255–8803). Women who crave silks, chiffons, and velvets that drape as langorously as they do, can count on this store for the goods.

Eileen Fisher Ninth Street (314 E. 9th St., between 1st and 2nd Aves., tel. 212/529–5715). This store predates the current era of Eileen Fisher ubiquity; it has the basic line of simply shaped clothes in soft fabric, plus close outs, samples, and seconds.

Endless Art Clothing (260 Park Ave. S, at 21st St., tel. 212/598–0875). Mostly from Indonesia, the unusual array of cotton and rayon clothes set out a stylish way to cope with sweltering New York summers. *Closed Sun.*

La Lumia (253 Church St., between Franklin and Leonard Sts., tel. 212/966–3923). A mixed bag of casual and work styles, the owners are notable for their willingness to work with you to design a skirt or vest made out of fabric you choose.

Laura Ashley (398 Columbus Ave., at 79th St., tel. 212/496–5110). The hallmark is old-fashioned frocks in the English manner, complete with straw boaters in season.

Legacy (109 Thompson St., between Prince and Spring Sts., tel. 212/966–4827). The kind of romantic, highly feminine yet sophisticated clothes that you imagined you'd wear when you'd finally grown up and could choose your own clothes.

Liberty House (2389 Broadway, between 87th and 88th Sts., tel. 212/799–7640). Natural fibers made into well-cut, comfortable, and distinctive clothes prove that grown-up hippies can dress for work without feeling like they've sold out. The sister store next door, **Liberty House Too**, offers quirky suits and ravishing special occasion dresses at slightly higher prices.

The Limited (691 Madison Ave., at 62nd St., tel. 212/838–8787). Considering the address, prices are moderate for handsome, casual clothing.

Paracelso (414 W. Broadway, between Prince and Spring Sts., tel. 212/966–4232). Amazing multihued chiffons, brocades, and rich velvets from India and America are made into skirts, blouses, jackets, and scarves and are swathed and draped around this squirrel's nest of a shop.

Putamayo (147 Spring St., between W. Broadway and Wooster St., tel. 212/966–4458). There's cool cotton clothing here, much of it made in warmer climes; it's crinkly and easy to care for.

Renell Boutique (2931 Broadway, between 113th and 114th Sts., tel. 212/749–4749). Masquerading as a small neighborhood store, this is actually a carefully chosen collection of attractive, touchable, and sexy clothing. The store also features a selection of pretty and affordable lingerie.

Discount **Bolton's** (225 E. 57th St., tel. 212/755–2527; 27 W. 57th St., tel. 212/935–4431; 1180 Madison Ave., between 86th and 87th Sts., tel. 212/722–4419; 2251 Broadway, at 81st St., tel. 212/873–8545; 53 W. 23rd St., tel. 212/924–6860; 4 E. 34th St., tel. 212/684–3750; 1191–93 3rd Ave., at 69th St., tel. 212/628–7553; and other locations). Moderately priced wardrobe basics are discounted by about a third at this chain, and sales drop prices even further.

Fine & Klein (119 Orchard St., between Delancey and Rivington Sts., tel. 212/674–6720). Domestic and imported handbags, reasonably priced, jam this unprepossessing landmark. *Closed Sat.*

Forman's (82 Orchard St., between Delancey and Broome Sts., tel. 212/228–2500). This attractive store discounts moderately priced clothing by Vittadini, Jones New York, Calvin Klein, Belle France, and others. Head to the branches at 94 and 78 Orchard for, respectively, petite and plus sizes. *Closed Sat.*

Loehmann's (236th St. at Broadway, the Bronx, tel. 718/543–6420; 101 7th Ave., between 16th and 17th Sts., tel. 212/352–0856). Traditionalists may still prefer to travel to the Bronx, but bargain hunters and shopaholics are rejoicing that the famous store has finally come to Manhattan.

S&W (165 W. 26th St., tel. 212/924–6656). Cheap it is not. But 40% off the latest by Dior and other well-known designers adds up to value that matches the selection. Other locations nearby stock furs, lingerie, and accessories. *Closed Sat.*

Larger Sizes **Ashanti** (872 Lexington Ave., near 65th St., tel. 212/535–0740). Velour leggings to velvet evening wear, with many stops in between, all in larger sizes. Look for dramatic and ethnic looks.

Daphne (467 Amsterdam Ave., between 82nd and 83rd Sts., tel. 212/877–5073). Daphne herself designs many of these funky, flowy clothes featuring bright colors, ethnic patterns, and rich fabrics. Check out their other store, four doors down, which specializes in lingerie and sleepwear.

The Forgotten Woman (888 Lexington Ave., at 66th St., tel. 212/535–8848; 60 W. 49th St., tel. 212/247–8888). Famous names like Dana Buchman and Tamotsu are among the business and evening wear here.

Soho Woman on the Park (32 W. 40th St., off 5th Ave., tel. 212/391–7263). Seasonless clothes cut to flatter (try the bias-cut skirts) and made in comfortable, lush cottons, rayons, and silks. *Closed Sun.*

Lingerie **Joovay** (436 W. Broadway, between Prince and Spring Sts., tel. 212/431–6386). Real silk bias-cut tap pants and teddies, lace-draped silk slips and chemises can be found in this tiny SoHo nook.

La Perla (777 Madison Ave., between 66th and 67th Sts., tel. 212/570–0050). Recently chosen best lingerie store by *New York Press*, this is a place for women (and their admirers) who know the power of seriously seductive underthings and don't mind if they come with a high price. *Closed Sun.*

Only Hearts (386 Columbus Ave., at 79th St., tel. 212/724–5608). Billing itself as a shop for the shameless romantic, this store has lacy lingerie and nightwear both comfy and seductive.

Peress of Madison Avenue (739 Madison Ave., between 64th and 65th Sts., tel. 212/861–6336). Despite its location, this family-owned store has a cozy atmosphere and offers a great selection of camisoles and panties from Hanro, the Swiss lingerie maker. *Closed Sun.*

Victoria's Secret (34 E. 57th St., between Park and Madison Aves., tel. 212/758–5592; 693 Madison Ave at 62nd St., tel. 212/838–9266; 565 Broadway, at Prince St., tel. 212/274–9519). Fancy undies and loungewear are affordable in these pretty shops.

Millinery **The Hat Shop** (120 Thompson St., near Prince St., tel. 212/219–1445). With hats by many makers in a variety of styles and prices, one is sure to be right for you. The amazingly friendly staff are happy to advise.
Lola (2 East 17th St., tel. 212/366–5708). Live out your film-noir-femme-fatale dreams in one of Lola's artful pillbox, netting, and flower creations. *Closed Sun.*
Suzanne (700 Madison Ave., between 62nd and 63rd Sts., tel. 212/593–3232). Hats change your personality, according to the nice lady at this tiny hattery. Cynics may feel that for $400–$500 each, a hat should also bring flowers and do the dishes, but they *are* handmade and awfully beautiful. *Closed Sun.*

Food

Bagels and **Ess-A-Bagel** (359 1st Ave., at 21st St., tel. 212/260–2252; 831 3rd
Bialys Ave., between 50th and 51st Sts., tel. 212/980–1010). The huge bagels here were recently deemed to have the highest calorie content of all New York bagels, but they are also frequently judged the best, with the perfect alignment of crisp crust and yielding center. The formidable fish counter offers appropriate accompaniments.
H&H Bagel (2239 Broadway, at 80th St., tel. 212/595–8003; 639 W. 46th, near 12th Ave., tel. 212/595–8000). These shops offer bagels in a dozen types, including sourdough, whole wheat, and the delectable "everything." Usually mobbed, but the line moves fast.
Kossar's Bialystoker Bakery (367 Grand St., between Essex and Norfolk Sts., tel. 212/674–9747). This lower Lower East Side bakery (It's practically in Chinatown.) is worth any detour if you need flat, chewy bialys and *perfect* onion board.

Breads **A. Zito and Sons** (259 Bleecker St., between 6th and 7th Aves., tel. 212/929–6139). The shop's tasty Italian whole-wheat bread—crunchy on the outside and soft on the inside—goes to many local restaurants.
Amy's Bread (672 9th Ave., between 46th and 47th Sts., tel. 212/977–2670). This breadmaker offers basic breads and loaves featuring olives, raisins, and, best of all, proscuitto, a delicious meal in it self.
D&G Bakery (45 Spring St., between Mulberry and Mott Sts., tel. 212/226–6688). Get here early to get the specialty: robust peasant loaves with chewy, crackly crusts.
Damascus Breads and Pastry (195 Atlantic Ave., Brooklyn, tel. 718/625–7070). For Middle Eastern breads, this is Mecca.
E.A.T. (1064 Madison Ave., between 80th and 81st Sts., tel. 212/772–0022). This store is owned by a Zabar, and though it carries all types of prepared food, the bread is the draw, including some of the best (and most expensive) sourdough loaves, rolls, and baguettes you'll ever sink your teeth into.
Ecce Panis (1120 3rd Ave., at 65th St., tel. 212/535–2099; 1260 Madison Ave., between 90th and 91st Sts., tel. 212/348–0040; 282 Columbus Ave., at 73rd St., tel. 212/362–7189). The air is perfumed with the scent of bread, the staff are friendly, and the focaccias, sourdoughs, pepper brioche, and hearty cookies here are divine.
Moishe's (181 E. Houston St., between Allen and Orchard Sts., tel. 212/475–9624). Old-fashioned Russian pumpernickel and other Old Country treats are sold here. *Closed Sat.*

Caviar **Caviarteria** (502 Park Ave., at 59th St., tel. 212/759–7410). Lunch at the elegant Champagne and Caviar Tasting Bar, then bring home (or send—they'll ship anywhere) some serious caviar or Icelandic gravlax for your loved ones.

Petrossian (182 W. 58th St., at 7th Ave., tel. 212/245–2217). Quite at home behind the building's grand Beaux-Arts facade, this café serves superb beluga, sevruga, and osetra caviar imported from Russia via Paris. Smoked salmon (try the "czar cut") and foie gras from the Périgord are also available. There are counters in front for takeout orders.

Cheese   **Ben's Cheese** (181 E. Houston St., between Allen and Orchard Sts., tel. 212/254–8290). Famous for the farmer's cheese, in your choice of baked, fresh, plain, or loaded with berries, raisins, vegetables, or nuts. *Closed Sat.*

DiPalo Fine Foods (206 Grand St., near Mott St., tel. 212/226–1033). Come here for heavenly Asiagos and Parmigiano Reggianos, freshly made mozzarella, and other Italian specialties. The kindly countermen dispense generous samples, too.

East Village Cheese (40 3rd Ave., between 9th and 10th Sts., tel. 212/477–2601). The specials at this tiny, cheese-crammed store are hard to beat. As they have expanded their stock to prepared meats and fresh breads, it's become a one-stop shop.

Murray's (257 Bleecker, at the corner of Cornelia, tel. 212/243–3289). A neighborhood fixture since 1940, this store offers about 300 varieties of cheese from around the world.

Chocolate and Candy   **Black Hound** (149 1st Ave., between 9th and 10th Sts., tel. 212/979–9505). If you want to give your sweet thing truffles or cookies in a perfectly cunning little box or tin, head right here.

Economy Candy (108 Rivington St., between Essex and Ludlow Sts., tel. 212/254–1531). Barrels, bins, and shelves overflow with candy that you've either never seen, or haven't seen in years. It's the cornucopia kids dream of. The slightly dingy atmosphere and low prices add to the experience.

Evelyn's Hand Dipped Chocolates (4 John St., off Broadway, tel. 212/267–5170). You'll understand what the fuss is all about when you taste Evelyn's nonpareils, which actually taste like chocolate. *Closed Sun.*

La Maison du Chocolat (25 E. 73rd St., tel. 212/744–7117). The (wealthy) purist's chocolate store, with geometric shapes, plain, beautiful wrapping, and unusual flavors (pineapple, fennel, tangerine). *Closed Sun.*

Leonidas (485 Madison Ave., between 51st and 52nd Sts., tel. 212/980–2608). Rich Belgian truffles in a multitude of fabulous flavors (orange and brandy, coffee hazelnut, nine kinds of praline) are flown in weekly for the delectation of New York's truffle hounds.

Li-Lac Chocolates (120 Christopher St., between Bleecker and Hudson Sts., tel. 212/242–7374). This unpretentious little shop, the Village's best source for sweets (especially their famous thin mints) for more than 70 years, features an assortment of chocolate delights.

Mondel Chocolate (2913 Broadway, near 114th St., tel. 864–2111). For over 50 years the Mondel family has won hearts with its handmade chocolates, including the old-fashioned butter crunch and the many novelty and holiday-themed chocolates.

Teuscher Chocolates (25 E. 61st St., off Madison Ave., tel. 212/751–8482; 620 5th Ave., at Rockefeller Center, 212/246–4416). Its best to think in terms of pieces, not pounds, at this pricey Swiss chocolatier, but the champagne truffle is so heavenly that one may not be enough.

Treat Boutique (200 E. 86th St., near the corner of 3rd Ave., tel. 212/737–6619). In a delicious example of gilding the lily, this shop turns fruit into candy, through the application of glacé and chocolate.

Coffee and Tea   **McNulty's Tea & Coffee Company** (109 Christopher St., between Bleecker and Hudson Sts., tel. 212/242–5351). The antique wood paneling of this tiny, aromatic shop says "Old New York"; the barrels of beans say Timor, Java, New Guinea. Fine teas are also available.

Porto Rico Importing Company (201 Bleecker St., between 6th Ave. and MacDougal St., tel. 212/477–5421; 40½ St.Marks Pl., at 2nd Ave., tel. 212/533–1982; 107 Thompson St., between Spring and Prince Sts., tel. 212/966–5758). Dark and atmospheric, these shops take coffee very seriously and the friendly staff will happily discuss the merits of each bean.

Fish, Meat, and Poultry

Citarella (2135 Broadway, at 75th St., tel. 212/874–0383). Justly famous for fresh fish, the store now also sells meat, freshly made pasta, and prepared foods, all as good as the fish. The window display, where a filet becomes fantasy, always merits a look.

Faicco's Pork Store (260 Bleecker St., between 6th and 7th Aves., tel. 212/243–1974) and **G. Esposito & Sons Jersey Pork Store** (357 Court St., Brooklyn, tel. 718/875–6863). Old-fashioned pork specialists offer freshly made sausage and other necessities.

Florence Meat Market (5 Jones St., at Bleecker St., tel. 212/242–6531). Known for its veal, the market was also recently cited by the *New York Times* for the excellence of its beef. *Closed Sun.*

H. Oppenheimer Co. (2606 Broadway, between 98th and 99th Sts., tel. 212/662–0246). Although the eponymous Harry Oppenheimer retired, the store still features kindly, courtly butchers, great meat, and advice on how to cook it. A West Side institution. *Closed Sun.*

Jake's Fish Market (2425 Broadway, at 85th St., tel. 212/580–5253). This small store wins raves for freshness and staff who don't mind giving cooking tips.

Grocers

Agata and Valentina (1505 1st Ave., at 79th St., tel. 212/452–0690). Everything looks great here, from the fresh fish (steamed on request) to the vegetable-heaped foccacias. Also produce, prepared foods, staples, cheese, and lots of samples.

Balducci's (424 6th Ave., at 9th St., tel. 212/673–2600). In this former mom-and-pop shop, food is displayed like art: mounds of baby carrots nudging scallions tickled by frilly lettuce leaves and feathery dill. You'll also find some of the city's best meats, fishes, cheeses, prepared foods and a cornucopia of imported delicacies.

Dean & Deluca (560 Broadway, at Prince St., tel. 212/431–1691). This huge SoHo trendsetter, all bright-white splendor, is basically a temple to food, with produce, amazing cheese, easy-to-idolize desserts, prepared food, and nearly everythng else you can think of. As in many religions, sacrifices may be required: these pedigreed edibles are pricey.

Fairway (2127 Broadway, at 74th St., tel. 212/595–1888; 2328 12th Ave., at 133rd and West Side Hwy., tel. 212/234–3883). Produce overflowing from the bins inside and out is the main attraction, but there's so much more. With meat, smoked fish, cheese and bread departments that rival nearby Zabar's (not to mention less attitude), this is a shopper's dream. The uptown branch has even lower prices, and a huge, refrigerated meat room (bring a sweater). Both stores are open daily til midnight, for night owl cooks.

Ferucci's Gourmet (171 1st Ave., between 10th and 11th Sts., tel. 212/529–7903). A small Italian grocery that frequently makes its way onto "Best of New York" lists, Ferucci's has a lot of cheese, freshly made sauces, breads, and appetizers at neighborhood grocery prices.

Gourmet Garage (453 Broome St., at Mercer, tel. 212/941–5850; 301 E. 64th St., between 1st and 2nd Aves., tel. 212/535–6271; 2567 Broadway at 96th St., tel. 212/663–0656. A wide range of excellent (and rarefied) produce and staples like vinegars, cheeses, olive oil, and artisanal breads can be found at these two stores.

Grace's Marketplace (1237 3rd Ave., at 71st St., tel. 212/737–0600). Grace Balducci of *the* Balducci family has created an exquisitely uptown selection of fresh produce, baked goods, and prepared foods in her own store.

Jefferson Market (450 6th Ave., between 10th and 11th Sts., tel. 212/ 533–3377). Beloved by villagers for its meat and fish and wide selection of imported items. A mellower alternative to the crush at nearby Balducci's.

Kam Man (200 Canal St., between Mott and Mulberry Sts., tel. 212/ 571–0330). The city's premier Chinese market, Kam Man is the best place to find dried foods, mushroom soy sauce, and all the items required for serious Chinese cooking.

Katagiri (224 E. 59th St., between 2nd and 3rd Aves., tel. 212/755– 3566). Hidden away a half-block from Bloomingdale's, Katagiri is a source for foods Japanese, including, fresh *mizuna* (peppery leafy greens), *uni* (sea urchin), green tea ice cream, and the other ingredients one might need for a Japanese feast.

Myers of Keswick (634 Hudson St., between Jane and Horatio Sts., tel. 212/691–4194). This store's stock is all British, including treacle, lemon shandy, toffee, bangers, and steak-and-kidney pie.

Sahadi Importing Co. (187–189 Atlantic Ave., tel. 718/624–4550). Spices, oils, lively, Middle Eastern specialities, a huge assortment of dried fruits and a festive atmosphere make this a festive place to shop. (Closed Sun.) Also worth a look is the neighboring **El-Asmar International Delights** (197 Atlantic Ave., tel. 718/855–2455), where absurdly nice staff serve fresh Middle Eastern salads and spices.

SoHo Provisions (518 Broadway, near Spring St., tel. 212/334– 4311). One flight up and virtually under Dean and Deluca's formidable nose, this store offers organic produce and Bhutanese red rice, dried Persian lemons, Muluhiyya leaves from Eqypt, and a host of other hard-to-find ingredients.

Union Square Farmers Market (17th St. at Broadway, tel. 212/477– 3220). One of the things New Yorkers list when they're thinking up reasons to stay in the city, this outdoor institution offers local farmers a market and local buyers a chance to snap up farm-fresh produce, cheeses, breads, flowers, and more. It's also a wonderful spot for people watching and celebrity sightings. Smaller neighborhood markets abound, call for locations. *Saturdays only.*

Vinegar Factory (431 E 91st St., tel. 212/987–0885). Assuming you have a table, plates, silverware, and a good bit of cash, you can get everything else you might need for a sumptous dinner party. Everything: Soup, olives, pasta, braised lamb shanks, vegetables, bread, fruit, coffee, pie, and nuts.

Zabar's (2245 Broadway, at 80th St., tel. 212/787–2000). A tradition on the West Side virtually forever, this store keeps expanding its offerings. Coffees and teas, jams and jellies, dried fruits, chocolates, crackers, oils and vinegars, and bottled and canned goods are on the main floor, along with a fragrant jumble of fresh breads and the cheese, meat, and (famously delicious) smoked-fish counters. Upstairs is one of New York's biggest selections of kitchenware. Take a number and enjoy the aromas.

Pastries   **Ceci-cela** (55 Spring St., between Lafayette and Mulberry Sts., tel. 212/274–9179). Tiny and French, this bakery offers authentic pastries, croissants, tarts, and truffles.

The City Bakery (22 E. 17th St, tel. 212/366–1414). Famous for its austerely beautiful tarts in inventive flavors like champagne peach, grape and hazelnut, plus the ever popular chocolate in several guises. Plan to grab a quick, nouveau lunch here before picking up that tart. *Closed Sun.*

Columbus Bakery (474 Columbus Ave., between 82nd and 83rd Sts., tel. 212/724–6880; 957 1st Ave., between 52nd and 53rd Sts., tel. 212/421–8413). The kind of place that makes people happy, whether they're picking up the perfect bread or sticking around for coffee, a light meal, or the succulent apple *tarte tatin* covered with cream.

Cupcake Cafe (522 9th Ave., at 39th St., tel. 212/465–1530). This bakery-restaurant has three tables and excellent waffles, but the real point is the buttery cakes and cupcakes and their lush floral icing.

Eileen's Special Cheesecake (17 Cleveland Pl., tel. 212/966–5585). This miniscule bakery more than lives up to its name: the cheese-cake, which comes in over 15 flavors (such as pumpkin, Rocky Road, and chocolate raspberry), may be the best in the city.

Little Pie Company (424 W. 43rd St., tel. 212/736–4780). Famous for what it can do for an apple. The one to buy is the sour cream apple walnut pie.

The Magnolia Bakery (401 Bleecker St., at 11th St., tel. 212/462–2572). This new bakery promises old fashioned desserts and delivers in a charmingly retro environment where you can order milk to wash down the treats.

Once Upon a Tart (135 Sullivan St., between Houston and Prince Sts., tel. 212/387–8869). Lovely tarts—cranberry pear, pumpkin, lemon, chocolate walnut—make the perfect dessert for two happy people or one person in need of a pick-me-up. Next door is a sit-down cafe offering desserts and light meals.

Pâtisserie J. Lanciani (414 W. 14th St., between 9th Ave and Wash-ington St., tel. 212/989–1213). Joseph Lanciani, the former chief pastry chef at the Plaza Hotel, now offers his exceptional confections here.

Poseidon Greek Bakery (629 9th Ave., between 44th and 45th Sts., tel. 212/757–6173). New York can't top it for baklava.

Pickles   **Guss's Pickles** (35 Essex St., between Grand and Hester Sts., tel. 212/254–4477). Watermelon rinds, cucumbers, peppers, and much more are pickled here and sold straight from the barrel. The sours are an essential New York experience. *Closed Sat.*

Smoked Fish   Some specialty stores happen to have smoked-fish counters, but these places major in the stuff: **Barney Greengrass** (541 Amster-dam Ave., between 86th and 87th Sts., tel. 212/724–4707) and **Murray's Sturgeon Shop** (2429 Broadway, between 89th and 90th Sts., tel. 212/724–2650) are neighborhood institutions and serve hordes of West Siders on the weekends. **Russ & Daughters** (179 E. Houston St., between Allen and Orchard Sts., tel. 212/475–4880), a Lower East Side old-timer, is beloved for smoked fish and its her-ring.

Spices and   **Aphrodisia** (264 Bleecker St., between 6th and 7th Aves., tel. 212/
Herbs   989–6440). The aroma here is part cardamom, part chamomile, part rose petals, and parts of the other 698 herbs and spices in glass jars shelved from floor to ceiling.

Flower Power (406 E. 9th St., between 1st Ave. and Ave. A, tel. 212/982-6664). Herbs for cooking, sure, but the real deal here is a huge variety of herbs and roots for ritual or healing purposes, including blessed thistle and eyebright.

Kalustyan's (123 Lexington Ave., between 28th and 29th Sts., tel. 212/685–3451). Deservedly voted best spice store by both *New York* magazine and *New York Press*, it offers a world of spices, plus teas, nuts, stuffed grape leaves, and freshly-made chutneys. Excellent selection and friendly staff make Kalustyan's the star of spice alley, but the aromatic and neighboring **Little India** (128 E. 28th St., tel. 212/683–1691), **Foods of India** (121 Lexington Ave., between 28th and 29th Sts., tel. 212/683–4419) and **Spice Corner** (135 Lexington Ave., at 29th St., tel. 212/689–5182) are crammed with Indian cooking necessities.

Specialty Shops

Antiques   **Lost City Arts** (275 Lafayette St., between Houston and Prince Sts.,
Architectural   tel. 212/941–8025). Taking home a genuine hunk of New York City
Details   can be fun, whether it's a gate, grillwork, or a gargoyle.

Clothing   **The Family Jewels** (832 6th Ave., at 29th St., 2nd floor, tel. 212/679–5023). Lillyan Peditto's upstairs shop is crammed with everything from '20s cloche hats and '30s crêpe dresses to '70s bell-bottoms.

Jean Hoffman (207 E. 60th St., between 3rd and 2nd Aves., tel. 212/535–6930). An extensive collection of wedding dresses, evening gowns, shoes, handbags, hats, parasols, walking sticks, and jewelry from the Gay Nineties to the Scintillating '70s, is offered for either purchase or rental. *Closed Sun.*

Eclectic **AstroTurf** (290 Smith St., between Union and Sackett Sts., Brooklyn, tel. 718/522–6182). A hearty supply of authentic '50s kitsch.

Kitschen (380 Bleecker St., between Charles and Perry Sts., tel. 212/727–0430). Vintage kitchenware, from the scary to the sublime, allows you to re-create the kitchen of your childhood.

Mood Indigo (181 Prince St., between Sullivan and Thompson Sts., tel. 212/254–1176). A crammed, friendly shop for all kinds of early 20th-century delights, from cocktail shakers and Fiestaware to vintage cigarette lighters, Bakelite jewelry, and 1939 World's Fair memorabilia.

orio-trio (248 Elizabeth St., between Prince and Houston Sts., tel. 212/219–1501). A carefully chosen and attractively displayed mix of home and kitchen items from the '20s through the '70s, some from China.

Susan P. Meisel (141 Prince St., between Greene and Wooster Sts., tel. 212/254–0137). Starring here are model ships and yachts of all sizes, plus wristwatches, furniture, and Deco-era ephemera.

Fun Stuff **Back Pages Antiques** (125 Greene St., between Prince and Houston Sts., tel. 212/460–5998). When you finally decide that you *need* that antique jukebox or slot machine, this is the place to go.

Second Childhood (283 Bleecker St., between 6th and 7th Aves., tel. 212/989–6140). For more than 25 years, it's been a source of mechanical banks, vintage dolls, wind-up and cast-iron toys, and Lilliputian battalions of European and American metal soldiers made between the 1900s and 1960s.

Furniture **Brian Windsor Art, Antiques and Garden Furnishings** (281 Lafayette St., between Houston and Prince Sts., tel. 212/274–0411). Wit and smart design predominate in this shop's stock of furniture, naive paintings, and American folk art. Look for 19th- and 20th-century garden pieces and other one-of-a-kinds.

c.i.t.e (100 Wooster St., near Spring St., tel. 212/431–7272). There's no telling what you'll find amid this mix of old and new, kitsch, odd, and genuine, but count on metal cabinets and containers, some gleaming, some rusty, plus handsome wood furniture from Indonesia.

Elan Antiques (345 Lafayette St., between Bond and Bleecker Sts., tel. 212/529–2724). This celebration of 20th-century design ranges from Mission to Moderne in furniture and decorative pieces.

Golden Oldies (132-29 33rd Ave., Flushing, near Shea Stadium and LaGuardia Airport, tel. 718/445–4400). It's worth the trek out here for the astonishing array of furniture—some antique, some vintage, some reproduction, some made in the decades just before and after World War II—scattered throughout a 65,000-square-foot warehouse.

Greene Street Antiques (65 Greene, between Spring and Broome Sts., tel. 212/274–1076). A well-chosen collection that runs from homey 19th-century Scandinavian to refined Art Deco, Art Nouveau, and Jugendstil pieces.

Jacques Carcanagues, Inc. (106 Spring St., at Mercer St., tel. 212/925–8110). A lovely open space filled with furniture and other wonders from India, Korea, the Philippines, and other distant lands.

John Koch Antiques (514 W. 24th St., between 10th and 11th Aves., 3rd floor, tel. 212/243–8625). Skylights here illuminate 4,000 square feet of usable antiques—many from estates.

Kentucky 7 (45 E. 7th St., tel. 212/533–0622). When you walk into this small space filled with rural american antiques arranged just so, you may want to take the entire stock, as is. For small pocketbooks, you'll surely find something you must (and can) have.

Peter Roberts Antiques (134 Spring St., between Wooster and Greene Sts., tel. 212/226–4777). Stickley and other luminaries of the American Arts and Crafts movement are well represented here.

Sarajo (98 Prince St., at Mercer St., tel. 212/966–6156). Eye-catching imports, from India and adjacent lands, include furniture, tribal art, and textiles.

Susan Parrish Antiques (390 Bleecker St., between Perry and W. 11th Sts., tel. 212/645–5020). The eponymous Susan Parrish has a great eye for quilts, folk art, and yellow ware from days of yore.

Wooster Gallery (86 Wooster St., between Spring and Broome Sts., tel. 212/219–2190). Sleek 20th-century furniture, emphasizing richly styled items from the '20s, '30s, and '40s.

Malls **Chelsea Antiques Building** (110 W. 25th St., between 6th and 7th Aves., tel. 212/929–0909). Kitsch, such as cookie jars, funky costume jewelry, and weird lamps like Aunt Clara had abounds, but there are real collectibles too—antique toys, old postcards, turn-of-the-century pottery and Oriental objets d'art.

Manhattan Art & Antiques Center (1050 2nd Ave., between 55th and 56th Sts., tel. 212/355–4400). More than 100 dealers, including some of the city's most amusing, are crammed onto three floors. The level of quality is not, as a rule, up to that of Madison Avenue, but then neither are the prices.

Posters and Prints **Pageant Book & Print Shop** (114 W. Houston St., between Thompson and Sullivan Sts., tel. 212/674–5296). A large selection of old prints, anatomical, botanical, and cartographical, can be found here at reasonable prices.

Philip Williams (80 Grand St., between W. Broadway and Wooster St., tel. 212/226–7830). A ramshackle treasure trove of posters from the turn of the century on, covering a huge range of subjects, including the circus, French and Italian film, food, travel, and magic.

Poster America (138 W. 18th St., between 6th and 7th Aves., tel. 212/206–0499). This shop—the oldest in the country devoted to this field—celebrates posters made here and abroad from late Victorian times to the mid-20th century. The movies, travel abroad, and the two world wars are a few of the poster themes. *Closed on Sundays during July and August.*

Art Supplies **Charrette** (215 Lexington Ave., at 33rd St., tel. 212/683–1401). For drafting supplies and other essentials for architects, engineers, and graphic artists, this is a great supermarket.

Lee's Art Shop (220 W. 57th St., tel. 212/247–0110). Uptown, this is the art-supply source. Framing is also available.

New York Central Art Supply (62 3rd Ave., at 11th St., tel. 212/473–7705). This excellent, full service art store, is distinguished by its upstairs room featuring origami paper, handmade paper from all over the world, and one-of-a-kind artist-made paper, all at reasonable prices. *Closed Sun.*

Pearl Paint (308 Canal St., between Church St. and Broadway, tel. 212/431–7932). A good art supply store has everything you need; a great one has things you never knew you needed, but suddenly can't live without. Pearl is massive, and most items are discounted, to boot.

Sam Flax (12 W. 20th St., tel. 212/620–3038; 425 Park Ave., at 55th St., tel. 212/620–3060). A wide range of high-end supplies, office furniture, drafting tables, and materials, and a custom framing department satisfy artists and those looking to jazz up home or office. *Park Ave. store closed Sun.*

Beads **Beads of Paradise** (16 E. 17th St., tel. 212/620–0642). Beads, amulets, charms, necklaces, and folk art from all over Africa make this a fascinating store. The friendly staff will string your bead purchases for you.

Margola Corp. (48 W. 37th St., tel. 212/564–9180). Austrian crystal in all sizes and colors, plus a wealth of beads of all types, from tacky to lovely. *Closed Sun.*

Books In addition to the stores mentioned below, the gift stores of museums are an excellent source for books on design, art, urban design, architecture, and all things visual. *See* Museum Shops *below*.

Architecture **Archivia** (944 Madison Ave., between 74th and 75th Sts., tel. 212/439–9194). An appropriately dignified place run by knowledgeable people, this store specializes in books published here and abroad that cover architecture, the decorative arts, and gardening.

Perimeter (146 Sullivan St., between Prince and Houston Sts., tel. 212/529–2275). The books here address the place where architecture and style meet. There's lots of European imports and the perfect gift for the urban aesthete on your list. *Closed Sun.*

Biography **Biography Bookshop** (400 Bleecker St., at 11th St., tel. 212/807–8655). This tidy, well-organized store stocks all manner of biographical material, including diaries and letters, from both major and minor publishers here and overseas.

Cookbooks **Kitchen Arts and Letters** (1435 Lexington Ave., between 93rd and 94th Sts., tel. 212/876–5550). For cooks, a small patch of heaven: owner Nach Waxman shares his wealth of knowledge with all who seek it. *Closed Sun.*

Gay and **A Different Light Bookstore** (151 W. 19th St., 212/989–4850). Lots
Lesbian and lots of books by, for, and about gays and lesbians. Late hours (till midnight every day), free readings and film series, and a small café expand the offerings.

Oscar Wilde Bookshop (15 Christopher St., between 6th and 7th Aves., tel. 212/255–8097). The oldest gay and lesbian book store in New York City—possibly in the world—carries a large selection of titles, including rare and out-of-print works.

General- **Barnes & Noble** (2289 Broadway, at 82nd St., tel. 212/362–8835; 675
Interest 6th Ave., between 21st and 22nd Sts., tel. 212/727–1227; 4 Astor Pl., east of Broadway, tel. 212/420–1322; 160 E. 54th, at 3rd Ave., in Citicorp Center, tel. 212/750–8033; 33 E. 17th St., tel. 212/253–0810; 1972 Broadway, at 68th St., tel. 212/595–6859; 600 5th Ave., at 48th St., tel. 212/765–0590; 1280 Lexington, between 86th and 87th Sts., tel. 212/423–9900). One of the world's largest book sellers has over a dozen branches in Manhattan. These are its superstores, carrying anywhere from 60,000 to 150,000 individual titles and a wide selection of periodicals on all topics, equipped with cushy sofas and Mission-style chairs and tables for leisurely reading. You can also peruse the wares at the pleasant (though often crowded) in-store cafés. The former main Manhattan store at 5th Avenue and 18th Street (tel. 212/807–0099) carries general works and buys and sells college texts and technical books.

Borders Books and Music (5 World Trade Center, tel. 212/839–8049). CDs, CD-ROMS, daily papers from the rest of the global village, a cafe, a grand schedule of readings and signings, the now obligatory easy chairs, and, yes, books, can be found in the first NYC branch of a midwest-based chain.

Coliseum Books (1771 Broadway, at 57th St., tel. 212/757–8381). A big, barn-like space, filled with an extensive stock, plus a great selection of remaindered titles.

The Corner Bookstore (1313 Madison Ave., at 93rd St., tel. 212/831–3554). A small, friendly bookstore with a knowledgable staff who are especially gifted at suggesting the perfect children's book. The selection of art and design books is excellent, and water and appropriate snacks are kept on hand for visiting dogs.

Crawford Doyle Booksellers (1082 Madison Ave., between 81st and 82nd Sts., tel. 212/288–6300). In the same space (though renovated and more navigable) and with some of the same staff as the old Burlington Books, this is a friendly place with a fine stock.

The Lenox Hill Bookstore (1018 Lexington Ave., at 73rd. St., tel. 212/472–7170). An offshoot of the uptown Corner Bookstore, this small, attractive store has an equally intelligent and inviting selection.

Madison Avenue Bookshop (833 Madison Ave., between 69th and 70th St., tel. 212/535–6130). Posh and a little clubby, the store contains a great many books in a small, well-designed space. *Closed Sun.*

Posman Books (1 University Pl., at Washington Sq., tel. 212/533–2665; 2955 Broadway, between 115th and 116th Sts., tel. 212/961–1527). Solid bookstores for dedicated readers, they feature a good selection of university-press books.

Rizzoli (31 W. 57th St., tel. 212/759–2424; 454 W. Broadway, between Houston and Prince Sts., tel. 212/674–1616; World Financial Center, tel. 212/385–1400). Once a piano showroom, the West Broadway store's Wedgwood-style ceiling is beautiful and seems to cast reflected glory onto the celebrated stock of international books on art, architecture, dance, and design, plus foreign publications and fiction.

St. Mark's Bookshop (31 3rd Ave., at 9th St., tel. 212/260–7853). Larger quarters make this Village standby easier to browse. Wide-ranging collection includes sections on cinema, anarchism, and nature/ecology, along with more standard fare and a discount table in the back.

Shakespeare & Co. (939 Lexington Ave., between 68th and 69th Sts., tel. 212/570–0201; 716 Broadway, at Washington Pl., tel. 212/529–1330). Current books, especially fiction and poetry, sold by a knowledgeable staff.

Spring Street Books (169 Spring St., between Thompson St. and W. Broadway, tel. 212/219–3033). Lots of periodicals and remaindered books, strong on art, style, and other appropriately SoHo-esque topics.

Three Lives & Co. (154 W. 10th St., tel. 212/741–2069). This cozy neighborhood bookshop illuminated by green-shaded reading lamps has a friendly staff and an excellent selection of books on gardening, design, art, gay and lesbian themes, mystery, plus city living.

Tower Books (383 Lafayette St., at 4th St., tel. 212/228–5100). A veritable supermarket of books (travel, music, and offbeat fiction are strong) upstairs and a great selection of magazines, both mainstream and not, downstairs.

Japanese **Kinokuniya Bookstore** (10 W. 49th St., tel. 212/765–7766). Even if you don't read Japanese, there's something for you here if you're interested in Zen Buddhism, Japanese culture, food, or business, or just looking for origami paper or groovy school supplies.

Mystery/ Suspense **Murder Ink** (1467 2nd Ave., bewteen 76th and 77th Sts., tel. 212/517–3222; 2486 Broadway, between 92nd and 93rd Sts., tel. 212/362–8905). The first store anywhere dedicated only to mysteries now has two branches, both packed with new, used, and rare mysteries.

Mysterious Bookshop (129 W. 56th St., tel. 212/765–0900). This store covers all things mysterious and criminal, with new, used, and rare books, including many first editions. *Closed Sun.*

Partners & Crime (44 Greenwich Ave., between W. 10th and 11th Sts., tel. 212/243–0440). Along with new, rare, and out-of-print books, this store also has a rental library, a resident troupe that performs old radio dramas, and a meeting room for crime afficionados. Check out the haunted fireplace.

Photography **Photographer's Place** (133 Mercer St., between Prince and Spring Sts., tel. 212/431–9358). This shop is an inspiration to amateur and professional picture-takers with its fine selection of current and out-of-print books devoted to great photographers. The **International Center of Photography bookstore** (*see* Museum Shops, *below*) is also good.

Revolutionary **Pathfinder Books** (214–16 Ave. A, between 13th and 14th Sts., tel. 212/328–1501; 167 Charles St., near West St., tel. 212/366–1973; 59 4th Ave., at Bergen St., in Brooklyn tel. 718/399–7257). Books by every manner of revolutionary, including Che Guevara, Castro, Malcolm X, Marx, Engles, and Rosa Luxemburg, among many others.

Science Fiction **Forbidden Planet** (840 Broadway, at 13th St., tel. 212/473–1576). It's a sci-fi haunt, a bastion of fantasy, horror, true crime, and comics. **Science Fiction Shop** (214 Sullivan St., between Bleecker and 3rd Sts., tel. 212/473–3010). This sci-fi specialist carries current and out-of-print titles.

Theater/Film **Applause Theatre Books** (211 W. 71st St., tel. 212/496–7511). Film and theater scripts, collections of reviews, biographies, and how-to books for the actor are among the works cramming the shelves of this roomy store devoted to the dramatic arts.
Drama Book Shop (723 7th Ave., between 48th and 49th Sts., 2nd floor, tel. 212/944–0595). One of the most comprehensive collection of scripts, scores, libretti, and theater crafts (outside of the Lincoln Center Library) can be found at this shop established in 1921 by the New York Drama League.

Travel **The Civilized Traveller** (2003 Broadway, at 68th St., tel. 212/875–8809; 2 World Financial Center, at the Wintergarden, tel. 212/786–3301). Travel books and accouterments, plus a house travel agent.
Complete Traveller Bookstore (199 Madison Ave., at 35th St., tel. 212/685–9007). The stock includes current and historic titles.
Rand McNally (150 E. 52nd St., between Lexington and 3rd Aves., tel. 212/758–7488). A solid selection of travel books is complemented by an array of detailed maps and other useful travel paraphernalia.
Traveller's Bookstore (Time-Warner Bldg., 22 W. 52nd St., between 5th and 6th Aves., tel. 212/664–0995). It's a local favorite. On weekends use entrance on the 51st Street side of building.

Used Books **Books and Bindings** (33 W. 17th St., tel. 212/229-0004). The newest addition to a neighborhood beloved by used book cogniscenti, this spacious store offers new, used, and out-of-print books and will repair or rebind your tattered treasures. Don't miss old standbys **Academy Book Store** (10 W. 18th St., tel. 212/242–4848), which has a broad range of books, records and CDs, especially classical and operatic music, and **Skyline Books and Records** (13 W. 18th St., tel. 212/759–5463), where you can get serious fiction and literary criticism, along with Jethro Tull's *Aqualung*, on vinyl.

Book Ark (173 W. 81 St., tel. 212/787–3914). Offering a wide variety of quality used books (think Didion, not Collins), the store is strong in art, drama, and foreign language titles.
Bookleaves (304 W. 4th St., off Bank St., tel. 212/924–5638). Interesting books in perfect condition can be found at this quiet store run by a booklover for booklovers.
Gotham Book Mart (41 W. 47th St., tel. 212/719–4448). This is one of those places that make New York so neat. New books mingle here with a good selection of used books. The Gotham has an astonishing history as the bookstore of choice for hordes of famous writers, and it's the one place in town where you can get all the Edward Gorey you need, often autographed. *Closed Sun.*
Strand (828 Broadway, at 12th St., tel. 212/473–1452; 95 Fulton St.,

between William and Gold Sts., tel. 212/732–6070). Eight miles of shelves house a million-plus books of all types at the main store, and the downtown store is no slouch either.

Fabric **B & J Fabrics** (263 W. 40th St., between 7th and 8th Aves., tel. 212/354–8150). With three floors of fabrics of all types, this store anchors a strip that should meet any fabricholic's needs—more than twelve stores in one block. (Plan to go on Saturday, as most are closed Sundays.)

Beckenstein Home Fabrics (130 Orchard St., off Delancey St., tel. 212/475–4525; closed Sat.) and **Long Island Fabrics** (406 Broadway, between Canal and Walker Sts., tel. 212/431–9510) both offer huge selections, not far from the city's leading zipper specialist, **Feibusch** (30 Allen St., between Canal and Hester Sts., tel 212/226–3964; closed Sat.). Equally important in this neighborhood is **Harry Zarin Co.** (72 Allen St., at the corner of Grand, tel. 212/966–0310), which claims it has the largest selection of upholstery fabrics in the world.

Handloom Batik (214 Mulberry St., near Spring St., tel. 212/925–9542). Batik fabric sold by the American branch of a family that has produced the cloth in India for seven generations. You can also get Indonesian Ikat fabric at this friendly store. Summer hours vary, so call.

Paron Fabrics (56 W. 57th St., tel. 212/247–6451) and **Paron II** upstairs, where already nice prices are chopped in half, have sumptuous fabric offerings, particularly silks. Neighboring **Weller Fabrics** (24 W. 57th St., tel. 212/247–3790) has an astonishing array of imported lace, while **Greenberg and Hammer** (24 W. 57th St., tel. 212/246–2835), though tiny, seems to have every kind of notion and needle a serious dressmaker might need, and **Tender Buttons** (143 E. 62nd St., tel. 212/758–7004) offers old and new buttons made of linen, velvet, shell, wood, horn, mother-of-pearl, soutache, among other substances, and hailing from Nepal, England, Italy, and Bali. *All stores closed Sun.*

Quilters can find cotton fabric, quilting notions, and information on classes at the **Gazebo** (114 E. 57th St., tel. 212/832–7077) and **Sew Brooklyn** (228 7th Ave., between 3rd and 4th Sts., Brooklyn, tel. 718/499–7383).

Florists **Fellan Company, Inc.** (1040 3rd. Ave., between 61st and 62nd Sts., tel. 212/421–3567). OK, the flowers in the windows are fake, but the ones in the store are real, beautiful, and long-lasting, with a great selection of orchids and flowering plants. *Closed Sun.*
Spring St. Garden (186½ Spring St., between Sullivan and Thompson Sts., tel. 212/966–2015). Depressed by too many generic florists? Drop by this tiny moss-filled store for an unusual and lovely arrangement. *Closed Sun.*
VSF (204 W. 10th St., between Bleecker and W. 10th Sts., tel. 212/206–7236). Gorgeous, painterly arrangements can be found here, and though they don't come cheap, there's a lot of floral bang for the buck. *Closed Sun.*

Fragrance and **Aveda Aromatherapy Esthetique** (456 W. Broadway, between Hous-
Makeup ton and Prince Sts., tel. 212/473–0280; 233 Spring St., between 6th Ave. and Varick St., tel. 212/807–1492). Emphasizing botanical essences and modern clinical research, these sleek shops offer light herbal compounds for face, hair, and body. The spas provide facials, body-waxing, hair-cutting, and scalp massage designed to beautify and relieve stress (and your wallet).
Bath Island (469 Amsterdam Ave., between 82nd and 83rd Sts., tel. 212/787–9415). This store, which perfumes the whole block, offers everything for your ablutions, from fragrances, unguents, oils, and powders to floating sponge animals and kid-pleasing tooth brushes.
Caswell-Massey (South Street Seaport, tel. 212/608–5401; 2 World

Financial Center, upper level, tel. 212/945–2630; 155 Spring St., between W. Broadway and Wooster St., tel. 212/219–3661). This is the place to come for sweet-smelling soaps, powders, perfumes, creams, sachets, and oils in soothing Old World packaging.

Crabtree & Evelyn (520 Madison Ave., between 53rd and 54th Sts., tel. 212/758–6419; 620 5th Ave., at 50th St., tel. 212/581–5022; 1310 Madison Ave., at 93rd St., tel. 212/289–3923). The pastel boxes for sale here, delicately inscribed with flowers and fruits and filled with sweetly scented toiletries, make fine presents for friends or yourself.

FACE Stockholm (224 Columbus Ave., between 70th and 71st Sts., tel. 212/769–1420; 110 Prince St., at Greene St., tel. 212/334–3900). Now in New York, this austere Swedish maker offers an extensive line of makeup.

Floris of London (703 Madison Ave., between 62nd and 63rd Sts., tel. 212/935–9100). This store boasts two appointments to the Royal Family (for fragrances and toilet preparations) and a nice selection of floral scents. Mainly for women, but "89" for men merits a sniff. *Closed Sun.*

I Natural (430 W. Broadway, between Spring and Prince Sts., tel. 212/965–1002). You can experiment with colors and shades on your own, or a nice lady, cotton ball in hand, will help you select the right cosmetics, fragrance, or skincare product.

Kiehl's Since 1851 (109 3rd Ave., at 13th St., tel. 212/677–3171). This family-owned spot provides an earthy, good-for-you line of makeup and skin-care products and 100+ essential oils, all plainly labelled, that exude a certain generic chic. *Closed Sun.*

M.A.C (113 Spring St., between Greene and Mercer Sts., tel. 212/334–4641; 14 Christopher St., between 6th and 7th Aves., tel. 212/243–4150). Whether you prefer shear, matte, or gloss lipsticks, face powders, or nail polish, this righteously activist establishment line will color you right.

Fun and Whimsy
B. Shackman & Co. (85 5th Ave., at 16th St., tel. 212/989–5162). Specializing in reproductions of Victorian cards and toys, this store will make you a hero to small children and to adults who crave some old-fashioned whimsy.

Evolution (120 Spring St., between Greene and Mercer Sts., tel. 212/343–1114) and **Maxilla and Mandible** (451 Columbus Ave., between 81st and 82nd Sts., tel. 212/724–6173). Two stores that offer uptowners and downtowners a chance to enjoy the natural world in all its splendor and oddity, from fossil fish to chinchilla, warthog and human skulls, mounted butterflies, shells, even glass eyes for taxidermy.

Little Rickie (49½ 1st Ave., at 3rd St., tel. 212/505–6467). A mind-boggling selection including glow-in-the-dark religious shrines, extensive Elvis paraphernalia, astronaut ice cream, holograms, and, of course, Silly Putty.

Love Saves the Day (119 2nd Ave., at 7th St., tel. 212/228–3802). If you're looking for G.I. Joe, or if you just want to dress like Malibu Barbie, stop by and appreciate how incredibly cheesy the '70s really were. The overflowing racks of clothes and the novelties from the Me Decade are astonishing.

Next Stop South Pole (Pier 17, South Street Seaport, tel. 212/962–2022). One-stop shopping for the penguin enthusiast: from mugs to videos.

Pandora's Box (Prince St., between W. Broadway and Thompson St., tel. 212/505–7615). You can't move in here for the plaster cherubs, griffins, Nefertitis, Corinthian columns, and many, many Elvises.

Star Magic (745 Broadway, between 8th St. and Astor Pl., tel. 212/228–7770; 275 Amsterdam Ave., at 73rd St., tel. 212/769–2020; 1256 Lexington Ave., between 84th and 85th Sts., tel. 212/988–0300). Astronomy and New Age meet here in a cosmic swirl of kaleidoscopes, crystals, stars, spaceships, and other gadgets—all accompanied by ambient music.

Games **Compleat Strategist** (342 W. 57th St., tel. 212/582–1272). Sci-fi, fantasy, mystery, military strategy, adventure, and many other games are sold here.

Game Show (474 6th Ave., between 11th and 12th Sts., tel. 212/633–6328; 1240 Lexington Ave., between 83rd and 84th Sts, tel. 212/472–8011). Board games for kids and adults in every imaginable variation.

Village Chess Shop (230 Thompson St., between Bleecker and 3rd Sts., tel. 212/475–9580). You'll find chessboards and pieces in ivory, wood, stone, pewter, brass, onyx, and marble—not to mention a crowd of chess fanatics who play here for hours.

Home Furnishings
Carpets/Rugs

ABC Carpet & Home (888 and 881 Broadway, at 19th St., tel. 212/473–3000). If it's woven and made to cover a floor, you'll probably find it here. (*see* Department Stores, *above*).

Central Carpet (426 Columbus Ave., at 81st St., tel. 212/787–8813; 81 8th Ave., at 14th St., tel. 212/741–3700). These two West Side stores feature discounted dhurries, hooked and contemporary rugs, Belgian-made Orientals, Chinese Art Deco, and more, all showcased by knowledgable employees.

Einstein Moomjy (150 E. 58th St., tel. 212/758–0900). One of New York's major sources for carpets, with a stock of broadlooms, dhurries and Orientals, and a good assortment of one-of-a-kinds.

Kalfaian & Son (475 Atlantic Ave., between Nevins St. and 3rd Ave., Brooklyn, tel. 718/875–2222). Serious rug-buyers count on Kalfaian for a good selection—and for Brooklyn prices on old Orientals.

Rug Warehouse (220 W. 80th St., between Broadway and Amsterdam Ave., tel. 212/787–6665). Antique Orientals are attractively priced at this West Side favorite.

China **Fish's Eddy** (889 Broadway, at 19th St., tel. 212/420–9020; 2176 Broadway, at 77th St., tel. 212/873–8819). Durable, industrial china made for hotels, restaurants, and clubs, along with charming, sturdy pieces made especially for the store, can be found here.

Lanac Sales (73 Canal St., at Allen St., tel. 212/925–7040) and **Goldman's Treasures** (655 6th Ave., at 20th St., tel. 212/924–4900) both discount major brands, such as Lenox, Noritake, Royal Doulton, and Stuart. What they don't have, Goldman's will special order for you at a 35% discount. *Closed Sat.*

Culinary Items **Bridge Kitchenware Corp.** (214 E. 52nd St., between 2nd and 3rd Aves., tel. 212/688–4220). Dust abounds, but so does every type of cookware and utensil in this store beloved by Julia Child and other chefs both home and professional. *Closed Sun.*

Broadway, Panhandler (477 Broome St., at Wooster St., tel. 212/966–3434). This is one of the city's premier pot, knife, and cookware shops.

Cathay Hardware Corporation (49 Mott St., between Mott and Mulberry Sts., tel. 212/962–6648). The store specializes in Chinese products.

Lechter's Housewares (1198 3rd Ave., at 69th St., tel. 212/744–1427; 55 E. 8th St., tel. 212/505–0576; 2151 Broadway, at 75th St., tel. 212/580–1610; 2503 Broadway, at 93rd St., tel. 212/864–5464; Manhattan Mall, 6th floor, tel. 212/268–7303; 250 W. 57th St., at Broadway, tel, 212/956–7290; and other locations). This housewares store offers pots, pans, tea pots, magnets, and most other kitchen basics at terrestrial prices.

New York Cake and Baking Supplies (56 W. 22nd St., tel. 212/675–2253). Everything for serious bakers, or anyone who, in a rash moment, volunteered to bake a wedding cake, complete with sugar flowers, multiple tiers, bride and groom, and frilled cake trays.

Williams-Sonoma (20 E. 60th St., tel. 212/980–5155; 1175 Madison at

86th St., tel. 212/289–6832; 110 7th Ave., at 17th St., tel. 212/633–2203; 1309 2nd Ave., at 69th St., tel. 212/288–8408). The retail outlets of the famous mail-order catalogue house have stylish cooking equipment, tabletop items, and a house brand of packaged foods like vinegar and spaghetti sauces.

Decorative Objects and Household Items

Adrien Linford (1320 Madison Ave., between 93rd and 94th Sts., tel. 212/289–4427; 927 Madison Ave., at 74th St., tel. 212/628–4500). In a pleasant setting, you'll find picture frames, serving pieces, ceramic objects, photo albums, candles, and other delicate items to add small accents in your house.

Alphabets (47 Greenwich Ave., between Perry and Charles Sts., tel. 212/229–2966; 115 Ave. A, between 7th and 8th Sts., tel. 212/475–7250; 2284 Broadway, between 82nd and 83rd Sts., tel. 212/579–5702). Great cards, sleek picture frames, luminescent Japanese tea cups, magnets, and all sorts of things you'll want once you see them. The perfect place to shop for affordable, unusual gifts.

Avventura (463 Amsterdam Ave., between 83rd and 84th Sts., tel. 212/769–2510). Fine glass and tableware for people who want to create an eye-catching and luxurious look. *Closed Sat.*

Bazaar Sabado (54 Greene St., at Broome St., tel. 212/941–6152). To add a Latin or Southwestern vibe to your home, browse through the Mexican, Peruvian, Guatemalan, and Santa Fe creations at this bright downtown shop. There are small one-of-a-kind pottery pieces and dazzling patchwork bedspreads.

The Clay Pot (162 7th Ave., between Garfield and 1st Sts., Brooklyn, tel. 718/788–6564). Everything here, from ceramics to scarves, earrings, and a huge selection of wedding rings, is handmade.

Craft Caravan Inc. (63 Greene St., between Spring and Broome Sts., tel. 212/431–6669). Contemporary African handicrafts such as textiles, barber shop posters, as well as decorative and functional objects made from tin cans, provide a glimpse of the vibrant African craft scene.

Felissimo (10 W. 56th St., tel. 212/247–5656). A Japanese-inflected store that offers lovely items for home and garden. Housed in a beautifully renovated turn-of-the-century townhouse, the New Age music, the sound of water everywhere, and the pretty tearoom, make this a serene shopping experience. *Closed Sun.*

Galileo (37 7th Ave., at 13th St., tel. 243–1629). Anywhere you look in this store, your eye will light on something beautiful. All you have to do is decide whether you need a vase, frame, leather box, etched glassware, or a woven straw hatbox.

Gracious Home (1217 and 1220 3rd Ave., between 70th and 71st Sts., tel. 212/517–6300). This may be the ultimate New York housewares store, with a range of products from ironing boards and dish drainers to decorative drawer pulls, glassware, and other, more design-conscious products.

Katagiri (224 E. 59th St., tel. 212/838–5453. This small shop has lovely Japanese imports, such as ceramics and some surprisingly efficient housewares.

Leo Design (413 Bleecker St., between W. 11th and Bank Sts., tel. 212/929–8466). Vintage pottery, antiquated prints in modern frames, extravagant chandeliers, and friendly employees to explain it all.

Mackenzie-Childs, Ltd. (824 Madison Ave., at 69th St., tel. 212/570–6050). Although it may be too precious for some, this store features its own line of pretty enamel tableware. Stop by just to visit the store chicken, who, though not free-range, seems quite happy. *Closed Sun.*

Mxyplyzyk (125 Greenwich Ave., between Jane and 13th Sts., tel. 212/989–4300). This store's goods are more streamlined than it's name. The emphasis is on clean, functional contemporary design in unexpected materials: wooden bud vases, tricycles of bright silver aluminum, and cardboard-and-steel filing cases.

Pottery Barn (117 E. 59th St., tel. 212/753–5424; 1965 Broadway, at

67th St., tel. 212/579–8477; 250 W. 57th St., tel. 212/315–1855; 600 Broadway, at Houston St., tel. 212/219–2420; 231 10th Ave., between 23rd and 24th Sts., tel. 212/206–8118; and other locations). Still dependable for basic tablewares, it now offers items for the whole house. Overstocks sell at cut prices at the 10th Avenue location.

Pull Cart (31 W. 21st St., between 5th and 6th Aves., tel. 212/727–7089). At this seventh floor atelier you actually make your own ceramics. You buy plain white ware, pay $6 per hour to paint it—there are books and picture files at hand—have it glazed and fired, and *voilà*—unique, inexpensive, custom-designed tableware.

Sam's Souk (979 Lexington Ave., at 70th St., tel. 212/535–7210; 321½ Bleecker St., between Christopher and Grove Sts., tel. 212/691–0726). Two tiny shops jam-packed with all manner of (mostly) Moroccan objects. Traditional painted glasses are especially lovely, and be sure to look up to see the hanging lanterns. *Uptown store closed Sun.*

Sara (952 Lexington Ave., between 69th and 70th Sts., tel. 212/772–3243). Pottery from Japan: some utilitarian, some decorative, all beautiful. Colors range from white to crackle-glazed greens that are almost luminous. *Closed Sun.*

Simon Pearce (120 Wooster St., between Prince and Spring Sts., tel. 212/334–2393; 500 Park Ave., at 59th St., tel. 212/421–8801). Ireland-born-and-trained Simon Pearce now works in Vermont, making sturdy glassware, wood bowls, and best of all, crackle-glazed celadon bowls, vases, and platters for this SoHo store.

Wolfman-Gold & Good Company (117 Mercer St., between Prince and Spring Sts., tel. 212/431–1888). Half antique and half contemporary in spirit, this chic SoHo shop always has something festive for the holiday table.

Zona (97 Greene St., between Prince and Spring Sts., tel. 212/925–6750). This airy, high-ceilinged store remains SoHo's bastion of the Southwestern look, with New Age music, bells, terra-cotta, woven wall hangings, expensive leather furniture and smaller items, all with the now-entrenched nouvelle farmhouse aesthetic.

Furniture/
Bedding

Boca Grande (66 Greene St., between Spring and Broome Sts., tel. 212/334–6120; 89 Spring St., tel. 212/966–7716). Furniture from all over the world, with some real beauties from India and Indonesia. Smaller items and bric-a-brac can be found at the Spring Street location.

Castro Convertibles (43 W. 23rd St., tel. 212/255–7000; 51 E. 34th St., tel. 212/679–6099; 1100 2nd Ave., between 57th and 58th Sts., tel. 212/421–8100). This old standby has sofabeds in spades.

Charles P. Rogers (899 1st Ave., between 50th and 51st Sts., tel. 212/935–6900). High-quality brass beds in traditional and contemporary styles are sold here.

Classic Sofa (5 W. 22nd St., tel. 212/620–0485). Classic styles abound, many with down cushions, and all made in New York.

Door Store (1 Park Ave., at 33rd St., tel. 212/679–9700; 1201 3rd Ave., between 69th and 70th Sts., tel. 212/772–1110; 123 W. 17th St., tel. 212/627–1515; 599 Lexington Ave., at 53rd St., tel. 212/832–7500; 134 Washington St., at Cedar St., tel. 212/267–1250). The specialty here is contemporary furniture at affordable prices.

E.J. Audi (160 5th Ave., at 21st St., tel. 212/337–0700). Several well-known lines are featured here, including Stickley Mission-style furniture and the James River Collection of 18th-century-style chairs and tables.

Jensen-Lewis (89 7th Ave., at 15th St., tel. 212/929–4880). The contemporary comfortable look comes with a gentle price tag here.

Knoll (105 Wooster St., between Prince and Spring Sts., tel. 212/343–4000). Come here for furniture made to the specifications of the masters such as Marcel Breuer and Mies van der Rohe.

Maurice Villency (200 Madison Ave., at 35th St., tel. 212/725–4840).

This store stocks expensive contemporary furniture, including up-holstered leather pieces.

Pompanoosuc Mills (470 Broome St., at Greene St., tel. 212/226–5960). Made in Vermont, these beds, armoires, dressers, tables, and chairs have simple, clean lines and are available in a variety of woods.

Portico Home (379 W. Broadway, between Spring and Broome Sts., tel. 212/941–7800). Updated, glossy yet comfortable versions of classic furniture, most produced by small, independent makers, are available here.

Scott Jordan Furniture (137 Varick St., at Spring St., tel. 212/620–4682). Smooth wood furniture, mostly cherry, and mostly made in Brooklyn and Vermont in Mission, Shaker, and other clean-lined styles are sold here at this large airy showroom.

Lighting **Just Shades** (21 Spring St., at Elizabeth St., tel. 212/966–2757). You have a choice here of 5,000 lampshades in dozens of different styles, and you can also custom order.

Lightforms (509 Amsterdam Ave., between 84th and 85th Sts., tel. 212/875–0407; 168 8th Ave., between 18th and 19th Sts., tel. 212/255–4664). Modern lamps and sconces in a variety of looks, from earthy to edgy.

Lighting by Gregory (158 Bowery at Delancey, tel. 212/226–1965). About a block's worth of discounted Lightolier products and a huge choice of track lighting.

Oriental Lamp Shade Co. (223 W. 79th St., tel. 212/873–0812; 816 Lexington Ave., between 62nd and 63rd Sts., tel. 212/832–8190). Unique and custom lamp shades and bases for every taste. Plus, they'll rewire or mount a beloved relic. *Closed Sun.*

Linens **Ad Hoc Softwares** (410 W. Broadway, at Spring St., tel. 212/925–2652). This cheerful shop features European sheets, India-print duvet and pillow covers, contemporary shower curtains, thick towels, and accessories for the home.

April Cornell (487 Columbus Ave., between 83rd and 84th Sts., tel. 212/799–4342; 860 Lexington Ave., between 64th and 65th Sts., tel. 212/570–2775). Formerly known as Handblock, these stores still offer richly decorated table linens and coverlets handprinted in India.

Eldridge Textile (277 Grand St., between Forsythe and Eldridge Sts., tel. 212/925–1523) and neighbor **Harris Levy** (278 Grand St., tel. 212/226–3102) offer selection and reduced prices on high-end linens. *Closed Sat.*

Laytner's Linen and Home (237 E. 86th St., between 2rd and 3nd Aves., tel. 212/996–4439; 2270 Broadway, near 82nd St., tel. 212/724–0180; 512 Broadway, between Broome and Spring Sts., tel. 212/965–9382). Laytner's has been around for years—but the selection of linen and good-looking furniture is kept so chic that you'd never know.

Pondicherri (454 Columbus Ave., at 82nd St., tel. 212/875–1609). A splashy spread of comfortably colorful duvet covers, table clothes, place mats, pillow cases.

Luggage **Altman** (135 Orchard St., between Delancey and Rivington Sts., tel. 212/254–7275). This shop discounts many major brands. *Closed Sat.*

Innovation Luggage (10 E. 34th St., tel. 212/684–8288; 300 E. 42nd St., tel. 212/599–2998; 1521 5th Ave., at 43rd St., tel. 212/986–4689; 1755 Broadway, between 56th and 57th Sts., tel. 212/582–2044; and other locations). Luggage of all shapes and sizes, including popular brands like Kiplinger and Hartman, is here.

Memorabilia and Themed Merchandise **The Ballet Company** (1887 Broadway, between 62nd and 63rd Sts., tel. 212/246–6893). Near Lincoln Center, this store carries programs, books, posters, videos, autographs, and T-shirts, for the balletomane.

Coca-Cola Fifth Avenue (711 5th Ave., between 55th and 56th Sts., tel. 212/418–9260). Imagine a store existing solely as variations on a logo: Some 600 items like radios, telephones, sweatshirts, toy trucks, and softballs all employ the magic words.

The Disney Store (711 5th Ave., at 55th St., tel. 212/702–0702; 147 Columbus Ave., at 66th St., tel. 212/362–2386; 39 W. 34h St., tel. 212/279–9890; 210 W. 42nd St., tel. 212/221–0430). The source for Disney characters on every possible object including t-shirts, mugs, sweat clothes, music boxes, and figurines.

Jerry Ohlinger's Movie Material Store (242 W. 14th St., tel. 212/989–0869). This shop specializes in posters and photos related to motion pictures from the Roaring '20s to the present, including many black-and-white stills.

Warner Bros. Studio Store (1 W. 57th St., at 5th Ave., tel. 212/754–0300). Nine stories of wildly interactive shopping madness. It all features Bugs Bunny, Porky Pig, and other Looney Tunesters and includes a 3-D theater, a light show, and wall-to-wall video screens.

Museum Shops These shops can all be enjoyed without paying museum admission.

American Museum of Natural History (Central Park West, at 79th St., tel. 212/769–5000). The spacious premises show off a collection of dinosaur models, crystals, handicrafts, nature books, and more.

Asia Society (725 Park Ave., at 70th St., tel. 212/288–6400). The selection of books on Asian art, traditions, and sacred places is excellent, and the Chinese tea pots, Balinese jewelry, and other crafts from the rest of the continent are carefully chosen.

The Brooklyn Museum (200 Eastern Pkwy., at Prospect Park, Brooklyn, tel. 718/638–5000). The museum's collection covers the world, and so does the shop, with Chinese batik, Mexican tin ornaments, Indian boxes, and a great selection of New York and Brooklynania. There's a separate store for kids, too. Midtowners can shop the small but charming branch at the Equitable Gallery (787 7th Ave., between 51st and 52nd Sts., tel. 212/554–4888).

Cathedral Church of St. John the Divine (Amsterdam Ave., at 112th St., tel. 212/222–7200). Unique to the spacious shop are handcut stone pieces made by artisans working on the still-uncompleted cathedral; the stock also includes books, toys, and cards.

The Cooper Shop at the Jewish Museum (1109 5th Ave at 92nd St., tel. 212/423–3211). An excellent source of Judaica, from books to games to artist-designed menorahs, mezzuzas, and other ritual items. *Closed Sat.*

Cooper-Hewitt National Design Museum (2 E. 91st St., tel. 212/860–6939). Always fabulous stock of design books, plus inspired arty objects and books related to the season or to current exhibits.

Guggenheim Museum Store (1071 5th Ave., at 88th St., tel. 212/423–3615; 575 Broadway, at Prince St., tel. 212/423–3875). Jewelry, decorative objects, scarves, books, T-shirts, posters, note cards, etc., are inspired by the museum's collection of modern art.

International Center of Photography (1130 5th Ave., at 94th St., tel. 212/860–1777; 1133 6th Ave., at 43rd St., tel. 212/768–4684). Browse here for excellent publications, posters, and postcards related to photography.

J. Pierpont Morgan Library (29 E. 36th St., tel. 212/685–0008). Art books are nestled among a selection of old-money objects including handsome desk items, Old Master reproduction drawings, facsimile editions of books and musical scores, and Morgan's own smoky-flavored tea.

The Library Shop at Mid-Manhattan (455 5th Ave., at 40th St., tel. 212/340–0839). A new venture for the library, this attractive store has books (about books, about New York, and for kids), plus great stationary and some original art inspired by the library's huge collection. The main branch at 42nd Street has a smaller store with different stock.

Metropolitan Museum of Art (5th Ave. at 82nd St., tel. 212/879–5500). Art lovers will appreciate the fine reproductions and the large selection of books. There are also well-stocked branches of the Metropolitan Museum shop at Rockefeller Center (15 W. 49th St., tel. 212/332–1360), on the Mezzanine at Macy's (34th St., between 6th and 7th Aves., tel. 212/268–7266), and in SoHo (113 Prince St., between Greene and Wooster Sts., tel. 212/614–3000).

Museum for African Art (593 Broadway, between Houston and Prince Sts., tel. 212/966–1313). A choice selection of traditional African handicrafts and contemporary artworks—jewelry, baskets, leather boxes, and textiles—as well as related books.

Museum of American Folk Art (2 Lincoln Sq., Columbus Ave. between 65th and 66th Sts., tel. 212/496–2966). The store carries clever cards, decoys, old-fashioned toys, and other pieces in the folk art tradition.

Museum of the City of New York (1220 5th Ave., at 103rd St., tel. 212/534–1672). Prints, posters, books, and toys that evoke old New York are crammed into this small shop.

Museum of Modern Art (11 W. 53rd St., tel. 212/708–9700). The stock features posters, books, reproductions from the collection, and thoroughly postmodern objects for the home. The overflow of high design items are across the street at the **Design Store** (44 W. 53rd St., tel. 212/767–1050), which has a trove of functional, but snazzily-designed, objects from housewares to watches and jewelry.

National Museum of the American Indian (1 Bowling Green, between Whitehall and State Sts., tel. 212/825–8093). The two shops here are a must for anyone interested in Native American crafts, history, or religious traditions, with books, jewelry, dolls, music, and more.

New York Transit Museum Gift Shop (Grand Central Terminal, Main Concourse, near 42nd and Park Ave., tel. 212/682–7572). The place for token cufflinks and earrings, histories of the transit system, and copies of those great Poetry-in-Motion subway posters. *Closed Sun.*

Studio Museum of Harlem (144 W. 125th St., between Lennox and 7th Aves., tel. 212/864–4500). The crafts on sale from Africa and black America range from trendy (Lucite pins) to magnificent (baskets from Botswana) to fun (dolls in 19th-century calico).

Whitney Museum of American Art Store Next Door (943 Madison Ave., at 75th St., tel. 212/606–0200). This small shop offers intriguing handmade jewelry, ceramics, wood boxes, and more.

Newspapers/ **Hotaling's** (142 W. 42nd St., between 6th Ave. and Broadway, tel.
Magazines 212/840–1868). Only New York could support a place like this, stocking just about every U.S. newspaper and magazine and many more from around the world.

See-Hear (33 St. Marks Pl., between 2nd and 3rd Aves., tel. 212/505–9781). Fanzines, rock-music magazines, and other must-haves for groupies of all ilk.

Paper/ **JAM Paper Outlet** (111 3rd Ave., between 13th and 14th Sts., tel. 212/
Postcards 473–6666; 611 6th Ave., at 18th St., tel. 212/255–4593; 1100 2nd Ave., at 58th St., tel. 212/980–1999). The place for inexpensive paper, cards, and envelopes in every imaginable color.

Kate's Paperie (8 W. 13th St., just off 5th Ave., tel. 212/633–0570; 561 Broadway, between Spring and Prince Sts., tel. 212/941–9816). Marbled and handmade papers, writing sets, boxes, journals, paper-based lamps, and a host of lovely items. Custom-made invitations and announcements, too. *13th St. closed Sun.*

Untitled (159 Prince St., between W. Broadway and Thompson St., tel. 212/982–2088). The specialty here is art postcards: Old Masters, Impressionists, Moderns, and others from collections around the world.

Pharmacies **Apthorp Pharmacy** (2201 Broadway, at 78th St., tel. 212/ 877–3480). This neighborhood stand-by, open 365 days a year, offers a unique service for those who can't swallow pills—any prescription can be compounded into a powder or a suspension. In addition, Apthorp has a range of beauty products, including hard-to-find French face powders.

In case you want to be welcomed there.

We're here to see that you're always welcomed at establishments everywhere. That's why millions of people carry the American Express® Card — for peace of mind, confidence, and security, around the world or just around the corner.

do more

In case you're running low.

We're here to help with more than 118,000 Express Cash locations around the world. In order to enroll, just call American Express before you start your vacation.

do more

And just in case.

We're here with American Express® Travelers Cheques and Cheques *for Two*.® They're the safest way to carry money on your vacation and the surest way to get a refund, practically anywhere, anytime.
Another way we help you...

do more®

AMERICAN
EXPRESS

Travelers
Cheques

Boyd's Madison Avenue (655 Madison Ave., between 60th and 61st Sts., tel. 212/838–6558). A dizzying display of hair ornaments, a wide range of makeup and imported toiletries, plus the pharmacy and typical over-the-counter preparations, make this a convenient option.

Zitomer (969 Madison Ave., between 75th and 76th Sts., tel. 212/737–5560). A pharmacy that has morphed into a small department store, you can browse through the kid's clothes and toys, lingerie, hats, and fancy toiletries while you wait for your prescription to be filled.

Records/CDs
General

Disco Rama (186 W. 4th St., between 6th and 7th Aves., tel. 212/206–8417; 40 Union Sq. E., between 16th and 17th St., tel. 212/260–8616). A narrow but cavernous music-shopper's paradise, Disco Rama has the most reasonable prices in New York on recent releases and a stunning selection of current alternative and soul recordings. A third store, at 146 West 4th Street (tel. 212/477–9410), offers classical and clearance selections.

HMV (2081 Broadway, at 72nd St., tel. 212/721–5900; 1280 Lexington Ave., at 86th St., tel. 212/348–0800; 565 5th Ave., at 46th St., tel. 212/681–6700; 57 W. 34th St., tel. 212/629–0900). These state-of-the-art record superstores, stocking 800,000 discs, tapes, and videos, are giving Tower a run for its money.

Tower Records (692 Broadway, at 4th St., tel. 212/505–1500; 1966 Broadway, at 66th St., tel. 212/799–2500; Basement of Trump Tower on 5th Ave., between 55th and 56th Sts., tel. 212/838–8110). These stores laid down the law for megachain retailers of records, cassettes, CDs (and technology not yet developed) of all kinds of music—rock, reggae, jazz, New Age, movie soundtracks, classical, and more.

Virgin Megastore (1540 Broadway, between 45th and 46th Sts., tel. 212/921–1020). A three-level media superstore, with music, videos, CD-ROMS, books, and a movie theater. Most of the space is given over to CDs and tapes, and there are a plethora of listening stations so you can try before you buy.

Rare and
Used

A-1 Record Shop (439 E. 6th St., between 1st Ave. and Ave. A, tel. 212/473–2870). Ignore the sullen staff and head for the bins, which are stuffed with a soul and rock collection that is breathtakingly comprehensive.

Bleecker Bob's Golden Oldies (118 W. 3rd St., between MacDougal and 6th Ave., tel. 212/475–9677). This Greenwich Village store, which started out as an oldies specialist, now covers punk, new wave, progressive rock, reggae, R&B, and electronic sounds. It's open until 1 AM.

Colony Music (1619 Broadway, at 49th St., tel. 212/265–2050). This theater-district institution houses an enormous selection of hard-to-find records and tapes of Broadway and movie tunes, as well as rare recordings from popular performers.

Footlight Records (113 E. 12th St., between 3rd and 4th Aves., tel. 212/533–1572). The out-of-print and much-searched-for titles here cover Broadway and film music, big band, jazz, imports, rock and roll, and country.

Gryphon Record Shop (251 W. 72nd St., 2nd floor, tel. 212/874–1588). Many knowledgeable listeners dub the 40,000-item rare-records selection the city's best.

Shoes

Arche (1045 3rd Ave., between 61st and 62nd Sts., tel. 212/838–1933; 995 Madison Ave., at 77th St., tel. 212/439–0700; 128 W. 57th St., tel. 212/262–5488; 10 Astor Pl., between Broadway and Lafayette St., tel. 529–4808). Supple, suede shoes that come in a rainbow of groovy colors.

Billy Martin's (812 Madison Ave., at 68th St., tel. 212/861–3100). Adorned boots and Western wear for those unafraid of being noticed.

Cole-Haan (667 Madison Ave., at 61st St., tel. 212/421–8440; 620 5th Ave., at 50th St. 212/765–9747). Beautiful, classically styled shoes can be found here.

Executive Leather Company (1482 3rd Ave., between 83rd and 84th Sts., tel. 212/772–7948). Notable for its excellent selection of Peter Kaiser shoes, the German-made shoes that are shaped on a wider last and combine comfort with au courant styling.

FreeLance (155 Spring St., between W. Broadway and Wooster St., tel. 212/965–9231). If you see a pair you like here, snap them up, because each style—mostly in black or brown leather, some classic with modern twists, some *very* trendy—at this Paris import is perfect of its kind and quickly walks off the shelf. (For women only.)

John Fluevog (104 Prince St., between Greene and Mercer Sts., tel. 212/431–4484). This Canadian-born designer makes the footwear for club kids and other hipsters.

Kenneth Cole (353 Columbus Ave., between 76th and 77th Sts., tel. 212/873–2061; 95 5th Ave., at 17th St., 212/675–2550; 597 Broadway, at Houston St., tel. 212/965–0283). Snazzy shoes here range from casual to dressy.

Maraolo (782 Lexington Ave., between 60th and 61st Sts., tel. 212/832–8182). The wide selection of classic heels, flats, and casual shoes for women, and of everything from sandals to dress shoes for men (many from European makers) make this a good stop for basic wardrobe enhancement.

Peter Fox (806 Madison Ave., between 67th and 68th Sts., tel.212/744–8340; 105 Thompson St., between Prince and Spring Sts., tel. 212/431–6359). This English shoemaker offers an up-to-date look enhanced with period flourishes. Also offers a popular (though pricey) bridal line.

Ritz (505 Park Ave., at 59th St., tel. 212/838–3319). Fashion's latest silhouettes, fabrics, and colors can always be found at this hip, Japanese-run store.

Tip Top Shoes (155 W. 72nd St., tel. 212/787–4960). Sure it's a little dowdy, but you can't beat it for the selection of *current* and comfortable shoes—from every Hush Puppy color to New Age Ecco hiking boots.

To Boot New York, Adam Derrick (256 Columbus Ave., between 71st and 72nd Sts., tel. 212/724–8249). A well of men's boots of all types helped this store make its name; tie shoes and loafers have been added to the mix.

Tootsie Plohound (1116 3rd Ave., at 65th St., tel. 212/249–0671; 137 5th Ave., at 20th St., tel. 212/460–8650; 413 W. Broadway, between Prince and Spring Sts., tel. 212/925–8931). Despite the silly name, Tootsie Plohound sells seriously fashionable, dapper send-ups of traditional styles from England, France, and Italy.

Sporting Goods/ Athletic Wear

Big City Kites, (1210 Lexington Ave., at 82nd St., tel., 212/472–2623). Kites in every color and shape, including box kites, dragons, sport kites, and the old-fashioned diamond kites you had as a kid, hang from the ceiling and walls of this small, festive store. *Closed Sun.*

Blades, Board, and Skate (120 W. 72nd St., between Broadway and Columbus Ave., tel. 212/787–3911; 160 E. 86th St., tel. 212/996–1644; 659 Broadway, between Bleecker and Bond Sts., tel.212/477–7350). This is where to buy in-line skates or to rent them by the hour or day.

Paragon (867 Broadway, at 18th St., tel. 212/255–8036). On its three floors, Paragon carries an in-depth selection of almost every type of equipment an athlete might want, from crossbows to kayaks, tennis rackets to exercycles, with the clothing and footwear to match.

Peck & Goodie (917 8th Ave., between 54th and 55th Sts., tel. 212/246–6123). This is the regular supplier of the highest quality blades, boots, and brackets for the likes of Olympic skaters Robin Cousins and Kathy Turner.

Pro Sports New York (333 6th Ave., near W. 4th St., tel. 212/645–9340). The young and hip come here for in-line skates, skateboards, and snowboards with the wildest colors and designs.
SCUBA Network (124 E. 57th St., tel. 212/750–9160; 175 5th Ave., between 22nd and 23rd Sts., tel. 212/228–2080). Everything for the scuba and snorkling enthusiast, including classes.
The Sports Authority (401 7th Ave., at 33rd St., 2nd floor, tel. 212/563–7195; 845 3rd Ave., at 51st St., tel. 212/355–9725; 57 W. 57th St., at 6th Ave., tel. 212/355–6430). A sports superstore with all the big-name brands.
Tents & Trails (21 Park Pl., between Broadway and Church St., tel. 212/227–1760). Seven floors of serious camping equipment can supply expeditions to the jungle or Antarctica.

Auction Exhibitions

Although you won't find auction action, the weekend is the perfect time to browse at pre-sale exhibitions at the city's major houses: **Christie's Park Avenue** (502 Park Ave., at 59th St., tel. 212/546–1000, 212/371–5438 for recorded schedules); **Christie's East** (219 E. 67th St., tel. 212/606–0400); **Sotheby's** (1334 York Ave., at 72nd St., tel. 212/606–7000, 212/606–7245 for recorded schedules); or **William Doyle Galleries** (175 E. 87th St., tel. 212/427–2730).

Flea Markets

There's no telling what you'll find at flea markets in black-topped school playgrounds and grungy parking lots. The markets run all year round, although selection may be weaker in deepest winter.

Annex Antiques Fair and Flea Market (6th Ave., between 24th and 27th Sts., tel. 212/243–5343). A great place to furnish your home cheaply or to complete that collection of cookie tins, Bakelite bracelets, or old linens. Some dealers come from as far afield as Pennsylvania to sell here, and local dealers come to buy what they'll later mark up.
I.S. 44 Market (Columbus Ave., between 76th and 77th Sts.). On Sundays, this school yard and cafeteria are jammed with 300 dealers. The draw is hand-crafted earrings, scarves, and hats, vintage jewelry and jackets, *enough* bric-a-brac, and a farmer's market.

Best Bets for Children

Books **Bank Street Bookstore** (610 W. 112th St., at Broadway, tel. 212/678–1654). The lower floor is filled with picture books and books for older kids, the upper floor has an excellent selection of books on parenting. Frequent buyers earn credits toward future purchases.
Books of Wonder (16 W. 18th St., tel. 212/989–3270). This cheerful store offers an excellent stock of new and antique children's books for all reading levels, mainly in hardcover versions. Oziana old and new is a specialty.

Clothing **Children's Place** (901 6th Ave., in the Manhattan Mall, tel. 212/268–7696; 173 E. 86th St., tel. 212/831–5100). Basic clothes at everyday prices, not an easy thing to find in this city.
Chocolate Soup (946 Madison Ave., between 74th and 75th Sts., tel. 212/861–2210). This shop offers handcrafted one-of-a-kinds and imports for infants to sixth-graders. *Closed Sun., winter–spring*.
Great Feet (1241 Lexington Ave., at 84th St., tel. 212/249–0551). A spacious store with shoes for infants and school-age kids. Friendly staff and lots of styles and sizes make life easier for busy parents.
Greenstones et Cie (442 Columbus Ave., between 81st and 82nd Sts., tel. 212/580–4322; 284 Columbus Ave., between 73rd and 74th Sts., tel. 212/501–8536; 1184 Madison Ave., at 86th St., 212/427–1665).

Even on sale, the prices make your head spin, but the stuff is all gorgeous.

Little Eric (1331 3rd Ave., between 76th and 77th Sts., tel. 212/288–8987; 1118 Madison Ave., between 83rd and 84th Sts., tel. 212/717–1513). Hipster kids and their fashion-conscious parents will surely find the right shoe at these two stores.

Morris Brothers (2322 Broadway, at 84th St., tel. 212/724–9000). Parents can find just about everything they need for children, from stretchies and baby bags for infants to labels to sew in for summer camp, to almost-hip clothing for teens.

Oilily (870 Madison Ave., between 70th and 71st Sts., tel. 212/628–0100). Boldly patterned, fanciful, unfussy (though not inexpensive) clothes for infants and children.

Peanut Butter & Jane (617 Hudson St., between W. 12th and Jane Sts., tel. 212/620–7952). PB&J lures parents in all the way from the 'burbs for comfortable, casual clothing, some of which is handmade exclusively for the shop. Lots of fun outfits, too: chaps for boys, tutus for girls, and some distinctive toys. The age range is from newborn to 10 years old.

Shoofly (465 Amsterdam Ave., between 82nd and 83rd Sts., tel. 212/580–4390). Whimsical shoes, hats, and socks can be found at this kid-friendly shop.

Spring Flowers Children's Boutique (1050 3rd Ave., at 62nd St., tel. 212/758–2669; 905 Madison Ave., between 72nd and 73rd Sts., tel. 212/717–8182; 410 Columbus Ave., between 79th and 80th Sts., tel. 212/721–2337). When grandparents come to town, or better yet, when they're paying, this store is the place for beautiful, traditional, and pricey clothes for children and infants.

Toys **Building Blocks** (1414 3rd Ave., between 80th and 81st Sts., tel. 212/772–TOYS; 812 Lexington Ave., between 62nd and 63rd Sts., tel. 753–TOYS). Lots of educational toys that kids will actually like, and knowledgeable staff with suggestions for clueless adults looking for the right gift.

Dinosaur Hill (306 E. 9th St., tel. 212/473–5850). Both toys and clothes are bright, cheerful, and a little homespun in this cozy, likable storefront.

Enchanted Forest (85 Mercer St., between Spring and Broome Sts., tel. 212/925–6677). This shop goes to the heart of bewitchment with its handmade toys and stuffed animals, folk pieces, and books of mythology and fairy tales.

F.A.O. Schwarz (767 5th Ave., at 58th St., tel. 212/644–9400). Waiting in line to get into this sprawling, two-level institution each December is a ritual to New York City kids. In the entrance is a wonderful mechanical clock with many dials and dingbats, and beyond that, all the stuffed animals in the world, dolls great and small, things to build with (including blocks by the pound), items for dress-up, computer games, board games, and kiddie cars that cost almost as much as the real thing.

Kidding Around (68 Bleecker St., between Broadway and Lafayette St., tel. 212/598–0228; 60 W. 15th St., between 5th and 6th Aves., tel. 212/645–6337). Two delightful stores, but the one on Bleecker is cozy and cramped, while 15th Street has more room to run around and try out all the toys. Both have lots of little items for under $5, as well as big, plush stuffed animals and other playthings.

Penny Whistle Toys (448 Columbus Ave., between 81st and 82nd Sts., tel. 212/873–9090; 1283 Madison Ave., between 91st and 92nd Sts., tel. 212/369–3868). Meredith Brokaw (wife of TV anchor Tom Brokaw) has assembled an intriguing array of high-quality toys here.

Toys "R" Us (1293 Broadway, at 34th St., tel. 212/594–8697; 24-30 Union Sq. E at 16th St., tel. 212/674–8714). City kids have their own megastore, three packed floors of everything from Tickle Me Elmo on up.

West Side Kids (498 Amsterdam Ave., at 84th St., tel. 212/496–7282). The thoughtfully chosen stock here ranges from blocks to books, dolls to trains, to art supplies and science kits. Lots of special events, and a birthday registry too.

For Babies Weekends are an excellent time to comparison-shop for cribs, strollers, high chairs, car seats, baby bottles, and larger-ticket essentials of Life with Baby. Prime destinations for these include:

Albee (715 Amsterdam Ave., at 95th St., tel. 212/662–5740). Albee claims to supply everything but the baby, and the selection of well-known brands is impressive.

Bellini (1305 2nd Ave., between 68th and 69th Sts., tel. 212/517–9233; 110 W. 86th St., tel. 212/580–3801). Styles are chic, the selection top-of-the-line—and you pay for what you get. *Closed Sun. in July and Aug.*

Hush-A-Bye (1459 1st Ave., at 76th St., tel. 212/988–4500). East Siders can acquire baby necessities close to home.

Schneider's (20 Ave. A, at 2nd St., tel. 212/228–3540). The selection is among the city's broadest, and the salespeople are friendly (passionate about Maclarens) and especially knowledgeable about all baby products. *Closed Sun.*

6 Where to Play

New Yorkers keep their noses to the grindstone on weekdays but they set aside weekends for R&R. In city parks—26,900 acres of parkland and playgrounds, malls and squares now in the midst of the most ambitious rebuilding program since the Great Depression—people hike and bird-watch, body-surf and windsurf, fly kites and toss Frisbees, bat baseballs and kick soccer balls, stroll, and picnic. Indoors, the competitive spirit flourishes at pool halls and backgammon, bridge, and chess clubs. Those who prefer to leave the gamesmanship to someone else, of course, can always stand on the sidelines and cheer for some of the biggest names in pro sports.

The Urban Outdoors

There are no spotted cows and weathered barns in New York's "country," and where there are forests, they are hemmed in by highways. Nevertheless, New York's parks constitute the largest urban forest in the nation. A recent project by the parks department's Natural Resources Group recorded more than 750 different native species of plants and animals here, including the American chestnut tree, the endangered peregrine falcon, the sharp-shinned hawk, and the white-tailed deer. Besides great works of landscape architecture, such as Central Park and Prospect Park, there are preserves more numerous than you might imagine, where nature follows its own path in salt marshes, scrubby areas, and forests.

Beaches

New York–area beaches are among the city's greatest year-round pleasures. State-of-the-art machinery has been introduced to eliminate debris, although it's still a good idea to call about swimming conditions. All city beaches are guarded in summertime, and entry to most, including the 15 miles under Parks & Recreation department supervision, is free. Only parking entails a fee.

Favorite **Fire Island,** a 16¼-mile-long sliver of sand south of Long Island
Strands proper, offers beaches at **Robert Moses State Park** (tel. 516/669–
Long Island 0449), on the western end of the island, and at **Smith Point County Park** (tel. 516/852–1316). Another 1,400 acres constitute the **Fire Island National Seashore** (tel. 516/289–4810). Fire Island is accessible by a train-and-ferry or train-and-bus combination (tel. 718/217–5477).
Jones Beach (tel. 516/785–1600) is one of the world's great manmade beaches. Built in 1929 by parks commissioner Robert Moses on the site of a much more unprepossessing strand, it is 6½ miles long and extremely wide, so even on weekends you can claim a patch of solitude of your own if you walk far enough. The Long Island Railroad (tel. 718/217–5477) runs regular trips to the beach in summer, going to Freeport by train and by bus from there.

New Jersey **Sandy Hook** (tel. 908/872–0115), now part of the Gateway National Recreation Area, is the home of the oldest operating lighthouse in the country and the site of a series of forts that protected shipping channels in Colonial days. The area today is much better known for its 7 miles of beaches, with terrific swimming and surf fishing. Dunes behind the strand shelter a holly forest that has no equal on the Eastern Seaboard.

Brooklyn **Brighton Beach** (tel. 718/946–1353), located in the Russian enclave known as "Odessa by the Sea," has an Old World atmosphere, with pushcart vendors and Eastern European sweet shops. Russian is spoke on every corner.
Coney Island (tel. 718/946–1353), once a sandy island that the Dutch named "Konijn Eiland" for its rabbit population, attracts millions every year, as it has ever since the 1830s, and there's nothing quite

like it for New York summer atmosphere: fried clams, skateboards, couples necking under the boardwalk, and an annual tattoo festival. It's home to the New York Aquarium, as well as one of the city's most unusual designated landmarks—the Cyclone roller coaster, a ride that offers two minutes of heart-stopping rolls and plunges. And you're just 3½ miles away by boardwalk from Brighton Beach. In winter, the beach is frequented by the stalwarts of the Polar Bear Club, who prefer their swimming when the water's icy.

Bronx   **Orchard Beach** (tel. 718/885–2275), on Long Island Sound, a grand mile-long sandy arc created in 1934 by the ubiquitous Robert Moses, is sometimes known as "the Riviera of the Bronx," attracting as many as 32,000 people on a scorching summer day. The borough's large Hispanic population gives the place a decidedly Latin beat, often enhanced with free salsa and Carib-flavored concerts on weekends. But the off-season is equally inviting for those in quest of a quiet winter walk along the beach or through the network of nearby nature trails.

Queens   **Jacob Riis Park** (tel. 718/318–4300), part of the Gateway National Recreation Area just west of Rockaway Park, was named for the Danish photographer who documented the lives of so many recent immigrants. The park stretches a full mile along the Atlantic surf, and facilities include softball fields, paddleball courts, and pitch-and-putt golf courses. In winter, the beach is given over to anglers and bird-watchers.
Rockaway Beach and Boardwalk (tel. 718/318–4000), 7½ miles of Atlantic strand, is the nation's largest municipal beach and the site of some of the city's best surf. Originally a weekend resort for Tammany politicians, it was once the "Irish Saratoga."

Staten Island   The entire southeast shore of the island is Atlantic Ocean beach, much of it part of either the New York City park system or the Gateway National Recreation Area. Terrific surf beaches are at **Wolfe's Pond Park** (tel. 718/984–8266) and **Great Kills Park** (tel. 718/351–6970), which, in addition to sandy shores, has a marina, fishing, and miles of trails for jogging and skating. The **Franklin D. Roosevelt Boardwalk** leads from Miller Field, part of the Gateway National Recreation Area (tel. 718/351–6970), along the ocean to Fort Wadsworth, under the Verrazano-Narrows Bridge, via Oakwood Beach, New Dorp Beach, Midland Beach, and South Beach—all popular, guarded strands.

Parks and Woodlands

Many New Yorkers would be surprised to learn that a full 13% of the five boroughs is parkland. A handful of nature centers access short, marked trails where you can see nature at its best.

Central Park   Created by Frederick Law Olmsted and Calvert Vaux beginning in 1858, this magnificent 843-acre park is unexpectedly full of natural splendors, considering its early 19th-century condition as a vile and barren bog full of oozy slime, polluted creeks, slaughterhouses, and bone-boiling works. Central Park was named a National Historic Landmark in 1965, and the nonprofit Central Park Conservancy, founded in 1980, has raised millions of dollars to restore the park's original landscape. Most recently, the park's scraggly and sometimes foreboding northern section was transformed into a walker's paradise, with streams, waterfalls, a new visitor center, and a romantic promenade beside the Harlem Meer.

On weekends, whatever the season, everyone turns out to make merry in the park. Salsa groups quick-step. Boom boxes reverberate. Folk dancers clap and circle. In-line skaters twirl and bop around Wollman Rink and zoom along park roads and promenades. Joggers huff and puff up the hills, while bicyclists whiz past in a blur of clicking gears. Some of the city's best sports facilities are here: baseball and softball fields, basketball courts, a lake for rowing, courts for lawn bowling, bridle paths, and 30 tennis courts (*see* Sports and Recreation, *below*).

For a detailed look, various tours—focussing on everything from bird-watching to Central Park's 19th-century history—are offered on weekends by the Urban Park Rangers (tel. 212/427–4040 or 800/ 201–7275).

Landmarks **The Pond** (near Scholars' Gate, at 59th St. and 5th Ave.) is a picturesque little body of water dominated by Overlook Rock, a massive outcropping of mica schist.

Central Park Zoo (*see* Zoos, *below*).

Delacorte Musical Clock (near the zoo) chimes on the half hour with an outburst of performing monkeys, bears, and other bronze figures twirling to nursery song chimes.

The Dairy (midpark at 64th St.), originally a working dairy, now holds the delightful park information center.

The Carousel (midpark at 64th St.) has been a favorite destination for generations of kids. This 1903 antique has 58 colorful hand-carved horses.

Sheep Meadow (midpark above 65th St.), the largest stretch of grass in Manhattan, makes up for Manhattan's dirth of beaches by providing a wide-open expanse for sun-worshipping. Sheep grazed here until 1934; they were sheltered for the night across the drive in the structure that is now the Tavern on the Green.

The Mall (just east of the Sheep Meadow), the park's formal promenade, is shaded by one of the nation's last great stands of American elms.

Bethesda Terrace and Bethesda Fountain (midpark at 72nd St.), at the northern end of the Mall, feature a magnificent stone staircase; wonderful willows, rhododendrons, and cherry trees; and a formal pool with Emma Stebbins's fine late-19th-century statue *Angel of the Waters*, at the center, surrounded by cherubs representing the Victorian virtues of Purity, Health, Peace, and Temperance.

Conservatory Water (east side of the park just above 72nd St.), the park's model boat pond, may be best known to youngsters as the site of the race in E. B. White's *Stuart Little*. Nearby are statues of Hans Christian Andersen and Alice in Wonderland—the latter worn shiny smooth by clambering children.

Cherry Hill Concourse (west of Bethesda Fountain) was once used as a turnaround for carriages. It's splendid in spring when the wispy blossoms of the cherry trees frill the hilltop.

Strawberry Fields (at W. 72nd St. entrance) covers 2½ acres landscaped with funds from Yoko Ono in memory of her husband John Lennon. The former Beatle was killed in 1980 in front of the building in which they lived, the Dakota, just across Central Park West. A black-and-white mosaic medallion in the garden reads simply "IMAGINE."

The Ramble (midpark north of the lake), 38 acres of shrubby, brushy woods, marks a transition to the less formal, more rustic northern part of the park. Bird-watchers congregate here year-round; some 275 of the 600 regularly occurring species in North America have been sighted here. Despite its woodsy appearance, the Ramble was carefully planned, right down to its "mountain torrent" and its "grotto."

Belvedere Castle (midpark at 79th St.), a fairy-tale stone structure, perches on one of the highest points of the park, Vista Rock, towering over turtle pond. There are splendid views from its terraces and turrets. The castle houses the recently opened Henry Luce Nature Observatory (tel. 212/772–0210)—which has telescopes, microscopes, and live animals—and a monitoring station for the U.S. Weather Bureau.

The Great Lawn (midpark between 81st and 84th Sts.), an immense meadow that was once a reservoir, was in sad condition after doing double duty for many years as the park's principal venue for concerts and other mega-events. (In 1995 100,000 kids and their parents gathered here for the Hollywood-style premiere of Walt Disney's Pocahanntas.) Recently, a major overhaul—involving underground engineering and tougher breeds of lawn grass—rejuvenated the turf.

The Jacqueline Kennedy Onassis Reservoir (midpark between 85th and 96th Sts.) is 106 serene acres of water ringed by a chain-link fence and a 1½-mile running path that offers glorious views of green against a backdrop of stately old apartment buildings, reflecting pink and gold in sunsets. In late fall, Canada geese and ducks speckle the water and call at each other above the distant hum of traffic.

Conservatory Garden (*see* Gardens, *below*).

The Charles A. Dana Discovery Center (110th St. and 5th Ave., tel. 212/860–1370) has hands-on exhibits about the park and offers environmental programs throughout the year. Located beside the beautifully restored Harlem Meer (meer is Dutch for lake), the center distributes free fishing rods. In what was once one of the park's least visited spots, kids now happily catch and release bass, bluegills, and catfish stocked here by the Parks Department.

Riverside Park This 324-acre strip of green along Manhattan's western edge, landscaped by Frederick Law Olmsted from 1873 to 1910, may not offer Central Park's natural breadth and variety, but it does have one thing the bigger park doesn't: the Hudson River. Flowing down from its headwaters in the Adirondack Mountains upstate, the Hudson once ran the gauntlet past chemical, electric, and sewage plants that dumped by-products (and worse) into the river. Since the passage of the Clean Water Act in 1972, the Hudson has slowly become cleaner and healthier, with fish, crabs, ducks, gulls, herons, and geese returning to the river and making Riverside Park a fine spot for contemplation. The park's wonderful promenades offer watery panoramas and terrific sunsets, and it's even more dazzling in spring when the crabapples and cherry trees are a pale pink froth. And unlike Central Park, Riverside doesn't draw people from outside its neighborhood with much frequency, so weekends here remain relatively tranquil.

Landmarks **The Boat Basin** (at 79th Street) is where several dozen New Yorkers live in houseboats ranging from funky to sleek. There's also a new small boat launch, from which kayakers and canoeists leave for short journeys up-river.

The Rotunda (at the 79th St. underpass) occupies a wonderful circular space punctuated by a fountain, flanked by stairways leading down from the road, and edged on another side by a colonnade and viewing platform over the Boat Basin. The acoustics are good, and in August, the Rotunda hosts the weekend-long Riverside Park Arts Festival.

Mt. Tom (at 83rd St.) is a boulder where Edgar Allan Poe often climbed to ponder the passing river scene.

Soldiers' and Sailors' Monument (at 89th St.), an imposing columned Civil War memorial fashioned after Athens's monument to Lysicrates, was designed by architect Paul E. M. Duboy, whose other works include the Ansonia apartment building (Broadway at 73rd St.).

91st Street Community Garden (at 91st St.), where local residents cultivate perennials for all to admire, is especially beautiful in spring and summer. Volunteer weeders are welcome on weekends; just speak to anyone who's working.

Joan of Arc Statue (at 93rd St.), a life-size bronze of the warrior on her horse, was erected in 1915 and was the first monument to a female historical figure in New York City. The sculpture's gothic marble base contains stone blocks from the Château de Rouen where Joan of Arc was imprisoned and from Rheims Cathedral.

Bird Sanctuary (116th to 120th Sts.) has been planted by the New York Audubon Society as shelter for small birds.

Grant's Tomb (Riverside Dr. at 122nd St.) was copied after Mausoleus's tomb in Turkey, a 4th century BC structure that was one of the Seven Wonders of the Ancient World. President Ulysses S. Grant and his wife lie in red marble sarcophagi beneath the soaring rotunda. This formal classical monument stands in fascinating contrast to the gaudy, 1960s-era mosaic benches that flank its terrace, and ongoing renovations are making the tomb gleam.

Grave of an Amiable Child (at 123rd St.) occupies a peaceful fenced area adjacent to Grant's Tomb and a few steps down. A five-year-old named St. Clair Pollack fell from this point in 1797; the grave has remained.

Manhattan's Other Parks

The city's newest parks are **Hudson River Park** (from Chambers to Vesey St.) and the adjacent 1¼-mile-long **Battery Park City Esplanade,** with views of the famous river, sailboats, ferries, seagulls, and—off in the distance—the Statue of Liberty. These parks are great for strolling, reading, and catching a bit of sea air. Filled with interesting design elements—such as a lily pond with baby turtles and the Lilliputian, cast-bronze "Real World" by artist Tom Otterness—both parks are meticulously maintained and also host concerts and readings during summer months. Stay to the water's side of the road: Weather permitting, joggers, bladers and bikers, unfettered by cars or streetlights, speed along the inside lanes.

For 20 years, **Bryant Park,** midtown's only major green space, was abandoned to the drug pushers. An incredible $9 million renovation, however, has made the park, between 40th and 42nd streets, delightful again. One-hundred-year-old plane trees shade upscale food vendors, visitors relaxing in folding chairs, and a lovely central fountain.

Carl Schurz Park, which runs between 82nd and 90th streets on the eastern edge of Manhattan, is the backyard of Gracie Mansion, the official mayoral residence. Situated on the East River, the park has fine views of Queens and the bridges, and it's a low-key place, perhaps because it's a bit out of the way.

North of Riverside Park is peaceful 66-acre **Fort Tryon Park,** which surrounds the Cloisters (*see* Chapter 4) and offers more wonderful views of the Hudson River. The central plaza honors Revolutionary War heroine Margaret Corbin.

Above Dyckman Street alongside the Harlem River, **Inwood Hill Park** covers 196 acres of incredibly quiet, hill-climbing woods. The park's most intriguing attraction, however, is its "Indian Rock Shelters," where centuries-old pottery shards from New York's native inhabitants have been uncovered. For trail guides, visit the park's nature center (tel. 212/304–2365), which is open most weekends 11–4.

The 12-acre **Peace Garden,** on the grounds of the United Nations (just east of 1st Ave. at 46th St.) has a lovely lookout over the East River. Lawns edged with hedges and punctuated with statues are crisscrossed by paths. The exquisite rose garden shows off 1,400 bushes in 37 species.

In an unlikely spot—atop a sewage treatment plant—**Riverbank State Park** (tel. 212/694–3600), stretching from 135th to 145th streets along the Hudson, was greeted with complete skepticism when it opened in 1993. But the Olympic-length swimming pool, complete track-and-field facility, ice-skating rink, Astroturf baseball diamonds, and health club–style gymnasium have helped to win people over. The windswept views of the Hudson River don't hurt either. Look for the Little Red Lighthouse (of storybook fame) hugging the Manhattan shore beneath the George Washington Bridge.

The tumultuous heart of the East Village is **Tompkins Square Park.** Between East 7th and East 10th streets and Avenues A and B, spread the 16 (relatively) serene acres which were the scene of riots in 1988, made into an unofficial shanty town by the neighborhood homeless, then cleaned up in 1991. Today, the square is mellower, but still busy; there's a dog run, basketball court, playground, and small pool.

Union Square Park, situated between 14th and 17th streets along Broadway, is an open and airy space with handsome subway kiosks and small patches of flowers. The sculpture of Lafayette is by Felix Bartholdi, better known for his *Liberty Enlightening the World*— the Statue of Liberty. But the park is best-loved in the neighborhood for its eclectic farmer's market (*see* Chapter 5).

A former vacant lot along Greenwich Street, between Chambers and Duane streets, has been landscaped into **Washington Market Park,** 1½ acres of lawn and meandering paths with an adventure playground and an airy Victorian gazebo.

At the foot of 5th Avenue stands **Washington Square Park,** a former potter's field and hanging ground that now bustles with families, kids, chess players, street musicians, students, and even a few aging hippies. Although drug dealers may occasionally inquire whether you're interested in some "smoke," plenty of police officers are on hand to keep the park safe. At the park's center is the landmark arch designed by Stanford White in 1892 to replicate an earlier structure commemorating the centennial of George Washington's inauguration. Around the park's perimeter are redbrick town houses that such luminaries as Henry James and Edith Wharton once called home.

Pelham Bay Park This 2,764-acre Bronx park, the city's largest, is one of the great surprises of New York. Once the fishing and hunting grounds of the Siwanoy Indians, it was named for Englishman Thomas Pell, who made peace with them in 1654.

Although its perimeters are crowded by high-rise housing projects, it is also a large and complex environment for wildlife: fish, egrets, salamanders, frogs, insects, raccoons and rabbits, owls, and even red fox. Many people consider its ragged 13-mile shoreline one of the most scenic of all public lands along the Atlantic. Along the shore, migrating ospreys dive for winter flounder, harbor seals dine on mollusks and crustaceans, and, in spring, fiddler crabs—one of several types that live here—lay their eggs on the pebbly beaches of Long Island Sound.

The park also includes tennis courts, baseball diamonds, a running track, a playground, a driving range, and a stable.

For more information, contact the Urban Park Rangers at the Pelham Bay Park Environmental Center near Orchard Beach (tel. 718/885–3466) or the park administrator's office (tel. 718/430–1890).

Landmarks **Rodman's Neck,** a meadow-and-scrub area southwest of Orchard Beach, is a favorite destination of bird-watchers and baseball players alike. It also contains a forest of European alder, a large concentration of white poplar, and nearly 5 acres of bayberry bushes. And it's home to the shooting range of New York City's Police Academy. **Thomas Pell Wildlife Refuge and Sanctuary** is one of the city's great outdoor classrooms for the study of nature, established in 1967. In addition to many acres of woodlands, it is the site of **Goose Creek Marsh,** the last 50 acres of ancient marshlands that once extended over 5,000 acres. **Split Rock Trail,** which winds through and around the marsh, passes the landmark **Split Rock,** a massive glacier-split boulder where poet Anne Hutchinson died in 1643 at the hands of marauding Siwanoy Indians. The **Central Woodlands,** full of red oak, black birch, and boxelder maples, shelter ruby-throated hummingbirds.

Glover's Rock bears a plaque commemorating the Battle of Pell Point, a Revolutionary War skirmish.

Bartow-Pell Mansion (*see* Historical Treasures *in* Chapter 4).

Hunter Island is a coastal area full of tidal wetlands, towering old oaks, uncommon native plants such as wild geraniums and wood betony (a type of mint), and the park's largest continuous forest. Huge rock outcrops incised by glaciers' movements 20,000 years ago, part of the Hunter Island Marine Zoology and Geology Sanctuary, can be seen along the Kazimiroff Nature Trail.

Van Cortlandt Park What's remarkable about this Bronx park is that all but 146 of its 1,146 acres are forests and wetlands. The pileated woodpecker feeds on insects in dead trees; the great horned owl hunts rabbits; and three types of bedrock jut out majestically: Fordham gneiss, Yonkers granite, and softer Inwood marble.

For more information or a list of weekend walking tours, call the Urban Park Rangers (tel. 718/548–7070) or the administrator's office (tel. 718/430–1890).

Landmarks **The Parade Ground,** with several baseball diamonds and plenty of space for football and soccer, is the center of the park's outdoor recreational activities. The highlight for spectators, however, are the numerous weekend cricket games, with players from around the world dressed in all-white cricket garb, exerting themselves with bats, balls, and wickets.

Van Cortlandt House (*see* Chapter 4).

Vault Hill, the burial ground of the Van Cortlandt family, rises 169 feet above sea level, offering fine views.

Van Cortlandt Lake, the largest expanse of fresh water (13 acres) in the borough was formed when Jacobus Van Cortlandt dammed Tibbetts Brook in 1699 to power two mills.

Tibbetts Brook flows into Van Cortlandt Lake through marshy areas that make for fine bird-watching; follow the mile-long **John Kieran Nature Trail** along Van Cortlandt Lake or the Old Putnam Railroad Track, abandoned since the early 1980s. The most notable denizens here are downy wood ducks.

Aqueduct Trail, another good path, was formed in the 1830s by workers who built the aqueduct to tap the Croton watershed north of the city. (The aqueduct itself was abandoned in 1897.) Fine forests of oak, maples, and tulip trees shade the trail.

Northwest Forest contains great stands of oaks and tulip trees interspersed with stunning outcroppings of Fordham gneiss. It can be explored on the **Cass Gallagher Nature Trail.**

Prospect Park Frederick Law Olmsted and Calvert Vaux, who collaborated on this 526-acre Brooklyn expanse of meadows, bluffs, boulders, glens, streams, and ponds, considered it even better than Central Park, their previous project. Located west of Flatbush Avenue and south of Grand Army Plaza, it is a beautiful place, with its 15,000 trees and shrubs and a network of winding roads and paths. As in Central Park, roads are closed to motor vehicles all weekend.

For information on volunteer activities, including half-day park cleanups and bulb-planting marathons for which the whole community turns out, call 718/965–8960. Call the Prospect Park events hot line (tel. 718/965–8999) for recorded information.

Landmarks **Grand Army Plaza** (intersection of Flatbush Ave. and Eastern Pkwy.), the stately and imposing northern entrance to the park, was designed by the architect Stanford White. The interior of the arch is open on selected weekends during warm weather; a spiral staircase to the top gives you a wonderful panorama of the park, south Brooklyn, and lower Manhattan.

Long Meadow (west side of the park) is the largest open space in an urban park in the entire United States. Frisbee, volleyball soccer, and lounging are all popular on this green expanse.

Vale of Cashmere (northern corner of the park), a natural amphitheater full of free-form ponds, offers cover for small birds amid its rhododendrons and azaleas.

Prospect Park Wildlife Center (*see* Zoos, *below*).

Prospect Park Carousel (near the zoo) was the dream of a Russian immigrant. Brooklyn's finest carvers created its 56 horses, chariots, lions, and giraffes. These and its stained-glass windows are now all restored to their 1912 splendor.

Music Grove, a pagoda-shaped bandstand, hosts summer concerts.

The Boathouse (*see* Chapter 4).

The Camperdown Elm (near the Boathouse), 125 years old and one of the city's most beloved trees, was immortalized by the poet Marianne Moore in her eponymous poem to the tree.

Quaker Cemetery (*see* Cemeteries, *below*).

Lefferts Homestead (*see* Chapter 4).

Alley Pond Environmental Center This preserve, improbably sited opposite a driving range, is what the Long Island sections of Queens looked like before suburbia: reed-edged glacial kettles, creeks, oak woodlands, and salt- and freshwater marshes. Although some of the metropolitan area's busiest highways surround you, they seem far away as you follow the short, marked trails in search of small mammals—rabbits, muskrats, opossums—and watch migrating birds by the hundreds in the wetlands in the fall. The center proper displays small live animals and hosts lively weekend children's programs (advance sign-up required). For details, contact the center (228–06 Northern Blvd., Douglaston, Queens, tel. 718/229–4000).

Jamaica Bay Wildlife Refuge Despite the fact that this part of Queens is a stone's throw from Kennedy Airport and within sight of Manhattan, during the past 40 years some 320 species of birds have been recorded on these 9,155 acres of salt marshes, fresh and brackish ponds, and open water. A wildlife refuge since 1953, it is now part of the Gateway National Recreation Area.

It's most exciting in spring, when hundreds of thousands of birds are nesting—including the great egret, snowy egret, and glossy ibis—and in fall, when ducks and geese making their way southward along the Atlantic flyway stop over on the two refuge ponds. Naturalists regularly lead walks through the refuge's 5 miles of trails. For information, call the visitor center (tel. 718/318–4340).

The Greenbelt Covering 2,500 acres of public and private land on Staten Island, the Greenbelt was conceived by great parks designer Frederick Law Olmsted, who owned a farm here. Although Staten Island has been getting progressively more built up since the Verrazano-Narrows Bridge was completed in 1964, the preserve protects five kinds of owls and shelters the most northerly example known of the sweetbay magnolia tree. Encompassing woods and meadows, ponds and wetlands, golf courses, cemeteries, and a couple of museums (Richmondtown Restoration and the Jacques Marchais Center of Tibetan Art; *see* Chapter 4), the area has 28 miles of trails.

For particulars, contact the main Greenbelt office (200 Nevada Ave., Staten Island, tel. 718/667–2165).

Landmarks **Todt Hill,** the high point (411 feet) of the park (at the intersection of Todt Hill and Ocean Terrace roads), is the highest tidewater elevation on the Atlantic seaboard south of Maine.

Hiking trails include the 13-mile Greenbelt Circular Trail, the 7-mile

La Tourette Trail, the 5¼-mile Richmondtown Circular Trail, the 4⅕-mile Willowbrook Trail, and the 5½-mile Amundsen Trail.

Reeds Basket Willow Swamp, 30 acres of trees, ferns, vines, and shrubs, flourishes in what used to be a glacial pond.

High Rock Park (at Nevada Ave., off Rockland Ave.), 94 acres of woodlands, swamps, and freshwater ponds, has its own network of six walking trails. The Urban Park Rangers (tel. 718/667–6042) sponsor regular guided walks here on weekends.

Moravian Cemetery (*see* Cemeteries, *below*).

Adjacent **Clove Lakes Park** (at Victory Blvd. and Clove Rd., tel. 718/390–
Parklands 8000), created by the damming of an ancient glacial valley, has three lakes, four bridges, and forests of oaks and beeches covering 195 acres.

Great Kills Park, on the Atlantic and part of the Gateway National Recreation Area (tel. 718/351–6970) is a good place for walking and for spotting shorebirds like killdeer, plover, and teal. Monarch butterflies stop here during their migrations to and from Mexico.

Gardens

New Yorkers who like to see nature pruned, planted, and blooming turn out on weekends to stroll, chat, and smell the flowers in the city's great gardens. Horticultural novices will no doubt encounter expert gardeners who are happy to share their passion and offer a tip or two.

Brooklyn With just 52 acres, this favorite New York green spot is smaller than
Botanic its Bronx counterpart but no less wonderful. In spring, its Daffodil
Garden Hill is like sunshine turned into flowers; when the 30 varieties of cherry and crab apple trees bloom, the Cherry Esplanade is one of the best shows in town. Lilacs burst forth when the cherries fade, followed by wisteria, azaleas, peonies, irises, and roses in a thousand varieties. The Japanese Hill and Pond Garden has a lakeful of goldfish and turtles, the Shakespeare Garden is full of plants immortalized by the Bard. The Steinhardt Conservatory lays out the Trail of Evolution through three domed and cupola-topped greenhouses, showing how plant life developed from the mosses and horsetails of billions of years ago to the plants of present-day deserts, temperate lands, and tropics. *1000 Washington Ave., Brooklyn, tel. 718/622–4433. Admission to grounds: $3 adults; $1.50 senior citizens; 50¢ children 6–16. Open weekends 10–6 (Oct.–Mar., 10–4:30).*

The Cloisters At the heart of this ersatz medieval monastery (*see* Chapter 4), some
Gardens 250 species of plants and flowers that would have been found in monastery gardens centuries ago flourish against the most colorful of backdrops: the Romanesque Cuxa Cloister, with its pink-and-white marble columns and octagonal fountain. The more austere Bonnefont Cloister has a fine view of the Palisades across the Hudson River. The Gothic Trie Cloister contains plantings of the 50 species identified in the museum's Unicorn Tapestries. The Saint-Guilhem Cloister, covered with a skylight, displays flowering bulbs and other greens in winter. Detour into Fort Tryon Park nearby to see the **Heather Garden,** just 600 feet long but wonderfully colorful thanks to original designs by Frederick Law Olmsted, Jr. *Ft. Tryon Park, tel. 212/923–3700. Suggested contribution: $8 adults, $4 students and senior citizens. Open Mar.–Oct., weekends 9:30–5:15; Nov.–Feb., weekends 9:30–4:45.*

Conservatory A colorful retreat, established as part of a WPA project in the 1930s,
Garden the Conservatory Garden is one of Central Park's showplaces. Just which of its three sections is loveliest is hard to say. Is it the central half-acre of verdant lawn flanked by allées of crab apple trees leading to a wisteria-twined pergola? Or the geometrically planted French parterre with its fountain of frolicking nymphs? Or the inti-

mate, naturalistic area full of magnolias, lilacs, annuals, and perennials, known as the Secret Garden after the Frances Hodgson Burnett children's classic? This is a gorgeous place, and the wrought-iron gates, from a now-demolished Vanderbilt mansion, make a stunning entrance. *5th Ave. at 105th St., tel. 212/360–2766. Admission free. Open weekends 8 AM–dusk. Free garden tours are given every Sat. (Apr.–Oct.) at 11 AM, rain or shine.*

New York Botanical Garden These 250 carefully tended acres are among New York City's most underappreciated delights—and recent renovations have made the garden even more appealing. Reopened in 1997 after a $24 million restoration in which 17,000 panes of glass were replaced by hand, the Enid A. Haupt Conservatory—an enormous Victorian-era glass house—once again shelters desert and tropical plant collections; and the all-new Everett Children's Adventure Garden, which includes a kid-sized laboratory, gives city youngsters a place to learn about plants, ecosystems, and the natural world. Other pleasures to be found outdoors include: formal gardens full of clematis, daylilies, and perennials; the geometrically planted herb garden with some 100 species; and the award-winning T.H. Everett rock garden, showing off thousands of delicate alpine flowers. There are also pines, spruce, and fir from all over the world; gardens of seasonal flowers; Rhododendron Valley, a blizzard of color in late May and early June; the Murray Liasson Narcissus Collection; Azalea Way; Cherry Valley; the T. A. Havemeyer Lilac Collection, whose huge white, pink, and lavender flower clusters perfume the air in May; and the Peggy Rockefeller Rose Garden, which blooms from late May until the first hard frosts. The surprising center of it all is the 40-acre NYBG Forest—the only uncut woodland in all New York City. Weekend walks and lectures are available on a regular basis, and special events, such as the spring flower festival and summer concerts, take place year-round. Don't leave without checking out the Shop in the Garden, which sells what are probably the healthiest plants in the city, along with other botanically inspired items. *200th St. and Southern Blvd., the Bronx, tel. 718/817–8700. Admission: $3 adults, $1 senior citizens, students, and children 6–16. Narrated tram tours: $1. Parking: $4. Open Nov.–Mar., weekends 10–4; Apr.–Oct., weekends 10–6.*

Queens Botanical Garden Brides, their attendants, and their mothers and mothers-in-law make summer weekends a constant swirl of ruffles, petticoats, and smiles at the Wedding Garden, with its weeping willows and water-lily pool; beyond that little corner, you can stroll through a bee garden, bird garden, herb garden, formal gardens of annuals, rose garden, and more. New demonstration gardens provide tips to urban horticulturists, and in late April and early May more than 10,000 tulips create a dazzling mass of color. *43–50 Main St., Flushing, Queens, tel. 718/886–3800. Admission free. Open Apr.–Oct., weekends 8–6; Nov.–Mar., weekends, 8–4.*

Staten Island Botanical Garden Situated on the 83-acre grounds of the Snug Harbor Cultural Center, this lush spread of sloping lawns and shapely trees has a Victorian air. The perennial garden is the area's largest; many other small gardens follow specific themes—one is for herbs, another for annuals, another to attract butterflies, and yet another full of roses. Tours are available. *1000 Richmond Terr., Staten Island, tel. 718/273–8200. Admission free. Open weekends dawn–dusk.*

Wave Hill Located on the Hudson River in Riverdale, the Bronx, this 28-acre estate, with 18 acres of gardens and 10 acres of woodlands, is a high point of horticultural New York. Directors of other public gardens come from all over the country to admire the plants and their unusual juxtapositions, which change from year to year. Free greenhouse and garden walks take place on Sunday afternoons at 2:15; there are also occasional nature walks, gardening workshops, family art projects, art shows, and concerts. A charming café serves drinks and snacks. *Independence Ave. at 249th St., Riverdale, the Bronx, tel. 718/549–3200. Admission: $4 adults, $2 students and senior citizens, children under 6 free; free mid-Nov.–mid-Mar. Open May 15–Oct. 14, weekends 9–5:30; Oct. 15–May 14, weekends 9–4:30.*

Zoos

The city's six zoos—known officially as wildlife conservation centers—are home to many, many species of mammals, birds, and reptiles. A recent $72 million capital modernization program has made them all the more attractive.

New York Aquarium for Wildlife Conservation This great institution on Coney Island's famous boardwalk has 10,000 specimens representing 300 different species of marine creatures. Among the more than 100 indoor and outdoor exhibits on the aquarium's 14 acres, you'll find Nuka—an 1,800-lb. Pacific walrus—who eats 400 pounds of squid, smelt, and herring each week, as well as sea turtles, sandtiger sharks, and baby beluga whales. At the popular Discovery Cove exhibit, a complex of coastal environments, there is a tidepool where youngsters can touch sea urchins and starfish and a 400-gallon "tidal wave" that crashes overhead every 30 seconds. Sea Cliffs, the aquarium's newest exhibit, re-creates the rocky Pacific coast and is home to walruses, seals, penguins, and dozens of different fish. Dolphins and sea lions perform for visitors in the aquarium's Aquatheater. *Surf Ave. at W. 8th St., Coney Island, Brooklyn, tel. 718/265–3474. Admission: $7.75 adults, $3.50 senior citizens and children 2–12, children under 2 free. Parking: $6. Open Memorial Day–Labor Day, weekends 10–7; Labor Day–Memorial Day, weekends 10–4.*

Central Park Zoo The country's oldest public zoo, first opened in 1864, is now state-of-the-art all the way: Animals live in tidy man-made biomes that re-create their natural habitats—even the lighting simulates the seasons. The focal point is a sea lion pool. Flanking it, and linked by a brick-and-glass colonnade, are three other substantial areas: the sky-lighted Tropic Zone building, which explores life in the rain forest from ground to treetops, amid ferns, moss, and steamy mists; the Temperate Territory, with its snow monkeys, Asian red pandas, and North American river otters; and the frosty Polar Circle, where you can watch the polar bears and penguins sporting below the water line as well as above. Artificial streams and fences hidden by vegetation replace bars. *Near 5th Ave. at 64th St. in Central Park, tel. 212/861–6030. Admission: $2.50 adults, $1.25 senior citizens, 50¢ children 3–12, children under 3 free. Open Apr.–Oct., weekends 10:30–5:30; Nov.–Mar., weekends 10–4:30.*

Bronx Zoo Only in a big zoo like this one, the largest urban zoo in the country, could you ride a camel, explore a jungle world of crocodiles and slumbering pythons, see snow leopards prowl Himalayan peaks, and penetrate the world of animal nightlife—all in the same afternoon. More than 600 species of animals are assembled here on 265 acres of woods, meadows, ponds, and streams, much of the grounds planted and contoured to re-create the landscapes of far-away places. Wild Asia, where elephants and tigers roam, is nearly 40 acres of open meadows and dark forests; in Jungle World, where only ravines, streams, and cliffs separate you from the narrow-nosed crocs and the 750-pound Malayan tapirs, waterfalls, and lush plantings add up to an indoor tropical forest. *Fordham Rd., the Bronx, tel. 718/367–1010 or 718/220–5141 for Friends of Wildlife Conservation walking tours. Admission: Apr.–Oct., $6.75 adults, $3 senior citizens and children 2–12; Nov.–Mar., $3 adults, $1.50 senior citizens and children 2–12. Parking: $6. Open Apr.–Oct., weekends 10–5:30; Nov.–Mar., weekends 10–4:30.*

Prospect Park Zoo This charming zoo focuses on small animals and is perfect for small children. Kids can get a nose-to-nose view of a prairie dog town, jump on lily-pad-shaped stepping stones across a marsh, walk in a 2,500 square foot aviary with free-flying birds, and sketch their favorite animals with drawing supplies provided by the zoo. *450 Flatbush Ave., Brooklyn, tel. 718/399–7339. Admission: $2.50 adults, $1.25 senior citizens, 50¢ children 3–12, children under 3 free. Open Apr.–Oct., weekends 10–5:30; Nov.–Mar., weekends 10–4:30.*

Queens Zoo With 250 animals and 40 species, the Queens Zoo displays North America's animals—including bison, mountain lions, black bears, and wolves—on pockets of wild habitat. Native woodland birds can be seen in a geodesic dome aviary, where a walkway winds from the forest floor into the treetops. And sea lions frolic on a "rocky California coast." There is also a petting zoo where kids can meet and touch domesticated animals, such as sheep, goats, and rabbits. *Flushing Meadows–Corona Park, Queens, tel. 718/271–1500 or 718/271–7761 for recorded information. Admission: $2.50 adults, $1.25 senior citizens, 50¢ children 3–12, children under 3 free. Open Apr.–Oct., weekends 10–5:30; Nov.–Mar., weekends 10–4:30.*

Staten Island Zoo The excellent collection of snakes—though they prefer the term "venomous reptiles"—is the highlight of this smallish (8-acre) zoo, but mammal fans like the new African savannah and rain forest exhibits (with ocelots and vampire bats). Children are enchanted by the animal hospital and its nursery viewing area, as well as by the children's zoo full of farm animals that can be petted and fed. *614 Broadway, Sunnyside (in Barrett Park), Staten Island, tel. 718/442–3100. Admission: $3 adults, $2 senior citizens and children 3–11, children under 3 free. Parking: free. Open weekends 10–4:45.*

Cemeteries

No description of the city's green places is complete without a mention of its cemeteries, where the shrub-scattered, tree-shaded lawns are punctuated at regular intervals by memorial headstones, monuments, and miniature temples. More peaceful than the parks on weekends, these graveyards also have fascinating stories to tell.

Manhattan **New York Marble Cemetery** (between 1st Ave. and the Bowery, 2nd and 3rd Sts.) is the last of more than three dozen cemeteries of Manhattan's early years. It's not open to the public, but through the gates you can read on its headstones names of such luminaries as Roosevelt, Varick, Scribner, and Beekman.

St. Mark's in-the-Bowery (10th St. at 2nd Ave., tel. 212/674–6377) claims Peter Stuyvesant as the most famous resident of its cobbled early 19th-century churchyard.

St. Paul's Chapel (Broadway at Fulton St., tel. 212/602–0874), a Georgian-style structure (circa 1766), once George Washington's place of worship and now Manhattan's oldest public building, is surrounded by a mossy, grassy, ivied churchyard. Its tumble of blackened headstones and monuments are incised with weeping willows and other funereal motifs of the day.

Shearith Israel, a Jewish congregation, has created three cemeteries over the years. The oldest (55 St. James Pl., opposite Chatham Sq.), in use 1682–1828, is full of faded inscriptions in Hebrew, English, and a Spanish-Hebrew known as Ladino. The second (76 W. 11 St., between 6th and 7th Aves.) was used 1805–1829, and the third (21st St., between 6th and 7th Aves.) 1829–1851. *Call 212/873–0300 for appointments to view these.*

Trinity Cemetery (between Amsterdam Ave. and Riverside Dr., 153rd to 155th Sts., tel. 212/368–1600) was established by Trinity Church (*see below*) in the 19th century, when this uptown site was farmland once owned by naturalist-artist John James Audubon. Rural peace still prevails on the grounds, which climb from the Hudson

River up to Amsterdam Avenue. Audubon's grave is here, as are those of the colorful Eliza Brown Jumel (who owned the Morris-Jumel Mansion; *see* Chapter 4); Charles Dickens's son, Alfred Tennyson Dickens; philanthropist John Jacob Astor; and clergyman Clement Clarke Moore, author of *'Twas the Night before Christmas.* The cemetery's walls, gates, and keeper's lodge were designed by the firm of Calvert Vaux, who worked with Frederick Law Olmsted on Central Park. The cemetery adjoins Trinity's former rural chapel, now the baronial Church of the Intercession.

Trinity Church (Broadway at Wall St., tel. 212/602–0800), downtown, is home to frequent concerts on weekdays. Weekends are best for savoring the churchyard's peace and for contemplating the sweep of New York City history revealed by the graves of Alexander Hamilton, William Bradford, steamship creator Robert Fulton, and Captain James Lawrence, the War of 1812 hero who exhorted, "Don't give up the ship!"

The Bronx **Woodlawn** (233rd St. and Webster Ave., tel. 718/920–0500) is considered by some people to be the most beautiful cemetery in the country; its 400 acres show off an incredible variety of trees—huge white oak and weeping beech, golden rain trees, and Kentucky coffee trees—and shelter some 120 species of birds. However, it's perhaps best known as the last resting place of a roster of tycoons, celebrities, and politicos so extensive that the cemetery actually publishes a map. The names read like a Who's Who of American civilization: meat-packer H. D. Armour, stockbroker Jules Bache, evaporated milk maker Gail Borden, Roaring '20s dancers Irene and Vernon Castle, patriotic song-and-dance man George M. Cohan, jazz greats Duke Ellington and Miles Davis, Admiral David Farragut, tycoon Jay Gould, impresario Oscar Hammerstein (the lyricist's father), bluesman W. C. Handy, composer Victor Herbert, railroad magnate Collis P. Huntington, dimestore kings Samuel H. Kress and Frank W. Woolworth, longtime New York City mayor Fiorello La Guardia, merchants R. H. Macy and J. C. Penney, newspaperman Joseph Pulitzer, women's rights crusader Elizabeth Cady Stanton, inventor Henry H. Westinghouse, and many others. The headstone of *Moby Dick* author Herman Melville, which bears the image of a blank slate, is near the oak where kidnapper Bruno Hauptmann received the $50,000 ransom for the Lindbergh baby. Woodlawn can be unexpectedly lively, with a dozen or so large Sunday concerts every year—jazz, choral music, George M. Cohan songs, Duke Ellington jazz, and Christmas carolers.

Brooklyn **Green-Wood** (5th Ave. at 25th St., tel. 718/768–7300) was designed by Henry Pierrepont, who laid out the streets of Brooklyn in 1835, a year after it was incorporated. He provided not only 11 parks for the new city but also, inspired by the rolling greenness of Paris's famous Père Lachaise and Boston's Mount Auburn, created a cemetery full of hills, ponds, lakes, and meandering drives. Its 478 acres have remained among the city's greenest and still offer some of the best bird-watching in the city. Along 22 miles of lanes and 209 paths bearing names like Sylvan Water, Lawn Avenue, Glade Hill, and Grassy Dell, the stones tell tales. An Indian princess said to have died from overeating when feted by New York society is buried here, as is the mad poet McDonald Clark, who is believed by some to have drowned himself in jail by letting a faucet drip down his throat. Better-known denizens are Governor De Witt Clinton; William Marcy "Boss" Tweed; piano manufacturer Henry Engelhard Steinway; soap magnate William Colgate; pharmaceutical kings Edward Squibb and Charles Pfizer; tobacco millionaire Pierre Lorillard; artists Nathaniel Currier, James Merrit Ives, Louis Comfort Tiffany, George Wesley Bellows, and George Catlin; newspapermen Henry J. Raymond (of the *New York Times*), Horace Greeley (of the *Tribune*), and James Gordon Bennett, Jr. (of the *Evening Telegram*); inventors

Samuel F. B. Morse (the telegraph), Peter Cooper (the steam loco-
motive), Elias Howe (the sewing machine), and "Soda Fountain
King" John Matthews (carbonated water); as well as gangsters Al-
bert Anastasia and Joey Gallo (gunned down at Umberto's Clam
House), and scattered secretaries of the navy, Civil War generals,
U.S. senators, and entertainers. Two-hour walking tours, which
cost $5, are given every Sunday in spring and fall (in nice weather) at
1 PM; call 718/469-5277 for details.

Quaker Cemetery (Prospect Park) is a landscape of big trees, old
gravestones, and pleasant hills; it's also the burial place of actor
Montgomery Clift, who died in 1966 at the age of 45. Although it's
inside a city park, the cemetery is closed to the public. However, occasional tours are given by the Urban Park Rangers (tel. 718/438-
0100).

Staten Island **Moravian Cemetery** (Richmond Rd. at Otis Ave. between Todt Hill
Rd. and Altamont, tel. 718/351-0136) boasts the tenancy of Commo-
dore Cornelius Vanderbilt, who germinated the seed of his great for-
tune by operating a ferry from Staten Island to Manhattan before
the War of 1812. He spent a million dollars here on an imposing
bronze-embellished mausoleum designed by the noted Richard Morris Hunt. His ancestor, Jacob Van Der Bilt, became a Moravian in
the 18th century and is buried on an adjacent plot; many others of
the sect are buried here, segregated according to sex. However, the
cemetery wasn't always a property of the United Brethren, and
many graves—including the first, of one Colonel Nicholas Britten,
dated 1740—are nonsectarian.

Group Outings

Appalachian Mountain Club (5 Tudor City Pl., New York, NY 10017,
tel. 212/986-1430). This popular hiking club schedules about a dozen
outings every weekend, year-round. Write or call for information
about membership and upcoming events.

New York City Audubon Society (71 W. 23rd St., tel. 212/691-7483).
The New York City chapter of the Audubon Society—the largest in
the nation—sponsors local wildlife walks.

Outdoor Singles (tel. 718/353-5506). This organization leads hikes
each weekend.

Outdoors Club (Box 227, Lenox Hill Station, New York, NY 10021).
Write to the club for a current schedule of walks, rambles, and
hikes.

Shorewalkers (Box 20748, New York, NY 10025, tel. 212/330-7686).
Club members regularly explore the city's waterfront and environs.

Sierra Club (Atlantic Chapter Outings, Box 880, Planeterium Station, New York, NY 10024, tel. 718/370-2096). The club's regional
chapter schedules city walks, hikes, treks, bike rides, and ski trips
year-round.

Wild Foods Walks (tel. 718/291-6825; or send a stamped self-
addressed envelope to 143-25 84th Dr., 6C, Jamaica, NY 11435 for a
schedule). "Wildman" Steve Brill leads botanical forays to identify
edible plants in parks in all five boroughs. Recipes provided.

Tours Led by The Urban Park Rangers of the New York City Department of Parks
Park Rangers and Recreation know about park history—both natural and
unnatural—and can take you to little-known green spots. For a current listing of weekend walking tours, call their hotline (tel. 800/
201-7275).

At the Gateway National Recreation Area—which encompasses
26,000 acres of bayshore, beach, open water, and protected wildlife
habitat—weekend walking tours are led year-round by national
park rangers. For a copy of their program guide, call the Jamaica
Bay Wildlife Refuge (tel. 718/318-4340) or the park's Staten Island
unit (tel. 718/351-6970).

Sports and Recreation

There's nothing quite like the exhilaration of victory, the agony of defeat, and the thrill of the game for completely obliterating all the real worries of the work week. The competitive spirit so dear to New Yorkers flourishes on weekends in dozens of private facilities and public parks.

Ballroom Dancing

Ballroom on Fifth (319 5th Ave., at 32nd St., tel. 212/532–6232) gives private and group lessons in waltz, tango, rumba, swing, mambo, merengue, and salsa. As demonstrated in the movie *Strictly Ballroom*, many of the dancers are competitors, but there are group classes for beginners too.

Roseland (239 W. 52nd St., tel. 212/247–0200), a glossy dance palace from back when, attracts a good Sunday crowd, mostly men and women over 50, with a sprinkling of younger newcomers. The bands play on from 2:30 to 11.

Sandra Cameron Dance Center (20 Cooper Sq., at E. 5th St., 6th floor, tel. 212/674–0505), owned by a three-time U.S. champion is a focal point for the resurgence of ballroom dancing, with classes in all ballroom styles and a tea dance from 2 to 6 every Sunday. Sandra Cameron also sponsors Saturday night ballroom and swing dancing at the 92nd Street Y.

Stepping Out (1780 Broadway, tel. 212/245–5200), another teaching studio that draws a crowd of ballroom specialists, devotes Saturday to private lessons in ballroom dancing, Latin, and swing, with group dancing in the evening.

Baseball

Playing fields in almost every park are largely reserved for leagues playing either softball or baseball. To guarantee playing time, you need a permit (call 800/201–7275 for information), but there are also pickup games here and there. Sometimes the game happens by chance, the teams made up of anyone within earshot, so take your mitt, and ask whether an extra is needed.

Solo hitters can practice in batting cages at **Hackers, Hitters & Hoops** (123 W. 18th St., tel. 212/929–7482).

Indoor batting cages can also be rented at the Field House at the **Chelsea Piers** (23rd St. and the Hudson River, tel. 212/336–6500).

Basketball

Shooting and dribbling action takes place at hundreds of outdoor courts. Those at **6th Avenue near 8th Street** draw real hotshots—and amazed onlookers. There's also lively play in **Riverside Park,** at the five-court complex between 104th and 114th streets and at another complex near 76th Street. **Hackers, Hitters & Hoops** (*see* Baseball, *above*) has an indoor court.

Bicycling

On weekend mornings, some 60 to 110 members of the **Century Road Club Association** (tel. 212/222–8062) turn out early—usually around 7 AM—for four- or five-lap races around the 6¼-mile circular drive in Central Park. Smaller packs of racing cyclists streak along at practically any hour on both Saturday and Sunday, although the park roads, closed to auto traffic, also have plenty of room for those who pedal at a more sedate speed. Early weekend mornings, city streets lend themselves perfectly to exploring by bike.

Manhattan While **Central Park** is the focal point of the city cycling scene, the **Riverside Park** promenade, between 72nd and 110th streets, with its Hudson River view, gets a more easygoing crowd. A new 3-mile bikeway along the Hudson River runs from 41st Street to **Hudson River Park**, the **Battery Park City Esplanade**, and **Battery Park**, where you can watch the sun set over the Statue of Liberty. Or circle through the winding streets of upper Manhattan in **Inwood Hill** or **Marble Hill**, where there are some terrific old brownstones, town-houses, and imposing apartment buildings. The entrance to the bike- and walk-way over the George Washington Bridge can be found at 178th Street and Cabrini Boulevard; from there, you can ride across the Hudson River, and connect with scenic River Road in New Jersey.

Brooklyn The trip across the **Brooklyn Bridge**, with its superb views of Man-hattan, is one of the most exhilarating in the city. The winding, syl-van roads in **Prospect Park**, closed to auto traffic as in Central Park, are also popular. Another good bet: the 2¼-mile-long bikeway along neighboring **Eastern Parkway**, once known as the Champs-Elysées of Brooklyn. The **Ocean Parkway** bicycle path, which runs from Church Avenue, near Prospect Park to Sea Breeze Avenue at Coney Island, is the oldest bikeway in the country, dating back to 1892; it's lined with benches, high-rise apartment complexes, and spreading maples, sycamores, and gingkos. The **Shore Parkway** bicycle path, a narrow strip of green from Owls Head Park in Bay Ridge to Kenne-dy Airport in Queens, offers a constantly changing vista—now the Verrazano-Narrows Bridge and Manhattan skyline, later Jamaica Bay and the Rockaways—but glittering water is always your com-panion. The **Coney Island Boardwalk** makes for a good ride provided you don't mind the bumps and get there before the crowds.

Staten Island Make tracks around the reservoir and on the roads in 209-acre **Silver Lake Park**, closed to motor vehicles on weekends. The golf course sets forth emerald vistas.

Rentals **AAA Bikes** (in Central Park's Loeb Boathouse, near E. 74th St., tel. 212/861–4137) is open weekends 9–7, closed in winter.
Canal Street Bicycles (417 Canal St., at 6th Ave., tel. 212/334–8000) is open Saturday 9:30–6:30 and Sunday 10–6.
Gene's Bicycles (242 E. 79th St., tel. 212/249–9218) is open weekends 9:30–7.
Metro Bicycles (1311 Lexington Ave., at 88th St., tel. 212/427–4450; 332 E. 14th St., tel. 212/228–4344; 546 6th Ave., at 15th St., tel. 212/255–5100; 231 W. 96th St., at Broadway, tel. 663–7531) are open Saturday 9:30–6:30 and Sunday 10–5, give or take an hour; call to confirm times.
Midtown Bicycles (360 W. 47th St., tel. 212/581–4500) is open Satur-day 10–6 and Sunday 10–5.
Pedal Pusher (1306 2nd Ave., between 68th and 69th Sts., tel. 212/288–5592) is open weekends 10–6.
West Side Bikes (231 W. 96th St., tel. 212/663–7531) is open week-ends 10–6, with shorter hours in winter.

Group Trips **Hosteling International–American Youth Hostels** (891 Amsterdam Ave., at 103rd St., tel. 212/932–2300) runs the Five Borough Bicyc-ling Club, which in addition to organizing day and weekend trips, sponsors the annual Five Borough Bicycle Tour in May, a 42-mile ride that takes 28,000 cyclists over usually cars-only roadways such as the FDR Drive, the Brooklyn–Queens Expressway, and the Verrazano-Narrows Bridge.
Staten Island Bicycling Association (tel. 718/815–9290) runs group tours on and off the island.
Transportation Alternatives (92 St. Mark's Pl., tel. 212/475–4600) sponsors group rides twice a month and publishes City Cyclist, a bi-monthly newsletter listing rides throughout the city. The group also

sponsors the Century, a five-borough bike marathon on the first or second Sunday in September.

Billiards and Pool

Although alcohol was prohibited in them until recently, new regulations now allow pool halls to serve beer, further lubricating the pool hall scene. Tables cost $7–$16 per hour, depending on the place, the time of day, and the number of players.

Amsterdam Billiard Club (344 Amsterdam Ave., between 76th and 77th Sts., tel. 212/496–8180), part-owned by comedian David Brenner, is particularly fashionable. There are 31 tables. *Open Sat. 11 AM–4 AM, Sun. 11 AM–3 AM.*

Amsterdam Billiard Club East (210 E. 86th St., between 2nd and 3rd Aves., tel. 212/570–4545) has 38 tables, an eight-ball league, a café, and an international beer bar. Open *Sat. 11 AM–4 AM, Sun. 11 AM–3 AM.*

The Billiard Club (220 W. 19th St., tel. 212/206–7665), with its velvet curtains and enormous bouquets, has a classy, turn-of-the-century look and 33 tables. *Open Sat. noon–3:30 AM, Sun. 1–1.*

Chelsea Billiards (54 W. 21st St., tel. 212/989–0096), with 53 tables on two floors, is one of the busiest. *Open 24 hrs.*

Corner Billiards (85 4th Ave., at 11th St., 212/995–1314) has 28 pool tables and a café in a brightly lit space. There's also a pool school and league play. *Open Sat. noon–3 AM, Sun. noon–2 AM.*

Julian's Famous Poolroom (138 E. 14th St., tel. 212/598–9884) has a quadrophonic CD jukebox, 29 pool tables, and eight Ping-Pong tables. *Open Sat. 11 AM–4 AM, Sun. 11 AM–2 AM.*

Le Q (36 E. 12th St., tel. 212/995–8512) has 28 tables, just off University Place. *Open 24 hours.*

Soho Billiards (56 E. Houston St., between Mulberry and Mott Sts., tel. 212/925–3753) offers 28 tables, a pool school taught by pros, and a snack bar. *Open Sat. 11–5 AM, Sun. 11AM–3 AM.*

West Side Billiard Club (601 W. 50th St., tel. 212/246–1060) has 12 pool tables, 8 Ping-Pong tables, and snacks. *Open weekends 11 AM–4 AM.*

Bird-Watching

When you think of Manhattan bird life, you may think first of pigeons, but in fact the city's green parks and woodlands provide a habitat for everything from Canada geese, summer tanagers, and fork-tailed flycatchers to buffleheads, Kentucky warblers, and common nighthawks. Since the city is on the Atlantic flyway, one of the country's four major spring and fall migratory routes, you can see birds that nest as far north as the High Arctic. May is the best season, when the songbirds are in their freshest colors, with so many singing at once you can hardly distinguish their songs. On a warm day with southwesterly breezes, an experienced birder who visits both shore and woodland can easily sight up to 100 species. To find out what's been seen where, call the Rare Bird Alert (tel. 212/979–3070). The **New York City Audubon Society** (71 W. 23rd St., New York, NY 10010, tel. 212/691–7483) offers outings most weekends as well as birding courses.

Manhattan **Central Park** has four prime birding areas: the promontory of the Pond near the southeast entrance, the Reservoir, the Loch at 104th Street in the center of the park, and the wild-and-woodsy Ramble on the north shore of the lake. Some 20 species of birds nest in the park, including cardinals, downy woodpeckers, eastern kingbirds, gray catbirds, and mallard ducks; others come through during migrations. The spring migration begins in March and climaxes in mid-May. You may see fish crows and iridescent common grackles in February; American robins and American woodcocks in March; ruby-crowned kinglets, blue-gray gnatcatchers, yellow-rumped warblers, brown creepers, black-and-white warblers, and hermit thrushes in April; and orioles, scarlet tanagers, rose-breasted grosbeaks, indigo buntings, and some 25 brightly colored species of warblers in May. The fall migration is less concentrated and less colorful because the birds aren't in their mating plumage—but it is the best time of year to look for hawks. Even bald eagles have been seen flying over the top of the park's Belvedere Castle, where hawk watches are held daily in October and November.

For more information about birding in Central Park, call the Henry Luce Nature Observatory in Belvedere Castle (tel. 212/772–0210), which sponsors birding tours through the Ramble, or the Charles A. Dana Discovery Center (tel. 212/860–1370), which hosts a family bird-watching club on the weekends.

The Bronx The best spots are the saltwater marsh and the lagoon in 2,764-acre **Pelham Bay Park,** where bald eagles, ospreys, and great horned owls have been sighted in recent years, and the freshwater marshes and upland woods in 1,146-acre **Van Cortlandt Park.**

Brooklyn The lakes and hilly terrain of 526-acre **Prospect Park** attract a bird population comparable to that of Central Park. It is known for the diversity of migrants, and some 22 species are known to nest here. Try the the Vale of Cashmere, Midwood, the shores of Prospect Lake, and Lookout Hill.

Other good bets in the borough include the 798-acre **Marine Park** marsh (near Ave. U, tel. 718/965–6551); the grassland habitat surrounding the abandoned runways at the city's first municipal airport, **Floyd Bennett Field** (tel. 718/338–3799); and **Green-Wood Cemetery.**

Queens The city's number-one spot for birding is the **Jamaica Bay Wildlife Refuge** (tel. 718/318–4340); its extensive bay shore and two large ponds are prime habitat for migrating shorebirds and wading birds such as herons, plovers, skimmers, oyster-catchers, and sandpipers. Spring and fall are the most rewarding times to visit, but flocks of avian visitors can be seen year-round from the refuge's well-kept trails. The woodlands and wetlands around the **Alley Pond Environmental Center** host a diverse population that includes egrets, herons, and Canada geese, as well as a fantastic array of small birds; Alley Pond is also the site of the **Queens County Bird Club's** monthly meetings (tel. 718/229–4000). Other good spots in Queens are **Flushing Meadows–Corona Park,** especially Meadow and Willow lakes; **Forest Park** (tel. 718/520–5316); and the 235-acre **Kissena Park,** which begins at the Nature Center (tel. 718/353–2460).

Staten Island Located surprisingly close to the Fresh Kills Landfill, the 260-acre **William T. Davis Wildlife Refuge** (off Travis Ave., New Springville, tel. 718/667–2165 for tours and trail maps) occupies a transition zone between salt marshes and glacial terrain full of hardwood forests, so it offers a wide range of birds, animals, and insects. Shrubby growths of viburnum and marsh roses provide cover for warblers and woodpeckers. This is an especially good place to sight hawks—red-tails, sharp-shinned, Coopers, and marsh hawks.

Wolfe's Pond Park (Holton Ave. at Hylan Blvd., tel. 718/984–8266) a fairly undeveloped 317 acres of wetlands, stretches around a pond that may be covered from shore to shore with ducks and geese during a migration; a stone's throw away, at the ocean, 200–300 birds—grebes, cormorants, and ducks—may land in front of you all at once.

Boating

The idea of boating around New York City conjures up images of a 19th-century lady twirling her parasol while her elegantly suited swain rows her across still waters. Only the costumes have changed, although the participants often have radios to serenade them when conversation palls. Go early.

In **Central Park,** the boats are rowboats (plus one authentic Venetian gondola) and the rowing terrain is the 18-acre lake. *Loeb Boathouse, near 74th St., tel. 212/517–2233. Open spring–fall, weekends 10:30– 6.*

In **Prospect Park,** the four-seater boats that scuttle across the 60-acre Prospect Lake and Lullwater are pedal powered. *Kate's Corner, near Wollman Skating Rink, tel. 718/282–7789. Open Memorial Day–Labor Day, weekends 11–6.*

Recently, public access to the Manhattan waterfront has improved, and several small boating clubs have begun to paddle on the Hudson River. The **Downtown Boathouse** (Pier 26, at N. Moore St. and the Hudson River, tel. 212/966–1852), open from 9 AM to dusk on weekends, has a small boat launch; and the **79th Street Boat Basin** in Riverside Park has a brand-new kayak launch and storage facility, where members of the **Hudson River Watertrail Association** (W. 79th St. Boat Basin, Box 46, New York, NY 10024) launch group paddles and host a spring Kayak Festival.

Boccie

There's more boccie than bowling in New York—100 city courts in the five boroughs. Of these, the easiest to get to from Midtown are at 96th Street and 1st Avenue, at East River Drive and 42nd Street, and at the Thompson Street Playground at Thompson and Houston streets in Greenwich Village. You'll also find boccie courts on Randalls and Wards islands, in Cunningham Park (718/217–6452) in Queens, and in Prospect Park, Brooklyn.

Bowling

Leagues are popular, so call before you come to make sure that open bowling is available.

Bowlmor has 44 lanes and a colorful Village crowd. *110 University Pl., between 12th & 13th Sts., tel. 212/255–8188. Open weekends 10 AM–2 AM.*

Leisure Time Bowling & Recreation Center offers 30 lanes on the second floor of the Port Authority Bus Terminal. *625 8th Ave., at 42nd St., tel. 212/268–6909. Open Sat. 10 AM–2 AM, Sun. 10 AM–11 PM.*

Whitestone Lanes offers good clean fun on 48 lanes. *30-05 Whitestone Pkwy., Flushing, Queens, tel. 718/353–6300. Open 24 hrs.*

Cross-Country Skiing

In **Central Park,** the Sheep Meadow, the Great Lawn, and the North Meadow are flat enough for even beginners to handle. In **Prospect Park,** Long Meadow and Nethermead are favorite destinations. Better skiers tackle various city nature trails: Bucks Hollow in **La Tourette Park,** Staten Island, winding through a former farm; the hardwood forests traversed by the Cass Gallagher Nature Trail in **Van Cortlandt Park;** and the woods in **Pelham Bay Park.**

For rentals, try **Scandinavian Ski & Sport** (40 W. 57th St., tel. 212/ 757–8524), open Saturday 10–7:30, Sunday 11–6:30.

Exercise and Yoga

Exercise studios do big business every day and, for many, weekends are the busiest time, attracting a mixed bunch of regulars, super-fit dancer types, and weekend athletes. Neighborhood favorites with classes all day include:

Classic Bodies Fitness (187 E. 79th St., tel. 212/737–8440). A solid range of classes—step aerobics, Hatha yoga, body sculpting, and "lean-and-mean" (a popular aerobics class mixing step and light hand-held weights)—are given all day Saturday, Sunday, and holidays.

Crunch Fitness (54 E. 13th St., between Broadway and University Pl., tel. 212/475–2018; 404 Lafayette St., below Astor Pl., tel. 212/614–0120; 162 W. 83rd St., near Amsterdam Ave., tel. 212/875–1902; 152 Christopher St., tel. 212/366–3725; and 1109 2nd Ave., between 58th and 59th Sts., tel. 212/758–3434) are decidedly hip places with fun classes, including aerobics, body sculpting, yoga, boxing, and kick boxing. There's also spinning (a stationary-racing-bike workout, complete with water bottle).

David Barton Gym (623 Broadway, between Bleecker and Houston, tel. 212/420–0507) is busy, with more than 90 classes every week, including step, yoga, body sculpting, indoor in-line skating, Tai-chi, Latin, "abs," and "Pregnant and Fit!"

Integral Yoga Institute (227 W. 13th St., tel. 212/929–0585) trains both body and mind toward fitness. The city's largest purveyor of the Hindu art, this spiritual exercise emporium, with adjacent natural food and vitamin stores, offers multiple classes from beginning to advanced on Saturday. The lotus position is just the beginning.

Integral Yoga Teaching Center (200 W. 72nd St., 4th floor, tel. 212/721–4000) has several 80-minute-long classes each weekend, focussing on posture and deep relaxation. Private meditation classes are also offered.

Jivamukti Yoga Center (149 2nd Ave., at E. 9th St., 2nd floor, tel. 212/353–0214) offers six classes a day on weekends, ranging from beginner to intermediate-advanced. Local celebrities are frequently spotted in this East Village ashram.

Steps (2121 Broadway, at 74th St., tel. 212/874–2410). Ballet, jazz, tap, and modern dance classes are offered for all skill levels, all day.

Yoga Zone (138 5th Ave., between 18th and 19th Sts., tel. 212/647–9642) has strengthening and toning classes in a sunny studio with a low-key atmosphere.

Fishing

Since the the city began fully complying with the federal Clean Water Act in the late 1980s, progressively cleaner, fish-filled waters have inspired a growing number of anglers to head for the city's 578 miles of shoreline.

Party Boats Brooklyn's **Sheepshead Bay,** a grand and stylish neighborhood at the turn of the century, is today salty, fish happy, and proud of its fleet, which is among the country's largest: Some 10–15 party boats go out every day year-round (weather permitting) and take evening trips in summer as well. A prime destination is the Mudhole, one of the world's great fishing grounds. Piers are along shore-hugging Emmons Avenue, and departure times are posted in the area—typically at 6, 7, and 8 AM for full-day trips, 8 AM and 1 PM for half-day outings. Tackle rentals and bait are provided. Call **Mike's Tackle & Bait Shop** (tel. 718/646–9261) for more information.

Small Boats On the Bronx's quaint City Island, **Jack's Bait & Tackle** (Cross St. and City Island Ave., tel. 718/885–2042) rents boats with 6-horsepower motors to go for flounder, bluefish, and striped bass. *Open May–Oct., weekends 5 AM–9 PM.*

Shore Fishing In the Bronx's **Pelham Bay Park,** regulars cast for black bass, flounder, fluke, and small blues from Orchard Beach (tel. 718/885–2275), and from nearby Hunter's and Twin islands. In Queens, **Rockaway Beach** (tel. 718/318–4000) can be good for bass, flounder, and porgies, and you can sometimes catch a big one from the **Breezy Point Jetty.**

In Brooklyn, the **Canarsie Pier** in the Gateway National Recreation Area (tel. 718/338–3799) is a favorite spot; occasionally the park management sponsors surf fishing master classes on weekends. If you just want to drop a line, try the catch-and-release program at Central Park's Harlem Meer, newly stocked with bluegills, bass, and catfish. Poles and bait are loaned out for the asking at the **Charles A. Dana Discovery Center** (110th St. near 5th Ave., tel. 212/ 860–1370).

For rods, reels, bait, tackle, and tips on where they're biting, try the following shops: **Capitol Fishing Tackle Co.,** on the ground floor of the famous Chelsea Hotel (218 W. 23rd St., tel. 212/929–6132), has everything you'll need for freshwater, saltwater, and fly fishing. *Open Sat. 9–5, closed Sun.*

The Urban Angler, Ltd. (118 E. 25th St., 3rd floor, tel. 212/979–7600) specializes in fly fishing, trip-planning, and local guide services. *Open Sat, 10–5, closed Sun.*

Golf

Courses The city's thousands of avid golfers jam the area's handful of well-tended city courses. Call 718/225–4653 to book tee times at any city course.

Long Island **Bethpage State Park** (tel. 516/249–0700), which also has tennis and polo, is about an hour and 20 minutes from Manhattan. Probably the best public golf facility in the area, it's home to no less than five courses, and the 7,065-yard par-71 Black is generally rated among the nation's top 25 public courses—the U.S. Open will be held here in the year 2002. Golfers without well-honed skills will find themselves in deep trouble on the Black's narrow fairways and small, well-bunkered greens. Other courses on the property include: the 6,537-yard Red, full of doglegs and long par 4s; the 6,513-yard par-72 Blue, with a tough front nine; the more forgiving 6,171-yard par-71 Yellow, a good beginner's course; and the 6,267-yard par-71 Green, the original course on the estate, which was acquired by the state in the early 1930s. Reservations for tee times on all five courses are accepted 24 hours a day on the park's automated reservation hot line (tel. 516/249–0707).

The Bronx **Pelham Bay Park** (tel. 718/885–1258 or 718/225–4653 for tee times) has two unexpectedly scenic 18-hole courses adjoining the Thomas Pell Wildlife Refuge and Sanctuary: the 6,405-yard Pelham course, noted for its wide fairways and gentle slopes, and the 6,492-yard Split Rock—rated New York City's most challenging course—with narrower fairways, more woods, and denser roughs.
Van Cortlandt Park is the home of the nation's first municipal golf course, established in 1895: the rolling 6,052-yard Van Cortlandt Golf Course (tel. 718/543–4595). There's also the attractive 9-hole, 3,200-yard Mosholu Golf Course (tel. 718/655–9164), with driving range, a practice green, and grass tees.

Brooklyn The 6,362-yard **Dyker Beach** course (7th Ave. and 86th St., tel. 718/ 836–9722 or 718/225–4653 for tee times) is a nice layout—tough yet forgiving.

The longest course in the city, the 6,866-yard **Marine Park Golf Course** (2880 Flatbush Ave., between Ave. U and Belt Pkwy., tel. 718/338–7113) has undergone a complete facelift in recent years and maintains some of the best greens around.

Queens The challenging 5,431-yard course at **Forest Park** (Forest Park Dr., tel. 718/296–0999) is tree-lined with rolling hills and a pro shop.

The flat, 6,263-yard **Clearview** course (202–12 Willets Point Blvd., tel. 718/229–2570 or 718/225–4653 for tee times) sees a lot of activity.

The 5,600-yard layout at **Douglaston** (6320 Marathon Pkwy. and Commonwealth Blvd., tel. 718/224–6566) is rolling, with small greens and narrow fairways.

Kissena (Booth Memorial Ave. and 164th St., tel. 718/939–4594) is relatively short at 4,665 yards, but it holds its own with decent-size hills and links-style fairways.

Staten Island At the 6,050-yard **Silver Lake** Course (915 Victory Blvd., near Forest Ave., tel. 718/447–5686), hills and tight fairways pose respectable challenges to good golfers.

The 6,366-yard **South Shore** course (Huguenot Ave. and Rally St., tel. 718/984–0101) is woodsy and recently renovated with new greens.

Historic 6,600-yard **La Tourette** (100 London Rd., at Forest Hill Rd. and Rockland Ave., tel. 718/351–1889) has long, wide, pretty fairways.

Driving Ranges In the Bronx, visit those at Turtle Cove Golf Complex in **Pelham Bay Park** and at the Mosholu Course in **Van Cortlandt Park.** In Brooklyn, there's **Gateway Sports Center** (3200 Flatbush Ave., tel. 718/253–6816), a concessionaire of the Gateway National Recreation Area, open summer weekends 8 AM–midnight and winter weekends 9–4:30. In Manhattan, the **Golf Club at Chelsea Piers** (23rd St. and the Hudson River, tel. 212/336–6400) has a 200-yard artificial fairway, a computerized tee-up system, and heated hitting stalls—so you can keep right on swinging even in winter.

Miniature Golf Miniature golf courses are another pleasant way to get away from city bustle.

Manhattan **Hackers, Hitters & Hoops** (123 W. 18th St., tel. 212/929–7482) has an indoor course.
Randall's Island Golf and Family Entertainment Center (1 Randall's Island Golf Center, tel. 212/427–5689), open weekends 8–8, has an outdoor course, as well as a night-lighted driving range.

Other Boroughs Featuring two miniature golf courses and about 75 stalls at its popular driving range, **Alley Pond Golf Center** (232–01 Northern Blvd., Douglaston, tel. 718/225–9187), open weekends 7 AM–10 PM, later in summer, can be found opposite the salt marshes of Alley Pond Environmental Center, just before the Nassau County line.

Gateway Sports Center (3200 Flatbush Ave., Brooklyn, tel. 718/253–6816), open weekends 9:30 AM–11:30 PM in summer, is extremely pleasant with its surrounding trees and shrubs and its views of Rockaway Inlet.

Handball

Many of the city's 854 playgrounds have handball courts, including those in **Central Park** at North Meadow Center (midpark at about 97th St.) and in **Riverside Park** at 72nd Street and 101st Street.

In the Bronx, you'll find courts in the **Orchard Beach** games area, among other locations. In Queens, go to Victory Field in bucolic **Forest Park** (Myrtle Ave. and Woodhaven Blvd.).

Horseback Riding

Weekends at the city's stables are busy, especially in spring and fall. Go early; horses are freshest in the mornings.

Manhattan There are 6 miles of bridle paths in Central Park, including the one around the Reservoir. Experienced English riders can rent a variety of mounts at the carefully run **Claremont Riding Academy** (175 W. 89th St., tel. 212/724–5100), the city's largest and oldest riding academy and Manhattan's only stable for riding horses. A National Historic Site, it's been in the same location since 1892, and it's the longtime home of the Central Park Hunt, an equestrian group that stages annual rides on certain holidays. Private lessons are available. The stable opens at 6:30 AM.

The Bronx An Olympic training facility with instruction for English riders, the **Riverdale Equestrian Center** (254th St. at Broadway, tel. 718/548–4848), open weekends 9–5, has three outdoor rings, one indoor ring, and $5 pony rides for kids. You can use English or Western saddles both in Pelham Bay Park on mounts from the **Pelham Bit Stable** (on Shore Rd. in the southernmost section of Pelham Bay Park, tel. 718/885–0551), which is open weekends 8 AM–dusk.

Brooklyn **Jamaica Bay Riding Academy** (7000 Shore Pkwy., tel. 718/531–8949) rents horses for beach riding and provides lessons in a large indoor ring. It's open weekends 9–5.

Queens To take trail rides through 538-acre Forest Park, try **Dixie Dew Stables** (88–11 70th Rd., tel. 718/263–3500), open weekends 7–5 or by appointment or **Lynnes Riding School** (88–03 70th Rd., tel. 718/261–7679), open weekends 9–4.

Ice Skating

Everyone becomes a kid when whirling across the ice. All city rinks schedule weekend sessions and provide lockers, skate rentals, music, and snack bars. Hours change seasonally.

Kate Wollman Rink (Prospect Park, Brooklyn, tel. 718/287–6431) features Caribbean Winter at the Rink and sessions for figure skaters, besides public skating.

Lasker Rink (Central Park, 110th St. and Lenox Ave., tel. 212/396–0388) is a well-kept secret. It has recently offered ice hockey as well as free-style skating areas, plus demonstrations and clinics.

Riverbank State Park (135th St. and the Hudson River, tel. 212/694–3600) has three-hour public skating sessions on weekends.

Rockefeller Center (50th St. at 5th Ave., tel. 212/332–7654) may be postage-stamp-size, but skating in the shadow of golden Prometheus may be the ultimate Manhattan skating experience. Rates tend to be higher than elsewhere.

Sky Rink (23rd St. and the Hudson River, 212/336–6100), with two rinks in the Chelsea Piers complex, is the city's biggest indoor skating spot and its only year-round skating venue. Both figure skating and hockey are taught at Sky Rink's skating school.

Staten Island War Memorial Rink (Clove Lakes Park, Victory Blvd., Staten Island, tel. 718/720–1010) is probably the best place to skate on Staten Island.

Wollman Memorial Rink (Central Park near 59th St., tel. 212/396–1010) is the largest city-owned skating facility, and there's no more beautiful spot on a clear day—or a snowy one.

World's Fair Ice Skating Rink (Flushing Meadows–Corona Park, Queens, tel. 718/271–1996) encourages ice hockey, but is also open for figure skating.

Jogging and Racewalking

The only essential for jogging is something the city has plenty of: pavement. And there's slightly less competition from cars and pedestrians on weekends.

Manhattan In **Central Park,** the route circling the Reservoir is a sociable place, busy from early in the morning until dark. You can do the upper track for water-and-woods views or the softer through-the-woods bridle path (about 1½ miles each) on the lower level. The park roads, closed to traffic on weekends, offer a more varied passing scene, with bicyclists and skaters as well as joggers. You can go longer distances on the roads without repeating your route—up to 6 miles if you go around the northern end of the park. Crime is generally not a problem as long as you jog when and where plenty of others do, which on weekends is nearly everywhere almost all day long.

Riverside Park (along Riverside Drive, beside the Hudson River) is gorgeous at sunset and at any time of day when the cherry blossoms bloom in May. From 72nd Street to 116th Street and back is about 4½ miles. There is also an outdoor track near 74th Street (8 laps equal 1 mile).

There is a ¼-mile track in **East River Park** (E. 6th St. at FDR Dr.) and ¼ mile track at **Riverbank State Park** (on the Hudson River at 135th St.). Other good routes are around **Gramercy Park** (⅕ mile), City Hall Park (½ mile), along the **Battery Park City Esplanade** (about a mile), and around the shore of **Roosevelt Island** (3½ miles).

Brooklyn   Here, the prime destination is **Prospect Park,** where the roads are closed to traffic on weekends. Also good are the 3-mile-long **Coney Island Boardwalk** to Brighton Beach and the 5-mile-long **Shore Road Promenade** along the Narrows in Bay Ridge.

The Bronx   **Pelham Bay Park** has a track-and-field facility that includes a-mile oval and an exercise trail. **Van Cortlandt Park** has a ¼-miler as well as a cross-country course, whose 3- and 5-mile loops begin and end at the Parade Ground.

Races and   The **New York Road Runners Club** (9 E. 89th St., tel. 212/860–4455)
Group Runs   offers a complete schedule of races and fun runs, including: group runs every Saturday at 10 AM, starting at the club's headquarters; a handful of New York City Marathon Long Training Runs; and the 5-kilometer *Runner's World* Nike Midnight Run, held on New Year's Eve. You don't have to be a member to participate.

Model-Airplane Flying

Designated fields are at the southern end of Flatbush Avenue in Brooklyn at **Floyd Bennett Field** (which, fittingly, is an abandoned airport), in the Bronx at **Ferry Point Park** (north of the Bronx-Whitestone Bridge) and in **Pelham Bay Park,** in Queens around Meadow Lake at **Flushing Meadows–Corona Park** and in **Forest Park,** and in **Great Kills Park** on Staten Island.

Model-Boat Sailing

The Conservatory Water in **Central Park** at E. 72nd St. hosts races and regattas every Saturday, April–November (weather permitting), from 10 AM–2 PM. At the park's model boathouse next door, members of the Central Park Model Yacht Club dry-dock dozens of high-tech, miniature boats—valued at more than $1,000 each. On rare occasions, otherwise sea-worthy vessels are scuttled by rampaging ducks.

Roller-Skating and Rollerblading

In-line skates have completely taken over traditional wheel-at-each-corner skates as the way to get around, and ever-growing crowds of skaters streak through **Central Park** every weekend. **Central Park Skate Patrol and School** (tel. 212/439–1234) gives free stopping lessons on the weekends and runs a reasonably priced skate school. Rentals are available at smooth **Wollman Rink,** which is given over to roller-skating from the beginning of warm weather to November (tel. 212/396–1010).

It's also fun on weekends to roll through **Riverside Park** from 72nd to 95th streets along the river, past the Boat Basin and along the Promenade; around **Roosevelt Island**; and along the new Hudson River bike- and blade-way which runs from 41st Street to **Hudson River Park**.

Two outdoor roller rinks at the **Chelsea Piers** complex (Pier 62 at 23rd St. and the Hudson River, tel. 212/336–6200) have free-skates, rentals, in-line skating classes, summer dance parties, and roller hockey. Meanwhile, the **Roxy** (515 W. 18th St., 212/645–5156), a downtown dance club, goes roller-disco on Tuesday (gay) and Wednesday (mixed) nights.

Lessons and rental skates, which come with protective wrist guards, kneepads, elbow pads, and helmet, are available at **Peck & Goodie** (917 8th Ave., between 54th and 55th Sts., tel. 212/246–6123), **Pro Sports** (987 8th Ave., at 58th St., tel. 212/397–6208), and from **Blades Board and Skate** which has several Manhattan stores, including: East (160 E. 86th St., tel. 212/996–1644), 2nd Avenue (1414 2nd Ave., tel. 212/249–3178), West (120 W. 72nd St., tel. 212/787–3911), and Tribeca (128 Chambers St., tel. 212/964–1944).

Sailing

The very established **New York Sailing School** (22 Pelham Rd., New Rochelle, NY 10801, tel. 914/235–6052) teaches basic sailing classes on Long Island Sound.

The Hudson River is also worth navigating. **Offshore Sailing School** (777 Green St., on the Hudson River in Jersey City, just opposite the World Trade Center, tel. 800/221–4326) offers a variety of instruction programs, including a basic learn-to-sail course. Intensive classroom study and on-the-water work are part of all courses. The school also has a club for experienced sailors.

Scuba Diving

The coast of New York, New Jersey, and Connecticut keeps divers busy with reefs, wrecks, and sunken subs. Dozens of head boats go out every weekend. **Pan Aqua Diving** (460 W. 43rd St., tel. 212/736–3483) starts new scuba instruction classes every week and plans local diving trips. **Scuba Network** (175 5th Ave., at 23rd St., tel 212/228–2080; 124 E. 57th St., tel. 212/750–9160) also teaches scuba and packages group dives.

Skateboarding

Skate kids will tell you that weekends in New York are cool; the obstacles and challenges that make the city so much fun for skateboarders are still there, but minus weekday crowds. Top spots include the banks underneath the **Brooklyn Bridge on the Manhattan side,** around the great buildings **downtown by Battery Park City,** around the cube at **Astor Place** in the East Village, **Union Square,** ramps set up at the roller rinks on the Hudson River's **Pier 62** at 23rd Streeet, and a new public skate park at **108th Street and the West Side Highway.** For gear, visit **Pro Sports** (987 8th Ave., at 58th St., tel. 212/397–6208; 333 6th Ave., tel. 212/645–9340) or **Blades Board and Skate** (*see* Rollerskating and Rollerblading, *above*).

Sledding

After a good snowfall, New York City children head for the nearest sledding hill. In **Central Park,** top spots are Pilgrim Hill, south of the Conservatory Water, and Cedar Hill, near 78th Street on the east side of the park. In **Riverside Park,** there's a good steep hill at 105th Street.

Brooklyn's **Fort Greene Park** has Monument Hill, which is long and smooth. **Prospect Park's** best slope is Paine Hill. Sledders in Queens head for **Crocheron Park** (Little Neck Bay, tel. 718/225–2620) or **Juniper Valley Park** (tel. 718/326–2877); in Staten Island, try the **La Tourette Golf Course** (tel. 718/351–1889).

Swimming

The recent construction of new public pools and the renovation of old ones means swimmers in Manhattan can get a serious workout. The YMCA and YWCA notwithstanding, there are a few other options to consider:

For a nominal annual fee ($25 adults, $10 senior citizens and young adults 13–17, free for children under 13), you can use the well-kept pools at either of these city-run recreation centers. The **Carmine Street Recreation Center** (7th Ave. S and Clarkson St., tel. 212/242–5228) has a newly renovated 23-yard indoor pool open Sept.– June, weekends 9 AM–4:30 PM and a 105-yard outdoor pool open weekends in July and August at similar times. **Asser Levy Recreation Center** (E. 23rd St., between the FDR Dr. and 1st Ave., tel. 212/447–2020) has a 64-foot indoor pool, open September–July, weekends 8 AM–4:45 PM, and a 129-foot outdoor pool open July–August. Lap swimming is scheduled in the early morning and afternoon.

Riverbank State Park (679 Riverside Dr., between 134th and 135th Sts., tel. 212/694–3600) has a 50-meter pool open on weekends 7 AM–9 PM, with lap swims for adults in the early morning. Admission for lap swimming: $3. Admission for free swimming: $1.25 adults, 75¢ for children 11 and under.

Asphalt Green (York Ave., between 90th and 92nd Sts., tel. 212/369–8890) is a fairly plush facility with a 50-meter pool, open weekends 8–8. Drop-in fee for the day is $15 for adults, $7 for children.

Surfing **Rockaway Beach** draws the crowds. To find out if the surf's up, call the local park beach (tel. 718/318–4000) or the **Rockaway Beach Surf Shop** (177 Beach 116th St., Rockaway Beach, tel. 718/474–9345), which has a huge stock of surfboards, boogie boards, and wet suits and is open weekends 10–6. In Manhattan, check out the surfboards and gear at **Island Sports** (1623 York Ave., tel. 212/744–2000).

Tennis

City Courts Permits are required for play in the warmer months; modestly priced at $50 a year, they're easy to get and are sold in every borough (tel. 212/360–8133 for information).

Manhattan **Central Park** (midpark near 96th St., tel. 212/280–0205) has 26 clay courts. Single-play admissions are available for $5 at the Tennis House adjoining the courts; play is free to season permit holders, who can make court reservations by telephone weekdays 1–4. You don't need a permit to take lessons, which are given on four adjoining hard courts.
East River Park (FDR Dr. at Broome St., tel. 212/529–7185) has 12 hard courts.
Fred Johnson Memorial Park (151st St. at 7th Ave., tel. 212/234–9609) has eight hard courts, the only lighted courts in Manhattan. On weekends they're open 8 AM–11 PM.
Inwood Park (207th St. and Seaman Ave., tel. 212/304–2278) has nine hard courts, open weekends 7 AM–8 PM.
Randall's Island (east of Downing Stadium, tel. 212/860–1827) has seven clay courts and four hard courts. Open weekends 8–8, the courts are busy after noon, but waits don't usually exceed an hour. From October to April, the hard courts are covered and are privately run (tel. 212/534–4845).

Riverside Park (96th St. at Riverside Dr., tel. 212/408–0266) has 10 red clay courts at 97th Street alongside the Hudson River. Park management also supervises 10 all-weather blacktop courts at 119th Street.

The Bronx **Pelham Bay Park** (Rice Stadium, Middletown Rd. and Bruckner Blvd., tel. 718/885–3368) has 10 recently renovated courts.
Van Cortlandt Park (beside Van Cortlandt Stadium, tel. 718/549–6494) offers eight clay courts and four all-weather courts, open weekends 8 AM–dusk.

Queens **USTA National Tennis Center** (Flushing Meadows–Corona Park, tel. 718/760–6200), the newly expanded site of the U.S. Open, has 27 outdoor courts (going up to 47 when the expansion is completed in 1998) and nine indoor courts, all Deco Turf II and all lighted for night play. On weekends they're open 8 AM–midnight.

Staten Island **Walker Park** (50 Bard Ave., Livingston, tel. 718/442–9696), to which tennis came from Bermuda in 1874, now has six well-kept hard courts; single-play permits are available. The courts are open weekends 8 AM–9 PM.

Clubs Many private tennis clubs are open to nonmembers as well. Weekends are busy, but it's usually possible to reserve a court in advance. Rates range from $32 to $100 an hour.

Manhattan **Crosstown Tennis** (14 W. 31st St., tel. 212/947–5780) offers four indoor hard courts that are air-conditioned in summer. *Open Sat. 6 AM–8 PM, Sun. 6 AM–midnight.*
HRC Tennis (Pier 13 and 14, East River at Wall St., tel. 212/422–9300) has eight Har-Tru courts under two bubbles, air-conditioned in summer. *Open weekends 6 AM–midnight.*
Manhattan Plaza Racquet Club (450 W. 43rd St., tel. 212/594–0554) offers five courts that are open-air in summer, under a bubble in winter, and lighted for play after dark. *Open weekends 6 AM–midnight.*
Midtown Tennis Club (341 8th Ave., at 27th St., tel. 212/989–8572) has eight Har-Tru courts—all under a bubble in winter and half under a bubble (and air-conditioned) in summer. *Open weekends 8 AM–10 PM.*
Roosevelt Island Raquet Club (281 Main St., Roosevelt Island, tel. 212/935–0250) has 12 air-conditioned green clay courts, lessons, clinics, a baby-sitting service, and game arranging. *Open Sat. 7 AM–11 PM, Sun. 7 AM–10 PM.*
Tennis Club (15 Vanderbilt Ave., at 42nd St., tel. 212/687–3841) has two year-round Deco Turf courts that usually aren't too busy on weekends. *Open weekends 7 AM–5 PM.*
Tower Tennis Courts (1725 York Ave., between 89th and 90th Sts., tel. 212/860–2464) has two indoor courts under a bubble. These courts get hot in summer, so reservations are only accepted for morning and evening play. *Open weekends 8 AM–8 PM.*
Turtle Bay Tennis Club (UN Plaza Hotel, 44th St. at 1st Ave., tel. 212/758–1234) has only one air-conditioned Uni-Turf court at its 38th-floor health club, but there's a fine view and court time is easy to get. *Open weekends 6 AM–10 PM.*
Village Tennis Courts (110 University Pl. at 12th St., tel. 212/989–2300) has two indoor Supreme-surface courts, a practice court, and a ball machine alley. *Open Sat. 7 AM–9 PM, Sun. 7 AM–10 PM.*

The Bronx **Stadium Tennis** (11 E. 162nd St., tel. 718/293–2386) has play on eight indoor-outdoor courts. *Open Oct.–Apr., weekends 7 AM–midnight.*

Brooklyn **Gateway Sports Center** (3200 Flatbush Ave., tel. 718/253–6816) offers eight hard courts. *Open weekends 10 AM–11 PM.*

Queens **Long Island City Indoor Tennis** (50–01 2nd St. at 50th Ave., Long Island City, tel. 718/784–9677) has two indoor Har-Tru courts. *Open weekends 7 AM–10 PM.*

Tennisport (Borden Ave. at 2nd St., Long Island City, tel. 718/392–1880) has 16 indoor red clay courts and 13 outdoor Har-Tru courts. *Open weekends 7:30 AM–8 PM.*

Windsurfing

The New York area is blessed with both smooth water for beginners and ocean surf for experts. Plumb Beach, Breezy Point, and Sandy Hook—all part of the Gateway National Recreation Area—offer excellent conditions. **Island Sports** (1623 York Ave., tel. 212/744–2000) goes out to Southampton, a couple of hours from Manhattan, every day in summer for day-long instructional sessions, with rental equipment provided.

Spectator Sports

The city's greatest spot for sports fans is probably **Madison Square Garden** (7th Ave., between 31st and 33rd Sts., tel. 212/465–6000), an institution that, in various buildings, has been a fixture of New York life since 1879. A jack-of-all-trades of the city's sports and entertainment scene (the writer O. Henry called it "the center of the Universe"), the Garden hosts everything from Ringling Bros. Circus and the Ice Capades to the Westminster Kennel Club Dog Show and the National Horse Show. Basketball, hockey, and many other sports are played here as well. The box office is open 11–8 on weekends; call there for tickets by phone or order through Ticketmaster (tel. 212/307–7171) at a hefty surcharge.

Baseball

The **New York Mets** play at Shea Stadium (Flushing Meadows–Corona Park, Queens, tel. 718/507–8499). The **New York Yankees** play at Yankee Stadium (E. 161st St. and River Ave., the Bronx, tel. 718/293–6000). Tickets are usually available at the box office; the best usually go to season ticket-holders.

Basketball

The **New York Knickerbockers** play home games in Madison Square Garden during the late-October–April season. Knicks tickets are hot and hard to come by at the box office (tel. 212/465–6000 for information). For the scoop on the latest action, phone the New York Knicks Hot Line (tel. 212/465–5867).

Football

The **New York Giants** play at Giants Stadium (East Rutherford, NJ, tel. 201/935–8111), as do the **New York Jets** (tel. 516/560–8100). Most seats for Giants and Jets games are sold on a season-ticket basis; remaining tickets for scattered singles occasionally are available at the stadium box office.

Hockey

The **New York Rangers** play at Madison Square Garden (tel. 212/465–6741, or call the Rangers hot line at 212/308–6977), the **New York Islanders** at Nassau Veterans Memorial Coliseum in Uniondale, Long Island (for tickets call 516/888–9000), and the **New Jersey Devils** at the Continental Arena in East Rutherford, New Jersey (tel. 201/935–6050 or 201/935–3900).

Horse Racing

A trip to the tracks, which (of the six days they're open), are busiest on weekends, shows off another side of New York City life—the horse-mad side, which is half passionate gamblers and half blue-blood types who invest thousands in a share of the thoroughbreds.

Aqueduct Racetrack (Rockaway Blvd. at 108th St. off Belt Pkwy., Ozone Park, Queens, tel. 718/641–4700), the largest thoroughbred race track in the United States, is a modern facility with a spate of new lawns and gardens. The season here runs from late October through April.

Belmont Park (Hempstead Tpke., Elmont, Long Island, tel. 718/641–4700), the grande dame of New York thoroughbred racing, is home of the third jewel in horse racing's triple crown, the Belmont Stakes. During its seasons (May–June and late Aug.–Oct.), breakfast at Belmont and afternoon tram tours provide pleasant weekend interludes.

The Meadowlands (East Rutherford, NJ, tel. 201/935–8500) has a trotter and pacer season January through mid-August and a flat track season Labor Day through December.

Yonkers Raceway (Central Ave., Yonkers, NY, tel. 212/562–9500) has a year-round trotter season.

Running

The city's biggest spectator sports event may be the **New York City Marathon,** which takes place annually on a Sunday in early November. Since the race's inception in 1970, the pack has grown from 127 (with 55 finishers) to 22,000 (some 16,000 of them finishing). Participants now include racewalkers, "jogglers" (who juggle their way through the 26 miles), oldsters, and youngsters, cheered on by the spectators lining rooftops and sidewalks, promenades and terraces all along the five-borough course. If you relish mob scenes, try to get near the finish line in Central Park. To enter, call the New York Road Runners Club (tel. 212/860–4455).

Tennis

The **U.S. Open,** a high point of the tennis buff's year, is held at the even larger and newly renovated National Tennis Center in Queen's Flushing Meadows–Corona Park at the end of the summer. The first weekend falls at the midpoint of the tournament, usually over Labor Day, and the second weekend sees the men's and women's finals. Finals tickets are available only to those who have planned well in advance, and the best seats go only to those who order box seats for the entire tourney. In the early rounds, however, tickets are easier to get, and there's action all day long. Strolling from one court to another is the real pleasure of a trip to the Open, which shows off the enthusiasm of the juniors and the aplomb of the over-30 players as well as the competitive spirit of players in their prime—the only group that TV covers. Buy a draw sheet as you enter the complex and decide which matches you want to see; your reserved-seat ticket to the stadium also admits you to all the other courts. For details, call the U.S. Open ticket office (tel. 718/760–6200). Tickets go on sale in spring by mail or through Tele-Charge (tel. 212/239–6250 or 800/524–8440).

The tennis year winds up with the **WTA** tourney in Madison Square Garden, culminating on a weekend in mid-November. WTA tickets go on sale in September (tel. 212/465–6000).

Best Bets for Children

Parks and Zoos In Central Park, favorite destinations include the **zoo,** the **carousel,** and the **Conservatory Water,** with its huge remote-controlled model boats and the climbable nearby statues of Alice in Wonderland and Hans Christian Andersen. Older children will enjoy roller-skating or ice skating, depending on the season, at Wollman or Lasker rinks. Hands-on activities at the **Henry Luce Nature Observatory** in **Belvedere Castle,** and the **Charles A. Dana Discovery Center** by the Harlem Meer will divert curious youngsters, and many of the weekend nature walks sponsored by the Urban Park Rangers are designed especially for kids.

In Brooklyn's **Prospect Park,** kite-flying on the Long Meadow is a great way to spend a spring Sunday with your kids; afterwards, head to the **Brooklyn Botanic Garden** and its fascinating Trail of Evolution in the Steinhardt Conservatory, or visit the prairie dog town at the newly restored **Prospect Park Zoo.** Short marked nature trails suitable for younger hikers can be found at the **Alley Pond Environmental Center** and **Jamaica Bay Wildlife Refuge** in Queens.

In the Bronx, don't forget the **zoo,** which is now the International Wildlife Conservation Park; younger children can wander through the Children's Zoo.

Playgrounds Manhattan has plenty, and they're state-of-the-art. These are some of the best:

Abingdon Square Park (Bleecker and Hudson Sts.), where West Village kids slide, climb, and play in the sandbox, is a friendly place, although perhaps not sophisticated enough to keep older brothers and sisters entertained.

Carl Schurz Park (near East End Ave. and 84th St.) is on two green blocks within sight of the East River esplanade.

Central Park has 21 playgrounds full of slides, bridges, bars, swings, towers, and tunnels, usually carpeted with sand or soft rubber matting and often cooled in summer by sprinklers and running water. The best are along 5th Avenue at 67th, 71st, 77th, 85th, and 95th streets. Along Central Park West, the best are at 68th, 81st, 85th, and 93rd streets. The Heckscher playground, mid-park at 62nd Street, is the park's largest and is a favorite with local school kids.

John Jay Park (off York Ave. near 77th St.), big and busy, offers swinging bridges, curving slides, a sprinkler, and a big sandbox.

Pearl Street Playground (Fulton, Water, and Pearl Sts.) is a postmodern playground with a couple of giant-size and multicolored capitals and a wall of glass blocks.

Playground for All Children (Flushing Meadows–Corona Park, Corona Ave. and 111th St., Queens, tel. 718/699–8283) puts children with disabilities and able-bodied children on an equal footing. Nature trails feature plaques in Braille as well as print, sandboxes are at wheelchair height, swings have extra-large seats and hand cords so swingers don't have to pump with their legs.

Riverside Park, edging Manhattan's West Side, has many playgrounds, but the best for small fry is at 76th Street, where a circle of elephants spraying water cools things down in summer.

77th St. at Amsterdam Ave., known in the neighborhood as the Wood Park, is the fanciful schoolyard park you've seen being built (more than once) on Sesame Street. Featuring a log castle, fortress, slides, and tire swings, it was built by parents and designed by kids working with a professional playground designer.

7 What to Sit Back and Enjoy

New York's arts scene is busy enough all week, but never are things livelier than on the weekends. On Saturdays alone, there are usually as many as two evening performances at most large theaters and concert halls. Athough Sunday may be a day of rest for some performers, there are more than enough matinees scheduled to take up the slack. And there are movies, lectures, readings, comedy, jazz, and more. Come summer, the city's artists take to the open spaces, joining in special music festivals or playing sporadic gigs in the parks.

How to Find Out What's On
One fabulous source of information is the Theatre Development Fund's **New York City On Stage** hot line (tel. 212/768–1818). Callers using touch-tone phones can choose from a menu that includes theater, dance and music, "family" entertainment, and events accepting the TDF voucher. With a little patience you can get not only listings but also lively descriptions of, for example, a particular play's plot, cast, and crew.

To find out what's going on in New York City parks, call the **Parks Special Events Hotline** (tel. 212/360–3456).

Lincoln Center has a hot line (tel. 212/546–2656) on which you can hear Beverly Sills dispense information about current performances. Two other arts organizations publish valuable calendars: the **Lower Manhattan Cultural Council** (5 World Trade Center, Suite 9235, New York, NY 10048, tel. 212/432–0900 weekdays only) and the **Queens Council on the Arts** (7901 Park La. S, Woodhaven, NY 11421, tel. 718/647–3377).

The New York Convention and Visitors Bureau also has information (2 Columbus Circle, tel. 212/397–8200).

Ticket Sources
Box Offices
For most events, ticket sellers at box offices make it their business to know their theaters and performance spaces and don't mind pointing out on a chart where you'll be seated. On weekends, most box offices open around noon, though it's advisable to buy your tickets before the day of the performance. For advance purchase, send the box office a certified check or money order, several alternate dates, and a self-addressed stamped envelope.

If you're charging tickets, call **Tele-Charge** (tel. 212/239–6200), **Ticketmaster** (tel. 212/307–4100), or **Ticket Central** (tel. 212/279–4200)—newspaper ads will specify which you should use for any given event. A $1–$5 surcharge per ticket will be added to the total, and your tickets will either be mailed to you or waiting for you at the theater's box office.

TKTS
The Theatre Development Fund's venerable TKTS booth (tel. 212/768–1818) on Duffy Square (Broadway and 47th St.) discounts day-of-performance tickets for Broadway and off-Broadway plays and some dance and other performing arts events by as much as one half, with a $2.50 surcharge. The names of shows available on that day are posted on boards near the ticket booth. On Saturday, the booth is open between 10 and 2 for matinees, and 3–8 for evening performances; for Sunday matinee and evening performances, hours are noon–8. Get there at least a half hour prior to assure yourself of some choices. TKTS accepts only cash or traveler's checks—no credit cards.

In the Wall Street area, there is another TKTS booth at 2 World Trade Center on the mezzanine. The booth is open Friday 11–5:30, Saturday 11–3:30. For weekend matinees, tickets go on sale the day before the performance. The lines at this TKTS location are often shorter than those at Duffy Square, though the offerings are sometimes limited.

TDF Vouchers
If you attend a great number of arts events, it will definitely pay to contact the Theatre Development Fund (1501 Broadway, Suite

2110, New York, NY 10036, tel. 212/221–0885 weekdays only) to get TDF vouchers, which cost $28 for four. When redeemed at the box office, the vouchers are worth full admission for dance, theater, and musical events at non-Broadway theaters. It's a good way to see up-and-coming groups at modest cost, and they will also occasionally buy you admittance to performances by better-known companies as well.

Theater

Nearly all of the approximately 250 legitimate theaters in New York have full weekend schedules. On Saturdays most theaters schedule two performances, and on Sundays Broadway shows generally hold matinees while Off- and Off-Off Broadway usually have evening performances. Weekends are such a popular time with theatergoers that lines at the TKTS discount tickets booth stretch around the block; the earlier you get there, the better.

Broadway

Historically, the nation's entertainment capital was once composed of almost 50 theaters that sprang up around Times Square between 1899 and 1925. Many of those showplaces have been gutted or turned into movie houses; those that remain as legitimate theaters are squeezed into an area bounded by 41st and 53rd streets between 6th and 9th avenues. In addition to the wonderful old jewel-box playhouses, you'll find **Theater Row,** six intimate Off-Broadway houses on the south side of 42nd Street between 9th and 10th avenues, and **Restaurant Row** (46th St. between 8th and 9th Aves.), where critics, actors, directors, playwrights, and regular starstruck Joes come to dine before and after the show.

Your major challenge will probably be choosing one show from the riches offered. When faced with the enduring threat of blockbusters like *Cats* ("Now and Forever"), remember, there's something special about seeing a low-key show in previews or seeing an already-panned play before it bites the dust.

What's Playing Broadway is well covered by the *New York Times;* the Friday Weekend section has "On Stage and Off," a special column devoted to theater news, and the Sunday Arts and Leisure section covers theater in depth. *Theater Week* lists Broadway as well as Off- and Off-Off-Broadway performances, and is available at many newsstands. The League of American Theatres and Producers publishes a twice-monthly *Broadway Theatre Guide*, available in theaters and hotels. *Playbill*, distributed in theaters and on sale at newsstands, wraps generic Broadway lore around each play's own program notes.

Tickets Discounts on long-running shows are often available if you can lay your hands on a couple of "two-fers." These discount ticket coupons can be found near cash registers around town, in line at TKTS, at the New York Convention and Visitors Bureau, and the office of the **Hit Show Club** (630 9th Ave., between 44th and 45th Sts., 8th floor, tel. 212/581–4211, open weekdays 9–4).

Ticket clubs designed to serve frequent theatergoers are also helpful. **Advance Entertainment New York** (tel. 212/239–2570), a telemarketing firm whose phones are manned by actors and actresses, provides updates on what's hot and gets tickets for members, sometimes at a discount and with special attention to the location of the seats. Membership costs $295 for a 3-year membership which includes your first pair of tickets; the service can also be used on a one-time, no-obligation-to-join basis, with a $5 per ticket service charge for nonmembers.

If money is no object and you are after some hot seats, go to a ticket broker. (A $65 ticket will cost about $100–$150 from the typical broker.) Try **Continental/Golden/Leblang Ticket Service** (tel. 212/944–8910 or 800/942–9455) and **N.Y. Theatre Tickets** (tel. 201/392–0999).

Theaters   Here is a selection of some of the more established Broadway theaters:

Ambassador (219 W. 49th St., tel. 212/239–6200).
Belasco (111 W. 44th St., tel. 212/239–6200).
Booth (222 W. 45th St., tel. 212/239–6200).
Broadhurst (235 W. 44th St., tel. 212/239–6200).
Broadway (1681 Broadway, at 53rd St., tel. 212/239–6200).
Brooks Atkinson (256 W. 47th St., tel. 212/307–4100).
Circle in the Square (235 W. 50th St., tel. 212/239–6200).
Cort (138 W. 48th St., tel. 212/239–6200).
Ethel Barrymore (243 W. 47th St., tel. 212/239–6200).
Eugene O'Neill (230 W. 49th St., tel. 212/239–6200).
Gershwin (222 W. 51st St., tel. 212/307–4100).
Helen Hayes (240 W. 44th St., tel. 212/228–3626).
Imperial (249 W. 45th St., tel. 212/239–6200).
John Golden (252 W. 45th St., tel. 212/239–6200).
Lincoln Center's Vivian Beaumont and **Mitzi E. Newhouse** (W. 64th St. at Broadway, tel. 212/239–6200).
Longacre (220 W. 48th St., tel. 212/239–6200).
Lunt-Fontanne (205 W. 46th St., tel. 212/307–4100).
Lyceum (149 W. 45th St., tel. 212/239–6200).
Majestic (247 W. 44th St., tel. 212/239–6200).
Marquis (1535 Broadway, at 46th St., tel. 212/382–0100).
Minskoff (200 W. 45th St., tel. 212/307–4100).
Nederlander (208 W. 41st St., tel. 212/307–4100).
Neil Simon (250 W. 52nd St., tel. 212/307–4100).
Palace (1564 Broadway, at 47th St., tel. 212/307–4100).
Plymouth (236 W. 45th St., tel. 212/239–6200).
Richard Rodgers (226 W. 46th St., tel. 212/307–4100).
Roundabout Theatre Company (1530 Broadway, at 45th St., tel. 212/869–8400).
Royale (242 W. 45th St., tel. 212/239–6200).
St. James (246 W. 44th St., tel. 212/239–6200).
Shubert (225 W. 44th St., tel. 239–6200).
Virginia (245 W. 52nd St., tel. 212/239–6200).
Walter Kerr (219 W. 48th St., tel. 212/239–6200).
Winter Garden (1634 Broadway, at 50th St., tel. 212/239–6200).

Off- and Off-Off Broadway

Off- and Off-Off Broadway, there are usually two performances each on Saturday and Sunday—one matinee in the afternoon and one evening performance. There are often seats available for all but the most phenomenal productions.

As Broadway ticket prices climb toward $100 and the hit mentality takes over, Off-Broadway has become a good place to catch Broadway smashes in the making (like *Bring In 'Da Noise, Bring In 'Da Funk*, which first appeared at the Public Theater). Major Off-Broadway enclaves are along Theatre Row and in the Village, though theaters turn up in out-of-the-way spots all across the municipal map, from Coney Island to Columbia Heights.

What's   The beyond-Broadway theater scene is especially well covered by
Playing   the *Village Voice*, in its helpful Choices section. The League of New York Theatres and Producers' twice-monthly *Broadway Theatre Guide*, available in most hotels and theaters, includes Off-Broadway entries as well.

Tickets Some smaller theaters handle their own ticket sales, either by phone or at the box office. Call ahead if going in person, since hours can be erratic. In addition, about 30 of the Off- and Off-Off-Broadway theaters share **Ticket Central** (416 W. 42nd St., tel. 212/279–4200). Normally, Off- and Off-Off-Broadway ticket prices average $10–$40.

Discounted tickets are also available. The **TKTS** booth in Duffy Square (*see above*) frequently handles Off-Broadway shows. The **Joseph Papp Public Theater** (*see below*) regularly sets aside tickets for sale at a discount through its Quiktix program. Quiktix go on sale at 6 PM for weekend night performances and at 1 PM for matinees, but lines form early—sometimes as early as 2 PM for a popular evening performance. **Classic Stage Company** (*see below*) also offers reduced rates for unsold tickets for the day of the performance.

Theaters **Theater Row,** a collection of houses of 100 seats or fewer on the downtown side of 42nd Street between 9th and 10th avenues, including **Harold Clurman Theatre** (412 W. 42nd St., tel. 212/594–2370), **Samuel Beckett Theatre** (410 W. 42nd St., tel. 212/594–2826), **Douglas Fairbanks Theatre** (432 W. 42nd St., tel. 212/239–4321 or 212/239–6200), **Intar** (420 W. 42nd St., tel. 212/695–6134), and the **Theatre Row Theatre** (424 W. 42nd St., tel. 212/886–1889).

Elsewhere:

American Jewish Theater (Susan Bloch Theatre, 307 W. 26th St., tel. 212/633–9797) presents plays and musicals that deal with the Jewish experience.

Cherry Lane (38 Commerce St., 1 block south of Bleecker St., tel. 212/239–6200), one of the original Off-Broadway houses, was the site of American premieres of works by O'Neill, Beckett, Ionesco, and Albee. .

Circle Repertory Company (159 Bleecker St., near Thompson St., tel. 212/239–6200), a venerable and warm little house, was founded in 1969 by, among others, Lanford Wilson, whose plays have often premiered here. Its fall to late-spring season provides first looks at works by some of America's brightest young playwrights, composers, and lyricists.

Classic State Company (CSC, 136 E. 13th St., between 3rd and 4th Aves., tel. 212/677–4210) often commissions fresh translations of classic plays and searches out directors with innovative approaches to well-known material. In recent years CSC has mounted acclaimed productions of works by Sophocles, Racine, Pinter, Chekhov, and Marivaux.

Ensemble Studio Theater (549 W. 52nd St., tel. 212/247–3405), a theatrical company in the truest sense of the word, has a stable group of actors, directors, and playwrights who collaborate on works-in-progress. EST actors, some of New York's best, are on view at an annual spring marathon of one-act plays.

Irish Arts Center (553 W. 51st., tel. 212/358–5174) features classic and contemporary Irish plays.

Jean Cocteau Repertory (Bouwerie Lane Theatre, 330 Bowery, tel. 212/677–0060), founded in 1971, presents international classics, intelligently performed by its resident acting troupe.

Jewish Repertory Theater (Playhouse 91, 316 E. 91st St., tel. 212/831–2000), started in 1974 by Ran Avni to produce plays about Jewish life, continues to thrive.

Joseph Papp Public Theater (425 Lafayette St., tel. 212/260–2400), renamed from the Public Theater in 1992 to honor its late founder and long-time guiding genius, continues its tradition of innovative theater. Its program includes new and classic plays, performance art, readings, and musical events. In the summer, the Public's Shakespeare Festival brings the Bard to Central Park's open-air Delacorte Theater.

La Mama (74A E. 4th St., between 2nd and 3rd Aves., tel. 212/475–

7710) grew from humble seeds—an East Village café opened by Ellen Stewart in 1961—into a grand avant-garde legend. La Mama, which has been called "the MGM of experimental theater," today stages productions in three different spaces: the Annex, First Floor Theater, and Club. La Mama alumni include Sam Shepard, Bette Midler, Andy Warhol, Nick Nolte, and Meatloaf.

Manhattan Theatre Club (City Center, 131 W. 55th St., tel. 212/581–1212) was started in the mid-1970s by actress Lynne Meadow, then fresh out of Yale School of Drama. The theater went on to feed *Ain't Misbehavin'*, *Crimes of the Heart*, and *Love! Valour! Compassion!* to Broadway and continues to produce some of New York's most talked-about plays by such accomplished playwrights as Terrence McNally, Arthur Miller, and Caryl Churchill.

New York Theatre Workshop (79 E. 4th St., between 2nd and 3rd Aves., tel. 212/460–5475), produces challenging new theater by American and international artists. This was the group that nurtured and premiered *Rent*.

Orpheum (126 2nd Ave., at St. Mark's Pl., tel. 212/477–2477), has been host to *Stomp*, the British performing troupe that makes a whole lot of noise, and keeps people coming back for more.

Pan Asian Repertory (Playhouse 46, St. Clement's Church, 423 W. 46th St., tel. 212/245–2660) is dedicated to giving stage space to Asian-American artists and plays.

Pearl Theatre Company (80 St. Mark's Pl., tel. 212/598–9802), focusses on a repertory of classics performed by resident players.

Playwrights Horizons (416 W. 42nd St., tel. 212/279–4200), one of the first Theater Row stages, develops new playwrights through readings, workshops, and full-scale productions. *Sunday in the Park with George*, *The Heidi Chronicles*, *Falsettoland*, and *Once on This Island* all got lift-offs here.

Primary Stages (354 W. 45th St., tel. 212/333–7471), presents startling new work by emerging American playwrights such as David Ives and more established ones such as John Patrick Shanley.

Promenade Theater (2162 Broadway, at 76th St., tel. 212/580–1313) has produced such celebrated works as the musical *Godspell*, Athol Fugard's *The Road to Mecca*, Simon Gray's *The Common Pursuit*, and Edward Albee's *Three Tall Women*. The Promenade is also the home of Theaterworks/USA (a children's theater company). Second Stage (tel. 212/787–8302), which reproduces recent plays that may not have been given a fair shake the first time around, owns space in the same building.

Repertorio Español (Gramercy Arts Theatre, 138 E. 27th St., tel. 212/889–2850), an award-winning Spanish arts theater, often mounts productions in Spanish with simultaneous translation into English via infrared cordless headsets, available for a small charge.

Sullivan Street Playhouse (181 Sullivan St., between Houston and Bleecker Sts., tel. 212/674–3838) continues to host *The Fantasticks*, the world's longest-running musical (since 1970).

Theater for the New City (155 1st Ave., between 9th and 10th Sts., tel. 212/254–1109), another theatrical experimenter with its roots in the 1960s, now offers 30 to 40 productions a year.

Vineyard Theater (Irving Dimson Theatre, 108 E. 15th St., tel. 212/353–3874), which relocated to brand new digs in 1989, is a small, nonprofit theater founded by a former cabaret singer. This theater is strong on new and revived musicals.

WPA Theatre (519 W. 23rd St., tel. 212/206–0523) showcases new American plays with up-and-coming actors and directors. Several WPA offerings have become feature films, including *Key Exchange*, *Steel Magnolias*, and *Jeffrey*.

York Theatre Company (Theatre at St. Peter's Church, 54th St. at Lexington Ave., tel. 212/935–5820) presents revivals of plays and musicals as well as new theater works. The company is noted for its excellent productions of Stephen Sondheim musicals.

Music

Whether you crave a late night jam session at a jazz club, a formal recital at Carnegie Hall or a rowdy rock experience, New York has musical events to satisfy the most eclectic tastes. Weekends resound with offerings at the major concert halls, downtown studios, parks, piers, and museums; the smoke even clears at some of the city's clubs when nocturnal musicians rise and shine for jazz brunch— a distinctive Sunday institution.

What's Playing   The *New York Times* Friday section includes selected information about music events worth catching around town. On Sunday, the *Times* Arts and Leisure section features longer articles on orchestras, opera stars, cabaret performers, composers, and jazz.

Tickets   Most major music halls have their own box offices.

Orchestral Music

New York is the home of several major orchestras and a principal stopping point for tours by out-of-town musicians, so every day of the week is lively on the concert scene.

Major Concert Halls   **Avery Fisher Hall** (Lincoln Center, 65th St. and Broadway, tel. 212/875–5030) brings to its stage the world's great musicians, and to its boxes the black-tie-and-diamond-tiara set. Designed by Max Abramovitz and opened in 1961 as Philharmonic Hall, it underwent a $5-million renovation in 1976, to improve acoustics, resulting in a 2,700-seat auditorium that follows the classic European rectangular pattern.

Brooklyn Academy of Music (30 Lafayette Ave., Brooklyn, tel. 718/636–4100) is America's oldest performing arts center, founded in 1859, though the present building dates from 1908. Here is where Isadora Duncan did her famous scarf dance, Sarah Bernhardt wrung out one of her last Camilles, Enrico Caruso suffered the throat hemorrhage that ended his career, and Garrison Keillor spun a few yarns. These days, the Brooklyn Philharmonic performs in BAM's 2,000-seat Opera House, and autumn's Next Wave Festival has put Brooklyn at the center of the avant-garde map.

Carnegie Hall (57th St. and 7th Ave., tel. 212/247–7800), in its century on New York's music scene, has witnessed the pianist Ignace Paderewski being attacked by crowds clamoring for kisses and locks of hair, a young Leonard Bernstein triumphing in his 1943 debut as a stand-in for New York Philharmonic conductor Bruno Walter, Jack Benny playing duets with Isaac Stern, and the Beatles taking New York by storm in 1964. Major renovation has left this busy international musical landmark in better acoustical and physical shape than ever—not just the Main Concert Hall but the small Weill Recital Hall, where bright young stars make their New York debuts.

City Center (131 W. 55th St., tel. 212/581–1212) has a large auditorium under its eccentric, tiled Spanish dome, built in 1924 by the Ancient and Accepted Order of the Mystic Shrine, saved from demolition by Fiorello La Guardia, and now renovated to sparkling splendor. City Center hosts concert versions of American musicals with its Encores series.

Colden Center for the Performing Arts (Kissena Blvd. and the Long Island Expressway, Queens, tel. 718/793–8080), a part of the Queens College complex, brings classical and other music groups to the city's largest borough. Recent performers have included the Boy's Choir of Harlem and the Urban Bush Women.

Symphony Space (2537 Broadway, tel. 212/864–5400) held an ice-skating rink, wrestling ring, and movie theater before volunteers from a drug rehabilitation center converted it to a concert space. Metropolitan Opera musical director James Levine has called it a

"West Sider's dream," with its fine acoustics and location in one of the city's musical hubs. Everyone from Itzhak Perlman to the Wretched Refuse String Band has appeared here, and in recent years, Symphony Space has become a major venue for dance, spoken word, and New Music as well.

Town Hall (123 W. 43rd St., tel. 212/840–2824), built in 1921, was designed by the renowned architectural firm McKim, Mead & White. This 1,500-seat midtown music enclave lets everyone feel close to the stage. Its bill is wide and a touch eccentric, with classical entries, ethnic sounds, occasional chamber revivals of dusty musical comedies, and downtown-style New Wave.

Smaller Ensembles

Metropolitan area concert halls specializing in chamber music echo with applause nearly every weekend of the year. If you make an effort, you can easily hear your favorite chamber music ensemble perform at a smaller, more intimate venue, such as Bargemusic in Brooklyn.

Chamber Music and More

Aaron Davis Hall (City College, W. 135 St. at Convent Ave., tel. 212/650–6900) hosts the way-uptown scene of iconoclastic musical events staged by the World Music Institute, as well as a variety of classical concerts.

Alice Tully Hall (Lincoln Center, 65th St. at Broadway, tel. 212/875–5050), an intimate "little white box" with seats for 1,096, is considered as acoustically perfect as concert houses get. It schedules many solo recitals and chamber music ensembles, including the Chamber Music Society of Lincoln Center, founded in 1969 by William Schuman, Alice Tully, and Charles Wadsworth—a group that almost single-handedly put chamber music on the Manhattan artistic map.

Bargemusic (Fulton Ferry Landing, Brooklyn, tel. 718/624–4061) has chamber music bubbling out of an old Erie Lackawanna coffee barge tethered along the East River every Sunday at 4 PM year-round. This self-proclaimed "floating concert hall" requires that you make reservations, although you pay upon arrival (no credit cards).

The Kitchen (512 W. 19th St., tel. 212/255–5793) has been, since 1976, a center for the avant-garde.

Merkin Concert Hall (Abraham Goodman House, 129 W. 67th St., tel. 212/501–3330), one of the city's newer auditoriums, is developing a reputation nearly as fine as that of its near neighbors at Lincoln Center. Lots of famous soloists claim the stage at this 457-seat hall, which also occasionally hosts the New York Philharmonic and the Chamber Music Society of Lincoln Center.

92nd Street Y (1395 Lexington Ave., at 92nd St., tel. 212/996–1100) is an East Side magnet for music, scheduling weekend performances by star recitalists and chamber ensembles.

Performance Space 122, or P.S. 122 (150 1st Ave. on the corner of 9th St., tel. 212/477–5288), called by the *Village Voice* the "petri dish of downtown culture," was converted from an old elementary school once attended by comedian George Burns. Concerts, exhibits, and productions come and go quickly, but seldom fail in freshness. Look for P.S. 122's annual performance marathon in February, during which scores of dazzling downtown musicians, dancers, alternative comedians and artists take the stage.

Sylvia and Danny Kaye Playhouse (Hunter College, 68th St. between Park and Lexington Aves., tel. 212/772–4448), presents a varied program of events, including distinguished soloists and chamber music groups, in a state-of-the-art concert hall.

Wave Hill (675 W. 252nd St., the Bronx, tel. 718/549–3200), a historic estate and garden with smashing views across the Hudson, holds musicales by classical and jazz groups. During the winter, performances take place once a month on a Sunday afternoon. Other music and dance programs occur throughout the year on both Saturdays and Sundays.

Weill Recital Hall (Carnegie Hall, 57th St. and 7th Ave., tel. 212/ 247–7800), formerly the Carnegie Recital Hall, was renamed and renovated in 1986, providing this intimate 268-seat auditorium with its own entrance on 57th Street. Three acoustic chandeliers imported from Holland warm up the sounds here, making it excellent for chamber music. The city's most promising new artists choose it for debuts; soloists, quartets, jazz, and early music are all on the weekend calendar.

Winter Garden Atrium (World Financial Center, Battery Park City, tel. 212/945–0505) frequently offers new and classical music concerts, among other events. The setting couldn't be prettier: an airy plaza full of polished granite and Italian marble, where 16 palms reach skyward into the barrel-vaulted glass roof. All weekend concerts and performances are free.

The Conservatories If you're interested in hearing youthful stars-to-be, check into the following: **Juilliard School** recitals (tel. 212/799–5000), held at Alice Tully Hall (65th St. at Broadway), Paul Recital Hall (144 W. 66th St.), and the Juilliard Theater (155 W. 65th St.); **Manhattan School of Music** (Broadway at 122nd St., tel. 212/749–2802); **Mannes College of Music** (150 W. 85th St., tel. 212/580–0210); and the **Brooklyn Conservatory of Music** (58 7th Ave., Park Slope, Brooklyn, tel. 718/ 622–3300).

Museum Concerts **Asia Society** (725 Park Ave., at 70th St., tel. 212/288–6400) features musicians from the far side of the Pacific throughout the year.

Brooklyn Museum (200 Eastern Pkwy., Brooklyn, tel. 718/638–5000) hosts occasional chamber concerts and New Music events.

The Cloisters (Fort Tryon Park, tel. 212/923–3700), the celebrated medieval branch of the Metropolitan Museum of Art, often imports early music groups on Sunday afternoons from Thanksgiving through Easter; during the Christmas season the Waverly Consort traditionally holds forth.

The Frick Collection (1 E. 70th St., tel. 212/288–0700), one of the city's most splendid little art museums, hosts Sunday concerts from October to May. Tickets to these are free but much in demand; call the museum three weeks prior to the concert to reserve seats.

Metropolitan Museum of Art (5th Ave. at 82nd St., tel. 212/535–7710) offers occasional weekend classical music concerts at its Grace Rainey Rogers Auditorium.

Museum of the City of New York (5th Ave. at 103rd St., tel. 212/534–1672) sometimes holds Sunday Rhythm in the City concerts which tie into the current program at the museum. Free with paid admission to the museum.

Museum of Modern Art (11 W. 53rd St., tel. 212/708–9480) hosts free Saturday evening concerts in the sculpture garden during the summer.

Queens Museum (Flushing Meadows, Queens, tel. 718/592–5555) offers chamber music on Sunday afternoons, free with paid admission to the museum.

Studio Museum in Harlem (144 W. 125th St., tel. 212/864–4500) showcases the works of African-American painters, photographers, and, occasionally, musicians.

Music in Churches Some of the city's best music takes place every Sunday in its churches—sometimes as part of worship services, sometimes at concerts or vespers held in mid- or late afternoon. A few institutions stand out; watch the newspapers for notices of concerts or call to have your name put on the mailing list.

Cathedral of St. John the Divine (112th St. and Amsterdam Ave., tel. 212/316–7540) has a lively musical program Sunday at 7 PM that includes weekly choral vespers by candlelight followed by an organ meditation.

Church of St. Ignatius Loyola (980 Park Ave., at 84th St., tel. 212/
288–3588) sponsors an organ recital series on occasional Sundays at
4. There are two masses every Sunday, at 11 AM and 12:30 PM; the
choir sings during the earlier service.

Holy Trinity Lutheran Church (Central Park West at 65th St., tel.
212/877–6815) has one of the most ambitious professional church music programs in the country, starring a Bach Vespers series from
late fall through Easter. This remains the only place in the country
where cantatas are regularly sung on the days of the liturgical calendar for which they were composed. On Sunday afternoons in winter
several Bach organ recitals star the church's three-manual 67-rank
pipe organ.

Madison Avenue Presbyterian Church (921 Madison Ave., tel. 212/
288–8920) features soloists and chamber music groups, such as the
St. Andrews Music Society, which has brought major choral works
and chamber music to the community. Performances are usually at
4, Oct.–Nov. and Jan.–May.

Metropolitan Baptist Church (151 W. 128th St., tel. 212/663–8990)
presents soul-stirring gospel music during its regular services on
Sundays at 10:45.

Riverside Church (Riverside Dr. at 122nd St., tel. 212/222–5900)
rings the 74 bells of the Laura Spelman Rockefeller Memorial Carillon every Sunday at 10:30, 12:30, and 3. The church has one of the
largest historic organs in the country. During Sunday services at
10:45, the 50-member choir performs. Also, on Sunday afternoons,
the church sometimes hosts chamber music concerts.

St. Ann and the Holy Trinity Episcopal Church (corner of Clinton and
Montague Sts., Brooklyn, tel. 718/875–6960) offers occasional organ
recitals on Sundays and popular music concerts on Saturdays.

St. Bartholomew's (Park Ave. at 50th St., tel. 212/378–0200), home
of the fifth-largest organ in the Western Hemisphere, presents concerts by visiting brass ensembles, choirs, opera companies, youth
orchestras, organists, and other groups, as well as its own choir
nearly every Sunday from fall through spring, except during Lent
(usually late Feb.–Mar.).

St. Michael's Church (225 W. 99th St., tel. 212/222–2700) features
the Great Organ, a mechanical action instrument with fine, majestic
sound, best heard during choral Eucharists at 11 AM on the first and
third Sundays of every month. The annual Christmas Festival of
Lessons and Carols, an ecumenical candlelight service, is modeled on
the one held in King's College, Cambridge.

St. Patrick's Cathedral (5th Ave. at 50th St., tel. 212/753–2261) presents guest organists from New York and around the world every
Sunday at 4:45. The choir at the 10:15 mass usually numbers at least
100, except during the summer and during the Christmas season.

St. Peter's Lutheran Church (Lexington Ave. at 54th St., tel. 212/
935–2200) offers a lively Sunday program of jazz vespers and jazz
and classical concerts at 5.

St. Thomas Church (5th Ave. at 53rd St., tel. 212/757–7013) stars its
celebrated boy's choir at choral evensong recitals Sundays at 4.

Washington Square Church (135 W. 4th St., tel. 212/777–2528) has
lively 11 AM Sunday services with a choir, thanks to its music director Paul Knopf, a professional jazz-gospel pianist. On occasional
Sundays the church has performing-arts vespers at 5:30.

Opera

In addition to the revered Metropolitan Opera and its livelier counterpart, the New York City Opera, smaller opera companies fill the
city's other halls. Vocal artists from all over the world consider New
York *the* place to make an operatic debut.

Amato Opera (319 Bowery, on the corner of E. 2nd St., tel. 212/228–
8200) performs at its intimate 107-seat downtown house. The season

typically includes several classics (such as *The Marriage of Figaro* or *La Bohème*) and American premieres of rarely performed operas. Performances take place on Saturdays at 7:30 and on Sundays at 2:30.

Brooklyn Academy of Music (30 Lafayette Ave., Brooklyn, tel. 718/ 636–4100), once the stage for all the world's great singers, has recently become active again in the field of opera. Its recent offerings have included new works by Philip Glass and Robert Ashley, and performances by the Kirov Opera of St. Petersburg. **Carnegie Hall** (57th St. and 7th Ave., tel. 212/247–7800) frequently offers vocal programs in its main concert hall. **Weill Recital Hall** presents new faces in opera, ready to receive roses on the occasion of their New York debuts.

Empire State Opera (62 Bay 8 St., Brooklyn, tel. 718/837–1176) boasts a 35-piece orchestra, professional leads, and lots of enthusiasm for a repertoire that includes *Il Trovatore* and *Romeo and Juliet*; the company stages three or four productions a year.

New York City Opera (Lincoln Center, Broadway at 65th St., tel. 212/870–5570) performs at the New York State Theater from September through November and in March and April, playing on Saturday matinees and evenings and Sunday matinees. In past years, the City Opera has widened its repertory to include new works (*Harvey Milk*, *The Turn of the Screw*), favorite musicals (*A Little Night Music*, *The Most Happy Fella*, and *Cinderella*), and time-tested classics (*Carmen*, *La Traviata*, and *Rigoletto*). Foreign-language operas are supertitled in English to help audiences follow the plots.

New York Gilbert and Sullivan Players (302 W. 91st St., tel. 212/769–1000; box office, tel. 212/864–5400) performs the lively operettas of the English masters of the form, usually at Symphony Space (95th St. and Broadway).

New York Grand Opera (154 W. 57th St., Suite 125, tel. 212/245–8837) mounts free summer performances of Verdi operas with a full orchestra and professional singers, at Central Park's annual Summerstage at Rumsey Playfield in Central Park at 72nd Street.

Repertorio Español (138 E. 27th St., tel. 212/889–2850) presents a diverse selection of performances in Spanish, ranging from comedic operas to flamenco dancing in the summer.

Jazz

Somehow jazz seems mostly the province of late weekend nights, when artists jam away until the wee hours, then pack up their instruments, go home, and conk out. But even jazz musicians can be persuaded to tune up whenever club managers and producers can bring in an audience. As a result, jazz erupts in clubs over brunch, in concert halls uptown and downtown, and at open-air festivals all day, all over the city. Greenwich Village is the city's jazz hub, but you'll find everything from fusion to Dixieland playing at plenty of truly serendipitous sites.

What's Playing   Apart from local newspaper and magazine listings, you can get information about current performances by stopping by any decent music store, where you'll find fliers about upcoming events and stacks of club passes.

Tickets   Jazz concerts and club gigs are usually priced at a fairly reasonable $10–$20, often several dollars less when you pay in advance, but some concert halls and clubs can also be quite expensive. Sometimes you'll find there's no charge for the entertainment at the clubs, but a drink minimum instead. Call the box office to obtain tickets, and check whether the club honors credit cards (many don't). Club music regulars offer two further cautions: Once upon a time, one admission fee covered the cost of a whole evening of jazz, but an increasing number of proprietors charge by the set, meaning that after the music temporarily dies down, you'll be herded toward the door. And concerning the matter of start-up, remember that time is surprisingly elastic in the music world. The ad may say the artists begin at 7:30, but that could mean 8 or 8:30—so be cool.

Jazz Concert   **Alice Tully Hall** (Broadway and 65th St., tel. 212/875–5050) presents
Spots   jazz concerts by renowned musicians as part of the Jazz at Lincoln Center series from September to May.

Apollo Theatre (253 W. 125th St., tel. 212/749–5838), the legendary Harlem showcase for black musicians and entertainers, schedules weekend shows.

Brooklyn Museum (200 Eastern Pkwy., Brooklyn, tel. 718/638–5000) hosts a series of Sunday jazz concerts in August.

Carnegie Hall (57th St. and 7th Ave., tel. 212/247–7800), decidedly at the tony (and thus, pricey) end of the New York jazz spectrum, schedules concerts with some of the greats in the field, such as tenor saxophonists Sonny Rollins and Branford Marsalis.

Jazzmobile (tel. 212/866–4900) is a kind of musical RV that rolls into parks (most often Riverside Park by Grant's Tomb) on balmy summer evenings.

JVC Jazz Festival New York (tel. 212/501–1390 or 212/496–9000), held in late June and early July, is the pinnacle of New York's jazz year. Concerts bring jazz greats to halls all over town, including Carnegie, Town, and Avery Fisher halls. For schedules, write: Box 1169, Ansonia Station, New York 10023.

Queens Museum (Flushing Meadows, Coronoa Park, Queens, tel. 718/592–5555) hosts occasional Sunday afternoon jazz concerts.

Studio Museum in Harlem (144 W. 125th St., tel. 212/864–4500) frequently offers jazz concerts on Sunday afternoons.

Symphony Space (2537 Broadway, at 95th St., tel. 212/864–5400) is a main stage for jazz uptown, particularly programs sponsored by the World Music Institute, a group dedicated to bringing music from the far corners of the globe to the Big Apple. The World Music Institute's season runs from September to June (for information call 212/545–7536).

Town Hall (123 W. 43rd St., tel. 212/840–2824) frequently books notables from the experimental jazz scene.

Winter Garden Atrium (World Financial Center, Battery Park City, tel. 212/945–0505), stylish and palm-shaded, sometimes showcases experimental music, including jazz, on weekends for free.

Jazz Clubs   Many restaurants serve jazz brunches, as noted in Chapter 2. In addition, the following clubs are worth checking out.

Birdland (315 W. 44th St., between 8th and 9th Aves., tel. 212/581–3080) is the place to find lots of up-and-coming groups, along with the requisite thick atmosphere.

The Blue Note (131 W. 3rd St., off 6th Ave., tel. 212/475–8592) is the quintessential jazz club—cramped, low-ceilinged, dim, and electric with musical excitement.

Detour (342 E. 13th St., at 1st Ave., tel. 212/533–6212) is a comfortable neighborhood bar that presents excellent free Sunday night jazz sessions beginning at 6.

Iridium (44 W. 63rd St., tel. 212/582–2121), a popular club and restaurant across from Lincoln Center, welcomes outstanding up-and-coming vocalists and combos. They also have a zippy jazz brunch on Sundays.

The Knitting Factory (74 Leonard St., between Broadway and Church St., tel. 212/219–3055) continues to feature fine avant-garde jazz in its Alterknit Theater.

Smalls (183 W. 10th St., at 7th Ave., tel. 212/929–7565), a lively addition to the jazz scene, jams from 10 PM Saturday night to 8 AM Sunday morning.

Sweet Basil (88 7th Ave. S, between Grove and Bleecker, tel. 212/242–1785) hosts some of the best line-ups in the city, for jazz brunches and on into the night.

Tavern on the Green (Central Park at W. 67th St., tel. 212/873–3200), with its charming setting in Central Park, features seasoned musicians doing classic tunes.

The Village Vanguard (178 7th Ave. S, at 11th St., tel. 212/255–4037), an old Thelonius Monk haunt in a smoky cellar, became a jazz mecca under the guidance of the late jazz impresario Max Gordon. It's pricey, but worth every penny.

Visiones (125 Macdougal St., at W. 3rd St., tel. 212/673–5576), a Spanish restaurant, attracts lovers of top-notch, avant-garde jazz.

Rock Clubs As a world-class city, New York attracts the top rock music acts in the business (*see* Madison Square Garden, *above*), but it's also the place to check out burgeoning (and not-so-burgeoning) talent.

Beacon Theatre (2124 Broadway, at 74th St., 212/307–7171) books older, more established rock acts like Billy Bragg and Robyn Hitchcock.

Brownies (169 Ave. A, between 10th and 11th Sts., 212/420–8392), a small, usually cramped East Village bar, consistently premieres newer talent for cheap.

CBGB's (315 Bowery, at Bleecker St., 212/982–4052) might be the most historic downtown rock club in New York. The Talking Heads and '70s punk acts first got their start in this dingy hole-in-the-wall. More mature folks now hang out next door at **CB's Gallery,** where relatively quieter rock groups play.

Coney Island High (15 St. Marks Pl., between 2nd and 3rd Aves., 212/674–7959) is a popular central East Village gathering place for the young alternative rock crowd. Expect severe hair and facial piercings.

Irving Plaza (17 Irving Pl., at 15th St., 212/777–6800), a fairly intimate club convenient to Gramercy Park and Union Square, has made a name for itself by booking great acts that are heading toward arena-sized audiences.

Luna Lounge (171 Ludlow St., between Houston and Stanton Sts., 212/260–2323), a spacious Lower East Side bar, has couches in the back room where you can relax and listen to bands play (often for free).

Mercury Lounge (217 E. Houston St., at Essex St., 212/260–4700) is a relatively new addition to the downtown nightlife scene. Up front is a dimly lit bar and in back are tables, which are often cleared away to make room for a rowdy mosh pit.

Sidewalk (96 Ave. A, at 6th St., 212/473–7373), an East Village restaurant, has a back room which is home to the anti-folk folk scene.

Webster Hall (125 E. 11th St., between 3rd and 4th Aves., 212/353–1600) is a club-kid's dream. This multi-floor dance complex hosts rave parties that go on way into the night.

Wetlands (161 Hudson St., at Laight St., 212/966–4225), in TriBeCa, is geared toward young Dead Heads who come to the bi-level bar to hear Grateful Dead cover bands, reggae acts, and established blues and folk musicians.

Dance

On weekends, dance lovers seek out companies both famous and obscure in the city's theaters and downtown studios. Performances by New York's American Ballet Theatre and New York City Ballet, and modern dance companies such as Trisha Brown, Merce Cunningham, Mark Morris, and the Alvin Ailey American Dance Theater draw an enthusiastic and loyal audience. Scores of other modern, ethnic, ad-hoc, and visiting dance companies also compete for attention. The three- and four-tiered theaters rarely sell out, but you may be disappointed if you arrive at the 472-seat Joyce Theater or another more intimate venue at curtain time.

The drama of ballet and its grandiose theaters can provide for a richly satisfying and romantic night on the town. The downtown dance scene is sparser in its productions, but audiences here look forward to the stimulation of the experimental and the unexpected. Some venues include a post-performance discussion session with the choreographer and the dancers.

What's Playing The *New York Times*, the *Village Voice*, and *Time Out* do their best to chronicle and critique all the dance that's going on in the city.

Tickets You can pay as little as $10 for dance tickets or as much as $70. Remember that in dance, seats close to the stage do not always provide the best vantage point on the intricate choreographic patterns, although you may be privy to the patter of pointe shoes and assertive exhales of the dancers. For discounted tickets, sometimes half-price, try the TKTS booths, and check whether TDF vouchers are valid for the dance events of your choice.

Major Venues **American Ballet Theatre** (Metropolitan Opera House, Lincoln Center, Broadway at 63rd St., tel. 212/362–6000) remains famous for its brilliant renditions of the great 19th-century classics (*Swan Lake*, *Giselle*, and *The Sleeping Beauty*), as well as for the unique scope of its contemporary repertoire, including works by 20th-century masters Balanchine, Tudor, Robbins, deMille, among others. The Company, now under the direction of Kevin McKenzie, has included such great dancers as Mikhail Baryshnikov, Natalia Makarova, Rudolf Nureyev, and Cynthia Gregory. Its 3-month New York season begins in the spring; no performances on Sunday.

Brooklyn Academy of Music (30 Lafayette Ave., Brooklyn, tel. 718/636–4100) presents American and foreign choreographers featuring their own companies or in collaboration with other performing artists. Donald Byrd, Susan Marshall, Pina Bausch, and Mark Morris have all performed recently. A bus service to the academy runs from mid-town Manhattan.

City Center (131 W. 55th St., tel. 212/581–7907) is where the moderns hold sway: Alvin Ailey American Dance Theater, Trisha Brown, Merce Cunningham, and Paul Taylor, among others.

Dance Theater Workshop (219 W. 19th St., tel. 212/924–0077) began in 1965 as a choreographers' cooperative and now showcases some of the city's freshest dance talent. The DTW's year-long season includes not only dance but contemporary music, video, theater, and readings.

Danspace Project (St. Mark's Church in the Bowery, 10th St. and 2nd Ave., tel. 212/674–8112) clears the honeyed wood floors in this church to present contemporary dance from September through June. The grounds and small square outside of the church and a peaceful East Village oasis.

Dia Center for the Arts (155 Mercer St., tel. 212/431–9232) hosts a number of performances by interesting local dancers.

Joyce Theater (175 8th Ave., at 19th St., tel. 212/242–0800), a former Art Deco movie theater in Chelsea, is a major New York dance center. Their eclectic international programming includes the fringe hotshots of dance in the Altogether Different festival. The Joyce is the unofficial home of the Feld Ballet/NY, founded in 1974 by an upstart American Ballet Theater dancer Elliot Feld. Also, **Joyce SoHo** (155 Mercer St., tel. 212/431–9233) features informal performances by local up-and-coming choreographers, often in shared concerts.

Merce Cunningham Studio (55 Bethune St., tel. 212/691–9751) hosts performances in the sacred space where the hallowed company rehearses. Dancers from established companies often test their own choreographic mettle here.

New York City Ballet (New York State Theater, Lincoln Center, Broadway at 63rd St., tel. 212/870–5570), now under the leadership of Peter Martins, was started by Lincoln Kirstein and George Balanchine in 1948. NYCB stresses the company's identity above that of individual dancers, though that hasn't stopped a number of principal dancers (Kyra Nichols, Darci Kistler, Damian Woetzel, and Jock Soto) from becoming stars. The company's repertory of 20th-century works is unmatched in the world. Its winter season runs from mid-November through February—with the beloved annual *George Balanchine's The Nutcracker* ushering in the December holiday season. The spring season lasts from late April through June.

P.S. 122 (150 1st Ave., at 9th St., tel. 212/477–5288) presents avant-garde local, national, and international choreographers. Occasionally, there are late shows on the weekend.

Repertorio Español (138 E. 27th St., tel. 212/889–2850) hosts the famed flamenco and modern dancer Pilar Rioja, who visits from Spain for three months each summer.

Sylvia and Danny Kaye Playhouse (Hunter College, 68th St., between Park and Lexington Aves., tel. 212/772–4448) presents national and international ballet and modern companies such as the Stuttgard Ballet, American Ballet Theatre Studio Company, and Eric Hawkins.

Symphony Space (2537 Broadway, at 95th St., tel. 212/864–5400) often features ethnic dance on its eclectic calendar of events.

Performance Art

When dance, drama, music, video, and other visual arts come together, the result is performance art, the enfant terrible of the avant-garde. New York is *the* place to sample the style, since it all started here—specifically downtown, in (what used to be) low-rent corners of SoHo, TriBeCa, and the Lower East Side.

Astor Place Theater (434 Lafayette St., near 8th St., tel. 212/254–4370) is where the ever-popular Blue Man Group—a trio of *extremely* physical comedians with bright blue shiny faces—has taken up residence for the last five years.

Brooklyn Academy of Music (30 Lafayette Ave., Brooklyn, tel. 718/636–4100) has built its current reputation on its annual Next Wave Festival of performance works, running from October to December and featuring the performance art elite, including Laurie Anderson, Mark Morris, and Robert Wilson, among others.

Dixon Place (258 Bowery, between Houston and Prince Sts., tel. 212/219–3088), an intimate loft space east of SoHo, is home to some of the more radical performing artists and young monologuists.

Franklin Furnace (112 Franklin St., between Church St. and W. Broadway, tel. 212/925–4671) has supported off-center arts since 1976. Eric Bogosian got his start here. Monthly exhibitions are at the Franklin Street address, while events are held at the Knitting Factory (74 Leonard St., tel. 212/219–3055) and P.S. 122 (*see below*).

Joseph Papp Public Theater (425 Lafayette St., 1 block east of Broadway, tel. 212/598–7150) frequently gives space to better-known performance artists such as downtown diva Ann Magnusson, David Cale, and Danny Hoch.

The Kitchen (512 W. 19th St., tel. 212/255–5793) is perhaps *the* Manhattan center for performance art, although video, dance, and music have their moments here, too.

La Mama (74A E. 4th St., between 2nd Ave. and Bowery, tel. 212/475–7710), a producing facility perpetually on the cutting edge of *something*, devotes both its Club and First Floor Theater to performance art.

P.S. 122 (150 1st Ave., at 9th St., tel. 212/477–5288), a vital force in downtown culture, usually has something experimental on tap. Look especially for its brief but dazzling February performance marathon, involving scores of downtowners and many artistic disciplines.

Surf Reality (172 Allen St., at Stanton St., tel. 212/673–4182), a new addition to the downtown avant-garde performance scene.

Readings and Lectures

Writers flock to New York, not only because it offers high-voltage stimulation but because it's one of the world's publishing centers. Lectures, workshops, and readings frequently staged at major auditoriums are attended by the literary and publishing big shots. For those interested in the written word, New York weekends can be counted on to produce a number of readings from which to choose. Consult the **New York City Poetry Calendar** (611 Broadway, Suite 905, 10012, tel. 212/260–7097), published monthly, for an extensive list of poetry and prose readings and writers' workshops around the city. The calendar is available by subscription and free at most Manhattan bookstores and public libraries.

A Different Light (151 W. 19 St., between 6th and 7th Aves., tel. 212/989–4850), the city's highest-profile gay and lesbian bookstore, frequently invites established writers to read from their most recent works.

alt.coffee (139 Ave. A, between St. Marks and 9th St., tel. 212/529–2233), an East Village internet café— coffee bar, hosts bi-weekly informal spoken word free-for-alls at which you're welcome to join in. Sign up at 8 for the 8:30 performance (which usually goes on until 10).

Cornelia Street Café (29 Cornelia St., between 6th and 7th Aves., tel. 212/989–9319), in the heart of Greenwich Village, has popular Sunday night readings of plays and new fiction nearly every week.

The Drawing Center (35 Wooster St., between Broome and Grand Sts., tel. 212/219–2166), an exhibition space in SoHo, frequently invites famous actors and writers to read aloud from their favorite fiction.

Ear Inn (326 Spring St., between Washington and Greenwich, tel. 212/226–9060), a bar-restaurant which has taken to calling itself a "dump with dignity," has a long tradition of presenting poetry readings on Saturday afternoons, from September to June.

Judith's Room (681 Washington St., between 10th and Charles Sts., tel. 212/727–7330), a feminist bookstore in the Village, often invites women writers to read on Sunday afternoons.

Metropolitan Museum of Art (5th Ave. at 82nd St., tel. 212/570–3930), like most museums, has a heavy lecture schedule all day on weekends. Artists such as David Hockney hold forth, as do the world's eminent art historians, on topics as varied as the museum's collections.

Nuyorican Poets Cafe (236 E. 3rd St., between Aves. B and C, tel. 212/505–8183) is the Alphabet City center for the convergence of poetry, performance art and music. The cafe has recently gotten popular for its competetive screenplay series as well as its legendary poetry slams.

The Poetry Project (St. Mark's in the Bowery, 2nd Ave. and 10th St., tel. 212/674–0910) frequently sponsors readings by prominent New York poets.

Unterberg Poetry Center (92nd St. Y, 1395 Lexington Ave., between 91st and 92nd Sts., tel. 212/415–5760) has been a prominent platform for poets, novelists, and playwrights since it was founded in 1939. Selected Sundays in fall and winter bring a popular Biographers and Brunch series.

Comedy and Magic

On weekends, most of the major comedy and magic clubs stand ready to welcome those looking for laughs or sleight of hand. Younger, more off-beat comedy acts as well as some more established per-coffee houses, so check theater and readings listings as well.

Boston Comedy Club (82 W. 3rd St., between Thompson and Sullivan Sts., tel. 212/477–1000) provides a place for Beantown comedians to test their stuff in the Big Apple. This place is popular with the N.Y.U. crowd.

Caroline's Comedy Club (1626 Broadway, between 49th and 50th Sts., tel. 212/757–4100), one of Manhattan's original comedy clubs, is still going strong at its uptown venue, attracting some of the top comics in the country.

Comedy Cellar (117 MacDougal St., between W. 3rd and Bleecker Sts., tel. 212/254-3480), located beneath the Olive Tree Cafe, presents a bill that's a good barometer of who's hot.

Comic Strip (1568 2nd Ave., between 81st and 82nd Sts., tel. 212/ 861–9386), with its corner-bar atmosphere and tiny, brilliantly lit stage, has a bill that's unpredictable but definitely worth checking out.

Dangerfield's (1118 1st Ave., at 61st St., tel. 212/593–1650) has been, since 1969, an important showcase for prime comic talent. It's frequently visited by its owner, Mr. D. himself.

Stand Up NY (236 W. 78th St., tel. 212/595–0850), a 175-seat, Upper West Side option for comedy devotees, books lots of bright faces coming off recent TV gigs. Stars drop in on occasion, too.

Movies and Video

The cinematic splendors glowing on screens in the dark of New York's movie theaters go far beyond the star vehicles and made-for-the-masses action-adventure films that monopolize auditoriums in most other towns. Unusual foreign offerings, small independent films, and classics both renowned and arcane—you can see them all on any day of the week, but weekends are prime time for film goers, especially Saturday night. Be prepared for lines that stretch around the block, though, especially for newly premiered titles.

What's Playing Most local publications list showtimes and include at least abbreviated reviews of current cinema. You can also find out about mainstream features by calling **MovieFone** (*see below*).

Tickets Go to the first show of the day, and you'll seldom have a wait; you may even get a discount. When buying tickets for a box-office hit early in its run, you may want to guarantee a seat by arriving at the box office an hour or so before show time. A good strategy is to pass by the theater, pick up tickets, have a meal and a stroll, and come back (a half hour before show time) to claim a place in the ticket holders' line.

You can also have your tickets waiting by calling ahead to **MovieFone** (777–FILM from area codes 212, 516, or 201), co-sponsored by the *New York Times* and WQHT 97 FM. For most movies, callers can track down the movie, the theater, the time, and order tickets in advance with a credit card; there's a $1.50 surcharge per ticket.

Museums **American Museum of the Moving Image** (35th Ave. at 36th St., Astoria, Queens, tel. 718/784–4520), housed in a building belonging to the historic Kaufman-Astoria Studios, presents a variety of programs annually, including major artist-oriented retrospectives (sometimes with personal appearances), Hollywood classics, experimental videos, and documentaries. (*See* Chapter 4.)

Museum of Modern Art (11 W. 53rd St., tel. 212/708–9480 for film information) is a treasure, with an extensive film archive founded by former museum director Alfred H. Barr, Jr., who believed that film is one of the most important art forms of the 20th century. A number of weekend screenings in two small, acoustically perfect auditoriums include offerings from cinema's earliest days to the present, encompassing films of all types, from all nations. (*See* Chapter 4.)

Museum of Television & Radio (25 W. 52nd St., tel. 212/621–6800) has a gigantic collection of 60,000 radio and TV shows, including popular nuggets of nostalgia like the Royal Wedding and Jackie Kennedy's tour of the White House. The library provides 96 consoles, where you can watch or listen to whatever you wish for up to two hours at a time. The museum has scheduled theater screenings, gallery exhibits, and children's series.

Festivals   **New Directors/New Films** (Museum of Modern Art's Roy and Niuta Titus Theatre, 11 W. 53rd St., tel. 212/877–1800, ext. 489), a joint project of MOMA and the Film Society of Lincoln Center, each spring presents the best work by up-and-coming directors.
New York Film Festival (Alice Tully and Avery Fisher halls, Lincoln Center, Broadway at 65th St., tel. 212/877–1800), the city's most revered film series, screens each September as many as 50 buzzworthy independent movies that may or may not wind up on screens anyplace else, plus special events and a video program at the Walter Reade Theater. (*See* Foreign Films, *below.*)

Something   **Angelika Film Center** (18 W. Houston St., at Mercer St., tel. 212/
Special   995–2000) and **Angelika 57** (225 W. 57th St., at Broadway, tel. 212/ 586–1900) draw film lovers for this foreign and independent fare; the downtown location has six screens and a lobby café which attracts (too much of) a beautiful crowd, so get your tickets early.
The Film Forum (209 W. Houston St., west of 6th Ave., tel. 212/727– 8110), offers a richly textured program embracing oldies, documentaries, and foreign and experimental films alike.
The Screening Room (54 Varick St., just below Canal St., tel. 212/ 334–2100), a spanking new bar and swanky restaurant complex with a screening room attached, shows independent and foreign films as well as the occasional midnight movie. Check out the "Dinner-and-a-Movie" special.

Revival   **Anthology Film Archives** (32–34 2nd Ave., at 2nd St., tel. 212/505–
Houses   5181), run by Fabiano Canosa (who used to manage the film program for the Public Theater) and longtime artistic director Jonas Mekas, is one of the city's most overlooked spots for finding a broad spectrum of auteur revivals and independent and experimental festivals.
Millenium Film Workshop (66 E. 4th St., between Bowery and 2nd Ave., tel. 212/673–0090) shows videos and films by experimental filmmakers, mainting a devotion to the "development and preservation of truly independent, personal cinema"—meaning: just about anything goes.
Symphony Space (2537 Broadway, at 95th St., tel. 212/864–5400), an Upper West Side performance center, has become popular with cineastes for its the Best Films of Our Lives and other themed film series.
Walter Reade Theater (Lincoln Center, 165 W. 65th St., tel. 212/875– 5600), run by the Film Society of Lincoln Center, is one of the best places to see old films in Manhattan. This comfortable, state-of-the-art gem presents several fascinating series that run concurrently, devoted to specific themes or a certain director's body of work; movies for kids are featured Saturday morning. Other good places to see revivals are: **American Museum of Moving Image**, the **Museum of Modern Art** (*see* Museums, *above*), and the **Film Forum** (*see* Something Special, *above*).

Big Screens   **Radio City Music Hall** (1260 6th Ave., at 50th St., tel. 212/247–4777) doesn't regularly show films, but they have recently inaugurated the annual Radio City Music Hall Film Festival to show off the 5,900-seat theater and its huge screen for a week during the month of September.
Sony Theatres Lincoln Square (Broadway and 68th St., tel. 212/336– 5000 or 212/595–6391) has 12 screens and an eight-story, 600-seat IMAX theater equipped for 3-D imagery.

The Ziegfeld (141 W. 54th St.,at 6th Ave., tel. 212/765–7600) is one of the few remaining grand (nearly 1,200 seats) theaters of New York that hasn't been torn down to make way for multiplexes.

Foreign Films The theaters noted above under Something Special and Revival Houses often schedule foreign movies. Other theaters that show foreign films include:

Carnegie Hall Cinemas (887 7th Ave., between 56th and 57th Sts., tel. 212/265–2520).
Eastside Playhouse (99 3rd Ave., between 55th and 56th Sts., tel. 212/755–3020).
Florence Gould Hall (55 E. 59th St., between Park and Madison Aves., tel. 212/355–6160).
Goethe House (5th Ave., between 82nd and 83rd Sts., tel. 212/439–8700).
Japan Society (333 E. 47th St., tel. 212/752–0824).
Lincoln Plaza Cinemas (30 Lincoln Plaza, Broadway at 62nd St., tel. 212/757–2280).
68th Street Playhouse (1164 3rd Ave., at 68th St., tel. 212/734–0302).
Sony Paris (4 W. 58th St., tel. 212/980–5656).
Quad Cinema (34 W. 13th St., between 5th and 6th Aves., tel. 212/255-8800).

Summer Arts

On weekends, particularly in summer, urban open spaces yield a harvest of cultural events, giving city folk plenty of reasons to stay in town and suburbanites plenty of reasons to visit. You might find the Big Apple Circus, the Metropolitan Opera, the Bread and Puppet Theater, or a Korean-American fest. The curtain goes up on Shakespeare in many a city park, not only in Central Park but in Brooklyn's Prospect Park, the Bronx's Van Cortlandt Park, Fort Tryon Park at Manhattan's northern tip, and Riverside Park at its western edge.

Note: Parks events are popular, so claim your seat or your parcel of lawn an hour or so before curtain time, then wait as the sun sets.

Outdoors

Celebrate Brooklyn (9th St. Bandshell, Prospect Park, Brooklyn, tel. 718/965–8969) presents dance events, Shakespeare, and classical, pop, and ethnic music on weekends from June to September. There's a suggested contribution of $1 for each adult.
Lincoln Center Out-of-Doors (Broadway at 65th Street, tel. 212/546-2656) transforms Manhattan's performing arts centerpiece into a virtual state fair of the arts during August. In recent years, as many as 300,000 people have attended some 100 events in one summer. Stages set up in the plaza accommodate jazz dancers, chamber orchestras, Broadway lyricists and composers, mimes, children's theater, and more.
New York Shakespeare Festival (Delacorte Theater, Central Park at 81st St., tel. 212/861–PAPP after mid-June, or contact the Joseph Papp Public Theater, 425 Lafayette St., tel. 212/260–2400) stages two plays every summer. Park breezes keep the Delacorte Theater cool on hot summer nights, as big-name stars such as Kevin Kline and Michelle Pfeiffer appear beneath the starry sky. Since 1954, when the late producer Joseph Papp launched the program, innovative productions of all kinds of classics have gone under the Shakespeare rubric. Although some of the tickets are sold in advance, most tickets are distributed free during the day—call for an estimate of the time you should arrive to wait in line, and bring a blanket to hold your place.

Summerfun (83 Acre Park, Snug Harbor Cultural Center, Staten Island, tel. 718/448–2500) brings a series of concerts to this gem of an arts complex, a quick trip by Bus S40 from the Staten Island ferry landing. Recent years have brought the Band, Don McLean, and Joan Baez. Tickets for major events (usually held on Saturdays at 8) can be ordered in advance from the center's ticket office. During the summer, there are free concerts on Sundays at 3.

Summerstage (Rumsey Playfield, Central Park at 72nd St., tel. 212/360–2756) sponsors free programs of music, dance, theater, and comedy, ranging from grand opera to polka to experimental rock. Performances are generally at 3 on Sundays, from June to August.

You Gotta Have Park! (Prospect Park, Park Slope, Brooklyn, tel. 718/965–8954) takes over Brooklyn's lush Prospect Park for 2 days during mid-May. In return for helping to clean the park, the public is rewarded with free entertainment—including paddle boat rides, a rollerblade derby, and storytelling time for kids.

Other Parks Elsewhere on municipal greenswards, weekends bring the **Bronx Arts Ensemble Concert Series** (with performances on both days at 2 PM in the Bronx's Van Cortlandt Park, tel. 718/430–1890), the **Orchard Beach Weekend Concert Series** (with musical groups tuning up at Pelham Bay Park's Orchard Beach, tel. 718/885–2275), and occasional musicalizing by the **Brooklyn Philharmonic** at Brooklyn's Seaside Park (tel. 718/965–8913).

Indoors

Mostly Mozart (Avery Fisher Hall, Lincoln Center, Broadway at 65th St., tel. 212/875–5135) enlivens city life for seven weeks during July and August with the music of Mozart and his contemporaries.

Lincoln Center Festival (W. 62nd to 66th Sts., Columbus to Amsterdam Aves., tel. 212/546–2656) is launching a new international performance festival to be directed by arts critic and writer John Rockwell. The festival includes classical music concerts, contemporary music and dance presentations, stage works, and non-Western arts and showcases guest artists and companies from New York and around the world.

Best Bets for Children

Weekends are youngsters' time to lay claim to the Big Apple, as concerts and theater presentations abound, parks and museums stage special programs, and children's performing arts groups burst into life. Many of these events are modestly priced or even free.

Arts in the Parks **Big Apple Circus** pitches its big top in Damrosch Park in Lincoln Center from October– January. Call for schedules and ticket information (tel. 212/874–8990).

Arts in Museums Since kids are out of school, children's museums are extra-lively on the weekends, with all kinds of special events. Check into the **Brooklyn Children's Museum,** the **Children's Museum of Manhattan,** the **Jewish Museum,** the **Children's Museum of the Arts,** and the **Staten Island Children's Museum.** Frequent programs for young visitors, often centered on the arts, are also offered at the **Museum of the City of New York, South Street Seaport,** and the **Queens Museum,** among others. *See* Chapter 4 for addresses, phone numbers, and hours.

Children's Theater **Brooklyn Academy of Music** (30 Lafayette Ave., Brooklyn, tel. 718/636–4100) presents an International Children's Theater Festival from March to June, including puppet shows, plays, and world music.

Henry Street Settlement (Louis Abrons Arts for Living Center, 466 Grand St., at Pitt St., tel. 212/598–0400), founded by a nurse in 1893 to care for the Lower East Side's sick and disadvantaged, now cares for the arts and mounts plays in its Arts for Family Series on Sundays at 2.

New York Childrens' Theater (Lincoln Sq. Theater, 250 W. 65th St., tel. 212/496–8009), dedicated to exposing kids to "realistic" theater, explores topics such as literacy and aging, with occasional Sunday performances in fall and winter.

The Paper Bag Players (tel. 212/362–0431) perform during the winter on Saturdays and Sundays at the Sylvia and Danny Kaye Playhouse (Hunter College, 68th St. and Lexington Ave., tel. 212/772–4448), presenting original plays like *The Horrible, Horrendous, Hideous Haircut*. It's been great fun for 40 years, and sellout crowds make advance ticket orders a good idea.

The **Puppet Playhouse** (Mazur Theater, Asphalt Green, 555 E. 90th St., tel. 212/369–8890) showcases magicians, musicals, puppet and marionette shows, and dance presented by a variety of companies.

Puppetworks (338 6th Ave., Park Slope, Brooklyn, tel. 718/965–3391) offers marionettes performing classic children's stories as well as hand-puppet shows on most weekends.

Swedish Cottage Marionette Theater (middle of Central Park, near W. 81 St., tel. 212/988–9093) presents highly popular one-hour marionette productions of classics such as *Cinderella*, in a small cottage right in Central Park on Saturdays at noon and 3 from October to July. Reservations are essential.

TADA! Youth Ensemble (120 W. 28th St., tel. 212/627–1732) is an amiable musical theater group made of New York City children who present all original musicals, often with a multi-ethnic perspective, during July and August and December and January.

Theatreworks (Promenade Theater, 2162 Broadway, at 76th St., tel. 212/677–5959), honored by the American Theater Association for "sustained and exceptional accomplishment in children's theater," serves up terrific original children's plays, like one recent adaptation of Jules Vernes' *Around the World in 80 Days*.

Story Hours   City bookstores often hold readings for children on weekends. But, your best best for story hours are at New York's public libraries. Check out the Children's Room at the Brooklyn Public Library (Grand Army Plaza, Brooklyn, tel. 718/780–7848), where they hold story hours regularly.

Barnes & Noble (2289 Broadway, at 82nd St., tel. 212/362–8835; 675 6th Ave., between 21st and 22nd Sts., tel. 212/727–1227; 4 Astor Pl., tel. 212/420–1322, and other branches) has regular story hours on weekends in the children's books section.

Books of Wonder (816 W. 18th St., between 5th and 6th Aves., tel. 212/989–3270), one of New York's finest children's bookstores, has story hours with writers and illustrators most weekends.

Other   The **92nd Street Y** (1395 Lexington Ave., at 92nd St., tel. 212/996–
Organizations   1100) is tireless about offering special programs for kids. The Metropolitan Opera's **Growing Up with Opera** program (tel. 212/769–7008) features special performances for families, which may take place on weekends. In addition, performances of the **Little Orchestra Society** in Avery Fisher and Alice Tully halls (tel. 212/704–2100) and other venues are ideal for families. The free summer arts festival, **Lincoln Center Out-of-Doors,** contains many offerings with child appeal. And don't forget December's great event, *The Nutcracker,* at the New York City Ballet (*see* Dance, *above*).

Index

A. A. Low Building, *89*

A Different Light Bookshop, *112, 174*

A. Zito and Sons (shop), *105*

AAA Bikes (shop), *144*

Aaron Davis Hall, *166*

ABC Carpet (shop), *99, 117*

ABC-TV building, *64*

Abercrombie & Fitch (shop), *97*

Abigail Adams Smith House, *90*

Abingdon Square Park, *158*

Abyssinian Baptist Church, *7, 64*

Academy Book Store, *114*

Ad Hoc Softwares (shop), *120*

Adrien Linford (shop), *99, 118*

Advance Entertainment New York (ticket club), *161*

Adventure on a Shoestring (tours), *73*

Agata and Valentina (shop), *107*

Aggie's (restaurant), *21–22*

Agnés B (shop), *101*

Agrotikon (restaurant), *28*

Aja (restaurant), *33*

Albee (shop), *127*

Alderbrook (mansion), *68*

Alexander Hamilton Custom House, *65*

Algonquin Hotel, *6, 37*

Alice Austen House Museum and Park, *71, 93*

Alice Tully Hall, *166, 170*

Alice Underground (shop), *101*

Alison on Dominick Street (restaurant), *21*

All-State Café, *48*

Alley Pond Environmental Center, *136, 158*

Alley Pond Golf Center, *150*

Alphabets (shop), *118*

alt.coffee (coffee bar), *174*

Altman (shop), *120*

Alva (restaurant), *34*

Amato Opera, *168–169*

Ambassador (theater), *162*

Ambassador Grill, *36*

America (restaurant), *34*

American Ballet Theatre, *172*

American Craft Museum, *83*

American Crafts Festival, *11*

American Festival Café, *40*

American Jewish Theater, *163*

American Museum of Natural History, *12, 93–94, 121*

American Museum of the Moving Image, *70, 83, 175, 176*

American Numismatic Society, *88*

Amerigo's (restaurant), *51*

Amici Miei (restaurant), *23*

Amsterdam Billiard Club, *145*

Amsterdam Billiard Club East, *145*

Amtrak, *2, 3*

Amy's Bread (shop), *105*

Angelica Film Center, *176*

Angelika 57 (movie theater), *176*

Angelika Kitchen (restaurant), *29*

Anglers & Writers Salon de Thé (restaurant), *30, 54*

Ann Taylor (shop), *97*

Anna Sui (shop), *103*

Annex Antiques Fair and Flea Market, *125*

Ansonia (restaurant), *48*

Anthology Film Archives, *176*

Antiques shops, *114–115*

Antiques shows, *10*

A-1 Record Shop, *99, 123*

Aphrodisia (shop), *109*

Apollo Theatre, *64, 170*

Appalachian Mountain Club, *142*

Applause Theatre Books, *114*

April Cornell (shop), *98, 120*

Apthorp (building), *65*

Apthorp Pharmacy, *15, 122*

Aquariums, *139*

Aqueduct Racetrack, *157*

Aqueduct Trail, *135*

Archdiocesan Cathedral of the Holy Trinity, *7*

Arche (shop), *123*

Architecture buildings, *61–62* lobbies, *62–63*

Archivia (shop), *98–99, 112*

Arizona 206 (restaurant), *42*

Armani (shop), *99*

Art Deco Society of New York, *73*

Art galleries, *86–87*

Art museums major museums, *78–82* small museums, *82* specialty museums, *83–84* world cultures, *84–86*

Art supply shops, *111*

Art Tours of Manhattan, *73*

Arthur Avenue, *68*

Arturo's (restaurant), *23*

Ashanti (shop), *104*

Asia Society, *84, 121, 167*

Asphalt Green (pool), *154*

Asser Levy Recreation Center, *154*

Astor Place, *67, 153*

Astoria, *70*

AstroTurf (shop), *110*

AT&T Building, *61*

Atlantic Avenue, *69, 99*

Auction exhibitions, *125*

Audubon Society, *142, 145*

Automotive Services, *14*

Aveda Aromatherapy Esthetique (shop), *115*

Avery Fisher Hall, *165*

Avventura (shop), *118*

Azzuro (restaurant), *46*

B & J Fabrics, *115*

B. Shackman & Co. (shop), *116*

B. Smith (restaurant), *38*

Baby-sitters, *14*

Baci (restaurant), *49*

Back Pages Antiques, *110*

Bagel and bialy shops, *105*

Balducci's (shop), *107*

Ballet, *12, 171–173*

Ballet Company (shop), *120*

Ballroom dancing, *143*

Ballroom on Fifth, *143*

Banana Republic (shop), *97*

Bangkok Cuisine (restaurant), *41*

Bangkok House (restaurant), *44*

Bank Street Bookstore, *125*

Bar Pitti (restaurant), *32*

Bargemusic (music hall), *166*

Barnes & Noble (shop), *112, 179*

Barney Greengrass (restaurant), *49, 109*

Barneys New York (department store), *12, 97, 99*

Bartow-Pell Mansion Museum, *91, 135*

Baseball participant, *143* professional, *156*

Basketball participant, *143* professional, *156*

Bath Island (shop), *115*

Battery Park, *144*

Battery Park City Esplanacle, *133*, *144*, *152*, *153*

Bayard Building, *67*

Bazaar Sabado (shop), *118*

Bazzini (shop), *66*

Beaches, *129–130*

Beacon Theater, *171*

Beads of Paradise (shop), *111*

Becco (restaurant), *38*

Beckstein Home Fabrics (shop), *115*

Bed, Bath & Beyond (shop), *99*

Beekman Place, *72*

Beijing Duck House (restaurant), *24*

Belasco (theater), *162*

Bellini (shop), *127*

Belmont, *68*

Belmont Park (racetrack), *157*

Belvedere Castle, *131*, *158*

Benny's Burritos (restaurant), *33*

Ben's Cheese (shop), *106*

Bergdorf Goodman (department store), *98*, *100*

Bernstein-on-Essex (restaurant), *26*

Bethesda Terrace and Bethesda Fountain, *131*

Bethpage State Park, *149*

Betsey Johnson (shop), *98*, *103*

Beverly (hotel), *6*

Bialystocker Synagogue, *66*

Bice (restaurant), *39*

Bicycling, *143–145*

Big Apple Circus, *178*

Big City Kites (shop), *124*

Big Cup (restaurant), *35*

Big Onion (tour), *73–74*

Bigelow Pharmacy, *15*

Billiard Club, *145*

Billiards, *145*

Billy Martin's (shop), *123*

Billy's (restaurant), *39*

Biography Bookshop, *112*

Bird Sanctuary, *133*

Bird-watching, *145–146*

Birdland (jazz club), *170*

Bistro du Nord (restaurant), *44*

Black Hound (shop), *106*

Black Sheep (restaurant), *31*

Blades, Board, and Skate (shop), *124*, *153*

Bleecker Bob's Golden Oldies (shop), *123*

Bloomingdale's (department store), *98*, *100*

Blue Nile (restaurant), *49*

Blue Note (jazz club), *170*

Blue Ribbon (restaurant), *22*

Blue Ribbon Sushi (restaurant), *23*

Bo Ky (restaurant), *24*

Boat Basin, *132*

Boat Building Shop, *89*

Boat Rental, *146–147*, *148*

Boat shows, *10*

Boathouse (museum), *88*

Boathouse Café, *42*

Boating, *146–147*

Boca Grande (shop), *98*, *119*

Boccie, *147*

Bolton's (shop), *104*

Bon 75 (restaurant), *49*

Book Ark (shop), *114*

Bookleaves (shop), *114*

Books and Bindings (shop), *114*

Books of Wonder (shop), *125*, *179*

Bookshops, *112–115*, *125*

Booth (theater), *162*

Borders Books and Music (shop), *112*

Boston Comedy Club, *175*

Bowling, *147*

Bowlmor, *147*

Bowne & Co. (shop), *89*, *97*

Bowne House, *70*, *92*

Box Tree (restaurant), *37*

Boyd's Madison Avenue (shop), *123*

Bread shops, *105*

Breezy Point Jetty, *149*

Brian Windsor Art, Antiques and Garden Furnishings (shop), *110*

Bridge Café, *20*

Bridge Kitchenware Corp. (shop), *117*

Brighton Beach, *129*

British Open (restaurant), *36*

Broad Financial Center, *65*

Broadhurst (theater), *162*

Broadway (theater), *162*

Broadway Panhandler (shop), *117*

Bronx
beaches, *130*
cemeteries, *141*
gardens, *138*
houses, *restored*, *91–92*
parks, *134–135*
restaurants, *51*
sightseeing, *68*
sports and recreation, *146–152*, *155–156*, *158*
zoos, *139*

Bronx Arts Ensemble Concert Series, *178*

Bronx Museum of the Arts, *82*

Bronx Zoo, *139*, *158*

Brooklyn
beaches, *129–130*
cemeteries, *141–142*
gardens, *137*
houses, *restored*, *92*
parks, *135–136*
restaurants, *51–52*
sightseeing, *68–69*, *72*
sports and recreation, *144*, *146–155*, *158*
zoo, *140*

Brooklyn Academy of Music, *165*, *169*, *172*, *178*

Brooklyn Botanic Garden, *137*, *158*

Brooklyn Bridge, *59*, *76*, *144*, *153*

Brooklyn Center for the Urban Environment, *74*

Brooklyn Children's Museum, *95*, *178*

Brooklyn Conservatory of

Music, *167*

Brooklyn Heights, *68–69*

Brooklyn Heights Promenade, *59*

Brooklyn Historical Society, *74*

Brooklyn Museum of Art, *79–80*, *94*, *121*, *167*, *170*

Brooklyn Philharmonic, *178*

Brooklyn-Queens Expressway, *57*

Brooks Atkinson (theater), *162*

Brookstone (shop), *97*

Brother Jimmy's BBQ (restaurant), *43*

Brother's Bar-B-Q (restaurant), *31*

Brownies (rock club), *171*

Bruno Bakery, *54*

Bryant Park, *76*, *133*

Bryant Park Music and Dance Half-Price Tickets Booth, *2*

Bubby's (restaurant), *20*

Building Blocks (shop), *126*

Bus tours, *75*

Bus travel
in New York, *3–4*
to New York, *2–3*
sightseeing from city buses, *75–76*

c.i.t.e. (shop), *110*

Cabana Carioca (restaurant), *38*

Cafe Beulah, *35*

Café Borgia, *22*

Café de Bruxelles, *31*

Café des Artistes, *46*

Café Español, *33*

Café Gitane, *25*

Café La Fortuna, *54*

Café Lalo, *55*

Café Loup, *31–32*

Café Luxembourg, *46*

Café Noir, *24*

Cafe on Clinton, *57*

Café Pierre, *42*

Café Word of Mouth, *55*

Caffé Dante, *54*

Caffé Reggio, *54*

Caffé Roma, *53*

Caffé Vivaldi, *54*

Cal's (restaurant), *35*

Calvary Episcopal (church), *7*

Calvin Klein (shop), 99, 101

Cammereri Brothers Bakery, 69

Camouflage (shop), 102

Camperdown Elm, 136

Canal Jean (shop), 102

Canal Street Bicycles, 144

Canarsie Pier, 149

Canton (restaurant), 24

Capitol Fishing Tackle Co. 149

Car rentals, 14

Car services, 14

Car travel
in New York, 4
to New York, 3

Carl Schurz Park, 133, 158

Carlyle Restaurant, 43

Carmine Street Recreation Center, 154

Carmine's (restaurant), 49

Carnegie Deli, 41

Carnegie Hall, 165, 169, 170, 177

Caroline's (comedy club), 175

Carousel, 131, 158

Carroll Gardens, 69

Carrot Top Pastries (restaurant), 55

Casa La Femme (restaurant), 23

Cass Gallagher Nature Trail, 135

Castle Clinton, 65

Castro Convertibles (shop), 119

Caswell-Massey (shop), 97, 115–116

Cat shows, 10

Cathay Hardware Corporation (shop), 117

Cathedral of St. John the Divine, 7–8, 65, 121, 168

Caviar shops, 105–106

Caviarteria (shop), 105

CBGB's (rock club), 171

Ceci-Cela (restaurant), 53, 108

Celebrate Brooklyn (summer event), 177

Cemeteries, 58, 67, 71, 133, 140–142

Cent'Anni (restaurant), 32

Central Carpet (shop), 117

Central Park
exploring, 130–132
playgrounds, 158
sporting activities, 144, 145–146, 147, 150–152, 153, 154, 158

Central Park Skate Patrol and School, 152

Central Park Zoo, 131, 139, 158

Central Woodlands, 135

Century Road Club Association, 143

Century 21 (shop), 100

Chalet Alpina (restaurant), 52

Chanin Building, 60

Charivari (shop), 98, 101

Charles A. Dana Discover Center, 132, 149, 158

Charles P. Rogers (shop), 119

Charrette (shop), 111

Cheese shops, 106

Chelsea
galleries, 87
restaurants, 35–36

Chelsea Antiques Building, 111

Chelsea Atelier (shop), 103

Chelsea Billiards, 145

Chelsea Commons (restaurant), 35

Chelsea Piers, 153

Chequepoint USA (currency exchange), 14

Cherry Hill Concourse, 131

Cherry Lane (theater), 163

Chez Ma Tante (restaurant), 31

Children
information on activities, 178–179
museums for, 94–95, 178–179
performing arts for, 178–179
recreational activities, 158
shops for, 125–127
sightseeing with, 76

Children's Museum of Manhattan, 95, 178

Children's Museum of the Arts, 178

Children's Place (shop), 125

Chin Chin (restaurant), 36–37

China Grill, 40

China shops, 117

Chinatown. *See* Little Italy and Chinatown

Chinatown History Museum, 85

Chinatown Ice Cream Factory (restaurant), 53

Chinese New Year, 10

Chocolate shops, 106

Chocolate Soup (shop), 99, 125

Christ Church and the Holy Family, 69

Christ Church United Methodist, 9

Christie's East (auctions), 125

Christie's Park Avenue (auctions), 125

Christmas events, 12

Chrysler Building, 60, 61, 62

Chumley's (restaurant), 30

Church of All Souls, 9

Church of Jesus Christ of Latter-Day Saints, 9

Church of the Incarnation, 8

Churches, 7–10
music in, 167–168

Circle in the Square (theater), 162

Circle Line (cruise ships), 73

Circle Repertory Company, 163

Circuses, 10, 178

Citarella (shop), 107

Citicorp Building, 70

The City Bakery (shop), 108

City Center (auditorium), 165, 172

City Crab (restaurant), 34

City Hall, 61, 65

City Hall Park, 65

City Island, 68

City Parks Events Hotline, 160

Civilized Traveller (shop), 97, 114

Claire (restaurant), 36

Claremont Riding Academy, 151

Classic Body Fitness, 148

Classic Sofa (shop), 119

Classic Stage Company, 163

Clay Pot (shop), 118

Clearview (golf course), 150

Clerical help, 14

Clinton Street, 69

Clock Tower (art gallery), 66

Cloisters (art museum), 83, 167

Cloisters Gardens, 137

Clothing shops
children, 125–126
men, 102–103
women, 103–105

Clove Lakes Park, 137

Clover Hill (restaurant), 51–52

Club outings, 142

Coach (shop), 97

Cobble Hill, 69

Coca-Cola Fifth Avenue (shop), 120–121

Coco Pazzo (restaurant), 44

Coffee and tea shops, 106–107

Coffee Shop, 34

Col Legno (restaurant), 29

Colden Center for the Performing Arts, 165

Cole-Haan (shop), 124

Coliseum Books, 112

Colony music (shop), 123

Columbia Cottage (restaurant), 50

Columbia University, 65

Columbus Avenue, shopping on, 98

Columbus Bakery, 98, 108

Comedy and magic, 174–175

Comedy Cellar (comedy club), 175

Comfort Diner, 36

Comic Strip (comedy club), 175

Comme des Garçons (shop), 97–98, 101

Community Church of New York, *10*

Complaints, *16*

Compleat Strategist (shop), *98, 117*

Complete Traveller Bookstore, *99, 114*

Computer stations, *14*

Coney Island, *129–130, 144, 152*

Coney Island High (rock club), *171*

Conference House, *93*

Conservatory Garden, *132, 137–138*

Conservatory Water, *131, 158*

Contrapunto (restaurant), *43*

The Cooper Shop at the Jewish Museum, *121*

Cooper Union (building), *67*

Cooper-Hewitt National Design Museum, *83–84, 121*

Cornelia Street Café, *174*

Corner Billiards, *145*

Corner Bistro, *30*

Corner Bookstore, *98, 112*

Cort (theater), *162*

Cotton Club (restaurant), *50*

Country Road (shop), *97*

Court House Square, *70*

Cowgirl Hall of Fame (restaurant), *31*

Crabtree & Evelyn (shop), *116*

Craft Caravan Inc. (shop), *118*

Crafts festivals, *11*

Crate & Barrel (shop), *99, 100*

Crawford Doyle Booksellers, *98, 112–113*

Crocheron Park, *154*

Crosstown Tennis, *155*

Crunch Fitness, *148*

Cub Room Cafe, *21*

Cucina di Pesce (restaurant), *28*

Cucina Stagionale (restaurant), *32*

Cuisine de Saigon (restaurant), *31*

Culinary shops, *117–118*

Cupcake Café, *54, 108*

Cupping Room Café, *22*

Currency exchange, *14*

D & G Bakery, *105*

Da Tommaso (restaurant), *41*

Daffy's (shop), *101*

Daily Forward Building, *66*

Daily News Building, *60*

The Dairy, *131*

Dakota (building), *65*

Dallas BBQ (restaurant), *48*

Damascus Bread & Pastry, *99, 105*

Dance, *171–173*

tickets, *172*

Dance Theater Workshop, *172*

Dancing, *143*

Dangerfield's (comedy club), *175*

Danspace Project, *172*

Daphne (shop), *104*

Darbár (restaurant), *41*

David Barton Gym, *148*

Dãwat (restaurant), *39*

De Robertis Pastry Shop (restaurant), *54*

Dean & DeLuca (restaurant), *22, 53, 98, 107*

Delacorte Musical Clock, *131*

Delivery services, *14*

Dentists, *15*

Department stores, *99–100*

Design Store, *122*

Designer's Resale (shop), *101*

Detour (jazz club), *170*

Dia Center for the Arts, *82, 172*

Dinosaur Hill (shop), *99, 126*

DiPalo Fine Foods (shop), *106*

Disco Rama (shop), *123*

The Disney Store, *121*

Dixie Dew Stables, *151*

Dock's (restaurant), *37*

Dock's Oyster Bar and Seafood Grill, *49–50*

Dog shows, *10*

DoJo (restaurant), *27*

Dok Suni's Korean Home Cooking (restaurant), *29*

Dominick's (restaurant), *51*

Door Store, *1192*

Doorway to Design (tours), *74*

Doral Court (hotel), *6*

Doral Park (hotel), *6*

Doral Tuscany (hotel), *6*

Doubleday Book Shop, *113*

Douglas Fairbanks Theatre, *163*

Douglaston (golf course), *150*

Downtown Boathouse, *147*

Drake (hotel), *6*

Drama Book Shop, *114*

The Drawing Center, *174*

Driving ranges, *150*

Due (restaurant), *46*

Dyker Beach, *149*

Dyker Heights, *12*

E.A.T. Café, *43*

E.J. Audi (shop), *119*

Ear Inn (restaurant), *22, 174*

East 50s restaurants, *38–39*

East River Park, *152, 154*

East 60s restaurants, *42–43, 54*

East Village and NoHo
restaurants, *26–29, 54*
shopping, *99*
sightseeing, *67–68*

East Village Cheese (shop), *106*

Ecce Panis (shop), *99, 105*

Ecco (restaurant), *20*

Ecco-La (restaurant), *46*

Economy Candy (shop), *106*

Edward Moran Bar & Grill, *19*

Edwardian Room (restaurant), *40*

18 de Julio Carnicería y Parrillada (restaurant), *53*

Eileen Fisher Ninth Street (shop), *103*

Eileen's (restaurant), *53*

Eileen's Special Cheesecake (shop), *109*

Einstein Moomjy (shop), *117*

Eisenberg and Eisenberg (shop), *103*

El Asmar International Delights, *99*

El Museo del Barrio, *85*

El Rincón de España (restaurant), *33*

El Teddy's (restaurant), *20–21, 66*

Elaine's (restaurant), *45–46*

Elan Antiques (shop), *110*

Eldridge Street Synagogue, *66*

Eldridge Textiles (shop), *120*

Elia's Corner (restaurant), *53*

Ellis Island, *88*

Emergencies, *15, 16*

Emily's (restaurant), *50*

Empire Diner, *35*

Empire State Building, *57, 61, 76*

Empire State Opera, *169*

Emporio Armani (shop), *101*

Enchanted Forest (shop), *126*

Encore (shop), *102*

Endless Art Clothing (shop), *103*

Ensemble Studio Theater, *163*

Ess-A-Bagel (shop), *105*

Ethel Barrymore (theater), *162*

Eugene O'Neill (theater), *162*

Evelyn's Hand Dipped Chocolates (shop), *106*

Evolution (shop), *116*

Executive Leather Company (shop), *124*

Exercise, *147–148*

Express (shop), *97*

Eyeglasses, *15*

F.A.O. Schwarz
(shop), *98*, *126*
Fabric shops, *115*
FACE Stockolm
(shop), *116*
Faicco's Pork Store,
107
Fairway (shop), *107*
Family Jewels (shop),
109
Fanelli (restaurant),
22
Fannie's Oyster Bar,
30
Far Upper West Side
restaurants, *50*
Feast of St. Anthony,
11
Feast of San Gennaro,
11
Federal Hall, *61*, *65*
Feibusch (shop), *115*
Felissimo (shop), *118*
Fellan Company, Inc.
(shop), *115*
Ferrara (restaurant),
25, *53–54*, *67*
Ferrier (restaurant),
47
Ferry Point Park, *152*
Ferucci's Gourmet
(shop), *107*
Fieldston, *68*
Fifth Avenue
shopping, *98*
walking on, *60–61*
Fifth Avenue
Presbyterian
(church), *9*
57th Street shopping,
98
Film Center Building,
62
Film festivals, *11*, *176*
Film Forum, *176*
Fine & Klein (shop),
97, *104*
Fiorello's Roman
Café, *47*
Fire Island, *129*
First (restaurant), *26*–
27
First Corinthian
Baptist Church, *64*
First Presbyterian
Church, *9*
First Shearith Israel
Graveyard, *67*
Fish, meat, and
poultry shops, *107*
Fishin Eddie
(restaurant), *48*

Fishing, *148–149*
Fish's Eddy (shop),
117
550 Madison, *61*
551 Fifth, *62–63*
570 Lex, *63*
Flatiron Building, *63*,
76
Flea markets, *125*
Florence Gould Hall
(cinema), *177*
Florence Meat Market
(shop), *107*
Florent (restaurant),
32
Floris of London
(shop), *116*
Florists, *115*
Flower District, *76*
Flower Power (shop),
109
Floyd Bennett Field,
146, *152*
Flushing Meadows-
Corona Park, *146*,
152
Foley Square, *65*
Food festivals, *10*
Food shops, *105–109*
Foods of India (shop),
109
Football, *156*
Footlight Records
(shop), *123*
Forbidden Planet
(shop), *114*
Ford Foundation
Building, *60*
Forest Park, *149*, *150*,
152
Forgotten Woman
(shop), *104*
Forman's (shop), *97*,
104
Fort Greene Park, *154*
Fort Tryon Park, *133*
44 (restaurant), *37*
42nd Street walking,
59–60
Fragrance and
Makeup shops, *115*–
116
Frank Stella Ltd.
(shop), *98*, *102*
Franklin D. Roosevelt
Boardwalk, *130*
Franklin D. Roosevelt
Drive, *4*
Franklin Furnace
Archives (gallery), *66*
Franklin Station
(restaurant), *21*
Fraunces Tavern
Museum, *65*, *76*

Fred Johnson
Memorial Park, *154*
FreeLance (shop), *124*
Frick Collection, *80*–
81, *167*
Friend of a Farmer
(restaurant), *34*
Friends' Quaker
Meeting House, *70*
Fujiyama Mama
(restaurant), *49*
Fulton Ferry Landing,
58
Fund for the Borough
of Brooklyn, *2*
Furniture shops, *110*–
111
Fu's House
(restaurant), *39*

Galileo (shop), *118*
Gallagher's
(restaurant), *40*
Game shops, *117*
Game Show (shop),
117
GAP Kids (shop), *97*
Garages, *5–6*
Gardens, *137–139*
Gargiulio's
(restaurant), *52*
Garibaldi Meucci
Museum, *93*
Gas stations, *14*
Gateway Sports, *150*,
155
Gay and Lesbian Pride
Parade, *11*
Gazebo (shop), *115*
Gem Spa (restaurant),
54
Gene's Bicycles, *144*
George Washington
Bridge, *3*, *58–59*
George Washington
Bridge Bus Station, *3*
Georgiou (shop), *97*
Gershwin (theater),
162
Gianni Versace (shop),
101
Gianni's (restaurant),
20
Gigino (restaurant),
21
Gino's (restaurant),
43
Giorgio Armani
(shop), *101*
Girasole (restaurant),
46
Glover's Rock, *135*
Godiva Chocolatier, *97*
Goethe House

(cinema), *177*
Golden Oldies (shop),
110
Goldman's Treasures
(shop), *117*
Golf, *149–150*
Golf Club at Chelsea
Piers, *150*
Good Enough to Eat
(restaurant), *48*, *55*
Goody's
(restaurant), *52*
Goose Creek Marsh,
134
Gotham Bar & Grill,
29
Gotham Book Mart
(shop), *114*
Gotham Lounge, Hotel
Peninsula
(restaurant), *54*
Gourmet Garage
(shop), *107*
Grace Church, *8*, *69*
Grace Court Alley, *69*,
72
Grace's Marketplace,
107
Gracious Home (shop),
118
Graduate Center
(CUNY), *60*
Gramercy Park,
Flatiron, and Union
Square *152*
restaurants, *33–35*
Gramercy Tavern
(restaurant), *33–34*
Grand Army Plaza
(Brooklyn), *69*, *135*–
136
Grand Central
Terminal, *60*, *61–62*,
76
Grant's Tomb, *75–76*,
133
Gray Line (tours), *75*
Great Feet (shop), *125*
Great Jones Street
Café, *27–28*
Great Kills Park, *130*,
137, *152*
Great Lawn, *131–132*
Greek Independence
Day Parade, *10*
Greenbelt (park), *136*
Greenberg and
Hammer (shop), *115*
Greene Street Antiques
(shop), *110*
Greenstone et Cie
(shop), *125–126*
Greenwich Village
sightseeing, *67–68*

Green-Wood Cemetery, *58, 141–142, 146*

Greetings Earthlings (shop), *97*

Grocers, *107–108*

Grotta Azzurra (restaurant), *25*

Grove (restaurant), *29*

Grove Court, *71*

Growing up with Opera, *179*

Gryphon Record Shop, *123*

Guggenheim Museum, *81, 121*

Guggenheim Museum SoHo, *82*

Guided tours, *73–76*

Guss' Pickles, *66, 109*

H & H Bagel (shop), *105*

H. Oppenheimer Co. (shop), *107*

Hackers, Hitters & Hoops, *143, 150*

Hamilton Park, *71*

Handball, *150*

Handloom Batik (shop), *115*

Harbor Lights (cruises), *73*

Harbour Lights (restaurant), *20*

Hard Rock Café, *40*

Harlem
restaurants, *50*
sightseeing, *64*

Harlem Renaissance Tours, *74*

Harlem Spirituals (tours), *74*

Harlem Week, *11*

Harlem Your Way! (tour), *74*

Harley Davidson Cafe, *40*

Harold Clurman Theatre, *163*

Harriet Love (shop), *102*

Harris Levy (shop), *97*

Harrison Street, *66*

Harry Zarin Co. (shop), *115*

The Hat Shop, *105*

Haveli (restaurant), *28*

Heartland Brewery (restaurant), *34*

Heather Garden, *137*

Helen Hayes (theater), *162*

Helicopter tours, *75*

Helmsley Building, *63*

Henderson Place, *72*

Henri Bendel (department store), *98, 100*

Henry Carlton Hulbert Mansion, *70*

Henry Luce Nature Observatory, *158*

Henry Street Settlement, Louis Abrons Arts for Living Center, *178–179*

Henry's End (restaurant), *51*

High Rock Park, *71, 137*

Hiking, *136–137*

Hi-Life Bar and Grill, *43*

Hit Show Club, *161*

HMV (shop), *123*

Hockey, *156*

Holland Tunnel, *3*

Holy Cross Roman Catholic Church, *60*

Holy Trinity Lutheran Church, *8, 168*

Home (restaurant), *29–30*

Home furnishing shops, *110–111, 117–120*

Honmura An (restaurant), *23*

Horse racing, *157*

Horseback riding, *150–151*

Horse-drawn carriage rides. *See* Sightseeing

Hospitals, *15*

Hosteling International-American Youth Hostels, *144*

Hotaling's (shop), *122*

Hotel packages, *6–7*

Houlihan's (restaurant), *55*

Houses, restored, *90–93*

HRC Tennis, *155*

Hudson River Club (restaurant), *19–20*

Hudson River Park Esplanade, *58, 65, 133, 153*

Hudson River Promenade, *133*

Hudson View Gardens, *72*

Hunan Balcony (restaurant), *50*

Hunter Island, *135*

Hunters Point Historic District, *70*

Hush-A-Bye (shop), *127*

I Natural (shop), *116*

I.S. 44 Market, *125*

Ice skating, *151*

Il Cantinori (restaurant), *32*

Imperial (theater), *162*

In Padella (restaurant), *28*

Indochine (restaurant), *29*

Innovation Luggage (shop), *120*

Intar (theater), *163*

Integral Yoga Institute, *148*

Integral Yoga Teaching Center, *148*

International Cat Show, *10*

International Center of Photography, *84, 114, 121*

International Delights (shop), *108*

Intrepid Sea-Air-Space Museum, *76, 88, 94–95*

Inwood Hill Park, *133, 144, 154*

Iridium (jazz club), *170*

Iris and B. Gerald Cantor Roof Garden, *58*

Irish Arts Center, *163*

Irving Plaza (rock club), *171*

Island (restaurant), *44*

Island Helicopter Sightseeing, *75*

Island Sports, *154, 156*

J. Crew (shop), *97*

J. Pierpont Morgan Library, *81, 121*

Jack's Bait & Tackle, *148*

Jackson Hole (restaurant), *42, 45*

Jacob Riis Park, *130*

The Jacqueline Kennedy Onassis Reservoir, *132*

Jacques Carcanagues, Inc. (shop), *110*

Jacques Marchais Museum of Tibetan Art, *85*

Jai Ya Thai (restaurant), *53*

Jake's Fish Market (shop), *107*

JAM Paper Outlet, *122*

Jamaica Bay Riding Academy, *151*

Jamaica Bay Wildlife Refuge, *136, 146, 158*

Japan Society Gallery, *85, 177*

Japonica (restaurant), *33*

Jazz, *169–171*

Jean Cocteau Repertory, *163*

Jean Hoffman (shop), *110*

Jefferson Market (shop), *108*

Jekyll & Hyde (shop), *102*

Jensen-Lewis (shop), *119*

Jerry Ohlinger's Movie Material Store, *121*

Jewish Museum, *85–86, 94, 178*

Jewish Repertory Theater, *163*

Jim McMullen (restaurant), *43*

Jivamukti Yoga Center, *148*

Joan and David (shop), *97*

Joan of Arc Statue, *132–133*

Joe Allen (restaurant), *37*

Joe's Shanghai (restaurant), *24*

Jogging and racewalking, *151–152*

John Fluevog (shop), *124*

John Golden (theater), *162*

John Jay Park, *158*

John Koch Antiques, *110*

John Street United Methodist Church, *9*

John's of 12th Street (restaurant), *28*

John's Pizzeria, *32*

Jones Beach, *129*

Joovay (shop), *104*

Joseph Papp Public Theater, *163*

Josephina (restaurant), *46–47*
Joyce Gold History Tours of New York, *74*
Judith's Room (shop), *174*
Judson Memorial Church, *8*
Juilliard recitals, *167*
Julian's Famous Poolroom, *145*
Jumel Terrace Historic District, *91*
Juniper Valley Park, *154*
Just Shades (shop), *120*
JVC Jazz Festival, *170*

Kalfaian & Son (shop), *117*
Kalustyan's (shop), *109*
Kam-Man (shop), *108*
Kaplan's (restaurant), *39*
Karyatis (restaurant), *53*
Katagiri (shop), *108, 118*
Kate Wollman Rink, *151, 152*
Kate's Paperie (shop), *122*
Katz's Deli, *26*
Kaufman Astoria Studios, *70*
Kaufman's Pharmacy, *15*
Kenneth Cole (shop), *124*
Kentucky 7 (shop), *99, 110*
Kidding Around (shop), *126*
Kiel's Since 1851 (shop), *116*
Kiev (restaurant), *28*
King Manor, *92*
Kingsland House, *92*
Kinokuniya Bookstore, *113*
The Kiosk (restaurant), *43*
Kissena Park, *146, 150*
The Kitchen (music hall), *166*
Kitchen Arts and Letters (shop), *112*
Kitschen (shop), *110*
Knickerbocker Bar & Grill, *30*
Knitting Factory (jazz club), *170*

Kossar's Bialystoker Bakery, *105*
Kramer's Reality Tour, *74*

L'Acajou (restaurant), *36*
La Bohème (restaurant), *30*
La Boîte en Bois (restaurant), *47*
La Bonne Soupe (restaurant), *41*
La Caridad (restaurant), *49*
La Colombe D'or (restaurant), *34–35*
La Focaccia (restaurant), *32*
La Fusta (restaurant), *53*
La Jumelle (restaurant), *23*
La Lumia (shop), *103*
La Maison du Chocolat (shop), *106*
La Mama E.T.C. (theater), *163–164*
La Tourette Park, *147, 150, 154*
Ladies' Mile, *63–64*
Lanac Sales (shop), *117*
Landmark Tavern (restaurant), *37*
Lanza Restaurant (restaurant), *29*
Lasker Rink, *151*
Laura Ashley (shop), *103*
Laytner's Linen (shop), *120*
Le Boeuf à la Mode (restaurant), *45*
Le Jardin Bistro, *25*
Le Madeleine (restaurant), *38*
Le Madri (restaurant), *36*
Le Parker Meridien (hotel), *6*
Le Q (billiards), *145*
Le Refuge (restaurant), *45*
Le Régence (restaurant), *42*
Le Relais (restaurant), *42*
Le Zoo (restaurant), *30*
Lechter's Housewares (shop), *117*
Lee's Art Shop, *111*
Lefferts Homestead, *92*

Legacy (shop), *103*
Leisure Time Bowling & Recreation Center, *147*
Lenge (restaurant), *47*
Lenox Hill Bookstore, *113*
Leo Design (shop), *118*
Leonidas (shop), *106*
Leroy Pharmacy, *15*
Les Friandises (restaurant), *54*
Les Halles (restaurant), *35*
Let There Be Neon (shop), *66*
Liberty House (shop), *103*
The Library Shop at Mid-Manhattan, *121*
Lightforms (shop), *120*
Lighting by Gregory (shop), *120*
Li-Lac Chocolates, *106*
The Limited (shop), *97, 103*
Limousine services, *15*
Lincoln Center, *2, 64, 178*
restaurants, *46–47, 54–55*
hot line, *160*
Lincoln Center Festival, *178*
Lincoln Center Out-of-Doors (summer event), *177, 178, 179*
Lincoln Center's Vivian Beaumont and Mitzi E. Newhouse theaters, *162*
Lincoln Tunnel, *3*
Linen shops, *120*
Little Eric (shop), *126*
Little India (shop), *109*
Little Italy and Chinatown restaurants, *24–26, 53–54*
sightseeing, *67*
Little Orchestra Society, *179*
Little Pie Company (shop), *109*
Little Red Lighthouse, *76*
Little Rickie (shop), *99, 116*
Live Bait (restaurant), *34*
Liz Claiborne (shop), *97*
Locksmiths, *15*

Loehmann's (shop), *104*
Lola (restaurant), *36*
Lola (shop), *105*
Lombardi's (restaurant), *25*
Longacre (theater), *162*
Long Island City, *70*
Long Island City Indoor Tennis, *155*
Long Island Fabrics (shop), *115*
Long Island Railroad, *2, 3*
Long Meadow, *136*
Lord & Taylor (department store), *12, 61, 76, 98, 100*
Lost and found, *16*
Lost City Arts (shop), *109*
Love Saves the Day (shop), *99, 116*
Lowell Hotel, *6*
Lower East Side restaurants, *26*
sightseeing, *66–67*
shopping, *97*
Lower East Side Tenement Museum, *67, 74, 90*
Lower Manhattan restaurants, *19–20*
sightseeing, *65*
Lower Manhattan Cultural Council, *160*
Lucky Strike (restaurant), *21*
Luggage shops, *120*
Luna Lounge (rock club), *171*
Luna Park (restaurant), *35*
Lunt-Fontanne (theater), *162*
Lusardi's (restaurant), *44*
Lyceum (theater), *162*
Lynnes Riding School, *151*

M.A.C. (shop), *116*
M & R Bar (restaurant), *24*
MacDougal Alley, *71–72*
Mackenzie-Childs, Ltd. (shop), *118*
Macy's (department store), *76, 100*
Madame Romaine de Lyon (restaurant), *42*

Madison Avenue shopping, *98–99*

Madison Avenue Bookshop, *113*

Madison Avenue Presbyterian Church, *9, 168*

Madison Square Garden, *2*

Magnolia Bakery (shop), *109*

Majestic (theater), *162*

The Mall, *131*

Man Ray (restaurant), *35*

Manhattan. *See also specific neighborhoods*
cemeteries, *140–141*
gardens, *137–138*
houses, *restored, 90–91*
orientation, *5*
parks, *130–134, 158*
science museums, *93–94*
sightseeing, *63–68*
sports and recreation, *143–158*
zoos, *139, 158*

Manhattan Art & Antiques Center, *111*

Manhattan Church of Christ, *7*

Manhattan Ocean Club (restaurant), *41*

Manhattan Passport (tours), *74*

Manhattan Plaza, *60*

Manhattan Plaza Racquet Club, *155*

Manhattan School of Music, *167*

Manhattan Theatre Club, *164*

Mannes College of Music, *167*

Mappamondo (restaurant), *32*

Maraolo (shop), *124*

Marble Collegiate Church, *9*

Marble Hill, *64, 144*

Margola Corp. (shop), *112*

Marine Park, *146*

Marine Park Golf Course, *149*

Marion's (restaurant), *27*

Maritime Crafts Center, *89*

Mark's (restaurant), *43–44, 55*

Marquis (theater), *162*

Marriott Marquis (hotel), *6*

Mary Ann's (restaurant), *36*

Match (restaurant), *22*

Matthew's (restaurant), *42*

Maurice Villency (shop), *119–120*

Maxilla and Mandible, Ltd. (shop), *98, 116*

Mayfair Hotel, *6*

McDonald's (restaurant), *19*

McNulty's Tea & Coffee Company (shop), *106*

Meadowlands (racetrack), *157*

Medical services, *15*

Mee Noodle Shop (restaurant), *38*

Meltemi (restaurant), *39*

Memorabilia shops, *120–121*

Memorial Arch, *58*

Menchanko-tei (restaurant), *41*

Menswear shops, *102–103*

Merce Cunningham Studio, *172*

Merchant's House Museum, *67, 91*

Mercury Lounge (rock club), *171*

Merkin Concert Hall, *166*

Mermaid Parade, *11*

Metro Bicycles (shop), *144*

Metro-North trains, *2, 3*

Metrocard, *4*

Metropolitan Life Building, *62*

Metropolitan Baptist Church, *64, 168*

Metropolitan Museum of Art, *12, 78–79, 94, 121–122, 168, 174*

Mezzaluna (restaurant), *44*

Mezzogiorno (restaurant), *23*

Mickey Mantle's (restaurant), *40*

Midtown Bicycles (shop), *144*

Midtown East restaurants, *36–37*

Midtown Tennis Club, *155*

Midtown West restaurants, *37–38, 54*

Mike's American Bar and Grill, *37–38*

Mike's Tackle & Bait Shop, *148*

Millenium Film Workshop, *176*

Milligan Place, *72*

Mimi Maternity (shop), *97*

Miniature golf, *150*

Minskoff (theater), *162*

Minter's Fun Food and Drink, *53*

Miracle Grill, *27*

Mitali East (restaurant), *28*

Mocca Hungarian Restaurant, *45*

Model Airplane Flying, *152*

Model Boat Sailing, *152*

Moe Ginsburg (shop), *103*

Moishe's (shop), *105*

Mondel Chocolates (shop), *106*

Montague Street, *68*

Montauk Club, *70*

Monte's Venetian Room (restaurant), *52*

Montgomery Place, *70*

Mood Indigo (shop), *110*

Moondance Diner, *22*

Moravian Cemetery, *71, 142*

Morgans (hotel), *6*

Moroccan Star (restaurant), *52*

Morris Brothers (shop), *126*

Morris-Jumel Mansion, *90–91*

Mo's Caribbean Bar & Grille, *43*

Moschino (shop), *99, 101*

Mostly Mozart (summer event), *178*

Motor cruises, *73*

Mott Street, *71*

Mt. Tom, *132*

MovieFone, *175*

Movies and Video, *175–177*

Mulberry Street, *67*

Municipal Art Society, *74*

Municipal Building, *65*

Murder Ink (shop), *113*

Murray's (shop), *106*

Murray's Sturgeon Shop, *109*

Museum Café, *48*

Museum concerts, *167*

Museum for African Art, *86, 122*

Museum Gallery, *89–90*

Museum of American Folk Art, *84, 122*

Museum of Chinese in the Americas, *67*

Museum of Modern Art, *81, 122, 167, 175, 176*

Museum of Natural History, *64*

Museum of Television & Radio, *176*

Museum of the City of New York, *74, 88–89, 94, 122, 167, 178*

Museum shops, *121–122*

Museums. *See also* Art museums
for children, *94–95*
cinema, *176*
historical, *87–93*
science-technology, *93–94*

Music, *165–171*
chamber music, *166–167*
for children, *179*
in churches, *167–168*
concert halls, *165–166*
conservatories, *167*
information, *165, 169*
jazz, *169–171*
museum concerts, *167*
opera, *168–169*
tickets, *165, 169–170*

Music Grove, *136*

Mxyplyzyk (shop), *118*

Myers of Keswick (shop), *108*

Mysterious Bookshop, *113*

Nadine's (restaurant), *30*

National Academy of Design, *82*

National Boat Show, *10*

National Museum of the American Indian, *86, 122*

Neary's (restaurant), *39*

Nederlander (theater), *162*

Negro Burial Ground, *65*

Neil Simon (theater), *162*

New Amsterdam (theater), *60*

New Directors/New Films (festival), *176*

New Jersey Devils, *156*

New Jersey Transit, *2, 3*

New Museum of Contemporary Art, *84*

New Republic (shop), *102*

New Victory (theater), *60*

New World Grill, *38*

New York Botanical Garden, *138*

New York Cake and Baking Supplies (shop), *117–118*

New York Central Art Supply (shop), *111*

New York Children's Theater, *179*

New York City Audubon Society, *142, 145*

New York City Ballet, *12, 172–173*

New York City Department of Parks & Recreation's Urban Rangers, *74, 142*

New York City Marathon, *12, 157*

New York City on Stage hotline, *160*

New York City Opera, *169*

New York City Poetry Calendar, *174*

New York Convention and Visitors Bureau, *2, 160*

New York County Courthouse, *65*

New York Division of Tourism, *2*

New York Film Festival, *11, 176*

New York Giants, *156*

New York Gilbert and Sullivan Players, *169*

New York Grand Opera, *169*

New York Hall of

Science, *94, 95*

New York Hilton, *7*

New York Is Book Country (event), *11*

New York Islanders, *156*

New York Jets, *156*

New York Knickerbockers, *156*

New York Noodle Town (restaurant), *25*

New York Magazine Movie Phone, *2*

New York Marble Cemetery, *140*

New York Mets, *156*

New York Public Library, *60, 61*

New York Rangers, *156*

New York Road Runners Club, *152*

New York Sailing School, *153*

New York Shakespeare Festival, *177*

New York Theatre Workshop, *164*

New York Thruway, *3*

New York Transit Museum Gift Shop, *122*

New York Yankees, *156*

Newspaper and magazine shops, *122*

Next Stop South Pole (shop), *116*

Nha Trang (restaurant), *26*

Nice Restaurant, *25*

Nicholas Roerich Museum, *84*

91st Street Community Garden, *132*

92nd Street Y, *74, 166, 179*

Ninth Avenue International Food Festival, *10*

Nobu (restaurant), *21*

NoHo. *See* East Village and NoHo

NoHo Star (restaurant), *27*

Northwest Forest, *135*

The Nutcracker, 179

Nuyorican Poets Cafe, *174*

NYC on Stage, *2*

Ocean Parkway, *144*

Odeon (restaurant), *20*

Odessa (restaurant), *52*

Office of the Queens Borough President, *2*

Offshore Sailing School, *153*

Old Devil Moon (restaurant), *27*

Old Navy (shop), *97*

Old Town Bar (restaurant), *34*

Olive's (restaurant), *22*

Ollie's (restaurant), *49, 50*

Omen (restaurant), *23*

Omni Berkshire Place (hotel), *7*

Once upon a Tart (shop), *109*

107 West (restaurant), *50*

One If By Land, Two If By Sea (restaurant), *29*

O'Neal's (restaurant), *47*

Only Hearts (shop), *104*

Opaline (restaurant), *27*

Opera, *168–169, 179*

Orchard Beach, *130, 150*

Orchard Beach Weekend Concert Series, *178*

Orchard Street, *66*

Oriental Lamp Shade Co. (shop), *120*

Oriental Town Seafood (restaurant), *25*

Original Yonah Schimmel Knishery, *26*

orio-trio, (shop), *110*

Orpheum (theater), *164*

Orso (restaurant), *38*

Oscar Wilde Bookshop, *112*

Osso Buco (restaurant), *32*

Our Lady of Lebanon Roman Catholic Church, *69*

Our Place (restaurant), *45*

Outdoors Club, *142*

P.S. 122, *173*

Pageant Book & Print Shop, *111*

Palace (theater), *162*

Palm Court, 5th Ave. (restaurant), *54*

Palm Court, 59th St. (restaurant), *40*

Pamir (restaurant), *43*

Pan Aqua Diving, *153*

Pan Asian Repertory (theater), *164*

Pandora's Box (shop), *116*

Pão! (restaurant), *24*

Paola's (restaurant), *46*

Paper Bag Players, *179*

Paper/postcard shops, *122*

Paracelso (shop), *103*

Parades, *10, 11*

Paragon (shop), *124*

Paramount (hotel), *7*

Park Avenue Synagogue, *8*

Park Bistro, *34*

Park East Synagogue, *8*

Park Events hot line, *2*

Park Slope, *69–70*

Parking, *5–6*

Parks
  Bronx, *134–135, 158*
  Brooklyn, *135–136, 158*
  Manhattan, *130–134, 158*
  Queens, *136, 158*
  Staten Island, *136–137*

Parks and Recreation Department Tours, *142*

Paron Fabrics (shop), *115*

Partners & Crime (shop), *113*

Party Boats, *148*

Pastry shops, *108–109*

Patchin Place, *72*

PATH trains, *2, 3*

Pathfinder Books (shop), *114*

Pathfinder Productions (tours), *75*

Pâtisserie J. Lanciani (shop), *108*

Patria (restaurant), *35*

Patricia Field (shop), *101*

Patsy Grimaldi's Pizzeria, *59*

Paul Smith (shop), *102*

Paul Stuart (shop), *102*

Peace Garden, *133*

Peanut Butter & Jane (shop), *126*

Pearl Paint (shop), *111*

Pearl Street Playground, *158*

Pearl Theatre Company, *164*

Peck & Goodie (shop), *124, 153*

Pedal Pusher (shop), *144*

Pelham Bay Park exploring, *134–135* sporting activities, *146, 147, 148, 149, 150, 152, 154*

Pelham Bit Stable, *151*

Peninsula (bar), *58*

Penny Whistle Toys (shop), *98, 126*

Peress of Madison Avenue (shop), *104*

Performance art, *173*

Performance Space 122 (auditorium), *166*

Performing arts for children, *178–179* comedy and magic, *174–175* dance, *171–173* movies, *175–177* music, *165–171* performance art, *173* readings and lectures, *174* summer arts, *177–178* theater, *161–164* tickets, *160–161*

Perimiter (shop), *112*

Personal and business services, *14-16*

Peruvian Restaurant, *38*

Pescatore (restaurant), *39*

Petaluma (restaurant), *44*

Peter Elliot Ltd. (shop), *102*

Peter Fox (shop), *124*

Peter Luger (restaurant), *52*

Peter Roberts Antiques, *98, 111*

Pete's Tavern (restaurant), *34*

Petrossian (restaurant), *40, 54, 106*

Pharmacies, *15, 122–123*

Philip Morris Building, *60*

Philip Williams (shop), *111*

Pho Bang (restaurant), *26*

Phone numbers, *2*

Photocopying and fax services, *14*

Photographer's Place (shop), *114*

Photographic services, *15*

Physicians, *15*

Piadina (restaurant), *32*

Picholine (restaurant), *47*

Pickle shops, *166, 109*

Pig Heaven (restaurant), *51*

Pink Tea Cup (restaurant), *31*

Pioneer (schooner), *73*

Pisces (restaurant), *27*

Planet Hollywood (restaurant), *40*

Playground for All Children, *158*

Playgrounds, *158*

Playwrights Horizons (theater), *164*

Plaza (hotel), *7*

Plaza Pharmacy, *15*

Plymouth (theater), *162*

Plymouth Church, *69*

Pó (restaurant), *32*

Poe Cottage, *91*

Poetry Center, *174*

Poetry Project, *174*

Pomander Walk, *72*

Pompanoosuc Mills (shop), *120*

The Pond, *131*

Pondicherri (shop), *98, 120*

Pools, *154*

Popover Café, *48*

Port Authority bridges and tunnels, *2*

Port Authority Bus Terminal, *2, 3, 60*

Portico (shop), *98, 120*

Porto Rico Importing Company (shop), *107*

Poseidon Greek Bakery, *109*

Posman Books (shop), *113*

Post House, *42*

Post Office, *16*

Poster America (shop), *111*

Poster shops, *111*

Pottery Barn, *118–119*

Pravda (restaurant), *24*

Pravinie Gourmet Ice Cream, *54*

Primary Stages, *164*

Primavera (restaurant), *45*

Primola (restaurant), *42–43*

Pro Sports New York (shop), *125, 153*

Promenade Theater, *164*

Prospect Park, *135– 136, 144, 146, 147, 152, 154, 158*

Prospect Park Carousel, *136*

Prospect Park Zoo, *136, 140, 158*

Provence (restaurant), *23*

Puerto Rican Day Parade, *11*

Puglia (restaurant), *25*

Pulaski Day Parade, *11*

Pull Cart (shop), *119*

Puppet Playhouse, *179*

Puppetworks, *179*

Putumayo (shop), *103– 104*

Quad Cinema, *177*

Quaker Cemetery, *142*

Quaker Meeting House, *92*

Quartière (restaurant), *53*

Queens beaches, *130* gardens, *138* houses, *restored, 92– 93* parks, *136, 146, 158* restaurants, *52–53* science museums, *94* sightseeing, *70* sports and recreation, *146, 149, 150, 155– 158* zoo, *140*

Queens Botanical Garden, *70, 138*

Queens County Bird Club, *146*

Queens County Farm Museum, *93*

Queens Festival, *11*

Queens Museum, *89, 167, 170, 178*

Queens Zoo, *140*

Queens-Midtown Tunnel, *3*

Quest Toys (shop), *97*

Quong Yeun Shing & Co. (shop), *67*

Races and group runs, *144, 152*

Radical Walking Tours, *74–75*

Radio City Music Hall, *12, 62, 176*

Radisson Empire (hotel), *7*

Rain (restaurant), *49*

Rainbow (restaurant), *40*

Rainbow Promenade (restaurant), *54*

The Ramble (wooded area), *131*

Randall's Island, *154*

Randall's Island Golf and Family Entertainment Center, *150*

Raoul's (restaurant), *23*

Ratner's Restaurant, *26, 67*

Readings and lectures, *174*

Record/CD shops, *123*

Reeds Basket Willow Swamp, *137*

Remi (restaurant), *41*

Reminiscence (shop), *102*

Renell Boutique, *104*

Repertorio Español (theater), *164, 169*

Republic (restaurant), *34*

Restaurants, *18–55.* *See also specific neighborhoods*

Richard Rodgers (theater), *162*

Richmond County Country Club, *71*

Richmondtown Restoration, *89*

Ringling Bros. Barnum & Bailey Circus, *10*

Rio Mar (restaurant), *33*

Ritz (shop), *124*

River Café, *51, 58*

River to River Downtown Walking Tours, *75*

Riverbank State Park, *133–134, 151, 152, 154*

Riverdale, *68*

Riverdale Country School, *68*

Riverdale Equestrian Center, *151*

Riverside Church, *8, 58, 168*

Riverside Park
exploring, *132–133*
sporting activities, *144, 150, 152, 153, 155, 158*

Riverside Park Festival, *11*

Riverview Terrace, *72*

Rizzoli Bookstore, *97, 113*

Robert Moses State Park, *129*

Rock Clubs, *171*

Rockaway Beach and Boardwalk, *130, 148, 154*

Rockaway Beach Surf Shop, *154*

Rockefeller Center, *60, 61, 62, 76, 151*

Rodman's Neck (meadow), *134*

Roller skating and rollerblading, *152–153*

Roosevelt Island, *152, 153*

Roosevelt Island Raquet Club, *155*

Rosa Mexicano (restaurant), *39*

Rose of India (restaurant), *28*

Roseland (ballroom), *143*

Rothman's (shop), *103*

The Rotunda (restaurant), *54*

The Rotunda (circular space), *132*

Roundabout Theatre Company at the Criterion Center, *162*

Roxy (dance club), *153*

Royal Canadian Restaurant and Pancake House, *48–49*

Royale (theater), *162*

Rug Warehouse, *117*

Running, *157*

Russ & Daughters (shop), *109*

Russian Samovar (restaurant), *41*

S & W (shop), *104*

Sabine Roy Florist (shop), *97*

Sahadi (shop), *99, 108*

Saigon House Restaurant, *26*

Sailing, *153*

Sailing tours, *73*

St. Ann and the Holy Trinity Episcopal Church, *8, 168*

St. Augustine's Roman Catholic Church, *70*

St. Bartholomew's (church), *8, 168*

St. Ignatius Loyola Church, *9, 168*

St. James (theater), *162*

Saint Laurie, Ltd. (shop), *103*

St. Luke's Place, *72*

St. Malachy's (church), *9*

St. Mark's Bookshop, *113*

St. Mark's in-the-Bowery (church-cemetery), *8, 67, 140*

St. Mark's Place, *67*

St. Martin's Episcopal Church, *64*

St. Michael's Church, *8, 168*

St. Patrick's Cathedral, *9, 60, 76, 168*

St. Peter's Lutheran Church, *9, 168*

St. Paul's Chapel, *140*

St. Philip's Church, *64*

St. Stephen's Methodist Episcopal Church, *64*

St. Thomas Church, *168*

St. Thomas the Apostle Church, *64*

St. Vincent Ferrer (church), *9*

Saks (department store), *98, 100*

Sal Anthony's (restaurant), *35*

Salaam Bombay (restaurant), *21*

The Saloon (restaurant), *47*

Sam Flax (shop), *111*

Sammy's Roumanian (restaurant), *26*

Sam's Souk (shop), *119*

Samuel Beckett Theatre, *163*

San Domenico (restaurant), *41*

Sandra Cameron Dance Center, *143*

Sandy Hook (beach), *129*

Sant' Ambroeus (restaurant), *44, 55*

Santa Fe (restaurant), *47*

Sara (shop), *119*

Sarabeth's Kitchen (restaurant), *45, 48*

Sarajo (shop), *98, 111*

Savann (restaurant), *48*

Savoy (restaurant), *22*

Sazerac House Bar & Grill, *31*

Scandinavian Ski & Sport (shop), *147*

Schneider's (shop), *127*

Science Fiction Shop, *114*

Scott Jordan Furniture (shop), *120*

Screaming Mimi's (shop), *102*

Screening Room, *176*

Scuba diving, *153*

SCUBA Network (shop), *125, 153*

Seagram Building, *62*

Sea-Hear (shop), *122*

Seaport Liberty Cruises, *73*

Seasonal events, *10–12*

Second Avenue Kosher Delicatessen, *28*

Second Church of Christ Scientist, *7*

Selwyn Theater, *60*

Serendipity 3 (restaurant), *42*

79th Street Boat Basin, *147*

77th St. Playground, *158*

Sew Brooklyn (shop), *115*

Sfuzzi (restaurant), *47*

Shabu-Tatsu (restaurant), *44, 49*

Shakespeare & Company (shop), *113*

Shakespeare in the Park, *11*

Shark Bar, *48*

Sharper Image (shop), *97, 98*

Shearith Israel (cemeteries), *140*

Sheep Meadow, *131*

Sheepshead Bay, *148*

Shoe shops, *123–124*

Shoofly (shop), *126*

Shopping
auction exhibitions, *125*

with children, *125–127*

clothing, *101–105*

department stores, *99–100*

flea markets, *125*

food, *105–109*

hours, *97*

museum shops, *121–122*

by neighborhood, *97–99*

specialty shops, *109–125*

Shore Parkway, *144*

Shore Road Promenade, *152*

Shorewalkers, *142*

Shubert (theater), *162*

Shun Lee Café, *47*

Siam Grill, *38*

Siam Square (restaurant), *29*

Sidewalk (rock club), *171*

Sierra Club, *142*

Sightseeing
architecture, *61–63*
with children, *76, 158*
city buses for, *75–76*
cul-de-sacs, *mews, exceptional blocks, and special streets, 71–72*
horse-drawn carriage rides, *76*
neighborhoods, *63–71*
tours, *73–76*
views, *57–58*
walks, *58–61*

Sign of the Dove (restaurant), *42*

Silver Lake Park, *144, 150*

Silvercup Studios, *70*

Simon Pearce (shop), *119*

Sistina (restaurant), *45*

68th Street Playhouse, *177*

69 Mott (restaurant), *25*

Skateboarding, *153*

Skiing, cross-country, *147*

Sky Rink, *151*

Skyline Books and Records (shop), *114*

Sledding, *153–154*

Small's (jazz club), *170*

Smith & Wollensky (restaurant), *36*

Smoked-fish shops, *109*

Smoking law, *18*
Sniffen Court, *72*
Snug Harbor Cultural Center, *71, 82*
Society of Friends (church), *9*
SoHo
galleries, *87*
restaurants, *21–24, 53*
shopping, *97–98*
sightseeing, *75*
SoHo Art Experience (tours), *75*
Soho Billiards, *145*
SoHo Kitchen (restaurant), *22–23*
SoHo Provisions (shop), *108*
SoHo Steak (restaurant), *23*
Soho Woman on the Park (shop), *104*
Soldiers' and Sailors' Memorial Arch, *69*
Soldiers' and Sailors' Monument, *76, 132*
Sony Paris (cinema), *177*
Sony Theatres Lincoln Square, *176*
Sony Wonder Technology Lab, *94*
Sotheby's (auctions), *125*
Souen (restaurant), *24, 29*
South Cove (esplanade), *65*
South Shore (golf course), *150*
South Street Seaport, *65, 76, 89–90, 178*
shops, *97*
South Street Seaport Walks, *75*
Spice and herb shops, *109*
Spice Corner (shop), *109*
Split Rock, *134–135*
Sporting-goods shops, *124–125*
Sports
participant, *143–156*
spectator, *156–157*
Sports Authority (shop), *125*
Spring Flowers Children's Boutique, *126*
Spring Street Books (shop), *113*
Spring Street Garden (shop), *115*

Spring Street Natural Restaurant, *22*
Stadium tennis, *155*
Stage Deli, *41*
Stand Up N.Y. (comedy club), *175*
Staple Street, *66*
Star Magic (shop), *116–117*
Staten Island
beaches, *130*
cemeteries, *142*
gardens, *138*
houses, restored, *93*
parks, *136–137, 144*
science museums, *94*
sightseeing, *70*
sports and recreation, *144, 146, 150, 151, 152, 155*
zoo, *140*
Staten Island Bicycling Association, *144*
Staten Island Botanical Garden, *138*
Staten Island Children's Museum, *95, 178*
Staten Island Ferry, *73*
Staten Island Institute of Arts and Sciences, *71, 94, 95*
Staten Island War Memorial Rink, *151*
Staten Island Zoo, *140*
Statue of Liberty, *90*
Stepping Out (dance studio), *143*
Steps, *148*
Stingray (restaurant), *48*
Story hours, *179*
Strand (shop), *114–115*
Strawberry Fields, *131*
Strivers' Row, *64*
Studio Museum of Harlem, *82, 122, 167, 170*
Subway, *4–5*
Sullivan Street Playhouse, *164*
Summer arts, *177–178*
Summerfun (summer event), *178*
Summersounds (summer event), *178*
Sun Wei Association (shop), *67*
Surf Reality, *173*
Surfing, *154*
Susan P. Meisel

(shop), *110*
Susan Parrish Antiques (shop), *111*
Sushi Hatsu (restaurant), *37*
Suzanne (shop), *105*
Swedish Cottage Marionette Theater, *179*
Sweet Basil (restaurant), *30, 170*
Swimming, *154*
Sylvia and Danny Kaye Playhouse, *166*
Sylvia's Soul Food Restaurant, *50*
Symphony Space (auditorium), *165–166, 170, 176*
Syms (shop), *101*

Table d'Hôte (restaurant), *44*
Tada! Youth Ensemble, *179*
Tahari (shop), *97*
Takahachi (restaurant), *29*
Takashimaya (department store), *98, 100*
Talk-A-Walk (tours), *75*
Tanti Baci Cafe, *33*
Tapas Lounge, *39*
Tap-O-Mania (dance event), *11*
Tavern on the Green (restaurant), *46, 170*
Taxis, *5*
TDF vouchers, *160–161*
Tea and Sympathy (restaurant), *31, 54*
Telecharge, *2, 160*
Telephone Bar & Grille, *28*
Temple Emanu-El, *8*
Tender Buttons (shop), *115*
Tennis
participant, *154–155*
professional, *157*
Tennis Club at Grand Central Terminal, *155*
Tennisport, *155*
Tents & Trails (shop), *125*
Teuscher Chocolates (shop), *106*
Thailand Restaurant, *25–26*

Theater, *161–164*
Broadway, *161–162*
children's, *178–179*
information, *161*
Off- and Off-Off-Broadway, *162–164*
outdoors, *177–178*
tickets, *160–161*
Theater for the New City, *164*
Theater Row, *60, 161, 163*
Theater Row Theater, *163*
Theaterworks/USA, *179*
Theodore Roosevelt Birthplace, *91*
31 Dim Sum House (restaurant), *25*
Thomas Pell Wildlife Refuge and Sanctuary, *134*
Thomas Scott's (restaurant), *30*
Three Lives & Co. (shop), *113*
Three of Cups (restaurant), *27*
Tibbetts Brook, *135*
Ticket Central, *160*
Ticket sellers, *2, 160–162*
Ticketmaster, *2*
Tiffany's (store), *76*
Time Café, *27*
Times Square, *60*
Tip Top Shoes (shop), *124*
Tiziano (restaurant), *36*
TKTS (ticket source), *160, 163*
To Boot (shop), *124*
Today's Man (shop), *103*
Todd Oldham Store, *101*
Todt Hill, *71, 136*
Tommaso (restaurant), *52*
Tompkins Square Park, *68, 134*
Tootsie Plohound (shop), *124*
Tortilla Flats (restaurant), *33*
Tours, *73–76, 142*
Tower and Home Apartments, *69*
Tower Books (shop), *113*
Tower Records (shop), *123*

Tower Tennis Courts, *155*

Towing services, *14*

Town Hall (auditorium), *166, 170*

Toy shops, *126–127*

Toys ""R"" Us (shop), *126*

Train travel, *3*

Transportation Alternatives, *144–145*

Trash and Vaudeville (shop), *102*

Trattoria dell'Arte (restaurant), *41*

Traveller's Bookstore, *114*

Treat Boutique (shop), *106*

TriBeCa restaurants, *20–21* sightseeing, *65–66*

TriBeCa Film Center, *66*

TriBeCa Grill, *20, 66*

Triborough Bridge, *3*

Trinity Cemetery, *140–141*

Trinity Church, *8, 65, 141*

Triplet's Roumanian (restaurant), *23*

Tudor City, *60*

Turtle Bay Tennis Club, *155*

12th Street Bar and Grill, *51*

20 Mott Street Restaurant, *24*

Twigs (restaurant), *36*

Two Boots (restaurant), *27*

Ukrainian Museum, *86*

Umberto's Clam House, *67*

UN Plaza–Park Hyatt Hotel, *7*

Union Square, *67, 153*

Union Square Cafe, *33*

Union Square Farmers Market, *108*

Union Square Park, *134*

United Nations, *60*

U.S. Courthouse, *65*

U.S. Open Tennis Championships, *11, 157*

USTA National Tennis Center, *155*

Universalist Church, *10*

Unterberg Poetry Center, *174*

Untitled (shop), *122*

Upper East Side restaurants, *43–45, 55*

Upper West Side restaurants, *47–50, 55* sightseeing, *64–65*

The Urban Angler, Ltd., *149*

Urban Park Rangers, *74, 142*

Uskudar (restaurant), *45*

V & T Restaurant, *50*

Vale of Cashmere (amphitheater), *136*

Valentine-Varian House, *91*

Van Cortlandt Lake, *135*

Van Cortlandt Museum, *92*

Van Cortlandt Park exploring, *135* sporting activities, *146, 147, 149, 150, 152, 155*

Vault Hill, *135*

Veniero's (restaurant), *29, 54*

Verbena (restaurant), *33*

Versace Boutique, *98*

Veselka (restaurant), *28*

Veteran's Day Parade, *12*

Veterinarians, *16*

Viceroy (restaurant), *35*

Victoria's Secret (shop), *98, 104–105*

Vietnam Veterans Memorial, *65*

The View (restaurant), *37*

Views, *57–58*

Village Apothecary, *15*

Village Chess Shop, *117*

Village Tennis Courts, *155*

Village Grill, *30*

Village Vanguard (jazz club), *170*

Vince & Eddie's (restaurant), *47*

Vincent's Clam Bar, *25*

Vinegar Factory (shop), *108*

Vineyard Theater, *164*

Virgin Megastore, *123*

Virginia (theater), *162*

Virginia Slims Tennis Championships, *12*

Visiones (jazz club), *170*

Visitor information, *2*

Vista International (hotel), *7*

Voulez-Vous (restaurant), *44*

VSF (shop), *115*

WPA Theater, *164*

Waldheim, *70*

Waldorf-Astoria Hotel, *7*

Walk of the Town (tours), *75*

Walker Park, *155*

Walker's (restaurant), *20*

Walking tours, *73–75, 142*

Walks, self-guided, *58–61*

Walter Kerr (theater), *162*

Walter Reade Theater (cinema), *176*

Warner Bros. Studio Store, *98, 121*

Washington Market Park, *134*

Washington Mews, *72*

Washington Square Art Show, *10*

Washington Square Church, *168*

Washington Square Park, *134*

Water Club (restaurant), *37*

Water Street, *65*

Wave Hill (estate), *68* gardens, *138–139* musicales, *166–167*

Webster Hall (rock club), *171*

Weill Recital Hall, *167, 169*

Weinfeld's Skull Cap Mfg., *66*

West End Collegiate (church), *9*

West 50s restaurants, *39–41, 54*

West Side Bikes (shop), *144*

West Side Billiard Club, *145*

West Side Highway, *4, 153*

West Side Kids (shop), *127*

West Village restaurants, *29–33, 54*

Westminster Kennel Club Dog Show, *10*

Wetlands (rock club), *171*

White Horse Tavern (restaurant), *30*

Whitestone Lanes, *147*

Whitney Museum of American Art, *81–82, 94, 122*

Wild Foods Walks, *142*

Wildlife refuges, *136, 139, 158*

William Childs Mansion, *70*

William Doyle Galleries, *125*

William T. Davis Wildlife Refuge, *146*

Windsor Pharmacy, *15*

Windsurfing, *156*

Windows on the World (restaurant), *19*

Winter Antiques Show, *10*

Winter Garden (theater), *162*

Winter Garden Atrium, *167, 170*

Wo Hop (restaurant), *25*

Wolfe's Pond Park, *130, 146*

Wolfman-Gold & Good Company (shop), *98, 119*

Wollman Memorial Rink, *151*

Women's wear shops, *101–102, 103–105*

Woodlawn (cemetery), *141*

Woolworth Building, *62, 65, 76*

Wooster Gallery, *111*

Workingmen's Cottages, *69*

World Financial Center, *65* shops, *97*

World Trade Center, *57, 76*

World's Fair Ice Skating Rink, *151*

WTA (tennis tournament), *157*

Wylie's Ribs & Co., *39*

Yaffa Café, *27*

Ye Waverly Inn (restaurant), *30–31*

Yeshiva University
  Museum, *86*
Yoga Zone, *148*
Yohji Yamamoto
  (shop), *101*
Yonkers Raceway, *157*

York Theatre
  Company, *164*
Yorkville
restaurants, *45–46*
You Gotta Have Park
  (event), *10, 178*

Zabar's (restaurant),
  55
Zabar's (shop), *64, 108*
Zarela (restaurant), *39*
Ziegfield (theater), *177*
Zinno (restaurant), *32*

Zitomer Pharmacy,
  15, 123
Zona (shop), *119*
Zoos, *139–140, 158*

NOTES

NOTES

NOTES

NOTES

NOTES

NOTES

Fodor's Travel Publications

Available at bookstores everywhere, or call 1–800–533–6478, 24 hours a day.

Gold Guides

U.S.

Alaska

Arizona

Boston

California

Cape Cod, Martha's
Vineyard, Nantucket

The Carolinas &
Georgia

Chicago

Colorado

Florida

Hawai'i

Las Vegas, Reno,
Tahoe

Los Angeles

Maine, Vermont,
New Hampshire

Maui & Lāna'i

Miami & the Keys

New England

New Orleans

New York City

Pacific North Coast

Philadelphia & the
Pennsylvania Dutch
Country

The Rockies

San Diego

San Francisco

Santa Fe, Taos,
Albuquerque

Seattle & Vancouver

The South

U.S. & British Virgin
Islands

USA

Virginia & Maryland

Walt Disney World,
Universal Studios
and Orlando

Washington, D.C.

Foreign

Australia

Austria

The Bahamas

Belize & Guatemala

Bermuda

Canada

Cancún, Cozumel,
Yucatán Peninsula

Caribbean

China

Costa Rica

Cuba

The Czech Republic
& Slovakia

Eastern &
Central Europe

Europe

Florence, Tuscany
& Umbria

France

Germany

Great Britain

Greece

Hong Kong

India

Ireland

Israel

Italy

Japan

London

Madrid & Barcelona

Mexico

Montréal &
Québec City

Moscow, St.
Petersburg, Kiev

The Netherlands,
Belgium &
Luxembourg

New Zealand

Norway

Nova Scotia, New
Brunswick, Prince
Edward Island

Paris

Portugal

Provence &
the Riviera

Scandinavia

Scotland

Singapore

South Africa

South America

Southeast Asia

Spain

Sweden

Switzerland

Thailand

Toronto

Turkey

Vienna & the Danube

Special-Interest Guides

Adventures to Imagine

Alaska Ports of Call

Ballpark Vacations

Caribbean Ports
of Call

The Official Guide to
America's
National Parks

Disney Like a Pro

Europe Ports of Call

Family Adventures

Fodor's Gay Guide
to the USA

Fodor's How to Pack

Great American
Learning Vacations

Great American
Sports & Adventure
Vacations

Great American
Vacations

Great American
Vacations for
Travelers with
Disabilities

Halliday's New
Orleans Food
Explorer

Healthy Escapes

Kodak Guide to
Shooting Great
Travel Pictures

National Parks and
Seashores of the East

National Parks of
the West

Nights to Imagine

Rock & Roll Traveler
Great Britain and
Ireland

Rock & Roll Traveler
USA

Sunday in
San Francisco

Walt Disney World
for Adults

Weekends in New
York

Wendy Perrin's
Secrets Every Smart
Traveler Should
Know

Fodor's Best Bed & Breakfasts

America

California

The Mid-Atlantic

New England

The Pacific Northwest

The South

The Southwest

The Upper Great Lakes

Compass American Guides

Alaska

Arizona

Boston

Chicago

Colorado

Hawaii

Idaho

Hollywood

Las Vegas

Maine

Manhattan

Minnesota

Montana

New Mexico

New Orleans

Oregon

Pacific Northwest

San Francisco

Santa Fe

South Carolina

South Dakota

Southwest

Texas

Utah

Virginia

Washington

Wine Country

Wisconsin

Wyoming

Citypacks

Amsterdam

Atlanta

Berlin

Chicago

Florence

Hong Kong

London

Los Angeles

Montréal

New York City

Paris

Prague

Rome

San Francisco

Tokyo

Venice

Washington, D.C.

Exploring Guides

Australia

Boston & New England

Britain

California

Canada

Caribbean

China

Costa Rica

Egypt

Florence & Tuscany

Florida

France

Germany

Greek Islands

Hawaii

Ireland

Israel

Italy

Japan

London

Mexico

Moscow & St. Petersburg

New York City

Paris

Prague

Provence

Rome

San Francisco

Scotland

Singapore & Malaysia

South Africa

Spain

Thailand

Turkey

Venice

Flashmaps

Boston

New York

San Francisco

Washington, D.C.

Fodor's Gay Guides

Los Angeles & Southern California

New York City

Pacific Northwest

San Francisco and the Bay Area

South Florida

USA

Pocket Guides

Acapulco

Aruba

Atlanta

Barbados

Budapest

Jamaica

London

New York City

Paris

Prague

Puerto Rico

Rome

San Francisco

Washington, D.C.

Languages for Travelers (Cassette & Phrasebook)

French

German

Italian

Spanish

Mobil Travel Guides

America's Best Hotels & Restaurants

California and the West

Major Cities

Great Lakes

Mid-Atlantic

Northeast

Northwest and Great Plains

Southeast

Southwest and South Central

Rivages Guides

Bed and Breakfasts of Character and Charm in France

Hotels and Country Inns of Character and Charm in France

Hotels and Country Inns of Character and Charm in Italy

Hotels and Country Inns of Character and Charm in Paris

Hotels and Country Inns of Character and Charm in Portugal

Hotels and Country Inns of Character and Charm in Spain

Short Escapes

Britain

France

New England

Near New York City

Fodor's Sports

Golf Digest's Places to Play

Skiing USA

USA Today The Complete Four Sport Stadium Guide

WHEREVER YOU TRAVEL, *H*ELP IS NEVER FAR AWAY.

From planning your trip to providing travel assistance along the way, American Express® Travel Service Offices are always there to help.

Weekends in New York

American Express Travel Service
New York Hilton Hotel
1335 Sixth Avenue
212/664-7798

American Express Travel Service
American Express Tower
200 Vesey Street
212/640-5130

American Express Travel Service
150 East 42nd Street
212/687-3700

American Express Travel Service
200 Fifth Avenue
212/691-9797

American Express Travel Service
New York Marriott Marquis Hotel
1535 Broadway
212/575-6580

American Express Travel Service
374 Park Avenue
212/421-8240

American Express Travel Service
JFK International Airport
Main Lobby
718/656-5673

Travel

http://www.americanexpress.com/travel

American Express Travel Service Offices are located throughout New York City. For the office nearest you, call 1-800-AXP-3429.